Frenemies

FRENEMIES

Feminists, Conservatives, and Sexual Violence

Nancy Whittier

OXFORD
UNIVERSITY PRESS

OXFORD
UNIVERSITY PRESS

Oxford University Press is a department of the University of Oxford. It furthers
the University's objective of excellence in research, scholarship, and education
by publishing worldwide. Oxford is a registered trade mark of Oxford University
Press in the UK and certain other countries.

Published in the United States of America by Oxford University Press
198 Madison Avenue, New York, NY 10016, United States of America.

Library of Congress Cataloging-in-Publication Data
Names: Whittier, Nancy, 1966–author.
Title: Frenemies : feminists, conservatives, and sexual violence / Nancy Whittier.
Description: New York, NY : Oxford University Press, [2018] |
Includes bibliographical references.
Identifiers: LCCN 2017022097 | ISBN 9780190235994 (hardcover) |
ISBN 9780190236007 (pbk.) | ISBN 9780190236014 (updf) | ISBN 9780190236021 (epub)
Subjects: LCSH: Sex crimes—Political aspects—United States—Case studies. |
Coalitions—United States—Case studies. | Politics, Practical—United States—Case studies. |
Feminism—United States. | Conservatism—United States. | United States—Politics and
government—1989–
Classification: LCC HV6592 .W45 2018 | DDC 364.15/30973—dc23
LC record available at https://lccn.loc.gov/2017022097

9 8 7 6 5 4 3 2 1

Paperback printed by WebCom, Inc., Canada
Hardback printed by Bridgeport National Bindery, Inc., United States of America

For my father, Carl Haycock Whittier (1929–2017), who helped instill my commitment to justice, and my children, Jonah, Eva, and Isaac Weigand-Whittier, who help maintain that commitment.

CONTENTS

ACKNOWLEDGMENTS

Portions of Chapter 3 and the Introduction appeared in different form in "Rethinking Coalitions: Anti-Pornography Feminists, Conservatives, and Relationships between Collaborative Adversarial Movements," *Social Problems* 61(2):175–93. Portions of Chapter 4 appeared in different form in "Carceral and Intersectional Feminism in Congress: The Violence Against Women Act, Discourse, and Policy," *Gender & Society*, 30(5):795–818.

I have relied on several student research assistants in assembling and managing the data for this project. Foremost among them is Elizabeth Williams, who assembled the initial hearings databases, legislative time-lines, much archival material, and countless other pieces of information. Without her work this project would not have been possible. Alison Langley and Dominique Adams-Romena also served as student research assistants.

The Center for Advanced Study in the Behavioral Sciences fellowship afforded me a year to work on this project and included many conversations over lunch that left their mark on my thinking about this. I presented a very early version there and especially appreciate comments from Gary Fine, Rhacel Parrenas, Damon Phillips, Carrie Rentschler, Jonathan Sterne, and Eric Worby. Amy Binder answered my sometimes naive questions about conservativism, and Elizabeth Borgwardt helped sort through legal searches and citations.

At the Center for Advanced Study in the Behavioral Sciences, Tricia Soto, librarian extraordinaire, helped locate electronic versions of congressional hearings and assisted with the search process for amicus briefs. She didn't bat an eye when my interlibrary loan requests included articles from *Playboy* and *Penthouse* alongside more traditional materials. In the Smith reference library, Sika Berger helped with locating congressional hearings and understanding their complicated cataloging system. David Podboy answered many questions about Refworks that took it well beyond what it was designed to do easily. Maida Goodwin at the Sophia Smith Collection helped locate materials in the *Ms. Magazine* and Gloria Steinem collections, as well as answering my questions about copyright. Thanks also to Thomas Rushford, Digital Historian in the U.S. House Historian's office, for helping me get access to some pdfs of House hearings, and to Lindsey Dawson for connecting us.

Morgan Lynn and Jane Palmer, both former students who work on issues of law and violence, posed and answered questions at an especially useful point in the work. Aliza Klein and participants in a meeting on child sexual abuse activism at the Ms. Foundation also contributed to my under-standing of how these issues fit together. Janice Irvine helped talk through some aspects of the sex wars, Sarah Soule gave useful advice on analyzing hearings, and Kim Voss suggested the idea of using amicus briefs as a data source. At Smith, Don Baumer answered my questions about congressional subcommittees and their functioning. Joseph Margulies commented on frenemies and the book's introduction. I am indebted to the many friends who weighed in on the book's title. I am also grateful to the reviewers from Oxford University Press for comments on earlier drafts and to anonymous reviewers for *Social Problems* and *Gender & Society* for comments on articles related to this project.

I am grateful to my editor, James Cook, for his enduring interest in this project and his advice along the way. Thanks also to Emily MacKenzie at OUP for her help as the manuscript went into production, to India Gray for her thorough copy-editing, and to Project Manager Tharani Ramachandran for shepherding the book through production. Thanks to Kate Weigand for constructing the excellent index.

Two scholarly groups were central to the final stages of writing. The Five College Social Movements Working Group has provided intellectual com-munity and workshopping for two of the chapters. I am especially grate-ful for comments and questions from Steve Boutcher, Mary Ann Clawson, Nicole Doerr, Rick Fantasia, Jasmine Kerrissey, Joya Misra, Daisy Reyes, and Marc Steinberg. My writing group, Susan Levin, Amy Rhodes, and Susan Voss, provided the encouragement to sit and write even at the busi-est times of the semester. Jo Reger helped talk through many aspects of the book, and her friendship sustained me through moments of doubt.

I owe the greatest debt to my family. Kate Weigand read and commented on parts of the manuscript and helped talk through others. She also did more than her share of carpool driving and other household tasks as I was finishing the manuscript. Her support has been indispensable. Jonah, Eva and Isaac Weigand-Whittier, despite their lack of interest in the content of the book, cheered its progress along. All of them provided the balance and richness that make life worthwhile.

LIST OF ACRONYMS

CAPTA	Child Assault Prevention and Treatment Act
CDL	Citizens for Decency through Law
CWA	Concerned Women for America
FACT	Feminist Anti-Censorship Task Force
FMSF	False Memory Syndrome Foundation
IMBRA	International Marriage Broker Regulation Act
NAACP	National Association for the Advancement of Colored People
NCCAN	National Center on Child Abuse and Neglect
NCMEC	National Coalition on Missing and Exploited Children
NCPCR	National Center for the Prevention and Control of Rape
NOEU	National Obscenity Enforcement Unit
NOW	National Organization for Women
NOW-LDEF	National Organization for Women's Legal Defense and Education Fund (later renamed Legal Momentum)
OVW	Office on Violence Against Women
SORNA	Sex Offender Registration and Notification Act
VAWA	Violence Against Women Act
VOCAL	Victims of Child Abuse Laws
WAP	Women Against Pornography
WAVPM	Women Against Violence in Pornography and Media

Frenemies

CHAPTER 1

Introduction

In the 1980s, some feminists and conservatives famously ended up on the same side of debates over pornography. In what has become a notorious case of supposed collaboration with the enemy, antipornography feminists worked to pass legislation that conservative antipornography activists also supported and lobbied for federal action by the Republican Justice Department. This splintered the women's movement, dividing opponents of pornography from advocates of sexual freedom, and proponents of working for change within existing political structures, even if controlled by conservatives, from those who saw such efforts as doomed to fail and as inevitably strengthening forces of inequality and power. Over time, the complicated interaction between feminists and conservatives against pornography became an apocryphal coalition between enemies, described as such in scholarship on social movement coalitions and in histories of pornography and censorship.

Pornography was not the only issue that brought together feminists and conservatives. In doing research on activism against child sexual abuse, I discovered that people from conservative evangelical Christian and feminist perspectives participated fairly harmoniously in the same organizations for survivors of child sexual abuse. And the Violence Against Women Act (VAWA) passed in 1994 with active cosponsorship from the most conservative and most liberal members of the U.S. Congress. While child sexual abuse and VAWA were lower profile than opposition to pornography, they seemed to represent the same kind of strange coalition between feminists and conservatives.

This book answers two questions about this kind of relationship between opponents with overlapping goals, whom I call frenemies in recognition of the fact that they are neither straightforward friends and nor die-hard enemies. First, what is the nature of these relationships? How can we conceptualize the interactions between feminists and conservatives? What do they tell us about how ideologically opposed activists interact and about the consequences of such relationships for the parties involved? Second, what are the consequences for their participants and for social change? What happens—what changes, who wins or loses—when erstwhile opponents work on the same issue? How have feminists and conservatives influenced law, policy, and culture regarding sexual violence? How has their mutual involvement shaped these outcomes?

Before I began my research, I assumed that I would be comparing three coalitions between feminists and conservatives to understand how different political contexts affected the leverage of each side over the ultimate outcomes. But when I started collecting data, I discovered to my surprise that none of them fits any extant definition of a coalition or any definition that I could reasonably propose. Conservative and feminist activists against pornography supported mostly different legislative and policy changes, did not possess overlapping networks, did not organize shared protests, retained distinct and opposed identities, and avoided coordinating strategy or tactics. Activists against child sexual abuse submerged political differences under the collective identity "survivor" and framed the issue as politically neutral, as did elected officials. This enabled many organizations and public policies to encompass divergent political views, while organizations that took explicitly feminist or religious conservative approaches kept largely separate, even as individuals participated across those lines. VAWA definitely involved a coalition of sorts between elected officials and feminist organizations, with active support from the most conservative and most liberal members of Congress, who both worked with women's movement organizations. This cooperation didn't carry over at the grassroots, however. Conservatives outside the state were opposed to VAWA, while most feminist activists supported it.

Across the board, the "strange bedfellows" were not in bed with each other. At best, they were like characters in 1960s sitcoms, sleeping in separate beds in the same room. Often they were even more distant. They sought change on the same issues but rarely fully converged and often worked in opposition to shape the specifics of legislation or policy. In contrast to collaboration between activists who share broad similarities, these cases are not coalitions. Their gains or losses in federal policy reflected their different power and influence, not their points of overlap. They interact in different ways, according to different logics, and are influenced by different forces and concerns. They are both oppositional and collaborative relationships.

Activists—especially critics of these campaigns—often assume that "getting in bed with the enemy" inevitably leads to defeat and cooptation.

Research on social movements shows, however, that the changes that activists achieve are a product of the receptivity of political decision-makers and the larger culture, as well as activists' own efforts and decisions. While few movements achieve unmitigated success, many achieve partial gains, and many have consequences that they could neither predict nor control. It is unlikely, therefore, that "getting in bed with the enemy" has the same consequences in all cases, let alone that it always leads to defeat.

Because feminists and conservatives converged on several issues related to sexual violence, understanding how this convergence enabled or restricted social change is particularly important. Feminists have poured considerable effort into trying to change cultural patterns, public policy, and law related to rape, domestic violence, and child sexual abuse. What they have achieved, and where they have encountered roadblocks, can tell us a lot about the long-term impact of the women's movement on American society. Focusing on how feminists and conservatives sought to influence federal policy on sexual violence from the 1980s to the 2000s, I explain how each issue played out in Congress and in activist contexts. From a feminist perspective, the involvement of conservatives along with feminists in these issues accounts for both some of the gains and for their limitations. (From a conservative perspective, feminists' involvement has done the same.)

Such relationships are not uncommon, although scholars have not studied them. Groups that are otherwise opposed have made common cause around issues ranging from government surveillance to same-sex marriage to prison reform. The term in common parlance for such relationships is "strange bedfellows," but this term implies a closer relationship than actually exists in many cases. Instead, because they were sometime-friends and sometime-enemies, often simultaneously, I call them frenemies. The term "frenemy" is widely used in popular culture and has been used since the 1950s to describe those who both support and undermine each other, including political opponents who work together. I employ it as an overall descriptor of this category of movement interaction that entails unexpected, unlikely, partial, and fraught collaboration between otherwise-opposed actors. It captures the complex nature of their antagonistic work toward similar but distinct ends. Like coalitions, relationships between frenemies vary in form and dynamics as well as outcomes. Each of the three case studies exemplifies a different form of relationship and a different balance of influence over the outcome. Together, they show how issues can be constructed to allow groups to support them for different reasons, how both the presence and absence of mass mobilization can facilitate unlikely collaborations, and how the structure of issue areas—in this case sexual violence and the complicated stew of gender, covert racism, and anticrime positioning that characterizes it—both shape and are shaped by engagement from different positions.

Opposition to pornography entailed true ideological opponents working on the same issue, which I call *collaborative adversaries*. Antipornography feminists and conservatives undeniably were engaged with some of the same governmental bodies during the mid-1980s, and they used some similar frames about pornography's negative effects on women and children. Yet they staked out distinct positions and rarely collaborated directly. What overlap they had was about expediency, as each side hoped to use the other to advance its own agenda. Ultimately, the feminist position never had much influence and quickly vanished from the public eye, while the conservative position gained. Elected officials and the Justice Department attempted to step up enforcement of obscenity law, but ultimately the effort failed as pornography became more widely accepted.

Campaigns against child sexual abuse entailed ideologically diverse activists uniting under an ideologically neutral umbrella, which I call *narrow neutrals*. Although many activists took explicitly feminist or religious conservative perspectives, the position that reached the broadest audience, including the state, defined child sexual abuse as nonpolitical or politically neutral, even as groups contained individuals of various political stripes. Whereas the pornography connection was based in expediency, the child sexual abuse overlap grew from proximity, as diverse people sought support and intervention under a unifying collective identity of survivor. In turn, the issue was supported by a broad range of elected officials who mostly accepted that it was neither a liberal nor a conservative issue, albeit one that could be turned to their own political advantage in various ways. The politically neutral definition of the issue facilitated legislation oriented toward crime control and punishment but foreclosed intervention in family structure and power from both the Left and the Right.

Activism for VAWA entailed feminist advocates gaining limited conservative support, which I call *ambivalent allies*. Opposition to rape and domestic violence as an issue was primarily "owned" by the women's movement. It originated in the women's movement, and it was feminists and some liberals who had it on their radar screen both inside and outside the state. Feminist activists crafted the legislation with staffers in liberal Democratic Senator Joseph Biden's office and yet gained strong support from the most conservative Republicans in Congress (Strebeigh 2009). The coalition in Congress was based in a pragmatic effort to secure votes and pass legislation. It was possible partly because conservatives outside the state who—unlike elected officials—opposed VAWA did not mobilize against the law. But their cooperation hinged on the frame of violence against women as a matter of gender

Table 1.1 TYPES OF RELATIONSHIPS BETWEEN FRENEMIES

Type of Relationship	Issue	Characteristics of Relationship	Overlapping Frame
Collaborative adversarial relationship	Pornography	Ideological opponents; covert and partial interaction, and overt opposition	Harm to women
Narrow neutrality	Child sexual abuse	Ideologically diverse participants under neutral umbrella	Abuse as beyond politics
Ambivalent alliance	VAWA	Coalition within Congress; disengaged movements outside the state	Gendered crime

and crime and did not extend to feminists' intersectional goals regarding how immigration, race, sexuality, or even gender shaped violence. Table 1.1 summarizes these three types of relationships between frenemies.

I focus on activism targeting the federal government from 1980 to 2013. It was in the 1980s that feminist activism turned toward the state and efforts by both feminists and conservatives to get a federal response on these three issues began in earnest. President Reagan and a Republican Congress were elected in November 1980, signaling a new political era. I take a close look at the interpretive processes that characterize movements' engagement with state actors, focusing on discourse and frames alongside legislation and policy. Both cultural and policy change are important, including how activists or elected officials talked about the issues, as well as the specific policies they advocated and the legislation or policy they implemented. While legislatures and elected executives have formal responsibility for changing the law and policy, they also contribute to changing cultural views of an issue through the way they discuss it. For example, federal legislation about sex offenders does not simply respond to the idea that they are intractably dangerous, it contributes to that idea. Cultural dynamics within the state include underlying discourses (large systems of meaning and assumption that shape how people talk and think), frames (specific ways of interpreting an issue and its importance), identity, and displays of emotion (Burns 2005; Haney 2000; Skrentny 2006).

My overall claims are straightforward. First, to understand all kinds of relationships between social movements, we must move beyond the concept of coalition to study a wider range of kinds of interactions. I develop a new model for analyzing the dynamics and paths of relationships between frenemies. These relationships are enabled by the construction of frames that can appear to reinforce the discourses and goals of otherwise-opposed groups. They are shaped by participants' jockeying for power and influence relative to each other, their concerns about the reputational costs of appearing to consort with the enemy, and the compromise or submersion of controversial goals in favor of areas of commonality. Second, the outcomes of these relationships for legislation, policy, and cultural change—including which side has greater success in shaping the outcome—vary depending on the relative power of participants, including mass mobilization, institutional ties, and structural inequalities of gender, race, and class. Because participants come from opposing movements, they differ in their support from other interested parties such as experts and elected officials; the resonance of their approach with existing frames and law; and the degree that each "owns" the issue through prevailing frames, constituency, movement infrastructure, and history.

The organization of the rest of the chapter proceeds as follows. First, I discuss the theoretical bases for my claims in depth, laying out a model of relationships among frenemies, showing how they developed over time, and outlining the factors that influence their consequences. Next, I discuss the growing, racialized criminal justice apparatus that set the context for these case studies and the strange alliances around them. I then explain my methods and data. The chapter concludes with an overview of the history and context for the three case studies and an overview of the organization of the rest of the book.

HOW SOCIAL MOVEMENTS INTERACT WITH EACH OTHER: FIELDS, COALITIONS, AND FRENEMIES

Activists and social movement organizations are embedded in fields that include other social movements that agree or disagree with them, institutional players, professions, cultural and media organizations and discourses, state agencies, legislative bodies, elected officials, and networks in daily life (Fligstein and McAdam 2012; McBride and Parry 2011; Ray 1999). Any given actor is part of multiple fields that are both overlapping (for example, the issues of child sexual abuse and domestic violence) and nested (for example, a local rape hotline and rape crisis services nationally) (Meyer 2003). Interaction and lines of power and outcomes flow through these fields (Armstrong and Bernstein 2008).

Social movement coalitions are a subset of fields, a particular type of interaction between social movement organizations that define themselves as allies and work together, ranging from a specific campaign to a long-term collaboration.[1] As Bystydzienski and Schact (2001:14) write, coalitions are "fluid sites of collective behavior where the blending of multiple personal identities with political activism interacts with structural conditions to influence the development of commitments, strategies, and specific actions." Coalitions may be ad hoc or ongoing and are fostered by a history of social or political ties between groups (Levi and Murphy 2006). They tend to build on individuals with ties to both movement organizations, whom Van Dyke and McCammon (2010:xvi) call "bridge builders" or hybrid organizations that combine two identities or movements, such as women's peace organizations (Heaney and Rojas 2014). Coalition partners use their overlapping networks to "exchange . . . information," coordinate actions, and develop "an agreed-upon framing of the issues" (Gilmore 2008:xvi).

Most coalitions grow from compatible ideology or shared collective identity between participants. In an analysis of a wide range of case studies, Van Dyke and McCammon (2010:307) found that a necessary condition for coalition was either "aligned organizational ideologies or the presence of a threat to movement goals." While a shared threat could activate preexisting social ties between organizations and lead to coalition work, even threat did not produce coalition across substantial ideological difference or in the absence of preexisting ties between groups. Even relatively small differences in ideology or collective identity, such as those between liberal and radical feminists (Bevacqua 2008), immigrant and welfare rights groups (Reese 2005), and labor and environmental organizations (Obach 2004) can make forming coalitions challenging.

Relationships between frenemies follow a different pattern. Looking at a full range of possible social movement interactions requires a new typology of their relationships. Separating congruence of ideology or identity from interaction, rather than assuming all movements that interact are ideologically compatible, distinguishes new types of movement-movement relationships.[2] Table 1.2 categorizes movements based on their ideological congruence (congruent, neither congruent nor opposed, and opposed) and their interaction with each other (interaction toward a shared goal, no interaction, or opposition).[3] Congruence of collective identity or ideology entails general compatibility, with some important shared values and beliefs, but not necessarily complete overlap. Radical and liberal feminists, or labor and environmental activists, would thus be congruent because of their shared membership in a progressive social movement sector.[4]

Table 1.2 TYPES OF MOVEMENT RELATIONSHIPS

Interaction between Social Movements	Congruence of Ideology and Collective Identity		
	Congruent	Neither congruent nor opposed	Opposed
Interaction toward shared goal	Coalition	Pragmatic coalition	Frenemies
No direct interaction	Spillover	Disengaged	Détente
Opposition	Niche competitors	Pragmatic opponents	Opposing movements

Treating movement interaction and congruence of ideology and collective identity as orthogonal dimensions yields nine types of movement-movement relationships. Coalitions occupy two of the squares, in which social movements that are congruent or neither congruent nor opposed in ideology or collective identity collaborate toward a shared goal. The other two types of relationships between ideologically congruent movements, spillover and niche competitors (rival organizations within the same movement), are recognized types of interaction distinct from coalition (Edwards and Marullo 1995; Meyer and Whittier 1994; Minkoff 1993). Movement organizations whose stances toward each other's ideology and collective identity are neither congruent nor opposed may not interact; when they do, their pragmatic alliance can be considered a coalition, but as McCammon and Van Dyke show, its path may be distinct and is facilitated by shared social ties, or bridging capital (McCammon and Van Dyke 2010; McCarthy 2005; Putnam 2000). Pragmatic opponents may have strategic differences or connections to opposed allies. Disengaged movement organizations are likely quite common within the overall social movement sector.

Among movements that oppose each other's ideology or collective identity, some do not interact (détente), and others work against each other (opposing movements (Meyer and Staggenborg 1996)). Frenemies are ideologically opposed yet interact toward a shared goal. Their interactions are more narrowly delimited than those of coalitions and are a mixture of cooperation and conflict.

As with coalitions, frenemy relationships vary in form. Some of this variation results from differences in the mode and quantity of interaction across different dimensions of social movements. While most work on coalitions focuses on how *organizations* work together (Van Dyke 2003; Van Dyke and McCammon 2010), in order to understand frenemies, we need to consider a wider range of social movement dimensions, including organizations, leaders, grassroots participation, collective identity, frames, specific campaigns, and overall goals. Movements may converge along each dimension fully, partially or covertly, or not at all. Interaction across different dimensions is related (i.e., movements whose leaders overlap are more likely to share frames or engage in shared collective action) but not determinative. Coalitions interact or are compatible in the majority of dimensions. Opposing movements generally do not overlap on any of them.

Frenemies interact along a narrower range of dimensions, and the specific dimensions of connection vary. They coordinate only covertly or partially on some dimensions and oppose each other along other dimensions. Their form varies depending on the dimensions of each social movement that interact. Some may entail interaction among leaders but not organizations; others may be connected primarily through rank-and-file or neighborhood networks. Each case study exhibits a different pattern, as the chapters of the book will show.

The logic and dynamics of relationships between frenemies differ from coalitions in part because participants are also part of opposing parent movements. Broad social movements are themselves internally diverse and coalitional, made up of numerous organizations with different specific goals, ideology, strategies, and tactics (Rochon and Meyer 1997). While coalitions may occasionally be movement-wide, they are more often confined to specific movement organizations. They do not lead to ideological critique or factionalism within the parent social movements, although there may be strategic disputes about resource allocation or tactics (Levi and Murphy 2006; Obach 2010). In contrast, interactions with "the enemy" may spark critique of participants and damage to their reputations, strategic disputes about the risks of strengthening opponents' larger agenda, and even factionalism within participants' parent social movements. The collaboration is exceedingly unlikely to extend to the larger movements as a whole. Participants must manage these tensions (Maney 2000). They do so through distancing strategies such as keeping direct collaboration covert, advocating for their goal in different locations or through separate elite allies, and explaining their distinct agendas. These strategies shift over time and may be deliberate or simply result from participants' preexisting differences.

The participants in each case study varied in their ties to and criticism from the larger feminist and conservative movements, ranging from organized feminist opposition on pornography, to nonorganized opposition from conservatives on VAWA, to little opposition from either side on child sexual abuse. Their strategies for distancing and reputation management varied accordingly. While antipornography feminists faced strong critique from other feminists, child sexual abuse activism's neutrality allowed both feminists and conservatives to participate without risking their reputations. Minimal conservative activism outside the state mitigated reputational risks for VAWA supporters on either side. Conservative lawmakers were rarely taken to task for supporting VAWA, and feminist supporters were not linked with conservative movement organizations.

The events recounted in this book take on different meanings for different actors. For feminists who opposed pornography and violence against women, this is a story of at least partial movement success, in placing pornography as a violation of women's rights on the agenda, and later recognizing rape and domestic violence as civil rights violations in VAWA. For other feminists, it is a story of how antipornography feminists bolstered a Puritanical sexual culture and how conservatives and the state used feminist concerns as a cover for initiatives that ultimately disempowered women and sexual minorities. For activists who oppose the punitive state, it is a story of how a concern with the protection of women and children legitimated the expansion of the prison system and the increasing incursion of the criminal justice arm of the state into communities and daily life, particularly those of people of color. For the religious Right, it is a story about the efforts of the government to protect women and children in the face of rising immorality and crime. For others on the Right, it is about a crackdown on lawlessness that suboptimally focuses on violence against women distinct from crime overall. For still other conservatives, it is about feminists' success in diverting taxpayer funds to support their radical attack on men and the family. For policy-makers and individuals working in the criminal justice system, it is a story of their growing understanding of how best to crack down on the crimes of rape, child abuse, and domestic violence. These are indeed strange bedfellows, with wildly disparate overall agendas and understandings of sexual violence. None achieved all they wanted, but their actions and interactions shaped the outcomes.

PATHS AND HOW SOCIAL MOVEMENTS DEVELOP OVER TIME

As Blee (2012) argues, movement organizations establish directions early on through initial decisions about membership, tactics, ideology, or collective identity. Over time, early decisions have consequences that make it harder for social movement organizations to change direction, but they remain open to choice and change. Combining this with the idea of various relationships among actors in a field, we can think about the unfolding of paths in relationships, whether between social movements or between movement and state actors. How groups initially frame an issue or the discourse they use to understand it influences understandings going forward. For example, because activists initially worked to reframe child sexual abuse as a serious crime rather than a shameful private matter, their ongoing efforts engaged more deeply with the criminal justice system. Because feminist opponents of pornography initially rejected a frame of obscenity in favor of a women's rights approach, they had difficulty persisting once the women's rights approach was overruled by the courts. When religious conservatives decried pornography's contribution to marital rape, they had trouble later opposing legal change in that area. The relationships among parties also followed paths shaped by initial connections and experiences over time. For example, advocacy organizations built ongoing relationships with Congress, in which initial testimony on one issue led to testimony on related issues over time.

The timing of each movement's engagement with the issue and the development of a professional sector shaped their influence. When one side organized first, it established initial "ownership" of the issue. When activist and professional engagement grow at the same time, activists' influence is diminished. In the case of *pornography*, both feminists and conservatives owned the issue, with divergent approaches to it. Feminists briefly mobilized large and passionate demonstrations, but conservatives had a longer history of organizing, deeper support from their parent movement, and a stronger organizational infrastructure (Bronstein 2011; Strub 2011). Conservatives also were strengthened by the lack of a significant professional advocacy sector on pornography, which left conservative legal advocacy organizations to take the lead. The separate bases and strength of these divergent movements promoted the collaborative adversarial model.

Opposition to child sexual abuse, in contrast, although originating with feminists, quickly drew broad participation and became more politically neutral; neither feminists nor conservatives strongly influenced public views of the issue. The relatively weak ties between activism against child sexual abuse and feminist, progressive, or conservative movements enabled the narrowly neutral relationship. Further, grassroots activism emerged only slightly before a rapidly growing sector of prevention and treatment professionals (Davis 2005; Whittier 2009). This time sequence and the movement's deliberate political neutrality left professionals with greater influence than activists within the state.

By the time VAWA was introduced, feminist mass mobilization had waned, but professionalized movement organizations, like NOW, feminist legal advocacy organizations, and organizations providing services for rape and domestic violence, dominated antiviolence advocacy. The professionals working on the issue of rape emerged after initial women's movement's activism on the issue and shared its basic agenda and framing. Conservatives' work against rape, in contrast, was minimal, but antipornography religious conservatives' condemnation of sexual and domestic violence left them with little room to oppose legislation on the topic. Rape as an issue was clearly owned by the women's movement and the women's movement was the stronger influence on VAWA, even at a time of relatively low feminist mobilization. Continuing along this path, feminists have been influential regarding Title IX enforcement against sexual assault on college campuses, sexual assault in the military, and international violence against women. The previous path inclines, but does not determine, future directions, and the ongoing involvement of conservatives and criminal justice discourses mean that outcomes could shift.

HOW SOCIAL MOVEMENTS ACHIEVE CHANGE

Short of revolution, few movements achieve their goals in full; instead, they achieve partial changes, at best. These partial changes almost always consist of the aspects of the movement's program that are most similar or least threatening to the existing order. For example, the idea that rape is a crime that should be taken seriously by police is more easily incorporated within prior discourse, law, and bureaucracy (as an instance of *crime*, a preexisting category) than the idea of rape as intrinsic to patriarchy, a means through which men maintain domination of women (Whittier 2009). Movements' attempts to influence federal government are filtered through the official designation of topics, selection of witnesses to testify before hearings, exercise of power in question-and-answer periods, winnowing processes of writing and passing legislation, construction of official statements, production of written reports, and numerous actions of units such as the Justice and Education Departments, as well as agencies such as the National Center on Child Abuse and Neglect (NCCAN) and Office on Violence Against Women (OVW). These selection processes, including language, access, and bureaucratic routine, favor advocates, frames, and goals that fit most neatly with existing discourses and legal frameworks, as well as advocates who are more powerful or tightly connected to those in power.

An extensive body of research deals with the outcomes of social movements. Generally compatible with my argument, previous work on the factors that shape movement impacts on federal policy finds that protest is particularly influential for getting an issue onto the policy agenda, while other forms of action like lobbying, testifying before congressional committees, and working with allies in state agencies are more influential in shaping the actual content and implementation of policy (Amenta et al. 2010; Banaszak 2010; Goss 2013). Indeed, all three issues were initially taken up by Congress at times of outside interest and attention, and ongoing engagement through testimony shaped policy content. In addition to a movement's own actions, the larger political context shapes outcomes. Political opportunities, including partisan control of Congress, divisions among elites that activists can exploit, and influential allies all increase the likelihood that movements will have an impact on policy (Amenta et al. 2010; Meyer 2004; Tarrow 1994). While frenemy relationships' inclusion of otherwise-opposed groups can therefore increase the likelihood that at least one member will have ties to powerful elites, their different allies and agendas can play out at cross-purposes.

While existing work emphasizes the importance of movements' ability to influence election results, disrupt normalcy through mass protest, or affect public opinion for persuading elected officials to support policy change (Kolb 2007), I also show the importance of advocates' cultural framing efforts. How organizations and political elites frame issues is central to shaping policy outcomes. Frames' effectiveness depends on their fit within existing discourses and frames for a particular issue (Ferree 2003; McCammon, Muse, and Newman 2007). Frames have to be credible to legislators and the general public (Amenta et al. 2010; Giugni 2007). For scholars of the policy process, "meaning" is often secondary to questions of the power of various policy-makers and interest groups, and measured mainly through public opinion (Burstein 2014; Skrentny 2006). Building on work about cultural change, I take a broader view (Whittier 2002). Just as movements' frames are more likely to be accepted into the wider culture when they resonate with existing understandings, the same is true in policy and law (Earl 2004; Rochon 1998). The discourses and frames that prevail in Congress limit the frames and associated policies that advocates can present before Congress (Burns 2005; Skrentny 2006). For example, even when activists organized outside criminal justice frameworks, their demands were filtered through the power of crime as a way of understanding violence and through bureaucratic routines that pursue enforcement.

John Skrentny (2006:1809) calls for unpacking the state's internal workings, arguing that we "should not treat the state as a black box . . . . The state is a textured entity of institutional structure and people; the people have agency, and that agency is powerfully mediated by cultural meanings." Rather than taking the state as a given or as primarily structural, I follow cultural theories that view the state as constituted through discourses, interactions, and emotion as well as structure (Aretxaga 2001; Aretxaga

2003; Haney 2000; Molotch and Boden 1985). In Abrams's (1988:76) now-classic view, the state can be viewed partly as an idea, an "ideological project" that legitimates the domination carried out in its name. Official routines, social practices, and meanings are central to the exercise of political power (Steinberg 2003). They justify, influence, and are influenced by policy and administrative action.

Official meanings are produced and displayed in a number of settings. Within Congress, a major location is congressional hearings and testimony, choreographed by staffers in committee chairs' offices who locate witnesses and help prepare their testimony. Agencies issue reports and studies about policy implementation and effectiveness. Presidents, presidential commissions, and executive branch officials make statements to the public, the media, and government players. In all of these locations, speech, symbolism, and displays or invocations of emotion produce and reflect meanings (Allahyari 1997; Aretxaga 2003; Gould, Timmons Roberts, and Lewis 2004; Molotch and Boden 1985; Naples 1997). Official meanings can be sincere, of course, but also reflect expediency, political concerns about public support, and horse-trading deals within Congress. Similarly, advocates' contributions reflect a mixture of genuine beliefs and strategic attempts to gain legislative support. Challengers participate in the construction of meaning within state contexts, and their influence is a potential movement outcome. They do not participate as equals, however; state actors retain more power, and some challengers and their frames have more access or power than others.

Political and discursive opportunities also are gendered, racialized, and classed. Discursive opportunities include beliefs about gender, race, and the nature of different groups of men and women; these beliefs are embedded in legal structures (McCammon, Muse, and Newman 2007). Similarly, political opportunities such as connections to elites and appearance of influence over elections or public opinion are shaped by structures of inequality, the underrepresentation of women and people of color in elected office, gender and racial gaps in voting, and the like (Bell 2014; Ferree and Mueller 2004). The entry of women into employment in federal government, for example, provided a ready-made network of supporters for the women's movement (Banaszak 2010; Katzenstein 1999), and Congress's fluctuating interest in women's issues affects access by the "women's lobby" to legislative influence (Goss 2013). Political and discursive opportunities often exclude intersectional approaches to policy and favor single-issue approaches (McBride and Parry 2011:14). Consequently, as I unpack the outcomes for the three case studies, I examine how these intersecting forces shaped them.

Analyzing outcomes for issues that draw together otherwise-opposed movements requires analyzing the relative influence, access to the state, and specific policy and cultural goals of each participating movement separately. Frenemies rarely have equal strength. Some movement actors, their parent movements, and the frames they promote are more powerful and influential in some contexts and times than others. Their relationship to those in power partially determines these differences, but so does their relationship to the dominant culture, the overall strength of their movement, institutional support, and opposition (Amenta et al. 2010). Of course success also depends on activists' own efforts, their ability to sustain themselves over a long haul, to gather the time and material resources to make themselves and their case visible, to communicate effectively, and to conceive and execute effective tactics (Meyer, Whittier, and Robnett 2002; Tarrow 1994; Tilly 2004). We have a tendency, however, to overemphasize these factors in cases of both success and failure. Movements' own characteristics and efforts interact with their contexts and the work of other movements in producing specific results and excluding others. Foremost among contextual factors for movements against sexual violence is the strong and growing criminal justice system.

VIOLENCE AND CRIME

Rape, child sexual abuse, and obscenity are all defined as crimes. Response to crime is central to the modern state. Crime provides a justification for the consolidation of state power to punish, surveil, and investigate and an emotional appeal that, through fear, increases popular support for authority (Margulies 2013). Simon (2007) argues that the United States increasingly "governs through crime," using a criminal model and fear of crime to regulate behavior in a host of institutions—including schools, families, and the workplace—and to justify the rise in the number of prisons and the increasing proportion of the population that is imprisoned. The consequences are well-known: shockingly high rates of incarceration, disproportionately high rates for Black and Latino people relative to whites, and even higher rates of contact with the criminal justice system if we include parole (Alexander 2010; Currie 2013; Richie 2012). These result from mandatory minimum sentences, "three strikes and you're out" laws that require long sentences after a third offense, the registration and civil commitment of sex offenders, "zero tolerance" policies that result in heavy sanctions in public schools, the trial of adolescents as adults, and draconian drug policies resulting from the "war on drugs." The federal role in crime has also increased dramatically, including a sharp increase in the number of federal crimes and in federal conditions and incentives to shape state criminal codes and practices (Margulies 2013).

The state is both a potential agent of violence, in the ever-present threat of use of force, and a potential protector from violence. Because maintaining order and preventing uncontrolled violence is a central function of modern states, failure to protect or intervene is itself an act of state violence, as Melissa Wright (2011) shows in her analysis of the murder of women in the Mexican–U.S. border region. States intervene in violence or fail to do so according to logics of gender, race, and national interest (Das 1996; Freedman 2013; McGuire 2010; Roberts 2001; Wright 2011). An effort to get the state to "do something" about an issue can thus represent a challenge to gender or racial equality. For example, McGuire (2010) shows that, prior to the 1970s, the rape of Black women was ignored by police and prosecutors. Bringing white rapists to justice was a major focus of pre-1960s civil rights activism in the South and beyond. Similarly, the antilynching movement sought state intervention and protection, working to define lynching as a crime and bring its perpetrators to justice (Giddings 2008; Hill 2009).

At the same time, calling for the state's protection also invokes its violence. Violence against women and children has long been used to justify the expansion of state power, especially to control people who are marginal by virtue of race, class, or sexual practice (Alexander 2010; Freedman 2013; Richie 2012; Rodriguez 2006; Rubin 1994; Sacco 2009). The US penal system took on its current expansive form—the "prison industrial complex"—alongside the criminalization of rape, domestic violence, and child sexual abuse, as well as a focus on victims of violence (Gottschalk 2006; Rentschler 2011; Whittier 2009).[5] The two trends shaped each other: Increasing intervention into sexual violence, especially against children, shaped and strengthened the penal system, and the growing penal system shaped the discourses used to explain and condemn sexual violence.

In all three cases, race intersects with gender to construct and legitimate state intervention. Crime in general is racialized in terms of both discourse (the association of whiteness with innocent victimization and of Black and Latino people and neighborhoods with crime) and policy (the disproportionate incarceration of African American and Latino people) (Alexander 2010; Gottschalk 2006; Richie 2012). This is true for sexual violence, as it is for other forms of crime. White women and children are often the face of victims or those at risk of crime (Baker 2013; Freedman 2013; Leon 2011; Rentschler 2011). Perpetrators, correspondingly, may be represented as or symbolized by men of color (Chancer 1998; Hollander 2001). But the relationship of social movements to these representations and policies is complex. The feminists working on all three issues engaged in different ways and to varying degrees with intersectional and white feminism. Conservatives, meanwhile, more consistently employed racist or unidimensional frames, but these varied in overtness.

Activists, legislators, and mainstream culture defined all three issues in ways that implicitly or explicitly rested on intersections of race and gender. This played out differently in the three cases. Antipornography feminists emphasized women's common gendered oppression through sexist imagery in pornography. Treating race as a factor that increased degradation of women of color, the mostly white antipornography feminist movement in a sense used racism as a way to enhance their argument that pornography was sexist (Nash 2008). Black feminists theorizing pornography during the 1980s and 1990s made similar arguments (Collins 2000; Harris 1989). While the women who appear in pornography were thus not constructed as predominantly white, antipornography feminism was not really an intersectional feminist movement either. Conservatives, on the other hand, emphasized the harm of exposure to pornography to children (constructed as innocent) and wives (who were presumed to be uninterested in pornography but sexually exploited by men influenced by pornography). While there was virtually no discussion of race or class in state contexts, the fact that feminists were not seeking to advance an intersectional feminist argument facilitated collaboration across ideological difference.

The child sexual abuse case also featured very little overt analysis of race and class or criticism of inequalities of race, class, or gender. As discussed, the narrow and neutral relationship depended on defining the issue as separate from any politicized questions or social movements on other issues. This included feminism but also critiques of the child welfare industry for targeting Black and poor families and of the patriarchal family (from the Left), or the association between race and the presumed greater criminality of nonwhite people (from the Right). While the image of threatened white children's innocence powerfully motivated legislation and public opinion, the focus on familial abuse meant that the vast majority of concrete examples in hearing narratives and of convicted offenders were white.

VAWA saw an explicitly intersectional feminist movement that came up against both unidimensional frames and reluctance to address structural racism in Congress. Activism on VAWA began later than feminist engagement with pornography and child sexual abuse, and the increasing centrality of intersectional approaches to the women's movement shaped its advocates' stance. So did the by-then-established history of concerted efforts to garner funding for anti-rape and domestic violence efforts in communities of color by framing these communities as "high crime areas" that produced more extensive alliances among women of color service providers and clients and the state (Gottschalk 2006:ch. 5). The centrality of race alongside gender in shaping both the issues of sexual violence and responses to them is underscored by the fact that Kimberle Crenshaw's (1991) groundbreaking theoretical article on intersectionality was based on an analysis of violence against women.

Overall, activism around child sexual abuse, pornography, and VAWA both challenged and reinforced the criminal state. Turning to the state and the criminal justice system for remedies to sexual violence has been a controversial strategy among feminists (Comack 2006). Many critics view the consequences of organizing within a criminal justice framework as inevitably regressive (Bernstein 2010; Bumiller 2008). Indeed, these consequences fall far short of radical transformation and are severely constrained by the state's interests in social control. Turning to the state for remedies against violence risks strengthening police and prison powers, themselves locations of violence, that are the core of the state's coercive power and pervaded with racial and class injustices. At a time when social welfare spending is severely reduced under neoliberalism, anticrime spending remains robust (Collier 2008; Gottschalk 2006). Criminal justice discourses and practices have changed from an emphasis on rehabilitation to a model of criminals as pathological and in need of containment, consistent with the neoliberal shift to individual rather than social definitions of problems (Beckett 1997). Feminist attempts to reshape government actions around sexual violence, thus, have been criticized as colluding with the rise of neoliberalism (Bernstein 2012; Bumiller 2008).

While these critiques are accurate, I suggest that they are only part of the story for two reasons. First, because control of crime is a central aspect of the modern state and the rule of law, activists concerned with violence and acts defined as crime cannot avoid the state. Even activism that does not directly engage with the state is often structured by its requirements (e.g., regulation and reporting mandates) and by the centrality of crime as the means for understanding violence. Culturally, when the state does not intervene against acts of violence, it sends the message that those acts are acceptable; thus, the dispossessed call for "equal justice" to invoke the protective powers of the state on their behalf. When an issue is a crime, this dilemma is inevitable. There is no simple solution to it.

Second, feminist activism alone does not determine policy outcomes around sexual violence. These policies are the product of a range of forces, including discourses about women as weak and in need of protection, power struggles among elites, and economic interests. Importantly, they include feminists' conservative frenemies. Conservative activists and institutional players push for action against sexual violence precisely to strengthen "law and order," control challenges from the poor and people of color (Beckett 1997), and justify political and military surveillance and control (Margulies 2013). While some activists argue that feminists and progressives should therefore abstain from attempts to influence policy, others take an incremental approach and attempt to shift policy directions. On these issues, as on many, there is no single, unified feminist movement.

Understanding the struggles between these movements and their varying influence over outcomes is thus central to understanding the rise and ramifications of public policy around sexual violence. Too often, debates about "getting in bed with the enemy" or targeting the state for change are not based in data about how such efforts have actually played out. By taking a close look at the evidence about modes of interaction between feminists, conservatives, and the state, and their consequences for culture, law, and policy, I both shed light on the events and dynamics at hand and suggest an approach that can be applied beyond these case studies.

STUDYING COMPARATIVE CASES: METHODS AND DATA

The comparative case design of this book draws on three long-lived, intersecting cases. Some of the same people, organizations, and governmental entities worked on all three cases, and the issues overlapped. For example, opponents of pornography often decried its use to promote child sexual abuse or rape; the commercial sexual exploitation of children in pornography also was subject to child sexual abuse punishment; VAWA included measures for addressing sexual assaults on minors; and sex offender registration and notification laws applied to sexual assault against adults as well as children. Actors' encounters with each other in one case—such as pornography—influenced how they approached each other and the issues in the other cases. All this developed and changed over time. Thus, rather than treating the cases as discrete (as in many studies based on a comparative case design), I use a dynamic, interactive, path-dependent approach, analyzing how actors, issues, discourses, and trajectories influence each other. At the same time, I draw out the differences among the cases to analyze the causal forces that shape their direction and outcomes.

I draw on a wide range of data and scholarly work. I rely mostly on contemporaneous sources rather than interviews conducted after the fact because these issues were so contentious and subject to reinterpretation over time. I do not try to determine the inner beliefs and motivations of participants but rather how they positioned themselves, in changing ways, in relation to each other and the issues at hand.

To understand activism by feminists and conservatives, I use contemporaneous news reports, writing in movement publications, organizational documents and other archival material, oral histories, memoirs, and secondary sources. I gathered materials through a search for all coverage of the three issues in the major movement publications from 1980 through 2010, using numerous related keywords and subjects. For the women's movement, the publications were *Ms.* and *off our backs*; for secular conservatism they were *Human Events* and the *National Review*; for religious conservatism they were *Commentary, Christianity Today, World Magazine,* and *American Spectator*.[6] These publications vary in religious and political outlook, as neither feminist nor conservative movements are homogeneous. I use these sources to look at movements' activities and goals, as well as frames and emotions about the issues. What did they want to achieve in terms of concrete policy changes and in terms of how lawmakers and the general public thought, talked, and felt about the issue? How did they position themselves in relation to other groups working on the issues? How did each publication frame the issues for their readership?[7] I use coverage from movement-aligned media, rather than data from mainstream media coverage of movement events because activism around the three case studies received little mainstream media coverage.[8] To supplement these media sources, I also draw on my own interviews with and observations of activists against child sexual abuse and activists in the early anti-rape movement.[9] For feminist opposition to pornography, I also draw on the archival papers of Women Against Violence in Pornography and Media, housed at the GLBT Historical Society in San Francisco, and the Gloria Steinem papers at the Sophia Smith Collection at Smith College. For activism against child sexual abuse, I draw on organizational documents, newsletters, and other print material from a range of groups active in the 1990s and 2000s (see Whittier 2009 for full discussion).

To understand activists' and other advocates' engagement with the state and elected officials' discourses, frames, and display of emotions, I draw on transcripts of congressional committee and subcommittee hearings. I compiled a comprehensive list of all congressional committee and subcommittee hearings on the three cases held between 1981 and 2013 using a subject search on Lexis-Nexis.[10] I coded hearings conducted during peak movement-involvement periods (outlined in the substantive chapters) to the witness level in order to analyze the number and composition of witnesses for the different cases and over time. For hearings conducted during other periods, I read through lists of witnesses and hearing subjects and coded hearings where key legislation was passed or important witnesses appeared to the witness level; the remaining hearings are coded only at the hearing level. This yielded 269 hearings between 1981 and 2013: 150 on child sexual abuse, 88 on pornography, and 31 on VAWA. One hundred and sixty-six hearings were coded to the witness level, with a total of 1,486 witnesses. Because a hearing could address more than one topic, there was some overlap, mainly between hearings on child sexual abuse and pornography.[11] I read and briefly annotated all hearings to assemble a comprehensive picture of legislation and testimony, and selected a sample of hearings for close qualitative analysis based on the appearance of antipornography conservative or feminist witnesses or the hearings' substantive importance.[12] Figure 1.1 shows the number of hearings on each issue over time.

Congressional hearings are a good indicator of policy-makers' interest in an issue (King, Bentele, and Soule 2007; Soule and King 2006). Congressional committee and subcommittee hearings are also a major location for the construction and circulation of discourse and a setting where advocates make their case as witnesses (Andrews and Edwards 2004; Holyoke 2009; King, Bentele, and Soule 2007; Sabatier 1991). Hearings are not a direct result of protest, but they do sometimes respond to protest (Olzak and Soule 2009) and to media attention and public opinion (Jones and Baumgartner 2004; Yongjoo and Haider-Markel 2001), which, in turn, can be influenced by movement mobilization. They are a setting where

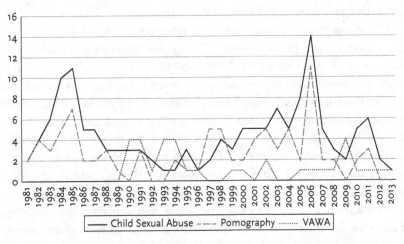

Figure 1.1 Number of Congressional Hearings on Pornography, Child Sexual Abuse, and VAWA, 1981–2013

activists from all sides, professionals, and elected officials talk about the issue (Diermeier 2000; Holyoke 2009). Elected officials and witnesses draw on existing discourses to frame the issues, display and invoke emotion, and construct authority according to various criteria. Legislators and witnesses interactively construct the meaning and worthiness of potential policies (Allahyari 1997). Lawmakers' conclusions are shaped by both testimony and their preexisting beliefs about the issue (Burns 2005; Campbell 2002; Jacobs and Sobieraj 2007; Skrentny 2006). Particularly in early hearings on an issue, dominant frames and final legislative form are not predetermined and testimony from advocacy groups can shape policy (Banaszak 2010; Burstein 2014; Burstein and Hirsh 2007; Lohmann 1998; Soule and King 2006). Hearings are thus a rich source of qualitative data on how witnesses and organizations articulate their positions and on their claims of connection to each other (Allahyari 1997; Brasher 2006; Gring-Pemble 2003; Holyoke 2009; Miller 2004; Molotch and Boden 1985; Naples 1997). Yet few scholars have analyzed them qualitatively across more than one or two hearings. (For an exception, see Burstein 2014.)

Framing in hearings is strategic, aimed at persuading diverse audiences; groups that differ politically may use similar language for different ends (Naples 1997). Frames also draw on underlying discourses that are less consciously articulated and can reflect deeper differences between speakers. All parties frame issues in ways that reflect both expediency (attempts to influence the result or to play to constituents) and underlying agendas. For example, a speaker who talks about rape as a violent crime may connect that to restrictions on women's freedom of movement (reflecting an underlying discourse about gender) or to an epidemic of violent crime in general (reflecting an underlying discourse about crime).

While congressional subcommittee hearings are not a backstage setting, most are low profile (Brasher 2006). Few draw an audience, almost none were televised before the 1990s, and most still are not. They are fully transcribed with hard copies available in many major libraries after up to a year or more past the hearing date; online availability is limited to a much smaller number of major research libraries. The official discourses, frames, and emotions displayed there are varied and changeable. Unscripted exchanges between members of Congress and witnesses and among witnesses are a unique window into the processes through which meaning is constructed in the state.

In addition to congressional committee and subcommittee hearings, I draw on documents, reports, and archival material from governmental agencies and officials, including the Department of Justice, the Attorney General's Office under Edwin Meese, NCCAN, and OVW. These include biannual reports, grant reports, public remarks, and some subcommittee and committee meeting minutes from OVW, mainly covering the years 2002–2012; the papers of Attorney General Edwin Meese (housed at the Hoover Institution), annual reports and grant reports from the NCCAN from its inception to 2004; reports and other material from the Department of Justice related to prosecution of obscenity and child pornography cases; the 1986 final report of the Attorney General's Commission on Pornography; and statements by the president and other executive branch officials. Finally, I identified amicus briefs for all Supreme Court cases dealing with the case studies using a subject search in Lexis-Nexis, collected all amicus briefs for the cases, and coded them by authors' affiliation.[13] These document collaboration by advocates from different perspectives and how they framed the issues.

THE CASES IN CONTEXT: THE HISTORY OF ACTIVISM AGAINST SEXUAL VIOLENCE

Feminists and conservatives have been central to virtually every era of activism around sexual violence (Breines and Gordon 1983; Freedman 2013; Sacco 2009; Whittier 2009). Rape, child sexual abuse, and pornography have been conceptually entwined since the Colonial Era and have long brought together ideologically diverse advocates, including feminists, conservatives, and religiously motivated reformers. These included moral reformers, antilynching activists, temperance groups, child welfare workers, suffragists, anarchists, antiracism groups, public health advocates, white supremacists, eugenicists, and religious Protestants and Catholics (Freedman 2013; Lindsay 2008; Lo 1982; McGuire 2010; Sacco 2009; Strub 2011), sometimes working together, sometimes separately. There is also a long history of state intervention regarding these issues, including federal, state, and municipal law, court cases, and criminal and social service interventions. Advocates of all stripes have worked inside and outside government (Banaszak 2010; Diamond 1995; Katzenstein 1999; Lindsay 2008). Feminists' involvement has also been criticized as moralistic, as reinforcing women's victimhood, and as playing into conservative goals, in an ongoing tension between "protection and equal rights" for women that has persisted to the present (Freedman 2013). The movements and changes of the 1980s and later built on this long history of activism and government intervention in sexual violence, obscenity, and sexual morality. In order to understand the context that frames the three case studies, this section provides a concise history of activism around all three issues and the broader feminist and conservative movements. It also sets the scene in terms of policy and law.

Race, as well as gender, is central to the social response to rape, child sexual abuse, and pornography (Freedman 2013; Friedman 2000; Sacco 2009; Whittier 2015). Denunciations of sexual violence and sexually explicit imagery have been used to justify lynching, to call for increased social resources for children, as evidence of immigrants' inferiority, and to reinforce the idea of white women's purity. Rape and child sexual abuse themselves have been used as weapons to control or punish women of color, especially African Americans and Native Americans, and as threats to restrict the mobility of women and children. White men historically could sexual assault Black, Native American, and immigrant women with impunity (Holland 2011); and child sexual abuse in "respectable" families has been mostly invisible while poor, immigrant, and families of color face excessive scrutiny (Sacco 2009).[14] Reformers' efforts to challenge sexual violence have been similarly inextricable from challenges to inequalities of race, class, and gender, and from their own race, class, and gender positions and the understandings that accompany them.[15]

Activism Combating Sexual Violence before the 1960s

During the Victorian and Progressive Eras, moral reformers upheld "a gender ideology that defined women by their purity," while using this ideology to gain "leverage to rein in white male sexual privileges" (Freedman 2013:51). Although modern definitions of feminism and conservatism cannot be meaningfully applied to this era, moral reformers were ideologically diverse. Some were more focused on "individual moral uplift or religious virtue," while others "identified men as the aggressors" and critiqued men's power (Sacco 2009:46). Working for child protection and age of consent laws, they saw considerable success (Freedman 2013). Intervention into mostly poor and immigrant families by both state agencies and charitable child protective organizations began on a large scale during this era (Sacco 2009). Moral reformers were not the only group working against sexual violence in the 1800s and early 1900s. Immediately after emancipation, freed Black women and men worked to address the problem of the rape of Black women and children (Freedman 2013). But the rollback of Black rights in the South after the rapid end of Reconstruction left African American women and girls vulnerable to rape and African American men subject to false accusations of rape and subsequent lynching.

Anti-obscenity activism also was widespread during this period, led by the same white Protestant demographic that animated the moral reform organizations. "Vice societies," led by Anthony Comstock and others, spurred the passage of the federal Comstock Act in 1873, criminalizing the distribution of obscene materials—defined broadly to include even information about birth control—through the mail. A focus on white women's sexual purity, including sexually transmitted diseases, prostitution, and obscenity, produced the Mann Act of 1910, which prohibited the transportation of girls across state lines for prostitution and remains in effect today, albeit with numerous revisions. The antiprostitution movement drew what we might now consider ideologically opposed participants, including "feminists, moralists, and civil libertarians" (Jabour 2013:144) and built on racialized imagery of white girls enslaved by immigrant or African American men. Overtly racist organizing, including among women, also grew. White supremacist groups supported moral reform efforts as a way of protecting white, native-born, Protestants from what they saw as immoral and dangerous immigrants and people of color (Blee 1991; Blee and Creasap 2010).

Activists in the 1980s referred to this past to delegitimize their opponents. Feminist opponents labeled antipornography feminists moralistic "New Victorians." Meanwhile, opponents of activism against child sexual abuse also complained about overreaching "child savers." Both sides framed the history of women's activism for sexual reform as serving the government's interest of social control that increased sexual repression and the oppression of women and sexual minorities.

Much of this ferment died down during and immediately after World War II, but three low-key developments of the 1950s laid the groundwork for the events that are this book's focus. First, African American organizing against lynching and sexual violence against African American women and girls grew in the 1950s and early 1960s and was closely connected to the civil rights activism of the time (McGuire 2010).[16] Campaigns against the prosecution of Black men on the one hand, and for the prosecution of white men on the other, encapsulate the complex politics of using the criminal justice system as a weapon against rape. While organizing aimed at protecting Black women from rape by white men had little success, it was important to the civil rights movement, which won significant victories in the 1950s and grew into a mass movement by the 1960s. Local communities and representatives of the NAACP sought to convince local law enforcement to arrest alleged rapists, but few did so and most were acquitted at trial. The few convictions resulted in very light sentences, which contrasted with the prevalence of the death penalty for Black rape defendants (McGuire 2010).

Second, the conservative movement grew dramatically during the post-war decades. In general, postwar conservatism's main preoccupations were opposition to the welfare state, advocacy of the free market, and a persistent anticommunism that focused on internal and international threats (Gross, Medvetz, and Russell 2011). After overall disengagement from worldly issues in the 1920s and 1930s, evangelicals began reengaging in politics and civic life in the 1940s. A meeting in 1942 led to the formation of the National Association of Evangelicals, a cross-denominational group headed by Billy Graham. Headquartered in Washington, DC, it published *Christianity Today* and sought to influence elected officials and public policy (Lindsay 2008). Their influence on federal politics grew with the 1944 founding of the DC-based evangelical group, The Fellowship, which became very influential in both domestic and international politics (Lindsay 2008). Several influential publications (*Commentary, Partisan Review, National Review*), founded in the 1950s, helped consolidate postwar conservatism (McGirr 2001). The *National Review* in particular sought to bring together diverse conservative factions and to increase their influence within the Republican Party (Diamond 1995). This "fusionist" approach, bringing together conservatives of different stripes, became the hallmark of the New Right in the 1960s and beyond. Women's involvement, including in conservative social issues, also grew, in what Nickerson (2012) calls "housewife populism."

Third, a mostly white feminist movement also was beginning to grow. An increasing number of women found employment in the federal government, where they helped spur the Presidential Commission on the Status of Women of 1961–1963. That group, in turn, coalesced a network of women who went on to found the National Organization for Women (NOW) in 1966 (Banaszak 2010). At the same time, young white, African American, and other women working in the civil rights movement began to talk about their experiences and marginalization in the Left, leading to the emergence of a wider women's movement by the late 1960s (Evans 1980).

Activism Against Sexual Violence and Pornography in the 1960s and 1970s

The 1960s saw the emergence of widespread social organizing around racial inequality, women's liberation, and opposition to the Vietnam War, and the emergence of a New Right movement that became increasingly powerful over the subsequent decades. In the 1970s, American society changed rapidly and profoundly as the changes wrought by these social movements affected major institutions, while organizing continued on the Left and the Right. Both feminists and conservatives engaged with the issues of pornography, rape, and child sexual abuse in these years, but in different ways and amounts. Their approach to these issues built on the paths established by their predecessors, particularly the seemingly similar but fundamentally different ideas of protecting women and children from male domination through violence and protecting women's purity from moral pollution and degradation. The growth of both movements shifted these paths, ultimately bringing both feminists and conservatives into closer contact with the state and with each other.

Women's Movement Organizing

The feminist women's movement, from its roots in the 1960s, grew large and diverse, containing national organizations such as NOW; grassroots consciousness-raising groups, bookstores, coffeehouses, and car repair collectives; and state and local groups focused on electoral politics, public policy, employment discrimination, reproductive rights, women's health, and countless other issues (Enke 2007; Rosen 2000; Whittier 1995). A vibrant Black feminist movement coalesced in the 1970s with both local and national organizations that focused on issues of reproductive rights, economic justice, sexuality, and health, and developed theory about what academics later called intersectionality (Springer 2005). Latina, Native American, and Asian American women also organized (Roth 2003). In national, state, and local organizations, all these feminist activists addressed issues of sexuality and violence, sometimes separately, sometimes together.

Rape was one of the very first issues that feminist activists raised in the late 1960s and early 1970s, and much of what we now take for granted about it grew from feminists' efforts, such as its commonality and the idea that it is an act of violence and domination that is neither the woman's fault nor the result of men's overpowering lust (Martin 2005; Matthews 1994). Feminist activists developed a new understanding of the causes and experience of sexual violence. This emerged from feminist consciousness-raising groups in which participants discussed their experiences, interpreted them in terms of collective, and therefore political, causes, and planned campaigns for change. Although this analysis was new to many feminists, and they were the first to publicize it widely, it was not new to longtime African American women activists, who had long understood rape by white men in similar terms (Freedman 2013; McGuire 2010).

Child sexual abuse and incest became an issue for feminists almost as early and grew directly out of anti-rape activism. As with rape, these early activists rethought the prevalence of child sexual abuse, especially within the family, and its causes and effects (Whittier 2009). Feminist activism on sexual violence was based on the view that violence against women and children was a manifestation of sexism, a systematic way that women and children were oppressed and made fearful, and a reflection of male domination.

By 1980, feminists had founded numerous organizations around the country to combat rape and child sexual abuse. The first rape crisis center was founded in Florida in 1972 and many others followed (Bevacqua 2000; Martin 2005; Matthews 1994). Bearing variations on the name "Women Against Rape," anti-rape organizations sprang up in most cities and towns around the country, from New York (Brownmiller 1999) to Columbus, Ohio (Whittier 1995), Lawrence, Kansas (Bailey 1999), Washington DC (Bevacqua 2000), and countless other locales. Most served simultaneously as support groups and outreach and change organizations seeking to improve societal responses to sexual violence. Major national feminist organizations also addressed the issue of rape during the 1970s, for example, NOW formed a Rape Task Force in 1973, and the National Black Feminist Organization cosponsored events with New York's Women Against Rape (Freedman 2013).[17] Activists also organized marches and self-defense training; some made vigilante threats to castrate rapists and used dramatic tactics like mailing blood or severed animal testicles to recalcitrant judges (Gavey 2009; McCaughey 1997; Whittier 1995). While many rape crisis centers were predominantly white, others were multi-racial. The Washington, DC rape crisis center was at the center of Black feminist organizing in the city and sponsored an influential 1980 conference on Third World Women and Violence (Bevacqua 2000), and the East Los Angeles Center was organized by and for Latinas (Matthews 1994).

Feminist activists who first started working against sexual violence were disinclined to trust official channels. Instead of allies, institutional actors were targets. Activists accompanied women who had been raped to the hospital and to interviews with police to ensure that they were treated with respect. When they discovered that evidence was rarely collected successfully, they pushed hospitals to do so. They shadowed rape trials, collecting evidence of judges' and prosecutors' bias. Outraged by exemptions for marital rape, they pushed for change in the law. Similarly, when law enforcement and social services ignored the sexual assault of children, they spoke out, helped children and nonoffending parents navigate the system, and sought to change what they saw as outrageously short statutes of limitations.

Ironically, all this brought feminist activists into closer connection with the state, mainstream social services, and activists of other ideological stripes. Efforts to change how police and hospitals responded to victims of rape and child sexual abuse led to contracts for training programs in which activists taught detectives, district attorneys, nurses, doctors, and teachers about how to respond sensitively and effectively to victims (Bevacqua 2000; Corrigan 2013; Rentschler 2011; Whittier 1995; Whittier 2009). Efforts to change the responses of child welfare agencies and psychotherapy led to similar—but smaller scale—training programs and also inspired substantial numbers of feminist activists to become credentialed therapists and social workers. Social workers and child protective workers began to develop professional specialties in serving abused children. They also called on self-help groups of survivors of child sexual abuse for their expertise (Whittier 2009). All this turned feminist activism against sexual violence onto a path of greater engagement with the state, whether state and local legislatures and agencies, federal agencies, or Congress and federal law.

As they sought to end sexual violence, many feminists turned their attention to its portrayal in mass media, and some focused on pornography as a particularly egregious example (Bronstein 2011). Initially, most feminists placed pornography on a continuum of violence against women as part of "rape culture," the context in which rape and sexualized male dominance were the norm.[18] Influential organizations formed in the 1970s to tackle depictions of violence against women in media and pornography: Los Angeles' Women Against Violence Against Women (WAVAW, 1976), San Francisco's Women Against Violence in Pornography and Media (WAVPM, 1976), and New York City's Women Against Pornography (WAP, 1979) (Bronstein 2011). These organizations quickly gained prominence in the women's movement and were hubs for exploring ideological and practical issues related to opposing pornography. But feminists hotly disagreed about the role of pornography in women's subordination and the wisdom of seeking state intervention.

Antipornography feminists' critique of pornography was, for some, connected to a broader critique of sexism in sexual practice. This, too, was controversial. Feminists from various ideological and organizational positions engaged with, argued about, and sought to change how they thought about and practiced sexuality. Some advocated a greater focus on lesbian sexuality; some encouraged sexual practices and desires that sought equality between sexual partners; and others articulated sexual practices and desires that eroticized power with an emphasis on consent and negotiation. Critique of pornography's depictions of women and sex naturally fit into this framework. Increasingly, other vocal feminists challenged the focus on pornography as central to women's oppression. The feminist debates over sexuality and pornography came to be called the sex wars. As we will see in the next chapter, they were vehement and only intensified as feminist opponents of pornography appealed to the state for intervention.

Like rape and child sexual abuse, the issues of pornography and sexuality ultimately drew feminists into debates regarding turning to the state. These debates fractured the women's movement and redirected the path of activism on all three issues. While their path ultimately led some feminists to advocate legal restrictions that would eliminate most pornography, including support for laws that conservatives also supported, this path was not predetermined or apparent in the early 1970s. It developed over time, as conversations progressed to positions, alternative legal strategies were foreclosed, and conflicts over sexuality splintered groups, leaving less ideologically diverse and more divided groups to engage the issue of pornography (Corrigan 2013; Bronstein 2011). The paths that were open in 1970 were entrenched by 1982. Both antipornography feminists and their feminist opponents had crystallized their positions, and the division between them was increasingly uncrossable. When feminist opponents of pornography sought state intervention shortly thereafter, the political and emotional divisions developed into full-scale battle, as we will see in the next chapter. This conflict spilled over into activism against rape and child sexual abuse more broadly (Bevacqua 2000; Corrigan 2013). At the same time, conservative organizing was growing to new heights, setting events in motion that would bring feminists and conservatives into closer contact.

Conservatism during the 1960s and 1970s

Conservative activists—both religious and secular—also opposed pornography and sought to protect women and children from sexual danger (Strub 2011). The conservative movement's, its greater inclusion of women, and its increasing focus on issues of sexuality and family, pulled it into contact with the same issues that feminists were targeting, setting the groundwork for both their points of overlap and their conflicts.

Although the 1960s and 1970s are known as a period of active social movements on the Left, they also saw the rise of the modern conservative movement. Evangelical Christianity grew and became more engaged with the political sphere and allied with conservative Catholics. This new Christian Right joined forces with the secular New Right (Diamond 1995). Secular New Right activists included "free market enthusiasts, libertarians, anticommunists, and social conservatives" (Blee and Creasap 2010:273). Their emerging alliance was cemented through opposition to common enemies of communists, the leftist movements of the 1960s, and secular humanism (Lindsay 2008; Nickerson 2012). These took form in campaigns opposing abortion, the Equal Rights Amendment, and gay and lesbian civil rights, issues that came together under the "pro-family" slogan and appealed to both religious and secular conservatives (Diamond 1995; McGirr 2001). Like movements of the Left, including the women's movement, the New Right mobilized grassroots participants, in contrast to the Old Right of the 1950s and before, which had relied on its strong leaders (Blee and Creasap 2010). But experienced leaders from the Old Right, like Phyllis Schlafly, were also crucial to the movement's survival and success (Blee and Creasap 2010; McGirr 2001). The Christian Right became more politically sophisticated throughout the 1970s and 1980s, "incorporat[ing] the trappings of secularism" to increase their political influence, building cross-denominational coalitions, and promulgating their own media outlets (Gross, Medvetz, and Russell 2011; Moen 1992:5).

Opposition to feminist goals, including the Equal Rights Amendment, abortion rights, and cultural changes regarding gender and sexuality, was central to the Right's effort "to wield moral authority through the state" (Blee and Creasap 2010). Building on evangelical Christian congregations and television ministries, organizers established the Moral Majority in 1979 to influence and elect Republican candidates (Diamond 1995). The Moral Majority grew rapidly and, with and other New Right organizations, became increasingly powerful in the Republican Party and the federal government.[19] Many women were active on the Right for the first time, in what came to be called "kitchen table activism," such as letter-writing campaigns (McGirr 2001). They mobilized around gendered and maternalist views of women as well-suited to upholding morality, children's interests, and the family (Benowitz 2015; Nickerson 2012). They worked against abortion and school desegregation, as well as for conservative political candidates (McGirr 2001).

Campaigns opposing pornography particularly drew conservative women's attention, although men, especially clergy, led these campaigns. Conservative antipornography campaigns, building on long-standing organizations, like Citizens for Decency through Law, were a visible part of rightwing activism during the 1970s. In fact, despite feminist ferment around the topic, outside observers in the 1970s rightly saw opposition to pornography as a conservative, not feminist, issue that was based on the belief "that the United States has morally disintegrated, evidenced by hippies, sex on television, crime, homosexuality, and secularism" (Lo 1982:126).

The most extensive organizing focused on pornography, but, by the mid-1980s, religious conservative organizations such as Moral Majority and Focus on the Family also engaged issues of family violence, simultaneously pushing to protect family "autonomy" against legal restrictions on corporal punishment, advocating nonviolent assertion of patriarchal authority over wives and children, and warning of the risks of child sexual abuse by step-fathers or in other nonmarital families. Like feminists, conservatives var-ied in their opinions on these issues (McGirr 2001), but their differences never rose to the level of intensity and factionalism seen in the women's movement. Their underlying reasons were founded on sexual morality and protecting the family rather than women's liberation. They disagreed vehe-mently with most feminist goals and viewed changes in women's status as undermining traditional sexual morality (Critchlow 2005; Schreiber 2008). Secular conservatives focused mainly on criminal enforcement on all three issues, but religious conservatives' engagement was broader.

Overview of the 1980s

By 1980, the women's movement had begun to affect societal attitudes toward sexual violence, but widespread change was still in its infancy, and the cultural and political climate was shifting decidedly to the Right. Prosecution of rape or child sexual abuse remained rare, services were underfunded, and federal attention to rape and child sexual abuse was just beginning. Liberalizing standards on pornography meant that sexu-ally explicit material was increasingly visible. President Reagan and a newly Republican-majority Senate were elected with support from an ascendant religious conservative movement, mass mobilization by feminists and other progressive movements was declining, and religious conservative groups like the Moral Majority seemed poised to reverse recent gains in women's status (Diamond 1995; McGirr 2001). The women's movement, in contrast, was shrinking and beset by conflict over sex and pornography, but despite the conservative climate, rape crisis phone lines, resource cen-ters, shelters, peer counseling services, court watch, and self-defense pro-grams serving adults and children who had been sexually assaulted grew steadily throughout the 1980s. Most originated from feminist organizing, but as they expanded to meet a huge untapped demand, the activists who ran them sought and gained funding and contracts with local, state, and federal government as well as from hospitals and schools. Feminist organ-izations struggled to balance their social change agendas with the deluge of cases and the bureaucratic requirements that came with government funding. By the late 1980s, many were absorbed by schools or hospitals and countless service organizations that were run by professionals with a relatively political neutral orientation flourished (Bevacqua 2000; Corrigan 2013; Gottschalk 2006; Martin 2005; Matthews 1994; Whittier 1995).

At the same time, a growing professional field focused on sexual violence (Cheit 2014; Davis 2005; Whittier 2009). Specialization in sexual assault developed in medicine, psychotherapy, social work, law, and academic research. Law enforcement developed special response and investigation teams, hospitals special staff, and multidisciplinary teams and professional associations connected child advocates. Many, but not all, such professionals came from feminist backgrounds. Individuals in these fields quickly became influential players and often eclipsed activists in influencing policy.

In terms of the *federal government*, after 1980 federal legislation and initiatives in all three issue areas expanded criminal justice, social welfare, and public health responses to sexual violence against women and children, and Congress engaged in extensive debate about them. All three issues are regulated through both state and federal law. Criminal law is the purview of states, with the federal government having jurisdiction over crimes that cross state lines or occur on federal or Native American land.[20] However, the federal government exerts an outsized effect on state law through requirements tied to federal funding and also provides funding for social services and law enforcement.

Federal attention to pornography—in Congress and in the agencies charged with enforcing laws against obscenity—spiked in the 1980s and percolated steadily after that. High-profile congressional hearings and the 1985 Attorney General's Commission on Pornography led to new legislation and enforcement initiatives. Government funding for antipornography efforts focused almost exclusively on governmental prosecution and interdiction. Although Republican congresspeople and presidents moved more aggressively against pornography, Democrats also engaged actively, and there was relatively little political division on the issue within the state. Over the next two decades, congressional debate on the topic—especially in relation to children—continued, but enforcement and other policy action diminished sharply.

In contrast, legislative attention to and funding for child sexual abuse occurred throughout the 1980s–2000s, under both Democratic and Republican control. Child sexual abuse had mostly separate funding streams through the National Center on Child Abuse and Neglect (established in 1974), and other federal agencies including Health and Human Services, the Centers for Disease Control, and the Victims of Crime Act. Besides the Child Abuse Prevention and Treatment Act (CAPTA), which is the central federal child abuse legislation, child sexual abuse also drove much of the congressional debate and legislation about pornography. Of all the case studies, child sexual abuse saw the least political or party division, as politicians of all stripes wanted to be seen as protecting children. By the 2000s, this entailed ever-stricter laws about sex offender registration and community notification that were supported by a very different set of advocates who still defined the issue as nonpolitical.

Overall, legislative attention to and funding for anti-rape initiatives were minimal before VAWA, although modest funding for rape prevention and treatment began in the mid-1970s and ebbed and flowed over the subsequent two decades (Bevacqua 2000; Martin 2005; Matthews 1994; Whittier 1995). Passed in 1994, VAWA funded numerous service, policing, and prosecution initiatives. It also contained a controversial provision allowing people to sue their assailants in federal court if an assault could be shown to be motivated by "gender animus." This provision was overturned by the Supreme Court in 2000, but the rest of VAWA was reauthorized and modestly expanded in 2000 and 2006 with strong bipartisan support. As conservative and feminist activists mobilized more outside the state and feminists pushed for expanded services for immigrant and LGBT victims of violence, the bipartisan consensus inside the state broke down and VAWA barely passed in 2013.

Across all these eras, feminists and conservatives engaged in different ways with cultural and legal opposition to pornography, child sexual abuse, and violence against women. While they rarely formed true alliances, they often worked in the proximity to each other, sometimes toward similar ends and sometimes at cross-purposes. Their indirect interactions and suspicion of each other are characteristic of noncoalitional relationships between frenemies. The next chapters of the book tell the story of their relationships in these three issue arenas and how both parties shaped what happened in policy, law, and culture.

ORGANIZATION OF THE BOOK

The book is organized into chapters on each case study. Chapter 2 focuses on the pornography case study, showing how the collaborative-adversarial relationship between feminists and conservatives opposed to pornography developed and how both sides interacted with governmental bodies, including municipal governments, the federal Attorney General's Commission on the Status of Pornography (aka Meese Commission), and Congress. Unpacking their actions and modes of influence, we see the selection processes that resulted in conservatives having more influence than feminists, and the surprising ways that feminists' concern with rape and child sexual abuse affected religious conservatives. The chapter takes us from the years of peak interaction and federal attention during the mid-1980s, to the 1990s and early 2000s, when conservative lobbying and federal action remained high but feminists had disengaged, to the later 2000s and early 2010s when the changed legal and social climate mitigated any deep opposition to pornography.

Chapter 3 deals with child sexual abuse. I show how this very different form of narrow-neutral relationship between frenemies coincided with relatively low influence by either feminists or conservatives on federal policy and culture regarding the issue. Instead, professionals and a single-issue survivors' movement defined child sexual abuse as nonpolitical. Moving from 1980 to 2013, the chapter shows how federal engagement with child sexual abuse expanded under the frame that the issue was beyond politics and how periodic challenges to this consensus emerged and were resolved. Attention to child sexual abuse shifted from a focus on violence within the family to a focus on child pornography and the control of sex offenders. But, despite the framing about dangerous strangers, the resulting legislation also applied to familial abuse. Experiential testimony, affirmed by ritualized expression of emotion, bolstered expert authority to bring together otherwise-opposed legislators and grassroots participants. The definition of child sexual abuse as beyond politics ensured a wide consensus on the issue and made challenging policy virtually impossible.

Chapter 4 examines the Violence Against Women Act and the activism that led to it. The chapter shows the importance of feminist organizations—and the absence of conservative ones—in drafting and promoting the legislation (Strebeigh 2009) and traces how support from conservative elected officials formed alongside opposition from conservative activists outside the state. VAWA emerged in the context of the burgeoning punitive state but also incorporated social service, civil rights, and prevention elements. With VAWA, as with the other cases, framing that supported ideologically opposed views was crucial and enabled the ambivalent alliance between feminists and conservatives in Congress. But the priorities of feminist advocates—who sought measures for immigrants, women of color, and LGBT people based on an intersectional understanding of violence—were marginalized under the power of criminal discourses and procedures in Congress. The relationship between these ambivalent allies entailed compromise on both sides.

Chapter 5, the book's conclusion, draws comparative theoretical lessons about frenemy relationships from all three cases and discusses their implications for ongoing policy regarding sex offenders, sex trafficking, and government surveillance. The well-trodden paths of feminist and conservative engagement with sexual violence have influenced recent approaches to sexual assault, including in the military and in colleges and universities. Feminists have influenced these developments, but not alone. Ideologically-diverse frenemies, including both feminists and conservatives, continue to be engaged in these issues and to shape their paths.

CHAPTER 2
Opposition to Pornography

Collaborative Adversaries

When I described this book to friends and colleagues, most immediately asked if I was writing about pornography. The most notorious case of alleged feminist-conservative coalition, opposition to pornography became a symbol of the dangers of feminist coalition with the Right. For activists and scholars alike, it has become a cautionary tale. The actual story is much more complex and helps us untangle the central questions of the book. How do opposed social movements interact with each other and governmental bodies when their goals share some common ground? How do they influence each other? What are the consequences of their actions for legislation, policy, and discourse?

The standard story about antipornography feminists goes like this: In the 1980s, some feminists formed an alliance with conservative antipornography organizations and government officials to pass antipornography legislation at the municipal level. They also made common cause with the ultra-conservative Attorney General's Commission on Pornography (known as the Meese Commission, after Attorney General Edwin Meese) and attempted to pass a federal version of the municipal ordinance. Conservatives cynically adopted feminist language about pornography as harmful to women to disguise their right-wing agenda and make pornography appear to be an issue of broader concern. This helped advance the Religious Right's agenda. The strange alliance was challenged by other feminists, who opposed censorship and embraced a wider range of sexual expression, in what is often termed the "sex wars." In the end, feminist and lesbian material became a target of censors' efforts, reinforcing the folly of antipornography feminism.

This story is virtually unchallenged in the writing of academics and activists.[1] For example, John Semonche (2007:226) writes about a "coalition" between Andrea Dworkin, Catharine MacKinnon, and "their newfound friends on the religious right." In a generally excellent account of antipornography feminism, Whitney Strub (2011:248–9) writes that Dworkin and MacKinnon were "valuable allies" to the Meese Commission, "did little to distance themselves from the Right," and "defen[ded] their conservative allegiances." Judith Levine (2002:xxiii) labels them "bedfellows" and calls the Meese Commission a "sort of summit" between "feminist sexual conservatives" and the Right. Participants in the sex and porn wars wrote extensively about the underlying conservatism and moralism of antipornography feminism, its cooptation by the Right, and, in Lisa Duggan's (1985:13) words, "the danger of coalitions."[2]

There are two main problems with this story. First, the relationship between the two movements was not a coalition. Second, the rightward swing of federal policy regarding pornography was due not to conservatives' cooptation of feminist language, but to their greater power compared to feminist activists and to the underlying structures and processes of the state. The story has been told this way because in the conflict among feminists over pornography, alliance with the Right was a damning accusation. The victors write history, and the anticensorship, anti-antipornography position won, leading to widespread acceptance of an oversimplified story. But antipornography feminists' accounts of the events are also a simplified story designed to gain support. Neither version reflects the complex nature of the relationship with conservatives and the forces shaping the end results. In this chapter, I rewrite the story of antipornography feminism and conservatism. In doing so, I show one form that relationships between frenemies can take, and explain how activists and other forces shaped federal policy on pornography.

Pornography is a large and complex field, including producers and distributors, multiple federal and state government agencies, laws, constitutional constraints and case law, mass media, activists from different perspectives, consumers, and technologies. Sexually explicit media can be regulated by zoning laws that confine it to certain areas and through obscenity law. Material that is legally obscene is not subject to First Amendment (i.e., free speech) protections; it can be seized and its producers, sellers, or consumers can be criminally charged. What is considered legally obscene has been defined in changing ways by the US Supreme Court. What is legally permissible has steadily broadened from the 1950s to the present.[3] Despite constitutional constraints, legislators have sought to regulate pornography. At the federal level, Congress holds hearings and passes legislation, presidents speak on the issue, executive branch agencies, including the Justice Department (under the attorney general), US Customs, the US Post Office, Federal Bureau of Investigation (FBI), Federal Communications Commission (FCC), and federal prosecutors all weigh in on pornography. National professional and industry groups such as the Free Speech Coalition (representing the adult industry), American Library Association, and American Booksellers Association engage. At the state or local level, prosecutors and police, state and municipal legislators, zoning boards, business associations, chambers of commerce, religious congregations, neighborhood associations, and interested citizens all engage. The field has altered over time as players interacted with one another and as a result of other social changes (for example, the rise of the Internet).

Before the mid-1980s, a feminist critique of pornography did not enter the federal policy process. Congress had addressed obscenity more broadly before 1970, but that approach was legislatively dead by the early 1980s. State approaches to pornography focused on venerable but unstable legal frames of obscenity, which were subject to constant court challenges, or on child exploitation. Despite conservative disapproval of all sexually explicit media, Congress did not approach pornography discursively or legislatively as a distinct problem apart from the exploitation of children. All congressional hearings that addressed pornography between 1977 and 1983 did so through the lens of child abuse, most often concentrating on the need for better social services to address the involvement of runaway children in prostitution and pornography. Such hearings included representatives of religious and conservative antipornography organizations, but not feminist ones.[4] But President Ronald Reagan's budget, which reduced funds for social services, blocked those avenues, as both Republicans and Democrats complained. Child pornography presented a more straightforward case, with a focus on criminal prosecution of producers and distributors. The prevailing frame and funds tilted toward criminal justice rather than social service solutions.

Although newly elected President Reagan pledged attention to the issue of pornography, he, like Congress, focused mainly on child pornography and its links to organized crime.[5] By 1984, as Reagan was gearing up for reelection, he ordered stepped up enforcement on obscenity by US Customs and the Postal Service and chartered the Attorney General's Commission on Pornography, which, as mentioned, reported to Edwin Meese.[6] As Whitney Strub (2011) argues, pornography was a relatively uncontroversial way for Reagan to curry favor with the Christian Right (see also Diamond 1995).

Conservative opponents of pornography saw an opportunity for influence. Meanwhile, antipornography feminists had built a sizeable movement at the local level but viewed the government's existing approaches as counterproductive.

Activism and congressional attention to pornography peaked during two separate and very different periods. First, between 1982–1988, feminists and conservatives were both highly mobilized on the issue and gained extensive congressional attention, federal action, and discursive change. Pornography sparked widespread response from the federal government in the Attorney General's Commission on Pornography, numerous congressional subcommittee hearings, and expanded enforcement divisions within several federal agencies. During this period, feminist frames emphasizing harms to women gained ground and legal obscenity enforcement grew.

Second, between 1997 and 2006, congressional attention peaked again, and Congress considered legislation to restrict pornography in new media and children's access to it. Conservatives remained active on the issue, but feminists were sidelined. Discourse framed pornography as harmful to children, rather than women, a morally protectionist approach that was prominent in both periods and grew from conservative frames. This chapter primarily focuses on the first time period, when feminists and conservatives were both engaged with the issue.

FRENEMIES, REPUTATION, AND OUTCOMES

Antipornography feminist and antipornography conservative social movement organizations shared a similar goal—the elimination of pornography—but they differed in the ideological and discursive bases for this goal and the specific legislative and policy changes they supported. Their networks did not overlap, their collective identities were incompatible, and they did not coordinate strategy or tactics. They explicitly opposed each other's larger agendas. Nevertheless, they interacted sporadically as their similar goals drew them into the same state contexts. Both participated in municipal legislative campaigns, congressional hearings, and hearings before the 1986 Meese Commission. Both sides hoped to affect how power-holders framed the issue, the discourses they used to understand it, and legislation and policy. Yet, even when they lobbied the same bodies, feminist and conservative opponents of pornography did not claim allegiance to each other or appear at the same time, nor did they usually support the same specific policy. Instead, each side defined pornography and its remedies according to their broader goals and beliefs. Antipornography conservatives wanted stronger enforcement and prosecution of obscenity statutes, to define obscenity broadly, and to expand zoning regulations to force pornography out of business, which they believed would promote sexual morality and strengthen families. Antipornography feminists advocated legislation defining pornography as a violation of women's civil rights, which, by allowing women to bring civil suits against distributors or producers of pornography, would force pornography out of business and thus change how society saw women and reduce sexual violence.

Their interaction had consequences for the individual movements, their reputations, and how they framed not just pornography but also violence against women. Conservatives, at times, were prone to incorporate versions of feminist frames, railing against the exploitation of women in pornography and its links to rape and spousal abuse, although they did so only during the few years when feminist opposition to pornography was prominent. Their primary frames remained religious and sexual morality. Over time, however, religious conservative publications increasingly covered rape and domestic violence even apart from the issue of pornography, suggesting that contact with feminist ideas helped increase visibility of these issues in evangelical contexts. In contrast, antipornography feminists, whose opposition to pornography was tightly linked to tackling violence against women, vocally disagreed with the conservative emphasis on morality and indecency and the corresponding policy reliance on obscenity law and zoning changes. They never incorporated conservative critiques about morality, social degeneration, or the importance of strong families. Nevertheless, they sometimes separated pornography from the rest of their program for social change or argued that sexually explicit media was uniquely harmful to women, creating what Gene Burns calls a "morally limiting frame" that could gain broader support (Bronstein 2011; Burns 2005; Strub 2011). Their occasional success in doing so, or in influencing how the state framed the issue, is evidence not of a coalition but of a social movement outcome.

Many feminists opposed antipornography feminism, unlike antipornography conservatism, which had no opposition from the larger conservative movement. Coalescing in the group FACT (Feminist Anti-Censorship Task Force), these feminists were opposed on freedom of expression grounds and out of concern that sexual freedom would be restricted for women, lesbians, gay men, and other sexual minorities (Duggan and Hunter 1995).[7] Even some feminists who were sympathetic to the critique of pornography were aghast at the idea of sharing ground with antifeminists and the state. Feminists on both sides of the debate over state intervention in pornography generally agreed that most pornography, like the rest of the mainstream media, was sexist. Antipornography feminists framed it in terms of violence against women; their feminist opponents, in contrast, understood pornography as a matter of sexual freedom and expression, an area in which state intervention was dangerous and linked to the history of censorship. Part of the dispute was about whether the state, newly in the hands of religious conservatives, could be trusted to advance women's interests.

For antipornography feminists, preserving their reputation in the face of accusations of being in bed with the enemy was a major challenge. Decrying unholy alliances, opponents of antipornography feminism constructed a plausible narrative how antipornography feminists were in bed with the Right. Conversely, antipornography feminists constructed a narrative in which their feminist opponents were promoting the sexual exploitation of women on behalf of pornographers. Conservatives, for their part, sometimes claimed alliance with or support from feminists yet sometimes claimed their approach to pornography was opposed to feminism. All these narratives had very real consequences for the reputations and relationships of the involved parties and, ultimately, for their parent social movements.

Besides influencing each other, antipornography feminist and conservative movements had some effect on policy and discourse regarding pornography. These effects were not a straightforward success for either side, but they tilted strongly Right because of conservatives' greater power and influence and the institutional and symbolic power of the state. Short term, increased obscenity enforcement by the Justice Department and congressional hearings and legislation on pornography regarding new media (i.e., cable television, home video, and computers) were disproportionately influenced by conservative control of the state and the close ties between conservative activists and the Reagan and Bush administrations. Feminist rhetoric, even mouthed by conservatives, was almost nonexistent in these contexts and mostly irrelevant to the outcomes. Long term, despite activists' efforts, legislation and prosecution crumbled under court challenges and discourse critical of pornography diminished in parallel with the rise in production and consumption across media.

The 1980s set activists on both sides and their parent movements on a particular path. Antipornography feminists' beliefs, strategic choices, and concern about their reputation foreclosed ongoing collaboration with conservatives in efforts to combat pornography through extending traditional obscenity enforcement to new media such as telephone and Internet pornography. But the discursive and legal emphasis on using civil rights legislation and frames to address violence against women persisted, eventually proving central to the Violence Against Women Act and the use of

Title IX against campus sexual assault. Conversely, the conflict left anti-censorship feminists loath to discuss sexism in pornography and took the issue largely off the table (Duggan and Hunter 1995). Antipornography conservatives' ties to federal elites remained strong, as they cycled in and out of the Justice Department, district attorneys' and other offices, and helped shape emerging legislation and enforcement against pornography. For example, the executive director of the Attorney General's Commission on Pornography was a federal prosecutor who went on to head Citizens for Decency through Law. But their use of violence against women as a bludgeon against pornography weakened their ability to oppose other legislation and policy on violence against women, as we will see in later chapters.

Next, after outlining initial antipornography activism by feminists and conservatives, I dissect the points of overlap in municipal campaigns for antipornography ordinances and antipornography feminist and conservative influence federally in Congress and the Meese Commission. I discuss the lasting effects of their activism, including the paths that led to feminists' marginalization and disengagement during the late 1980s and beyond, and the decline of both feminist influence and their relationship with conservatives as the federal government acted on conservative goals. Finally, I show the consequences of their relationship for feminists and conservatives.

CONSERVATIVE AND FEMINIST OPPOSITION TO PORNOGRAPHY: BUILDING ORGANIZATIONS, MOBILIZING PROTEST

Conservatives had been fighting pornography for decades.[8] Although opponents of pornography crossed the political spectrum, conservatives were the best organized throughout the 1950s and 1960s. Citizens for Decent Literature, later named Citizens for Decency through Law (CDL), was established by Charles Keating in 1955 and remained a major player through the 1980s. Grounded in Catholicism, the group was overtly non-denominational and had numerous white, suburban women members despite an overwhelmingly male leadership. It grew rapidly, subtly courting Far Right support while cultivating a "moderate image" (Strub 2011:98). The group used legal strategies and, in a tactic that proved both successful and persistent, produced films and brochures with excerpts from sexually explicit products to "arouse" the concerns of viewers (Strub 2011).

Antipornography conservatives defined pornography broadly, to include virtually any representation of sexual activity or nudity. Pornography was objectionable to conservatives because of its depiction of nonmarital sexuality and its incitement of lust and masturbation. While religious conservatives saw these as part of a larger set of sinful challenges to the family and children's innocence, secular conservatives saw them as undermining the strong families and values necessary for the nation's success (Strub 2011). Sexually explicit media became more widespread and socially acceptable throughout the 1970s and 1980s; items that had been suppressed previously were no longer considered legally obscene, and conservatives were frustrated with what they saw as inadequate enforcement. The 1970 Johnson Presidential Commission on Pornography, which had found it to be largely harmless, infuriated conservatives and undermined the rationale for state intervention (Gerhard 2001). The use of zoning regulations to confine pornography to particular areas nevertheless permitted it to flourish in isolated neighborhoods, and attempts to zone pornography out of entire cities did not pass court muster (Strub 2011).

Reagan's election raised the hopes of the Religious Right for significant change, including action on obscenity (Diamond 1995; Willentz 2008), and antipornography conservative organizations grew following 1980. The rising strength of the Religious Right enlivened well-established organizations, such as CDL and Morality in Media, and spawned new ones, such as the Religious Alliance Against Pornography. The movement was closely connected to larger conservative organizations such as the Moral Majority and Focus on the Family as well as evangelical Christian congregations.

Meanwhile, feminist opposition to pornography also was growing. Feminist opposition to pornography emerged in the 1970s from the movement against violence against women and sexism in mass media (Bronstein 2011; Strub 2011). In the 1970s, feminist discourse placed pornography on a continuum of violence against women as part of the "rape culture," the context that rationalized rape and in which male dominance was the norm in sexual relationships and elsewhere. Some feminists came to see pornography as an ideological linchpin in this system because of its portrayal of women as sex objects who enjoyed rape and physical pain, which they believed shaped the larger view of women as less than human and promoted violence against women. Unlike conservatives, they defined pornography by its promotion of sexual violence and exploitation of women, not simply in terms of sexual explicitness. It was problematic not on moral or familial grounds, but because of its role in women's oppression.

Major antipornography feminist organizations emerged on both coasts, including Women Against Violence in Pornography and Media in San Francisco (WAVPM, 1976), and Women Against Pornography in New York (WAP, 1979). Charismatic leaders, often unaffiliated with major social movement organizations, also were central to antipornography feminism, and included Catharine MacKinnon, Andrea Dworkin, Susan Brownmiller, Gloria Steinem, and Robin Morgan. Early feminist opponents of pornography, unlike conservatives and later antipornography feminists, were ambivalent about legal change. They were open to some legal strategies, including zoning, but debated legal restrictions on pornography.[9] Debate over censorship occurred regularly at WAVPM general membership meetings in the 1970s, and members held a wide range of opinions.[10] In addition to discussions at meetings, WAVPM held a 1979 workshop on the First Amendment, which included "the possible dangers of relying on patriarchal legal system to accomplish our ends,"[11] and established a study committee on the First Amendment in 1980, which discussed both pros and cons of advocating ordinances restricting pornography. (Cons included alienating "civil liberties people," and "could this kind of thing be used against gay or good sex stuff?")[12] Although members thought that pornography contributed to a "climate in which rape, battery, child molestation and sexual assault are considered acceptable and "cool' by the culture,"[13] they generally aimed not to ban pornography but to build "a movement of women [that could] change the economics and social norms in this country."[14]

Women Against Pornography, which formed shortly after WAVPM, focused more narrowly on pornography rather than sexism in other media, and its members were quicker to advocate state intervention. Located in New York City and led by feminist luminaries including Gloria Steinem, Susan Brownmiller, and Robin Morgan, WAP quickly became the most visible and influential feminist antipornography organization. It sought and received extensive mainstream media coverage, focusing on the idea that pornography both promoted and was itself violence against women. In 1979, WAP organized a massive conference and march in Times Square, and by 1982 boasted 3,500 members (Bronstein 2011). Like WAVPM, WAP distinguished itself from conservative opponents of pornography, but it was less conflicted about seeking legal change or trying to influence the state, as we will see later in the chapter.

In emphasizing women's shared oppression through pornography and sexual violence, WAP and WAVPM paid relatively little attention to differences among women. WAVPM tried persistently, with mixed success, to recruit women of color, but their minimal focus on racism in pornography made this difficult (Bronstein 2011:291–92). WAP's attempts in this direction were more muted, and their emphasis on universal sisterhood prompted critiques from women of color (Bronstein 2011:245). Given the racial separations and conflicts in the women's movement (Breines 2002; Roth 2003) and the long-standing activism by Black women against rape, this gap is both predictable and unfortunate. Antipornography feminists and Black feminists both pointed to the intensified degradation and dehumanization of Black and other women of color in pornography, but this did not develop into a fully intersectional antipornography feminist critique or campaign (Collins 2000; Harris 1989; Nash 2008).

Even before antipornography feminists turned to the state, other feminists began to mobilize a "pro-sex" anticensorship women's movement (Bronstein 2011). A 1982 conference at Barnard, planned to counter what organizers saw as a conservative shift in the women's movement's approach to sexuality, erupted into conflict and helped coalesce the nascent network of pro-sex/anticensorship feminists. Two edited volumes containing conference papers circulated widely in women's studies classes and feminist bookstores and fed debates in local communities over the politics of sexual practices and representations (Snitow, Stansell, and Thompson 1983; Vance 1984).[15]

Both feminist and conservative movements against pornography engaged in collective action outside the state, but not together. The majority of feminist antipornography activism during the late 1970s and 1980s focused on direct action, writing, and persuasion. New York's WAP and San Francisco's WAVPAM organized marches in red-light districts, ran tours aimed at increasing opposition to pornography, and presented slideshows of pornographic images to raise awareness about pornography among community groups. WAP estimated that they gave 2,500 tours of the sex industry in Times Square in their first year (Brownmiller 1999). Activists poured blood or ink on pornographic magazines, boycotted businesses that advertised in *Playboy*, and wrote books and pamphlets arguing that pornography constituted "woman hating," in Andrea Dworkin's words (Brownmiller 1999; Duggan and Hunter 1995; Dworkin 1976; Dworkin 1991 [1979]). Meanwhile, antipornography conservative activists organized pickets and boycotts of 7-Eleven (ostensibly the nation's largest retailer of pornographic magazines) and other businesses. These were framed by participants as based in Christian conservatism and did not include feminist participants (Frame 1984; Rabey 1984; Selle 1984).

The protests organized by antipornography feminists were larger and received more publicity than those organized by their conservative counterparts (Bronstein 2011). Not surprisingly, some conservative individuals and organizations sought to join them. WAP's landmark 1979 march in Times Square drew conservatives among the estimated 5,000 marchers, but feminist "marshals scuffled with police to keep willing conservative allies out of their ranks" and destroyed their signs (Bronstein 2011:68; Potter 2012). Feminists worked to distance themselves from conservatives.

In Pittsburgh, for example, local antipornography conservatives sought to "claim common ground with feminists to disguise their sexist goals," but in response, the Pittsburgh group changed their name from Women Against Pornography to Women Against Sexist Violence in Pornography and Media to discourage affiliation attempts by the Right who, they wrote, "are right now trying to use us and our slideshow to push their repressive anti-porn bill" (Bronstein 2011:276–77). WAP also received and responded to many letters of interest from antipornography conservatives, some of whom may have joined the organization as paper members (Bronstein 2011).[16] Certainly politically diverse constituencies attended their Times Square tours. Brownmiller (1999:306) listed attendees, including high school and college classes, the Anti-Defamation League, a "study group of Chinese-American women . . . [and] whole groups of foreign tourists who'd heard that we offered the best sightseeing bargain in town." Brownmiller (1999:306–7) alone describes WAP members' "paying a courtesy visit" to Father Morton Hill, the president of Morality in Media. Even then, they were concerned about reputation. She recounts, "In our terror at being lumped with religious conservatives, 'abortion' and 'gay rights' were the first words out of our mouths." Nevertheless, she describes Hill as "a good, kindly man, and very knowledgeable about our mutual interests." Neither she nor any other source describes further collaboration, but Morality in Media member (later president), Robert Peters, described having had a great time with an interfaith group "at that huge demonstration in Times Square" (Potter 2012:68).

However, conservative organizations never affiliated with WAP or cosponsored protests. On the other side, feminist antipornography groups did not participate in conservative demonstrations or organizations. The groups did not publicize or praise each other's protests, either. No articles about WAP's red-light district tours or slideshows appeared in the conservative press, nor about the conservative protests at 7-Eleven in the feminist press.[17] Antipornography feminists and conservatives both wanted to drive pornographic outlets out of business and were using similar tactics. These tactics were appealing to at least some on the Right, until they realized the affiliation with the women's movement (Bronstein 2011). Although they shared a similar target, their differences of identity, ideology, and network were too great to allow them to work in coalition.

As some feminist organizations began to focus on pornography more narrowly, the potential for overlap grew. But it only materialized when antipornography feminists proposed legal change. As feminist and conservative opponents of pornography sought to harness the power of the state for their own ends, they turned first to municipal legislation and then to federal government. As I show next, antipornography feminism briefly changed the landscape, through municipal ordinances, the Attorney General's Commission on Pornography, and mid-1980s Congressional hearings. The changes were dramatic as feminist and conservative opponents of pornography briefly converged. Their fraught interaction began in Minneapolis in 1984.

MUNICIPAL ANTIPORNOGRAPHY ORDINANCES

A municipal ordinance campaign in Minneapolis, Minnesota, was ground zero for the pornography wars, the first time that antipornography feminists tried in earnest to harness governmental power. Feminists were quickly joined by conservatives who were interested in this new, potentially constitutional, way of restricting pornography. Just as quickly, opponents of the ordinances mobilized, including the ACLU and the newly formed Feminists Anti-Censorship Task Force (FACT). The interactions between antipornography feminists and conservatives around the municipal ordinances illustrate the complexities of relationships between movements that are neither friends nor enemies.

Ordinances defining pornography as a violation of women's civil rights and providing civil means of enforcement passed in Minneapolis in 1983 and 1984 and in Indianapolis in 1984. The Minneapolis mayor issued a veto both times, while the Indianapolis ordinance was signed into law but promptly ruled unconstitutional (Downs 1989; Strub 2011). Similar ordinances were later introduced unsuccessfully in Los Angeles, Cambridge, Massachusetts, and the Massachusetts State Legislature.[18] Grounded solidly in a feminist rationale, the approach initially drew support from feminist activists and liberal-to-moderate politicians in Minneapolis but quickly caught the attention of conservatives in Indianapolis and nationally. Developed by feminists Catharine MacKinnon and Andrea Dworkin, the ordinance likely appealed to conservatives because they hoped it might allow them to sidestep First Amendment limitations to obscenity law (Downs 1989).

But although both feminists and conservatives worked for the ordinances, they did not do so in coalition. Feminist activists (but not conservative) mobilized in Minneapolis, while conservative activists (but not feminist) mobilized in Indianapolis. The ordinance campaign in Indianapolis also entailed limited and covert collaboration between one antipornography feminist leader (MacKinnon) and a Republican councilwoman who worked with supporters on the Right. These were covert, backstage interactions between leaders without interaction between rank-and-file members. This, plus the separation in time and space between the feminist-supported Minneapolis campaign and the conservative-supported Indianapolis one allowed leaders in both movements to embrace an identical goal.

The ordinance emerged from a collaboration between Dworkin and MacKinnon, who co-taught a course at the University of Minnesota law school in the fall of 1983 titled "Pornography." The course outline and readings built the conceptual and legal approach employed in the ordinance. The class was described as "[a] feminist inquiry into the issues of equality and freedom, coercion and consent, morality and politics," which examined, "the nature and structure of male power, sexual objectification, women as whores, the political meaning of force, the Sexualization of race, the use of children, the nature and meaning of sexual shame, and the significance of penetration." The course was intellectually and emotionally intense, and the students—56 women and 4 men—found an outlet in the Minneapolis ordinance campaign.[19]

Minneapolis Legislative Campaigns: Feminist Supporters and Sympathetic Officials

The Minneapolis campaign makes the ordinance's grounding in the women's movement crystal clear. Interested by MacKinnon and Dworkin's approach, Minneapolis city counselors asked them to draft a law (MacKinnon 1997:4). Dworkin wrote at the time, "Kitty and I have written a statute that we think just completely works on every level: meaning legal and political in feminist as well as broader terms."[20] Councilwoman Charlee Hoyt, a moderate Republican who supported women's issues, was the original sponsor and a key mover for the ordinance and worked closely with MacKinnon and Dworkin in the lead-up to the hearings (Downs 1989:ch. 3).

The ordinance barred "trafficking in pornography," defined as "the production, sale, exhibition, or distribution of pornography," and permitted any woman to bring action against producers or distributors of pornography "as a woman acting against the subordination or women" (MacKinnon and Dworkin 1997:429).[21] Enforcement would occur if someone filed a civil rights complaint with the municipal or state Office of Equal Opportunity or brought a civil suit against producers or distributors of pornography.[22] The ordinance did not provide for criminal charges, in contrast to obscenity law.

Pornography was defined in terms of women's oppression, as "the sexually explicit subordination of women, graphically depicted" that included specific features:

> [W]omen are presented as sexual objects, things, or commodities . . . in postures of sexual submission or sexual servility, including by inviting penetration; women's body parts—including but not limited to vaginas, breasts, and buttocks— are exhibited, such that women are reduced to those parts; sexual objects who enjoy pain or humiliation . . . experience sexual pleasure in being raped . . . tied up or cut up or mutilated or bruised or physically hurt, or as dismembered . . . being penetrated by objects or animals . . . in scenarios of degradation, injury, torture, shown as filthy or inferior, bleeding, bruised, or hurt in a context that makes these conditions sexual. (MacKinnon and Dworkin 1997:428–9)

After the mayor vetoed the ordinance the first time, a revised ordinance included a slightly narrower definition of pornography that focused on violence or coercion rather than simply objectification. The revised definition of pornography aimed to assuage concerns about First Amendment issues by making the definition of pornography closer to what would legally be considered obscenity (and thus not protected by the First Amendment), and was intended to give the appearance of exempting "soft-core" magazines such as *Playboy*. Antipornography feminist leaders, however, explained privately that they believed *Playboy* and similar magazines would not be exempt, writing in an unsigned document sent to Gloria Steinem, "The new part of the definition (conquest, domination, exploitation, possession, use, etc.) does, in our view, cover *Playboy, Deep Throat*, etc."[23]

The Minneapolis campaign centered on feminist principles and advocacy. Far from attempting to build a coalition with conservatives, organizers sought to confine the campaign to feminists and the City Council. Dworkin wrote to Gloria Steinem that they were keeping their strategy quiet, explaining, "*This has to remain pretty secret* because we don't want the pornographers in here fighting it . . . . So please keep it very quiet now."[24] They were optimistic about the ordinance's passage. MacKinnon reported in a November,18, 1983, letter to Steinem: "We are incredibly excited about this legal idea of making pornography a form of sex discrimination. . . . It feels world-historic in so many ways."[25]

MacKinnon, Dworkin, and their students worked to line up testimony through feminist networks, including "battered women's shelters, rape crisis centers, women's and neighborhood groups" (Brest and Vandenberg 1987:620–21). They lined up at least 29, and up to 34, of the 36 witnesses who spoke at City Council in favor of the ordinance. Many of these supporting witnesses (16) recounted personal experiences, mainly the use of pornography by men who raped them, including fathers, husbands, boyfriends, strangers, and pimps. Some (9) supported the ordinance from a feminist but not personal perspective, mostly based on their experience as therapists, staff in battered women's shelters, professionals working with sex offenders, or researchers. Only one conservative spoke in support of the bill, Morality in Media's Eugene Conway, and he later retracted his support and pushed for traditional obscenity enforcement instead.[26] Relatively little opposition emerged at the hearings. While 36 witnesses testified in favor, only eight witnesses spoke against the bill; the opposed Minnesota Civil Liberties Union lobbied the Council directly instead of testifying (Downs 1989:84–85).[27] Over 200 supporters attended the hearings; they "reacted to unsympathetic testimony with booing and hissing, moaning and crying" (Brest and Vandenberg 1987:621). Candlelight vigils during the votes and a sit-in at Council voting chambers led to arrests (Downs 1989:87).

For MacKinnon, Dworkin, and their supporters, the hearings were not just a means to an end. They "gave pornography's survivors a forum, an audience, and a concrete opportunity to affect their world" (MacKinnon 1997:4). Often graphic and emotionally intense, the testimony represented a feminist "giving voice," in which telling the story of one's victimization is meant to change one's own feelings as well as the larger world (Whittier 2009; Whittier 2012). Council members commented on the difficulty and importance of listening to such testimony. In a typical exchange, Council Chair White told one witness, "I recognize that this was difficult with all the ears that were here, for you to sit here and make that kind of statement. Thank you . . . . It takes a lot of guts." Councilwoman Barbara Carlson commented similarly, "I would like to preface my question by thanking the people that have shared their stories tonight. I know it was extremely painful for them, for me, for the women to share their stories" (MacKinnon and Dworkin 1997:103, 120). This ritualized—albeit sincere—expression of emotion by officials after witness testimony was typical of the other case studies and other contexts as well, as I will discuss in Chapter 3.

The bill passed December 30, 1983, only to be vetoed by the mayor, who cited First Amendment concerns. After revisions (and after Council elections), the ordinance came before Council again in July 1984. Supporters attempted to gain the mayor's support and a veto-proof majority on the Council. The lobbying by supporters was intense. Demonstrations, "intense and often hostile, depicting non-supporters as enemies or traitors to women's causes," preceded the Council's vote, and numerous protesters were present when the mayor vetoed the ordinance a second time

(Downs 1989:64–65). So high were passions on the issue that a 23-year-old Minneapolis antipornography feminist immolated herself in a "pornography bookstore" on July 10, leaving a statement that said, "Sexism has shattered my life . . . . Because of this, I have chosen to take my life and to destroy the persons who have destroyed me."[28] Further afield, Dworkin and MacKinnon sought help from Gloria Steinem in lobbying the Minneapolis Council for passage, although it is not clear how much she actually did. Before the vote someone, probably Dworkin, sent Steinem a 23-page document with detailed information on the ordinance and on each Council member, including lengthy talking points for Steinem.[29] The talking points included "how important the bill is for women's rights," "the national NOW resolution supporting" the ordinance, "the interconnectedness of all feminist issues," and "feminist solidarity and how sometimes feminist hopes come to rest on a specific issue at a given time."[30] The tactics for approaching potential supporters and likely opponents alike involved appealing to their collective identity as feminist, so that supporting one feminist issue meant supporting this one. The bill passed, but Mayor Fraser vetoed it again because of constitutional concerns and the expense of defending the ordinance in court.

Accounts of the political alliances surrounding the ordinances vary wildly depending on the partisan alignment of the author (e.g., Brownmiller 1999; Douglas 1986; Downs 1989; MacKinnon and Dworkin 1997; Strossen 2000). Local and national feminists on both sides and antipornography conservatives closely followed both votes, especially the second. Phyllis Schlafly endorsed the ordinance in her newsletter (Downs 1989; Strub 2011). Save for the withdrawn testimony by Eugene Conway of Morality in Media, no hands-on collaboration with conservatives developed. The lack of coalition with or support from conservatives in Minneapolis is generally omitted from accounts of the "alliance," which focus primarily on Indianapolis.[31] It is clear, however, that publicity about Minneapolis brought the approach to the attention of conservatives nationwide and led to its consideration in Indianapolis. Along with increased activism by feminists opposed to censorship, Indianapolis was central to what became the dominant narrative of coalition with the Right.

Indianapolis: Conservative Supporters, Backstage Feminists

At the same time that Minneapolis was considering the second version of the ordinance, Indianapolis voted on a virtually identical version, but in a very different political climate, where the city, City Council, sponsor, mayor, and supporters were conservative. Indianapolis was home to at least two religious conservative antipornography groups, Citizens for Decency through Law (CDL), and Citizens for a Clean Community, the latter headed by a cofounder of the Moral Majority, as well as neighborhood antipornography groups. Two members of CDL's executive committee also served on the City Council (Downs 1989:104–5). The bill's sponsor, Beulah Coughenour, was quite conservative, opposing marital rape laws and the ERA, and worked closely with the mayor, religious conservative William Hudnut. Hudnut was committed to cracking down on pornography and was praised in the conservative religious press for his concerted efforts to do so, ordering police to "use every available resource within the limits of the law" against pornography and prostitution (quoted in Downs 1989:99; Rabey 1984).

The Indianapolis ordinance was the moment of greatest collaboration between antipornography feminists and conservatives, but this collaboration was circumscribed and fraught for both sides. Councilwoman Coughenour invited MacKinnon to work with her, and MacKinnon apparently helped substantially with the ordinance's content, spoke before the City Council to introduce and explain it, and assisted with arranging witnesses who testified to the effects of pornography. According to Downs, MacKinnon "worked more behind the scenes" to avoid "alienating the council with her radical feminism" and did not lobby individual members. In fact, some council members reported, "MacKinnon came across as conservative, and they did not know about her background" (Downs 1989:112–16). Council and CDL member David McGrath said, "MacKinnon portrayed herself as an ultra-conservative" (quoted in Downs 1989:121). MacKinnon's testimony, however, clearly showed the ordinance's grounding in a concern with women's subordination as manifest through sexualization; it is hard to imagine how anyone listening to the testimony could have construed her as an ultra-conservative (MacKinnon and Dworkin 1997:269–75). More likely, McGrath wanted to avoid the appearance of crossing political lines himself.

Unlike Minneapolis, feminist organizations and individuals did not protest or lobby in Indianapolis. Even a fundraising letter that Steinem sent out at the time was addressed to Minnesota citizens and framed solely in terms of the Minneapolis ordinance, with no mention of Indianapolis.[32] Local conservative groups, in contrast, worked hard for passage, although not until after the initial public hearing. According to an interview conducted by FACT leader Lisa Duggan with Indianapolis's Reverend Dixon, a former Moral Majority head, Coughenour did not notify him about the public hearing for tactical reasons. But conservatives became active before the vote, organizing a petition drive and mobilizing an estimated 200 supporters through congregations to attend the Council vote. Two members of CDL, Ron Hackler and Jack Lian, spoke in support.[33] Lian reported that CDL had several hundred signatures on the petition and that "there must have been a thousand people at City Hall showing support for the ordinance"(Downs 1989:118; Duggan 2006).[34]

Conservative supporters worried about collaborating with feminists. Coughenour told a journalist at the time that the feminist connection "does give me real pause for thought because I'm a world apart. It is dangerous. It's very dangerous." Similarly, CDL's Lian said, "I probably had some difficulties with this ordinance standing by itself" due to its feminist underpinnings (quoted in Downs 1989:110, 127). Supporting Council members did not particularly agree with the feminist focus on women's rights, but voted for the ordinance because of a general opposition to pornography and conservative supporters' mobilization, despite their individual preference for a more traditional obscenity approach. For example, one member, William Dowden, saw the issue with pornography as rooted in the problem of lust and therefore "as a great deal more than a violation of woman's rights. Pornography, to me in my own social-moral value system, is demeaning to men and women. And I didn't want to see it categorized in such a narrow framework" (quoted in Downs 1989:108). It was not only feminists who worried about getting in bed with the enemy.

Immediately after the ordinance passed in Indianapolis, a group of media distributors and civil liberties advocates challenged it in court.[35] The ACLU, Indiana Civil Liberties Union, and American Library Association filed amici curiae briefs on behalf of the plaintiffs, and Catharine MacKinnon filed the sole supporting brief. Federal District Judge Sarah Evans Barker ruled against the ordinance, concluding, "even [a]ccepting as true the City-County Council's finding that pornography conditions society to subordinate women, the means by which the Ordinance attempts to combat this sex discrimination is nonetheless through the regulation of speech." (*American Booksellers Association v. Hudnut* 598 F. Supp. 1316 [S. Dist. Ind. 1984]). On appeal, Morality in Media and other antipornography conservative organizations filed supporting briefs, as did MacKinnon, Andrea Dworkin, and the Neighborhood Pornography Task Force. FACT also filed an amicus curiae brief, signed by 80 prominent feminists, that was widely circulated and reprinted (Duggan and Hunter 1995). The Appellate Court upheld the overturning of the ordinance on the same grounds (*American Booksellers Association v. Hudnut* 771 F.2d 323 [7th Cir. 1986]).

Actual interaction across ideological lines included limited backstage interaction between two leaders, MacKinnon and Coughenour, and a shared target and goal. Several factors enabled this overlap despite the movements' differences. The geographically separate and sequenced nature of the ordinance campaigns allowed both sides to support an identical goal. Flexible framing placed the ordinance within each group's distinct self-definition; as each side framed pornography primarily in terms of its harmful effects on women, they retained but downplayed their divergent ideologies and the connection between ending pornography and their differing goals. Simultaneously, the movements' profound differences of ideology and collective identity, lack of shared social ties, and different outside allies precluded extensive collaboration.

Antipornography feminists' involvement in the municipal ordinance campaigns exemplifies particular dynamics of engagement with the state. Because the landscape of municipal politics is smaller, with greater access for citizens, antipornography feminists had an outsized ability to shape the ordinance. This was particularly the case in the first consideration of the ordinance in Minneapolis, where national organizations on either side were not yet engaged, most antipornography conservatives were not yet aware of the process, civil liberties groups were just beginning to engage, and feminists on the other side had not yet mobilized. By the Indianapolis vote and the second vote on the ordinance in Minneapolis, liberal and feminist opponents of the ordinance were mobilized, as were conservative supporters. The antipornography feminists who had so much influence over the process in the beginning lost control of it. MacKinnon's involvement in Indianapolis did not bring a radical feminist frame to what Indianapolis conservatives saw as their own fight, albeit with potentially dangerous feminist implications. So it is when activists of any stripe engage with the state. Their opportunities for influence—on legislation, its enactment, and on official discourse—are greatest early on when other powerful players are absent. Success brings involvement from opponents and from supporters with different agendas.

Dworkin had hoped that the ordinance would "rearrange the political place of pornography."[36] It did, but not in the sense she imagined. Instead, it galvanized opposition from feminists and others, and animated the narrative about antipornography feminists' alliance with conservatives, carving powerful and lasting fault lines between feminists. It introduced conservatives to antipornography feminist arguments and developed the frames and materials that all sides used at the federal level. And finally, the ordinances briefly catapulted MacKinnon and Dworkin onto the national stage and brought them to the attention of conservatives.

Antipornography Feminist and Conservative Influence in the Federal Context

The two movements converged on the same federal bodies in the mid-1980s. For a brief moment, antipornography feminism received an official hearing. Contrary to the accepted story, this was not solely due to an alliance with the Right. Instead, officials responded to the presence of a mass feminist antipornography movement and publicity about the innovative strategy of the civil rights ordinance, which itself was driven by the women's movement. Congressional committees and the Meese Commission called antipornography feminists as witnesses because of this publicity. This is not unique to the issue of pornography. Members of Congress are driven by public opinion, and social movements signal public concern with an issue (Campbell 2002; Jones and Baumgartner 2004; King, Bentele, and Soule 2007; Soule and Olzak 2004). Without a mass movement, the ordinance, antipornography feminist federal influence, and influence on conservatives would not have occurred.

The 1985 Meese Commission became a flashpoint for the growing activism on all sides after the Indianapolis ordinance battle. Indeed, the Commission was important, but so were less publicized work by Congress on pornography and policy implementation by federal departments. Across the board, antipornography feminist presence was confined to a few years and settings, while antipornography conservative influence spread throughout federal contexts and ultimately affected federal policy and discourse far more than its feminist counterpart.

Antipornography Feminism in Congress

Overall, 90 hearings dealt with pornography between 1981 and 2011. The number of hearings varied substantially over time. During the 1980s, the number of hearings on pornography rose between 1982 and 1988; they increased again in 1997 and 1998, 2001–2004, and 2006, as Figure 2.1 shows. Here, I focus on the hearings from 1981 to 1991, during the administrations of Presidents Reagan and Bush I. I discuss later hearings at the end of the chapter. From 1981 to 1991, there were 33 hearings, with a total of 263 witnesses.[37] Republican-controlled subcommittees held slightly less than half of those hearings (45.5 percent), disproportionate to their control of 25 percent of chambers in the House and Senate combined.[38] Republican and Democratic committee chairs called about the same number of witnesses per hearing, on average (9.13 and 9.81, respectively), and

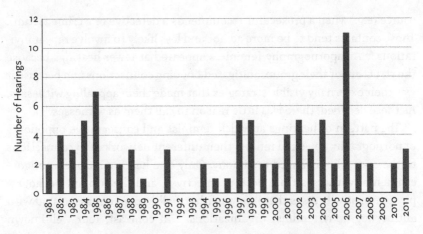

Figure 2.1 Number of Congressional Hearings on Pornography, 1981–2011

both Republicans and Democrats used similar frames for opposing pornography. The vast majority of these hearings focused on child pornography or the risks of children's access to pornography; only 7 of the 33 hearings during this period did not.

Overall, equal numbers of antipornography feminists and conservatives appeared before Congress between 1981 and 1991, with 13 nongovernmental witnesses from each perspective.[39] However, antipornography feminist witnesses appeared only after 1984 and at only four hearings, with the majority (8) concentrated in one hearing, a 1984 Senate hearing on "Effects of Pornography on Women and Children." Antipornography conservatives, in contrast, appeared at most hearings that addressed pornography at length, under both Democratic and Republican chairs. Most were from religious conservative organizations such as CDL, and many of the same individuals testified repeatedly. While all except one of the conservative witnesses were affiliated with antipornography organizations, only four of the feminist witnesses were affiliated with a women's social movement organization.[40] Representatives of organizations have more pull in influencing policy since they can cite the support of members and their structures facilitate ongoing lobbying.

Potential witnesses come to the attention of Congress through organizations that have established relationships with staff or congresspeople (DeGregorio 1994; Diermeier 2000). Larger, staffed organizations, such as CDL, are able to maintain such relationships and reliably provide witnesses over time. Smaller organizations or individuals come to the attention of congressional staff mainly if their activities gain extensive publicity (e.g., through the city ordinances) or because they are referred by an established source (e.g., when a prosecutor recommends a detective or a crime victim). Those contacts tend to be more ad hoc and less likely to involve repeat invitations.[41] Antipornography feminists appeared at fewer hearings because the structure of their groups mitigated ongoing connections and because it was their externally visible strategies that made them appealing witnesses. As these declined, there was little reason to call them as witnesses.[42]

The pattern of hearings at which feminist and conservative opponents of pornography appeared reflects their different networks and connections to the staff who arranged testimony. Only one hearing included nongovernmental witnesses from both perspectives, and the two antipornography feminist witnesses there were neither well-known nor associated with antipornography feminist organizations.[43] In contrast, four well-known spokesmen from major antipornography conservative organizations testified.

Even when testifying on the same legislation, feminist and conservative witnesses made distinct arguments. Conservative witnesses merged a view of pornography as harmful to women with their own broader opposition to sexually explicit media, but feminists did not return the favor, never using conservative frames about morality, religion, or the sanctity of the family. The relative "purity" of antipornography feminist witnesses' testimony and the lack of overlap or coordination between antipornography feminist and conservative witnesses or their organizations underscores their lack of coalition.

For example, many antipornography feminist luminaries testified at Arlen Specter's 1984 Senate hearings on "The Effect of Pornography on Women and Children." (Specter, a moderate Republican, chaired the Senate Judiciary Subcommittee on Juvenile Justice, under whose jurisdiction child pornography fell.) Over four days of hearings, Specter called many of the same categories of witnesses as the ordinance campaigns, including people who had appeared in pornography, people who had been sexually assaulted by assailants using pornography, and law enforcement officials, but he called no witnesses from antipornography conservative organizations.[44] Many of the law enforcement officials made strong arguments in favor of increased obscenity enforcement, but they did not make the antipornography conservative points about immorality, family breakdown, and the like. In contrast, Specter called numerous antipornography activists who were explicitly feminist: Andrea Dworkin, Catharine MacKinnon, Judy Goldsmith of NOW, Linda Marchiano (later Linda Boreman, the pornography actress turned antipornography activist who was working with MacKinnon and Dworkin at the time), author and activist Katherine Brady, and Susan Brown of Women Against Pornography.

In the hearings, Specter sought to oppose pornography yet frequently challenged antipornography feminists over issues of free speech. His exchange with feminist witness Dorchen Leidholdt, a leader of NY WAP, was typical. Leidholdt laid out the antipornography feminist critique of pornography and of the obscenity approach, following Specter's query about magazines like *Playboy*:

Senator Specter: What do you suggest that we do with those magazines?

Ms. Leidholdt: I think that we really ought to consider that these magazines may indeed be sex discrimination, may indeed foster the second-class status of females in the society.

Senator Specter: Do you think they are obscene?

Ms. Leidholdt: The problem with the whole concept of obscenity is it does not identify the harm. It does not identify who is being hurt . . . and the fact that primarily it is women and children.

Specter went on to challenge the argument that pornography violated women's civil rights.

Senator Specter: Excuse me. You think that women as a class are . . . having their legal rights violated by the way women are depicted in magazines like Playboy?

Ms. Leidholdt: I think we are having our civil rights violated and I also think that we are also having our human rights violated because much pornography literally depicts the torture of women.

Senator Specter: And it leads to abuse of women by people in society who read the magazines?

Ms. Leidholdt: I think it leads to very systematic sexual abuse of women and children and I also think it keeps women as second-class citizens. It keeps women inferior. It keeps men perceiving and treating women as inferior and therefore it keeps us inferior in society.

Senator Specter: It is a far-reaching theory that you articulate . . . . You are really making a very broad attack on some very deeply ingrained institutions in our society which currently have protections under the first amendment.[45]

Leidholdt, like other feminist witnesses, did not modify her position in response to Specter's challenges, retorting that she indeed thought these First Amendment protections were wrong.

Other antipornography feminist witnesses took a similar approach. NOW's Judy Goldsmith proclaimed that "no rights are absolute" and led Specter to compare the impact of pornography on women with "racism."[46] Three women testified about their experiences, using a feminist frame to explain how being sexually assaulted as children or used in child pornography led to their ongoing sexual exploitation as prostitutes and in relationships as adults. For example, Peggy Smith, from Minneapolis, told of her childhood sexual abuse by a neighbor who used pornography "to show me how to be, and what to do," her abuse by a pornography-using husband and other men in adulthood, and the role of pornography in the sexual abuse of her daughter and son. She attributed her newfound realization about "how pornography is being used against women all the time in this country" to the Minneapolis activism.[47]

The hearings began August 4. By the time MacKinnon and Dworkin appeared at the third day of hearings in late September, Specter was full of questions about the municipal ordinance and its constitutional implications. At that point, the ordinance's fate was unclear. It had passed in Indianapolis and the district court had issued an injunction, but the district ruling against it would not be issued until November 19. Specter explored constitutional questions with MacKinnon and the ACLU's Barry Lynn at some length.[48] These exchanges were much more contentious than the reception that the Meese Commission would later give MacKinnon and Dworkin. For example, in questioning Andrea Dworkin's claim that women should have a civil remedy (i.e., the ability to sue for damages) if they have "pornography forced on them," Specter asked:

> Wait a minute. Back up. You are saying that if a man forces a woman to duplicate what is in a magazine, that your ordinance gives the woman a cause of action against the man who so forces?. . . I would suggest to you that if someone today forces a woman . . . there is a cause of action that a woman has under those circumstances. Do you disagree with that?
>
> Dworkin: I entirely disagree with that, sir. I think there is virtually no real legal remedy yet for battery—
>
> Specter: . . . Battery is a civil tort . . .
>
> Dworkin: The fault with battery is with enforcement. One of the things that pornography does is make the woman's word worthless in the legal system, as well as in society at large . . . .
>
> Specter: I don't think a new law is going to change that. I think hearings like this may.
>
> Dworkin: . . . One of the reasons we do not want the State empowered to do this, that we want women empowered to bring these suits, is because in our view the state has failed to stop this kind of violence against women in any way.

Specter went on to ask Dworkin for examples in which battery cases had been thrown out of court, Dworkin repeated that women "can't get an injunction," while Specter pushed, "Now, answer my question" (U.S. Senate 1984a:231). Ultimately, MacKinnon, the next scheduled witness, spoke up, and Specter followed her testimony with similarly challenging questioning. In contrast, when Specter questioned a witness from a shelter for homeless teens about child pornography, he was more satisfied with the narrower definition of obscenity and civil compensation that would apply to child pornography. As the witness responded to each question, Specter simply moved on to his next question, without debating or follow-up questioning (U.S. Senate 1984a:197–98).

Despite the contention, Specter did partially endorse the idea that pornography caused harm to women, repeating Dworkin's assertion: "As we sit here today there will be many women across the United States injured as a result of pornographic material which you can't identify who they will be, but there will be injuries to women and that women as a class are degraded by these obscene materials" in a subsequent speech to Congress (Specter 1984). Later, he introduced legislation that appeared to be based on these hearings, as we will see below. The link between antipornography feminists and this legislation has been traced, inaccurately, to the more visible Meese Commission, where feminist-conservative ties were slightly closer.

The Meese Commission

Shortly after Specter's hearing, President Reagan tapped his attorney general, Edwin Meese, to establish a Commission on Pornography, commonly referred to as the Meese Commission.[49] It was charged with examining the social effects of pornography and recommending government action. It held hearings around the country in 1985 and 1986, studied pornographic movies and magazines, and gathered testimony from numerous witnesses. Its lengthy 1986 report, reprinted for the mass-market with an introduction by conservative religious journalist Michael McManus, was promoted in conservative publications as a shocking exposé that landed the definitive blow against pornography (Minnery 1987; Nordlinger 2001).

The Commission tilted strongly Right. Made up of a range of experts and advocates, the Commission was chaired by conservative prosecutor Henry Hudson, and its executive director was Alan Sears, who became the legal counsel for Citizens for Decency through Law after the Commission. Both had made their names prosecuting obscenity cases. Of the Commission's ten other members, six were outspoken opponents of pornography; the remaining four had expertise or interest in sexual assault or deviance (Attorney General's Commission on Pornography [hereafter AGCP] 1986;

Vance 1986b). None identified publicly as a feminist. The women members were somewhat less opposed to pornography than the men: three had not spoken against pornography prior to the Commission, and two ultimately issued a joint statement dissenting from some of the Commission's recommendations, generally opposing increased enforcement and penalties for obscenity (AGCP 1986).[50] In other words, antipornography conservatives had strong ties to several Commission members. Antipornography feminists, in contrast, lobbied but did not successfully ally with conservative members and found a sympathetic ear only in Frederick Schauer. There is no evidence to suggest that antipornography feminist and conservative organizations or leaders coordinated with each other around the Meese Commission.

The pattern of witnesses before the Meese Commission was similar to Congress, with 11 antipornography feminist witnesses and 16 antipornography conservative witnesses testifying (AGCP 1986). All the conservative witnesses were affiliated with organizations, compared with only five of the feminist witnesses. Further, many of the organizations with which feminists were affiliated were small or ad hoc groups that never appeared before Congress, compared with larger and enduring groups on the Right, such as CDL and Morality in Media that were regularly part of the policy process. Twenty-nine additional witnesses testified about their personal experiences; most of these represented a conservative religious antipornography position, but some reflected antipornography feminism's emphasis on the links between pornography and violence against women. Three or four witnesses came from a list of 28 potential witnesses that WAP had suggested to the Commission chair.[51] Anticensorship feminists also testified.

The majority of witnesses who opposed pornography took a religious conservative approach. They decried pornography's effects on family life, causing men to abandon their roles as providers and husbands for an obsession with sexual deviation that they often imposed on their wives and sometimes on their children. They included women who had appeared in pornography and since converted to evangelical Christianity and men who condemned their own excessive use of pornography from an evangelical Christian perspective (AGCP 1986). For example, Brenda MacKillop, a former Playboy bunny, explained that, "*Playboy* is more than a pornographic magazine with pictures of naked women. It is a philosophy that enticed me to throw aside my Judeo-Christian ethic of no premarital sex and no adultery and to practice recreational sex with no commitments" (Schlafly and U.S. AGCP 1987:92–93). Some witnesses simply described how pornography had led their husbands or fathers to sexually assault them without explicitly religious or political language. For example, Diann testified: "I was coerced into acting out certain sexual fantasies which [my husband] had, many times, from reading pornographic literature or viewing certain pornographic movies" (Schlafly and U.S. AGCP 1987:84–85).

Antipornography feminists appearing before the Commission included Dworkin, MacKinnon, Leidholdt, and Therese Stanton of Minneapolis's Pornography Resource Center. They staunchly promoted their own views. Dworkin, in words that were prominently featured in the Commission's report, described misogyny in pornography and its effects on women, recounting how pornography objectified, humiliated, and violated women:

> I live in a country where if you film any act of humiliation or torture, and if the victim is a woman, the film is both entertainment and it is protected speech. Now that tells me something about what it means to be a woman citizen in this country, and the meaning of being second-class. . . . [Pornography] keeps us socially silent, it keeps us socially compliant, it keeps us afraid in neighborhoods; and it creates a vast hopelessness for women, a vast despair. One lives inside a nightmare of sexual abuse that is both actual and potential, and you have the great joy of knowing that your nightmare is someone else's freedom and someone else's fun.

She called on the Commission to act on the side of feminist goals:

> I am asking you to help the exploited, not the exploiters. . . . I am asking you as individuals to have the courage . . . to go and cut that woman down and untie her hands and take the gag out of her mouth [referring to a photograph the Commission viewed], and to do something, for her freedom. (AGCP 1986:198–99)[52]

Leidholdt showed the commission the WAP slideshow and provided them with copies of the testimony from the Minneapolis ordinance. MacKinnon defended the civil rights approach's constitutionality and emphasized the problems with obscenity law (MacKinnon and Dworkin 1997). In contrast to conservatives, they framed their opposition to pornography in terms of their version of feminism, emphasizing the pervasiveness of rape, child sexual abuse, and domestic violence, the ubiquity and sexualization of male power, and the centrality of pornography to women's subordination.

The Commission process clearly included feminist opponents of pornography alongside conservatives, although the latter were more numerous. The final report reflects this. The influence of antipornography feminist witnesses and perspectives is most marked in the lengthy section of the report entitled "Victim Testimony." In addition to testimony before the

Commission itself, the report quotes extensively from testimony before the Minneapolis ordinance hearings and from written statements sent to the Commission from WAP.[53] The final report also reflects the antipornography feminist approach to race, framing it as "an intensifier" of the harms of pornography, in which women of color are "represented 'worse' than white women" (Nash 2008:18, 55). The only discussion of race in the final report, besides the listing of titles with racial descriptors, is in Dworkin's statement decrying the "trade in racism as a form of sexual pleasure" and in the recommendation summarizing the harms of pornography, which notes that gender is "often aggravated by . . . age, race, disability, or other vulnerability" (AGCP 1986:198, 189). Feminist frames for opposing pornography also made their way into commissioners' individual statements, mainly in reference to Dworkin's testimony. For example, Park Dietz, a middle-of-the-road commissioner who was a psychiatrist, drew directly on antipornography feminist frames:

> When Andrea Dworkin challenged us to find the courage "to go and cut that woman down and untie her hands and take the gag out of her mouth, and to do something, to risk something, for her freedom," I cried. . . . I ask you, America, to strike the chains from America's women and children, to free them from the bonds of pornography, to free them from the bonds of sexual slavery, to free them from the bonds of sexual abuse, to free them from the bonds of inner torment that entrap the second-class citizen in an otherwise free nation.

From the other end of the (limited) political spectrum represented on the Commission, conservative evangelical James Dobson of Focus on the Family combined antipornography feminist and antipornography conservative language:

> Pornography is degrading to women . . . . Remember that men are the purchasers of pornography. Many witnesses testified that women are typically repulsed by visual depictions of the type therein described. It is provided primarily for the lustful pleasure of men and boys who use it to generate excitation . . . . Pornography is the theory; rape is the practice.

Dobson blended his surprisingly literal adoption of Robin Morgan's memorable phrase with typical conservative critiques of pornography for its role in promoting "disease and homosexual activity" and its "significant harm to the institution of the family and to society at large."

While antipornography feminists influenced the Commission's frames, conservatives influenced its policy recommendations. The policy recommendations do include a section on "civil remedies," which briefly summarizes the municipal ordinances, affirms that pornography is "a violation of human rights" and under some conditions is "discrimination on the basis of sex," and recommends that Congress hold hearings on the question. It departs from the feminist civil rights approach, however, in recommending that, because of the overturn of the Indianapolis ordinance, the definition of pornography must "pass constitutional muster," that is, that it must be legally obscene (AGCP 1986:186–89).[54] Most of the Commission's recommendations focused on obscenity law and enforcement, goals supported solely by conservatives.

SHIFTING FRAMES ON THE RIGHT

Conservative opponents of pornography strategically used parts of feminist frames about pornography's harms to women in the Meese Commission and before Congress, but their discussion of sexual violence seemingly ended with pornography. In general, antipornography conservatives pointed to pornography's harmful effects on women as a moral justification for stepped-up action against pornography, but they did not promote women's rights or a feminist analysis. For example, Meese Commission Executive Director Alan Sears, who had since become legal counsel for CDL, testified in 1987 before the Democratic-controlled House during the "Hearing on Women, Violence, and the Law." Sears made liberal use of selected parts of antipornography feminist frames by repeatedly emphasizing the range of harms that pornography produced for women. He combined these themes with antipornography conservative frames, listing several social harms due to pornography verbatim from the Meese Report: "loss of jobs or promotions, sexual harassment at the work place, financial losses, defamation, loss of status in the community, the promotion of racial hatred, the loss of trust within the family . . . . Obviously, the related divorces, the promiscuity, compulsive masturbation, prostitution and other sexual harassment" (U.S. House 1987:53). While many of these themes address effects, they simultaneously emphasize men's loss of status due to their pornography use. The corruption of men through pornography was a strong focus in conservative discourse and allowed critics to make an argument about pornography's harms that relied on a religious conservative ideology rather than on feminist critiques of sexism.

Even this partial incorporation of antipornography feminist frames was short-lived. In a 1988 hearing, after antipornography feminism had declined in visibility, Sears continued to give nominal attention to negative effects on women, but based the argument entirely on conservative frameworks. Rather than focusing on violence against women, he emphasized effects of pornography on the "health of women" through the negative effects of gay sex on family life, claiming that men go to adult bookstores to have sex with other men, "after having anonymous sexual activity and exposing themselves at great risk to sexually transmitted diseases, including ... AIDS, then return to their homes and further transmit these diseases to their innocent family or girl friends" (U.S. House 1988:419). Similarly, antipornography conservative Jerry Kirk summarized the "victims" on whose behalf he worked, proclaiming, "Every one of those little children, every one of those young people, and women, and marriages, and families are worth it" (U.S. House 1988:101). Women were one among many categories of victim, and women's rights had dropped out of the picture, replaced by concern marriage, family, and children. Even the superficial consideration of race seen in the Meese Report was absent.

Outside the state, in publications and congregations, Christian conservatives also incorporated feminist rhetoric about pornography as degrading to women, as wrongly presenting them as sex objects, and as promoting rape, including marital rape (a major focus of antipornography testimony), and child sexual abuse. They did this alongside rhetoric about the sanctity of marriage, men's role as head of the household, and the importance of sheltering children from exposure to sexuality. For example, a 1981 article in *Christianity Today* argued, "The image of women so relentlessly propagated by pornography is that they are . . . a gender ordained for the sexual pleasure of men, and are principally distinguished by their possession of genitalia offering rich possibilities for male gratification" (Christenson 1981). A 1986 *Christianity Today* editorial made the standard moral argument that one of pornography's negative aspects was its status as the "first step to adultery," yet also proclaimed, "It is no wonder, then, that the feminist movement has been especially aggressive in its condemnation of pornography. Women are the primary victims of it. Pornography not only degrades and dehumanizes women, but it leads to outward aggression and violation of their personal rights" (Kantzer 1986). Religious conservatives often quoted MacKinnon or Dworkin in such articles but used their statements only to describe the contents of pornography before asserting a religious conservative critique. A typical 1986 article in *Christianity Today* entitled, "Pornography: The Human Tragedy: Must a Moral Society Tolerate the Burgeoning Market for Perversion?" began by quoting Dworkin's testimony before the Meese Commission, identifying her as "a prominent feminist opponent of pornography" who "testified: 'Women are bound, battered, tortured, humiliated . . .'" Yet most of the article focused on how the

Commission found, "[a]stonishing evidence" of "the destructive attitudes toward sexuality and family life, and the brutal physical damage that pornography engenders, particularly to children and women" (Minnery 1986). Such articles made a clear distinction from feminist reasons for opposing pornography.

Sometimes the distinction from feminism was drawn more explicitly, as in a 1986 *Christianity Today* article about an interdenominational Christian conference on pornography. The author complained:

> Feminist speakers linked pornography to women's civil rights. "The image of male dominance is . . . at the root of all forms of sexual violence," said United Methodist minister Beth Ann Carey in the conference's opening sermon . . . . She said the root problem is that "we make our God into a man." Theological conservatives, of course, found this untenable. (Frame 1986)

Despite the ongoing differences and distinction between themselves and feminists, over time, the religious conservative press somewhat changed its approach to child sexual abuse, rape, and domestic violence: writing about them outside the context of pornography, describing them as common, and discussing implications for women and congregations. For example, a 1992 article debunked rape myths and argued that the Church had a responsibility to respond to allegations and ensure victims get help. Since this went beyond the expertise of most pastoral counselors, the author advocated referral to external rape crisis services, noting "most victim-assistance programs and literature have been initiated by feminists, but they still may offer great help" (Walters and Spring 1992). Other articles criticized domestic violence, argued that "male headship" should not mean "male domination," and examined the issue of "patriarchy" in theological terms (e.g., Tracy 2003).

This cultural change was likely due partly to Christian conservatives' exposure to feminist analyses of sexual violence through the pornography debates. Feminist attention to rape, child sexual abuse, and domestic violence especially resonated among religious conservative women who had experienced sexual violence. In *Righting Feminism*, Ronnee Schreiber (2008:57) shows that the conservative women's organization Concerned Women for America (CWA) opposed pornography because it "causes men to inflict physical and emotional harm on women" and that its rhetoric on the issue was much closer to that of feminism than on the other issues it prioritizes.[55] Substantial differences from feminist approaches to violence against women remained, of course. Critique of patriarchy entailed reframing male headship of the family, not rejecting it; and the nuclear family and sexual morality were still elevated.

THE END OF THE FRENEMY RELATIONSHIP: FEDERAL ANTIPORNOGRAPHY OUTCOMES AFTER THE MEESE COMMISSION

Feminist opposition to pornography peaked in its influence on both the state and conservatives in the mid-1980s, with congressional hearings, local ordinances, and the Meese Commission. But even at its peak, its influence was limited. Conservatives and, ultimately, the state held discursive and structural power that feminists could not access. In contrast to the dynamics in coalitions, where movements merge frames, antipornography conservatives strategically emphasized pornography's harms to women alongside its other ills, but they did so in terms of degradation rather than oppression and did not retain these frames over time. By the end of the 1980s, any relationship between feminists and conservatives had dissolved.

Outcomes reflected conservative rather than feminist goals. Most congressional hearings continued to take child sexual exploitation as the primary context in which pornography was discussed and included no feminist leaders, organizations, or frames. The Justice Department, under the leadership of the attorney general, had charge of implementing the recommendations of the Meese Commission and did so by proposing new legislation and increasing prosecution for obscenity. It was conservative advocates who were part of this policy process, and it was they who shaped the outcomes. This is evident in both discourse and legislative proposals as the Justice Department moved forward from the Meese Commission. Feminists' exclusion from this process is clear in the tenor of banter about sexuality in official contexts, the relationship between the Religious Right and the Justice Department, and amicus briefs to pornography-related cases before the Supreme Court. I show how this unfolded below, unpacking how state power operated to shape outcomes for discourse and legislation.

Legislation and Congressional Hearings

The signature legislation drafted by the Justice Department was the Child Protection and Obscenity Enforcement Act. Coordinated by Assistant Attorney General William F. Weld, the legislation was drafted in 1987 and revised under Meese's personal direction. It was the main official response to the Meese Commission's recommendations; 7 of the bill's 11 provisions codified Commission recommendations.[56] Congressional testimony in favor of the Act came entirely from conservatives, including representatives of CDL, the Religious Alliance Against Pornography, and the

Southern Baptist Convention's Christian Life division, as well as prosecutors. Witnesses rarely mentioned rape or child sexual abuse, and mostly focused on the law's provisions for improving prosecution of obscenity, not why obscenity was objectionable (U.S. House 1988; U.S. Senate 1988b).[57]

The Child Protection and Obscenity Enforcement Act passed in 1988.[58] The provisions prohibiting obscenity on cable television and increasing penalties for "dial-a-porn" were overturned in court. The record-keeping requirement for producers of pornography provision also was overturned, but a revised version passed in the following Congress and has been upheld since.[59]

Most of the other legislation that came before Congress after 1986 expanded obscenity law and did not involve feminists. The exceptions were two similarly named Acts, the Pornography Victims' Protection Act and the Pornography Victims' Compensation Act. Both nodded rhetorically to the antipornography feminist position but did not codify it. First introduced in 1986 by Republican Senator Specter, and reintroduced in subsequent years, the Pornography Victims *Protection* Act would have allowed children or adults coerced into appearing in pornography to bring civil suit in federal court. A similar version was introduced in the House by William Green for several years beginning in 1986.[60] Republican Senator Mitch McConnell introduced the Pornography Victims' *Compensation* Act in 1989. It would have permitted civil suits by victims who could prove that a specific obscene item was a proximate cause of sexual assault, *if* the offender was criminally convicted of the assault and the item was shown to be obscene through criminal conviction. This was much more restrictive than the municipal ordinances, which permitted civil suits based on other kinds of harm besides sexual assault and did not require showing proximate cause, assailant conviction, or legal obscenity. Only the Protection Act was ever introduced in the House, whereas both eventually were considered simultaneously in the Senate. Neither passed, despite being introduced regularly in the House and Senate.[61]

The Compensation Act is cited as evidence of antipornography feminist influence and coalition with the Right (while the Protection Act is not discussed) (Semonche 2007; Strub 2011). In fact, antipornography feminists were divided on both easily confused Acts and the alliances around them differed. The Protection Act initially drew support from a group called Feminists Fighting Pornography, several local feminist antipornography organizations, some chapters of NOW, and a host of child welfare and domestic violence organizations, but was not supported by WAP.[62] Although MacKinnon called the Protection Act "a version of the ordinance's coercion provision" and the Compensation Act "a rendition of the ordinance's assault provision," she complained that the sponsors of both "compromised their bills fundamentally" (1997:16–18). Feminists' and conservatives' divergence in viewpoint led to differences over the ability of performers in pornography to consent. Antipornography feminists argued that free consent was impossible in a sexist society and that women in pornography had been either directly forced, blackmailed, or sexually assaulted beginning in childhood. The Protection Act, in contrast, codified the idea that performers who consented to appear in pornography could not sue. Similarly, Meese Commission Chair Henry Hudson argued that protections against forced participation were important, but "[i]f they fully consent and fully agree to it, that's fine."[63] In discussing modes of coercion, federal officials described "a regimen of physical abuse and hardships" as well as "hard drugs," in a gender-neutral frame that they applied to boys as well as girls and women.[64]

The Compensation Act was not supported by any major feminist groups and drew its major support from conservatives. Antipornography conservative organizations and individuals actively supported it, with supporting testimony from Sears, former Meese Commissioner and Covenant House director Bruce Ritter, members of the Religious Alliance Against Pornography, and many clergy.[65] The major feminist antipornography organizations opposed it, as did some chapters of NOW. Dworkin, proclaiming, "This is not our bill," critiqued the Compensation Act in a 1992 interview.[66] Only Feminists Fighting Pornography, led by former WAVPM member Page Mellish, supported the Compensation Act. Despite the name, the group took positions that were closer to conservatives than to the rest of antipornography feminism. For example, Mellish was quoted in the *Washington Times* in a 1990 article about NEA funding of a performance by Annie Sprinkle, "Post-Porn Modernist," asking, "Why is tax money being used to present this pornography?"[67] Mellish likely coordinated with local conservative antipornography groups; she provided a list of endorsements to the Senate in 1991 under the Feminists Fighting Pornography letterhead, including the most arch-conservative antipornography groups from around the country.[68] While Mellish seemingly tried to build a feminist-conservative coalition, the antipornography feminist movement distanced itself. This failed legislation, widely cited as an example of feminist influence on conservatives, was not only peripheral to antipornography feminism, it was also inconsequential in comparison to enforcement and prosecution efforts.

Obscenity Prosecution

In addition to legislation, the Justice Department dramatically stepped up its prosecution of obscenity cases in the late 1980s. Meese established a multidisciplinary center on obscenity prosecutions within the Department of Justice to assist federal, state, and local prosecutions and formed the National Obscenity Enforcement Unit (NOEU), a task force within the attorney general's office. He directed the Organized Crime Strike Force and U.S. attorneys around the country to increase investigation and prosecution of obscenity cases.[69] The number of investigations, indictments, and convictions grew substantially, especially prosecution of child pornography. Little scholarly work or journalism has examined these trends; most focuses instead on case law, not on routine obscenity enforcement. My conclusions on the Reagan Justice Department's numbers come from internal Justice Department memos. In 1985, the director of the FBI told the Meese Commission that the Bureau had investigated 2,484 cases of obscenity and sexual exploitation of children from 1978 to1985, with 137 indictments, 118 convictions, fines of $1,085,000, and "recoveries, restitutions, and . . . forfeitures" of $6,109,267.[70] Shortly afterward, in 1987, there were 80 federal obscenity *indictments* in just one year. Child pornography prosecutions skyrocketed from 3 in 1983 to 249 in 1987.[71] Meese touted over 100 successful child pornography prosecutions in 1985 and 1986 and a vast sting operation (with Customs and the Postal Service) in 1987, yielding more than 150 indictments.[72]

Increased sentencing was also a priority. The U.S. Sentencing Commission, with encouragement from the NOEU, increased the sentencing guidelines for obscenity and child pornography and eliminated the possibility of parole. Whereas in 1985, 44.6% of people sentenced under federal child pornography charges received no prison time, with an average sentence of 19.9 months for those who did, the new guidelines meant that even a low-level defendant with no prior felony convictions would receive a sentence of 70–87 months with no parole.[73] The NOEU regularly offered prosecutors tips to increase the sentence, such as including any sadomasochistic material in the charges, showing that the defendant was in a managerial position, and considering RICO (the federal statute covering organized crime) and child sexual abuse charges.[74] This was consistent with the Reagan administration's overall emphasis on aggressive prosecution and harsh sentencing for crimes across the board (Simon 2007). It contradicted antipornography feminists' consistent opposition to obscenity law as a strategy.

Official Discourse

By definition, obscenity is a criminal offense, and Attorney General Meese and others in the Justice Department consistently framed pornography in terms of *crime* and preferred the term "obscenity" to "pornography." For example, Meese asserted, "this crime is [not] any different than a lot of other crimes that we prosecute."[75] By 1988, Meese was even referring to "the Obscenity Commission, the Commission on Pornography, as it was formerly known," underlining the distinction between pornography (legal if indecent) and obscenity (a criminal offense).[76] Often the definition of obscenity was tautological, demonstrated by Meese's statement that "there will be no censorship by the Department of Justice as long as I am Attorney General" but "unlawful materials that come within the Supreme Court's definition of obscenity . . . are unlawful."

Obscenity was rightly criminal, Meese maintained, because it had victims, including "exploited and molested" children, "families who are destroyed by the sexual abuse of children and women," and "people who are intimidated by gangsters" from the "organized criminal enterprises" behind the production and distribution of obscenity.[77] The Justice Department occasionally connected concern with pornography to rape and child sexual abuse in speeches to the public. For example, the talking points prepared for Meese before the press conference announcing the Commission's members include the Commission's consideration of "the relationship between pornography and sex-related crimes such as rape and child abuse."[78] President Reagan, meanwhile, said that obscenity "exploits women, children, and men alike," incorporating women but not as a unique category.[79] Similarly, at an "advanced pornography seminar" for prosecutors in 1988, Meese proclaimed that "dehumanized men, battered women, abused children and ruined lives . . . are the inevitable result of hard core obscenity," and included the problems of rape and child molestation, marital rape, and adolescent sexual exploitation as outcomes of pornography.[80] Overall, the problem was broader than the effects on women.

Officials also drew on discourse about public health and organized crime. For example, a 1988 commentary in the *Obscenity Enforcement Reporter* defended the harsh RICO charges brought against the owner of video rental stores and bookstores that sold pornography not only on the grounds that the owner was a "career criminal" but also that the material depicted "many of the acts today's public health officials warn us against: casual, anonymous sex, violent anal intercourse, rape, group sex, sadomasochism, torture, bondage and more."[81] They also occasionally analogized obscenity to illegal drugs. For example, speaking to a seminar for prosecutors and others in 1988, Meese proclaimed, "Obscenity is about the same thing as drugs; that is the defense of human decency and dignity in the face of degrading, destructive habits that cause crime, that are themselves a crime, and that contribute lots of dollars to the criminals . . . . Obscenity, just like drugs, creates addicts . . . [and] can lead to horrendous personality changes."[82] These were all frames that were prevalent in conservative anti-pornography organizations of the time but were at odds with the perspectives of feminists and other progressives of all stripes.

Sexuality in the State

Official discourse was nonsexual, but innuendo and joking periodically invoked the embodied sexual experience of male government officials in a way that would have been antithetical to antipornography feminists. For example, at the first press conference on the Commission's Report, Meese refused to answer questions about its contents on the grounds that he had not yet read it; consequently, reporters asked instead for his personal views. One, addressing the report's suggestion that even depiction of "normal sex between married couples" could be harmful to viewers, asked Meese if he had ever "publically attended a display of normal sex and had the sensation that your sexuality was harmed in any way?" Meese, to laughter, replied, "Well, I'm not going to comment substantively until I've read the report."[83] When Commission Chair Henry Hudson was questioned at the press conference, the same reporter asked, "Assume you had been exposed to pornography and obscenity growing up over the years, how did it harm you?" Hudson addressed the question more directly than Meese, admitting, "like I'm sure everyone in this room, I have examined pornography and obscenity" but not "the types of materials contained in Categories 1 and 2; namely, sadomasochistic materials and materials involving coprophilia, bestiality" and not "with any degree of regularity." When the reporter followed up to ask about whether exposure to other categories of pornography had harmed him, Hudson replied, "I don't believe they have" and also noted that the report did not indicate they were harmful.[84] Reporters periodically qualified statements about the contents of pornography with disclaimers like "now—I haven't looked at them in a while" to general laughter.[85]

Meanwhile, the statue of Lady Justice with one breast bared appeared directly behind Meese during the press conference; when a reporter asked whether it could be considered pornographic, Meese replied that he didn't know.[86] At a subsequent press conference on the implementation of Commission recommendations, a reporter jokingly queried, "Is there any particular reason why we are meeting in this room instead of that lovely hall across the street where we met the last time?" and Meese replied, to general laughter, that the hall was busy and "I wasn't able to get the statue moved over in time."[87] Such minor moments underscore how the state remained the domain not only of men but also of men who—unlike anti-pornography feminists—saw much pornography as innocuous material to joke about, not as evidence of women's sexualized subordination.

Justice Department Alliance with Conservatives and the Religious Right Outside the State

Meese approached conservatives as his natural allies, deriding liberals who say, "anything no matter how dangerous or how exploitative of children ought to be allowed, because it's only . . . consenting adults." In contrast, Meese told prosecutors, "you are the friends . . . of the normal, traditional, the decent, the ordinary people." As the Justice Department worked with conservative organizations, many "normal, traditional, decent" people from conservative religious perspectives wrote to Meese to support his efforts.

Conservative antipornography organizations had close ties with the Justice Department. Although the Commission's report encouraged boycotts and other pressure tactics to drive pornography outlets out of business, Meese was cautious about endorsing the approach in public and claimed that the Justice Department's resource center would not provide resources to citizen groups.[88] In actuality, the Reagan administration actively encouraged activists in the conservative antipornography movement. The Religious Alliance Against Pornography was invited to the White House in 1986 for a briefing, where Meese exhorted them to "take up the battle and join full force in a coordinated effort against the traffickers of these sordid materials."[89] The NOEU sent its publication *Obscenity Enforcement Recorder* and updates on its activities to "citizen leaders" including leaders from Morality in Media, CDL, National Coalition Against Pornography, and National Federation for Decency. NOEU staff also spoke to numerous organizations, including Concerned Women of America, the Ohio Coalition Against Pornography, Pennsylvania vs. Pornography, the Morality in Media National Conference, Morality in Media of Wisconsin, the Orange County Coalition Against Pornography, the Christian Legal Society of North Carolina, and the Pittsburg Coalition.[90]

Meese and Reagan reportedly received over 150,000 letters regarding the Commission and obscenity enforcement. Almost all the letters preserved in Meese's personal papers support a crackdown on pornography.[91] Writers praised Meese's efforts and the Commission and demanded additional enforcement. The vast majority used religious conservative language.

One typical writer asked Meese "to enforce vigorously the laws against obscenity and to invoke the blessing of Almighty God on this important endeavor,"[92] while another decried that "purveyors of man's lowest carnality are allowed to force their immorality on the people under the guise of constitutional rights."[93]

Although it is possible that individual letter-writers embraced a feminist opposition to pornography, none identified themselves as such, and no letters from feminist organizations are in the files. A few writers did mention negative effects on women but only in conjunction with religious language. For example, a Washington woman wrote, "As a woman, I have felt it degrading, demeaning and threatening. I will not sit through movies, read books, or listen to coarse jokes that portray women the way the pornography industry does." She promised to "pray for" Meese.[94] A similarity in the wording of many letters suggests organized letter-writing campaigns. The antipornography feminists who sought to influence federal policy were not part of such campaigns.

Changing Goals and Amicus Briefs

Although they shared the broad goal of eliminating pornography, feminists and conservatives advocated different specific policies: zoning and obscenity prohibitions versus codifying the view that pornography violated women's civil rights. After the Indianapolis civil rights ordinance was deemed unconstitutional, conservatives focused on obscenity and zoning, which antipornography feminists continued to oppose. As we have seen, legislation introduced during this period paralleled conservative policy goals and conservative organizations—but not antipornography feminists—testified in favor.

This legislation has been subject to extensive litigation. The amici curiae briefs for cases before the Supreme Court confirm the minimal collaboration between antipornography feminists and conservatives. Between 1981 and 1991, eight cases before the Supreme Court focused on pornography, for which 40 amici curiae briefs were filed by nongovernmental parties. Of these, 11 briefs supporting increased measures against pornography were filed by religious conservative antipornography organizations. No briefs were filed by feminist organizations or individuals.[95] Antipornography feminists' disengagement reflected the cases' orientation toward conservative policy goals. The cases dealt with attempts to expand zoning restrictions or obscenity law, such as by seizing profits through RICO, forbidding nude barroom dancing, expanding definitions of child pornography, or making telephone sex lines illegal. These were approaches that antipornography feminists opposed.

Two cases before lower courts saw antipornography feminists and conservatives briefs on the same side of the same case. The more prominent was the Indianapolis ordinance case, in which MacKinnon, Morality in Media, and other conservative antipornography organizations filed briefs at the appellate level (*American Booksellers Association v. Hudnut* 771 F.2d 323 [7th Cir. 1986]).[96] Second, three 1988 libel cases against *Hustler* magazine, brought by feminists Andrea Dworkin and Dorchen Leidholdt and conservative antipornography activist Peggy Ault were argued separately at the district level, but Dworkin's's appellate case included two amicus briefs, one from CDL and one from Gloria Steinem and Susan Brownmiller (867 F. 2d 1188 [1988]). All three cases were argued at the appellate level by the same Wyoming attorneys.[97] Other than these two cases, court cases saw no overlap between antipornography feminists and conservatives.

Whereas earlier feminist opposition to pornography was situated in opposition to violence and sexism in media in general, by the mid-1980s, at least some feminist antipornography leaders saw sexually explicit media as distinct from other sexist media (Bronstein 2011). In theory, this position might have made it possible for antipornography feminists to support obscenity prosecution and zoning restrictions, but their focus on distinguishing themselves from conservatives foreclosed that path. Further, because the power to enforce a criminal law rests in the hands of the state, antipornography feminists argued, obscenity law weakened women and strengthened the very forces that oppressed them.

A coalition, in which the parties share specific goals, ideology, collective identity, or frames, would entail support for at least some of the same policy goals. Frenemies who share a specific policy goal, such as opposing the Patriot Act or the Defense Against Marriage Act, are more likely to file joint or concurring amicus briefs even if their broader goals diverge. Indeed, we see slightly more overlap in the child sexual abuse and VAWA cases. In the case of pornography, the parties' disagreements on the specific policies through which to achieve their shared goal, and the risks to their reputations of appearing too close, made this overlap impossible.

Outcomes in the 1990s and Beyond

Although Women Against Pornography survived until 1993, its mass mobilization declined along with its engagement in the policy process (Bronstein 2011; Potter 2012). As feminists working against sexual violence moved into new arenas, the antipornography effort lost visibility. Conservative groups, meanwhile, continued picketing stores that carried pornography and protesting the Holiday Inn and Marriott for offering in-room adult films (Nordlinger 2001).[98] However, they had never mobilized the same level of mass protest as antipornography feminism, and the 1990s were no different. Instead, the conservative movement's strength was in its formal organizations, which survived and continued to play a role in the policy process, appearing at hearings, filing amicus briefs, and providing information to local chapters and congregations. With the rise of the Internet, revelations of religious conservative clergy and laypeople viewing pornography became common, and the conservative Christian media increasingly framed the problem as "pornography addiction." Less about inciting sexual violence, pornography addiction entailed betraying wives, sexual sin, and financial irresponsibility ("Gardner 2001; Kennedy 2008; Minnery 1985; "We've Got Porn" 2000). Its solutions at the individual level were prayer, 12-step programs, and medicalized addiction treatment (Irvine 1995). At the policy level, conservatives continued to push for legal enforcement.

The proliferation of pornography through technology and its dangers to children became the central preoccupation of both the state and conservative antipornography organizations throughout the 1990s and 2000s. Virtually all legislative consideration of pornography entailed a focus on children. From 1992 to 2011, only two hearings did not focus on harms to children from access to or inclusion in pornography. There were substantially fewer hearings per year under Presidents George H. Bush, Clinton, and Obama than under Reagan and George W. Bush. Party control of the House or Senate continued to make a difference, with 74% of hearings on pornography between 1992 and 2011 held in chambers controlled by Republicans.[99] Issues related to women came up only a handful of times. Four Black feminist witnesses testified at three hearings about misogyny and racism in rap music; this was also the only significant consideration of racism in any hearing. No other witnesses from feminist organizations testified on pornography between 1992 and 2011.[100]

Regulating sexually explicit material on the Internet proved constitutionally difficult. Multiple legislative attempts fell under court challenge (Heins 2001; Semonche 2007; Strub 2011).[101] Proving material obscene also became more difficult because under the *Miller* rule, material could be found obscene only if it violated community standards (see endnote 3). Defense teams were able to cite large numbers of video rentals or Internet downloads as evidence that sexually explicit material did not violate community standards. As a result, regulation and prosecution of obscenity became almost impossible by the late 1990s. The battle shifted instead to limiting access by minors and in public settings like libraries and schools.

The extensive court cases on pornography that followed saw briefs by numerous conservative antipornography organizations, including Citizens for Decency Through Law, Morality in Media, and Concerned Women of America. On the other side, a host of civil liberties, freedom of expression, and media organizations filed briefs. The group Feminists for Free Expression, which included prominent feminists who took a civil liberties approach, was the only feminist organization that filed an amicus brief, and it opposed increased regulation.[102] In line with the different kinds of relationships across the case studies, child sexual abuse pulled ideologically conservative and nominally ideologically neutral groups together more than pornography alone. Two cases dealing with child pornography in 1993 and 1994 included antipornography conservative organizations, child welfare, and child sexual abuse survivors organizations as amici on the same side.[103] Feminist antipornography organizations and activists did not weigh in on any of these cases, including the child pornography cases. They did file briefs in cases on other issues, including abortion rights and sex work.[104] In other words, antipornography feminists had the ability to use legal activism but turned their focus away from pornography.

Prosecution and penalties for child pornography have continued to be substantial. Thousands of people are arrested and charged each year in connection with child pornography.[105] Other federal obscenity prosecutions, however, after growing dramatically under Reagan, decreased dramatically over time. Unlike child pornography, pornography involving adults is subject to constitutional protections.[106] Although President George W. Bush ramped up prosecutions, few resulted in convictions, and the Obama administration instituted no new prosecutions (Gerstein 2011; Gerstein 2013). Some conservatives complained about the lack of "adult obscenity" investigations under Obama, but the difficulty of obtaining convictions was at least as important in causing the decrease as Obama's political affiliation (Gerstein 2011).

Why Conservatives Had More Influence than Feminists

The larger context shaped the relative influence of each movement on their shared target. Not only did conservatives have stronger and more numerous supporters in government, a typical indicator of political opportunity, they also were positioned more favorably culturally and in relation to the discursive and procedural power of the state. The Commission and

Congress determined the *topical focus and location* of their hearings. They emphasized law enforcement, production and distribution of pornography, the role of organized crime, Customs and Postal Service interdiction, links to prostitution, and teenage runaways. As feminist critic Carole Vance (Vance 1986a) wrote about the Commission, "The narrowly drawn hearing topics effectively minimized testimony on important topics like censorship, the First Amendment, or sexuality." Congressional hearings did address First Amendment considerations both because Congress was more politically diverse than the Commission and because legislation, unlike the Commission's recommendations, had to consider Constitutional constraints. But a broader consideration of sexuality was rare in Congress as well.[107]

Witnesses were recruited according to the governmental body's priorities. Most were critical of pornography. They disputed how best, and how far, to control pornography, but not its abhorrent nature. Witnesses' remarks before governmental bodies were structured and constrained by the prevailing understandings and processes in Congress and the Meese Commission, filtered through the prevailing understandings of the issues.[108] Congresspeople and Commissioners asked the questions, exerting a powerful influence on what could be said and heard. The Commission reportedly cross-examined anticensorship witnesses more rigorously and treated anti-pornography witnesses more favorably (Califia 1986; Lynn and American Civil Liberties Union 1986). As we have seen, the question and answer with feminist antipornography witnesses before Congress was more pointed, highlighting the difference between the legal frame of obscenity and women's rights, while accepting conservative antipornography stances with less contention.

The Commission's ability to *frame witnesses' testimony* included how it was presented in the final report. Only the "Victim Testimony" section contains excerpts of any length from witnesses' testimony. Voices of witnesses who opposed regulation of pornography, or testified about their experiences in a way that did not emphasize victimization, are thus categorically excluded in the final report. For example, the brief section on the civil rights approach frames it as "civil remedies" and does not discuss other objections to this approach, although some witnesses presented them.[109]

Overall, interpretations of pornography that *resonated* with existing ways of understanding pornography were more influential than others, in a typical dynamic of cultural change (Rochon 1998; Snow and Benford 1998; Whittier 2009). Across state bodies, obscenity is the major legal and discursive means of understanding pornography. This assumes that the decisions to be made are about how much sexual explicitness is permissible and in what contexts. An obscenity approach does not depend on negative effects on the viewer or others, but instead varies depending on legal constraints and community standards of acceptability. Closely associated with the understanding of the problem as obscenity was the connection to child exploitation, as state actors discussed the relationship of pornography to child prostitution and non-feminist opponents of pornography emphasized these and other dangers to children. During the peak of feminist and conservative antipornography ferment, state actors tried on different frames and occasionally their underlying discourses, as we see in exchanges with witnesses as they attempt to understand how women are affected by pornography (feminist frames), their sympathy for complaints about the detrimental effect of sexually explicit media on parents' control of their children's sexuality (family and child protection frames), and the corrosive effects of sexual immorality (religious conservative frames). As we have seen, feminist frames quickly subsided as feminist witnesses no longer appeared before Congress and conservative witnesses dropped feminist language from their own testimony. What persisted were obscenity and child protection frames, buttressed by often-submerged notions of sexual immorality and the need to protect children's (implicitly white) purity.

Unsurprisingly, antipornography feminists were marginalized in the antipornography efforts of the 1990s and beyond, whereas conservatives continued to play an important role. Legislative and policy outcomes from the Commission and Congress entailed increased obscenity enforcement and little else, following conservative, rather than feminist, goals. The success of conservatives was due not to the influence of antipornography feminists, but to their marginalization in a context where bureaucratic procedure, and structural power shape what social movements can achieve.

IDENTITY BOUNDARIES AND REPUTATION DEFENSE

The effects of the interaction between antipornography feminists and conservatives on the women's movement were striking. Feminist participants faced threats to their reputation and entered into disputes over the boundaries of the collective identity "feminist." This was intensified by the challenge from the feminist counter-movement, led by the Feminists Anti-Censorship Task Force (FACT). Both sides claimed that they were the true feminists and that the other side was collaborating with the enemy. These internecine battles were hotter and more bruising than those between either side and the Right. Simmering for some time, they intensified and came to a head around the ordinances and the Meese Report (Potter 2012).

The debates centered around feminist identity (who could properly claim it), coalitions (which side had formed alliances with unsavory allies), and outcomes (influence on public policy). Such conflicts are unique to relationships between frenemies, in which managing and defending reputation is a significant challenge.

Identity claims

It is hard to convey the depth of mutual anger and contempt between antipornography and anti-censorship feminists. Antipornography feminists' efforts to define themselves as the true feminists often entailed the assertion that their opponents were not feminists at all. For example, a letter signed by many leaders of antipornography feminism in the wake of FACT's amicus brief in the Indianapolis ordinance case stated: "FACT and its supporters ... degrade and caricature the word feminism by using it to describe their defense of pornography" (Brest and Vandenberg 1987:65–66).[110] MacKinnon and Dworkin regularly referred to their opponents as "feminists" (using quotation marks to challenge feminist credentials), a "tiny, noisy elite of women who defend pornography professionally," who were associated with the "pro-pimp lobby," "female mouthpieces" speaking for "the corporate interests of the entertainment industry" (MacKinnon 1997:11–12).

Conversely, opposed feminists termed antipornography feminists "the New Victorians," argued that they were "anti-sex," and analogized them to the temperance movement in their zeal for prohibition. Nadine Strossen, a feminist attorney, signatory of the FACT statement and ACLU President, wrote scathingly about the "McDworkinites" and their "traditionalist-feminist antisex juggernaut" (Strossen 2000:29). FACT member Lisa Duggan took on Catharine MacKinnon's impending marriage to a man as hypocritical, writing, "Antipornographers construct a wacky feminist world in which heterosexual monogamous marriage (the kind that Catharine MacKinnon's reported engagement to Jeffrey Masson has prepared her to enter), is not suspect as 'patriarchal,' but lesbian sex is . . . because it's 'male'!"(Duggan and Hunter 1995:9–10). Their statements about each other reveal a disagreement over the definition of feminism as well as the strategic and ideological importance of distinguishing their positions.

Antipornography feminism was very controversial in the broader women's movement. Even coverage of the pornography ordinances and the Meese Commission in *Ms. Magazine* and *off our backs* was controversial. For example, MacKinnon and Dorchen Leidholdt wrote angry letters after an even-handed 1985 *Ms.* cover story (Blakely 1985), "Is One Woman's Sexuality Another Woman's Pornography?"[111] They complained that FACT was using the article in its publicity and asked what steps would be taken to, in Leidholdt's words, "undo some of the damage that the April Ms. has done to our movement?"[112] They objected because it legitimated the idea that feminists might disagree over pornography. In their view, anyone who did not support the ordinance and the notion that pornography was instrumental in women's oppression could not lay claim to the identity feminist. The heated rhetoric and the personal nature of criticism of sexual desire, deepened the rift until the sides viewed each other with mutual mistrust and even hatred.

Coalition Claims

Accusations about coalitions were at the center of the dispute. Anti-censorship feminists charged that anti-pornography feminists were in bed with the Meese Commission and Reagan administration. For example, Rosemarie Tong (1986:8) wrote about the Indianapolis ordinance, "the feminist anti-pornography campaign has encouraged . . . dangerous political alliances . . . . Feminist anti-pornographers were playing with fire and perhaps brimstone by working with groups like the Eagle Forum, the Moral Majority and the National Federation for Decency . . . " The suggestion that antipornography feminism was allied with and equivalent to right-wing censorship, prudery, and moralism was widely espoused.

Leidholdt reportedly said that she was "not embarrassed to be in agreement with Ed Meese" (Vance 1986b:80), but most antipornography feminists took pains not to be seen as in bed with the enemy. They did this by minimizing the conservatism of antipornography conservatives, disclaiming coordination with them and suggesting that women on the Right might ultimately make common cause with feminists based on gender solidarity.

Some antipornography feminists—particularly MacKinnon, who had the closest connection with conservatives—sought to emphasize antipornography conservatism's opposition to pornography and deemphasize its conservatism. They did so in defense of their reputations, strategically acknowledging some cooperation while reframing it. MacKinnon frequently argued that the individuals and bodies involved were less conservative than critics charged. For example, she argued that the Commission was "named 'the Meese Commission' by a hostile press in order to discredit it" and that Meese "did not originate it and did virtually nothing with its results" (MacKinnon and Dworkin 1997:14). She did not mention that the leadership and majority membership of the commission were from right-wing backgrounds, nor that the commission itself was formed at President Reagan's request. With regard to the municipal antipornography ordinances, MacKinnon argued that "of all the sponsors of the bill in all the cities in which it has been introduced, only one—Beulah Coughenour of Indianapolis—has been conservative. Work on one bill with an independent individual is hardly an alliance with a political wing" (MacKinnon and Dworkin 1997:10).[113]

Disagreements often entailed disparate views of the truth about the nature of the relationship between feminists and conservatives.[114] For example, it was well-documented that a local Moral Majority leader supported the Indianapolis ordinance and got his supporters to lobby the Council. Yet MacKinnon (1997:10) wrote flatly that, "Neither Rev. Dixon nor his followers appear to have spoken at the Indianapolis hearing. No one has said that Rev. Dixon or his group had any other contact with the process. Thus it was that the outcome of a legislative vote came to be attributed to the presence of some who came to watch as others cast it." This is a disingenuous statement, as MacKinnon herself well knew the value of behind-the-scenes lobbying and visible support; given the conservatism of the bill's sponsor (Coughenour), Mayor Hudnut, and CDL City Council members, it defies logic to think that they were not in contact with the well-organized local Moral Majority.

Some antipornography feminists made the case that women's shared interests justified connections with conservative women, who might even become feminists themselves. As MacKinnon (1997) declared, "exactly what is sinister about women uniting with women across conventional political lines against a form of abuse whose politics are sexual." Some even called openly for coalition with right-wing women. Ann Ferguson made such a call to, " . . . ally with New Right women to push for the civil rights of women against pornography" while trying to "convince individual conservative women to overcome some of their homophobic and puritanical feelings about sex." She hoped to convert women on the right who, "like us, are caught in the conflict of emotional intimacy and sexual pleasure" (see also Dworkin 1983 [1978]; Ferguson 1986). Despite such hopes, the collaboration these writers dreamed of never materialized.

Antipornography feminists also cited FACT's alliance with the ACLU as evidence that they were abandoning women's interests in favor of collaboration with male liberals and even pornographers themselves. Leidholdt (1985:26) wrote that she told a *Crossfire* producer that she would not debate FACT on the program because it was "a small group of lesbians that defends pornography and sadomasochism . . . [and] fronts for the ACLU, which, in turn, fronts for and is partially funded by the pornographers."[115] Nan Hunter and Lisa Duggan of FACT refuted these claims as gay-baiting "truly inventive falsehoods" and rightly placed the origin of FACT in the feminist sexuality debates, not the ACLU.[116] In general, however, FACT and its supporters spilled less ink directly defending themselves, instead publishing extensively on their own critique of antipornography feminism.

Influence claims

We have seen that antipornography feminism had minimal influence on policy outcomes. Nevertheless, even as leading antipornography feminists complained that the Meese Commission had wrongly emphasized obscenity law, they simultaneously claimed to have influenced its recommendations. MacKinnon and Dworkin proclaimed victory with a press release when the Meese Report was issued, stating, "For the first time in history, women have succeeded in convincing a national governmental body of a truth women have long known: pornography harms women and children." Similarly, Leidholdt proclaimed: "We commend the Commission for being the first federal government body to report on the systematic campaign of abuse, terror and discrimination being waged against over half the citizens of this country." Even in 1997, long after it was clear that the Reagan Justice Department had not endorsed a civil rights approach to pornography, MacKinnon claimed that the Commission "substantially adopted the civil rights approach in its approach, findings, and recommendations" (MacKinnon and Dworkin 1997). At the same time, antipornography feminists critiqued the Commission for "recommending extension and escalated enforcement of obscenity laws" which Leidholdt said, "misconceive the harm of pornography as an affront to sensibilities instead of an injury to women's lives" and MacKinnon and Dworkin called the Commission "anti-woman, anti-gay, beside the point and ineffectual" (Douglas 1986).

For once, anticensorship feminists agreed, charging that antipornography feminists had significantly influenced the Meese Commission. FACT and other opponents made the Meese Commission and the local ordinances the centerpiece of their critique of antipornography feminists, denouncing their alliance with the Meese Commission as providing political cover to the right wing (Califia 1986; Duggan and Hunter 1995; Vance 1986b; Vance 1990).

In fact, feminist influence has been overstated by both sides. The single approved ordinance in Indianapolis was overturned and opponents prevailed in the other cities. While the Meese Commission's actions were important on a symbolic level, with high-theater hearings and a final report full of denunciations, its conservative legal experts must have known that its recommendation of a civil approach—one of its many legal recommendations—was unlikely to hold up in court. But this symbolic, discursive power was important to feminists on both sides. The Meese Commission's "recognition" that women are harmed by pornography resonated with MacKinnon and her allies even as it chilled opponents. But concrete, less visible policy effects of the Meese Commission were untouched by feminism. And the legislation and enforcement efforts that did ensue were opposed by antipornography feminists.

Ultimately, FACT and other opponents of antipornography feminism prevailed in how the history of these conflicts was written. But, as Potter (2012:76) writes, "this does not mean that its [antipornography feminism's] adherents were, or became, conservative. It demonstrates only that they lost to another faction whose repertoire was more persuasive." In the dispute over the identity and ideology "feminist," the boundaries ultimately excluded antipornography feminists, successfully defining them as conservative. This was largely because of the damage done to their reputations by the charge of coalition with the Right. The Right was also affected by the relationship and faced reputational and identity concerns, as we have seen.

In sum, both movements affected each other. They worked to distinguish between themselves and the opponent since both sides stood to lose credibility by association. They did this by outlining what was "feminist" or "Christian" about their positions and by criticizing the other side in general, if not always in relation to pornography. Unlike conservatives, antipornography feminists also had to defend themselves against an active counter-movement of feminists. Their efforts to distinguish themselves from one another and to defend their reputations were as influential in shaping their longer term paths as their overlapping targets and goals.

CONCLUSION

In the end, despite the efforts of both feminists and conservatives, pornography continued to proliferate. Although some federal legislation passed relating to child pornography and online availability of sexually explicit media to minors, most was overturned. The pornography industry grew larger and more mainstream, sexually explicit images became more widespread in other media, and sexually explicit imagery was arguably as sexist as ever (Jensen 2007; Levy 2005). Conservatives, women, and the highly religious consume pornography at significant rates (Ogas and Gaddam 2012). While conservatives seemed to be winning during the 1980s, neither they nor antipornography feminists had a deep or lasting effect on sexually explicit media.

Neither movement remained highly mobilized over time. Antipornography conservative organizations, such as CDL, continued to testify before Congress, but extra-governmental mobilization diminished. Religious conservatives, facing disclosures of pornography use by clergy and others, focused on pornography addiction and efforts to help men resist and families recover from pornography consumption. Antipornography feminist organizations, under fire from other feminists, were defunct by the early 1990s. Individual activists shifted to other issues related to sexual violence and commercial sex, such as sexual harassment, rape, prostitution, domestic violence, and human trafficking.[117]

These outcomes were not inevitable, but they were overdetermined. The movements' decisions at turning points, including their relationship with each other, set them on particular paths (Blee 2012). Coupled with legal constraints, reputational threat, and the actions and influence of the myriad players in the field, the movements operated within a limited range of possibility increasingly constrained over time. Antipornography feminists' decision to focus on pornography as a distinct issue from other violent and sexist media was one such turning point. Committing to the initial ordinance campaign in Minneapolis was another. Combined, these made it very likely that turning to the state for recourse would prevail as a strategy. While it would have been possible to turn away from a legislative focus after the ordinance was overturned, the decision to try to influence the Meese Commission committed antipornography feminism to a state-focused strategy by 1985. Because it raised the possibility of cooperation with ideological opponents and posed serious risks for activists' reputation in the larger women's movement, the focus on the state proved demobilizing for antipornography feminism. Their primary legislative goal was quickly taken off the table by the courts, while their ideological commitments and reputational concerns prevented working with conservatives on obscenity law, leaving them marginal to the ongoing policy debates. The internal feminist fights left them marginal in the women's movement as well. The foreclosure of a civil rights approach to pornography did not preclude this approach in other arenas, however. It saw daylight in VAWA, antitrafficking efforts, and requirements for colleges and universities to address sexual violence under Title IX.

The longer term consequences for the women's movement overall were marked. "The women's movement," like most broad-based social movements, is itself a coalition (Cole and Luna 2010; Rochon and Meyer 1997). At its peak in the 1970s, the women's movement coalition was broad, pulling in a range of activists with different ideological, identity, and issue positions. By 1980, fault lines over race, sexuality, and strategy were deepening. Feminists of color organized autonomously and critiqued the white feminist movement for racism, focus on issues most relevant to white and middle-class women, and exaltation of a falsely unified sisterhood (Combahee River Collective 1983; Freeman 1975; Richie 2012; Roth 2003; Whittier 1995). The divisions over race did not parallel those over pornography. Many prominent Black feminists opposed pornography, seeing it grounded in the historical exploitation of Black women's bodies, even as antipornography organizing remained mostly white (e.g., Collins 2000).[118] The heated arguments about sexuality, pornography, and the turn to the state, further ruptured the women's movement coalition. These events set feminists on a particular path for dealing with sexual violence. Burned by the sex and pornography wars, much of the women's movement moved away from organizing against sexual violence, and the dangers of working with the state became a truism.

Conservative antipornography activists faced a smoother road with less dramatic consequences for their parent movement. They had support from the broader conservative movement, well-established organizations, and faced congenial targets. After the Indianapolis court decision made it clear that the feminist antipornography legal approach would not succeed, conservatives promptly returned to their own strategy, working with Congress, pressuring unsupportive presidents, and promoting sexual morality through congregations and organizations (Strub 2011). Feminists remained almost entirely absent from these efforts. FACT and other feminists opposed to antipornography feminism did not vocally oppose these conservative-backed restrictions on sexually explicit material. Instead, opposition came from broad civil liberties organizations like the ACLU.

The relationship between antipornography feminists and conservatives also had its own path. During the 1980s, the two movements engaged with the same issue (the municipal ordinances) in mostly separate locations, and with the same governmental bodies (the Meese Commission and Congress) in different ways. They were separate and opposed, but influenced each other. In fact, the entry of feminist critiques of rape into conservative opposition to pornography was one of the significant outcomes of the antipornography feminist movement. Their complicated relationship underscores the inadequacy of simple concepts of coalition or opposition. The standard story about their alliance was a rhetorical charge by their feminist opponents, rather than a description of reality. But the narrative became accepted by scholars and activists alike, repeated in work on coalitions and on feminism.[119]

Many who have written about the relationship between antipornography feminists and conservatives also charge that antipornography feminists strengthened the conservative position or moralistic opposition to pornography more generally by providing political cover to the Religious Right and making opposition to pornography seem like a mainstream cause rather than an effort by religious fanatics (Heins 2001; Semonche 2007; Strossen 2000). As we have seen, this vastly overstates antipornography feminist influence. Antipornography feminist discourses and frames made slight inroads into the state in the 1980s but vanished almost entirely by the end of the decade, while conservative discourse about morality, family, and child protection frames remained strong. Feminists' impact was greatest for a short time, when the definition of pornography and the approach to the issue was in flux and when feminists were mustering large antipornography demonstrations. Over time, their influence was minimal, and they had little social movement power to back them up, as both pornography and state intervention were controversial in the larger women's movement. Conservatives did not need feminist cover since they had powerful allies in the president, attorney general, and Congress. Ultimately, feminist cover or no, conservative antipornography efforts failed as well.

Much of what happened in Minneapolis, Indianapolis, within Congress, and even in the Justice Department was cultural rather than legislative. The testimony of witnesses about pornography, debates over constitutional constraints and the causal relationship between pornography and violence, and Justice Department publicity aimed at "concerned citizens" are all ways that citizens and different arms of the state express their disapproval of sexually explicit media, sexism, or lawlessness. It matters whether pornography is defined through criminal law as obscenity, as a crime against children, or as a cultural expression of misogyny. The discursive power of the idea of pornography as obscenity made other interpretations of pornography less likely to take hold, even when activists eloquently stated them. But the power of obscenity as an approach also comes from its constitutional underpinnings and from the agencies that enforce it. Culture, legislation, state structure, and power all matter.

Antipornography feminists made much of the idea that their model ordinance used civil rather than criminal law, claiming that this put the power in the hands of women rather than the government to bring suit, as if this would somehow prevent invoking the power of a patriarchal state (MacKinnon 1997). Indeed, the criminal penalties attached to obscenity, including prison terms, fines, and seizure of assets, are severe. But the distinction is less important than it seems. Both civil and criminal law entail bringing the power of the state to bear, whether through prosecutors or civil judges, and both carry similar risks. In either case, activists face the question of whether to invoke the protective or punitive power of the state, with the knowledge that that power may very well be turned against them next. In the case of rape and child sexual abuse, activists grappled with questions about victims' autonomy to make decisions about prosecution, counterproductive sex offender registries, and the implications of strengthening a highly punitive and inequitable prison system. But it is also the state's discursive power—the condemnation that comes with criminalization—that motivates activists' efforts to pursue intervention by the criminal justice system.

CHAPTER 3
Beyond Politics

Child Sexual Abuse and Narrow Neutrality

The idea that child sexual abuse is not an inherently political issue or the domain of one ideology or movement may seem self-evident, but it is not inevitable. Feminists argue that child sexual abuse is fundamentally about power and oppression of women and children, religious conservatives see it as the consequence of the decline of the family, and many on the Left and Right claim that concern about child sexual abuse is an overblown excuse for expanding state power. Yet individuals from diverse perspectives and legislators of all persuasions agreed that child sexual abuse should be beyond politics—politically neutral—and worked together to combat it. Approaching abuse as a single issue, without linking it to other inequalities or social forces, they collaborated narrowly.

What produced this narrowly neutral relationship? The dominance of medical and criminal discourse, the invocation of experience, and shared emotional rituals produced and maintained narrow neutrality in Congress, activist and professional groups, and media representations. Prevailing discourse in mainstream culture and in Congress defined child sexual abuse in terms of pathology or crime. This was reinforced by the structural fact that congressional consideration of child sexual abuse usually occurs in the House and Senate Judiciary Committees, which are charged with issues that are considered crimes. Personal stories of child sexual abuse were especially important, and all parties treated experience as a highly credible basis for understanding child sexual abuse. Expert testimony and scientific research also provided information with a veneer of objectivity that reinforced the idea that child sexual abuse was not a matter of politics. Congressional hearings on child sexual abuse were also emotional, but in structured and ritualized ways, as legislators and witnesses invoked emotion according to recognized routines that served to legitimate the issue's importance. All this enabled grassroots activists and members of Congress to connect across political lines and display their commitment to working against child sexual abuse.

The construction of child sexual abuse as beyond politics enabled the cross-ideological engagement with the issue that I call narrow neutrality. Narrow neutrality facilitated the passage of legislation and foreclosed the conflicts and politicized agendas and discourses that might have produced different outcomes. Narrow neutrality also pulled policy and advocacy toward criminal justice and punitive treatment and away from challenges to children's powerlessness or the patriarchal family, an emphasis on preserving the traditional family, or a critique of false accusations. Congressional processes picked up on, amplified, and translated narrowly neutral frames and underlying discourses into law, and ignored, silenced, or structurally excluded other approaches from both the Right and the Left.

As I show in this chapter, advocates inside and outside Congress strategically emphasized the idea that child sexual abuse was a problem in families across race and class. This impulse stemmed partly from advocates' desire to counter long-standing stereotypes about people of color, poor people, and immigrants as more prone to child abuse. It also was a means of sidestepping congressional opposition to social welfare funding by suggesting that funding to combat child sexual abuse would benefit a broad socioeconomic spectrum (Nelson 1984). But it also reflected the involvement of white and middle-class women and men in the survivors' movement, who were speaking out about sexual abuse in their families. As criminal enforcement against child sexual abuse grew, offenders were (and are) predominantly white, in contrast to virtually every other kind of crime. As the rhetorical emphasis shifted to nonfamilial abuse, the specter of the stranger pedophile reinforced other aspects of racialized discourse, particularly the idea of the innocent, vulnerable, white victim and, Lancaster (2011) and Leon (2011) argue, consolidated the idea that the (implicitly-white) community is threatened by outside danger, justifying the extension of state crime control into even affluent white communities. None of this meant that more traditional forms of racial inequality were not also present. White offenders, especially familial ones, receive disproportionately favorable sentencing and rehabilitation options, youth of color and working-class youth are "adultified" and thus less likely to be seen as innocent victims (Corrigan 2006; Ferguson 2000; Freedman 2013;

Meiners 2009; Roberts 2001; Whittier 2015), and expertise and authority are shaped by race and class.

Members of Congress from across the political spectrum sponsored hearings and supported laws on child sexual abuse. The topic of child sexual abuse had the greatest amount of federal legislation, congressional hearings, and mass media coverage of the three case studies. These hearings included professionals from all disciplines, adults who had been sexually abused as children, and parents of abused children, and a small number of activists. Those working on the issue differed in their ideologies, movement affiliations, and larger agendas, but they largely put these differences aside as irrelevant to child sexual abuse, which they repeatedly stated was beyond politics. Legislators, witnesses, and activists uniformly decried abuse even when they opposed specific legislation.

The narrowly neutral umbrella depended on the exclusion of larger political agendas. In contrast to the other two case studies, few witnesses officially represented activist groups, even if they were part of them. Many witnesses testifying before Congress were accountable to community organizations, but these connections were rarely articulated. Specifically, some witnesses had feminist or other political perspectives or commitments, but most muted these in congressional testimony. Many professional and advocacy organizations were deliberately apolitical or politically neutral and included members from a wide range of ideological leanings. Others, such as law enforcement officials or health-care providers, had ongoing relationships with rape crisis or child abuse advocacy organizations in their communities or were involved in multidisciplinary teams that included activists, social workers, and others. These connections had reputational implications, but to a much lesser degree than the questions of reputation that dogged antipornography or VAWA activists.

Cooperation under the narrowly neutral umbrella required that conservatives downplay their traditional rhetoric about the pathology of the inner city or underclass, and liberals and feminists downplay their commitments to social change around gender, race, and class. They avoided ideological conflict by virtually never discussing gender, race, or class. Instead, they came together around protecting children (with the implicit idea that some children were more vulnerable and innocent than others) from the especially heinous crime of child sexual abuse. But there were unintended consequences for both sides. In terms of state programs, punitive approaches prevailed rather than preventive or service approaches and the offender population was predominantly white. In terms of discourse, the notion that some victims were more worthy and some offenders more able to be rehabilitated was implicit but powerful.

In terms of authority, some kinds of experiential and expert authority were more persuasive than others (Naples 2003). Race, gender, and class were inextricably linked to all of these (Roberts 2001).

Interactions among diverse or otherwise-opposed groups were not a simple matter of finding the "lowest common denominator." They rested on commonalities that were important and highly salient to participants. At the grassroots, activists explicitly constructed the collective identity "survivor" as a shared childhood experience and adult trajectory that transcended other differences. In Congress, legislators expressed strong commitment to working against child sexual abuse; while one can never know whether elected officials are genuinely concerned about issues they champion, their discourse and framing emphasized the great importance and significance of the issue, which was, undoubtedly, genuinely important to their constituents.

NARROW NEUTRALITY AT THE GRASSROOTS: THE SURVIVORS' MOVEMENT AND THE FIELD

Among activists, narrow neutrality meant that they understood the shared identity of "survivor" of child sexual abuse as a powerful commonality that transcended forces that might ordinarily divide people. While many groups formed around specific shared experiences (Black survivors, men, lesbians, Christians, etc.), major organizations pulled together individuals from across these categories and featured overt discussion of commonality and empathy for each other's experiences—the "neutral" element. After the mid-1980s, almost all organizations focused on child sexual abuse as a single issue—the "narrow" element. Media coverage of the single-issue movement also emphasized this unifying identity of survivor and recruited individuals from across the social spectrum to participate in the organizations that were publicized in the articles or simply to think of themselves in these terms.

The first feminist child sexual abuse organizations, emerging from anti-rape activism around 1980, built a feminist self-help movement that focused on rethinking child sexual abuse and developing peer techniques for assisting individuals with its effects. As their ideas reached a broader audience and professionals, journalists, and government officials began to address the issue, a larger movement of survivors emerged. This broader movement focused on child sexual abuse as a single issue, more than as a manifestation of larger systems of inequality. Its members focused on self-help and peer support, and worked to raise public awareness about child sexual abuse. These activists included both men and women who thought of themselves as "nonpolitical" as they encouraged survivors to speak out. Because child sexual abuse cuts across political allegiances, women and men from diverse perspectives and backgrounds identified as survivors and often participated in the same groups.[1]

Activism against child sexual abuse was at its peak in the 1980s and early 1990s as it consolidated this narrowly neutral model. It achieved considerable visibility and influence and self-help groups spread around the country. Eventually some of these groups developed into professionally staffed organizations that included individuals and groups from otherwise-opposing perspectives, such as conservative evangelical Christians and lesbian feminists. A large professional sector, including psychotherapy, social work, medicine, academic research, law enforcement, and clergy developed specializations in working with children and adult survivors of child sexual abuse. Some professionals came to this work from experiences with feminist organizing against child sexual abuse and rape, especially early on, but many others followed professional paths, influenced, but not defined, by feminist work on child sexual abuse.

Single-issue organizations managed their diverse constituencies by eschewing ideological and political stances beyond child sexual abuse. Organizations like VOICES (loosely interpreted to stand for Voices of Incest Survivors Can Emerge and renamed Voices in Action in the late 1990s), the Healing Woman, Incest Survivors Resources International, and the American Coalition on Abuse Awareness covered state and federal legislation on issues like statutes of limitation for abuse prosecution in their publications but rarely attempted to influence legislation directly. The main influence of the survivors' movement was indirect, through raising media attention and visibility, which in turn influenced congressional attention to the issue. Professionals working on child sexual abuse were more important in actually initiating and shaping legislation, as were quasi-state organizations made up mainly of professionals like the National Association for the Prevention of Child Abuse and the National Center on Missing and Exploited Children (NCMEC).

Mass media coverage of child sexual abuse grew rapidly during the 1980s as activists working to bring public attention to the issue garnered coverage in magazines, newspapers, books, and television. Mainstream media, especially magazines aimed at women, presented personal narratives of survivors, including celebrities, and emphasized the importance of visibility and breaking silence about abuse as a means of personal healing from its effects. Articles recounted both incest and abuse outside the family, as well as suggesting ways to prevent child sexual abuse. Mass media sources were likely to portray female victims and male offenders, but the gendering of the issue was almost always implicit rather than explicit. In other words, the framing of child sexual abuse in mainstream media reflected the gender-neutral approach of the self-help wing. By the later 1980s, more articles in mainstream media dealt with false accusations, false memories, and acquittals in daycare or ritual abuse cases.[2]

Overcoming silence and stigma through personal and cultural visibility was central to the movement's goals regarding child sexual abuse, and the resulting attention helped change culture and policy. Members of Congress discussed media coverage and even framed hearings around highly publicized media events like a TV movie about incest (U.S. House 1994a). Yet, although activists brought the issue to public attention, they could not control how the media portrayed child sexual abuse. Overtly political elements, like activists' critique of the family or children's powerlessness, rarely reached a mainstream audience. Media coverage reflected movement frames that child sexual abuse was widespread and that children were not to blame, but presented medical and criminal solutions rather than broader social solutions or the peer support many activists favored. As we will see, this was the approach in law and policy as well.

The publicity about incest and child sexual abuse also affected public opinion. Survey data shows that the openness encouraged by the survivors' movement had an impact. While few social scientists have studied public opinion about child sexual abuse in the United States, 41 percent of respondents to a 1984 *Glamour* poll reported having been sexually abused as children, almost all by relatives or acquaintances ("This Is What You Thought" 1984:47). A later survey of undergraduates found that 63 percent knew someone who had been sexually abused, and only 8 percent of this sample thought that most offenders were strangers (Fuselier, Durham, and Wurtele 2002:277). Surveys also suggest that beliefs about abuse reflected mass media accounts. The two surveys to examine the question found that the vast majority of respondents believed (accurately) that male parents, relatives, or family friends were the most frequent offenders and that children are usually truthful about sexual abuse (Calvert and Munsie-Benson 1999; Fuselier, Durham, and Wurtele 2002).

By the early 1990s, these gains sparked an influential countermovement. It, too, was ideologically diverse. Led by the False Memory Syndrome Foundation (FMSF), it was made up of parents who had been accused of sexual abuse by their adult children and professionals who supported their cause. It focused on false accusations by adults and children and the unreliability of children's testimony. Mustering scholarly evidence for the unreliability of childhood memories, the FMSF reshaped public opinion about the truth of adults' recollections of childhood sexual abuse. The FMSF and its allies also questioned children's reports of abuse and won numerous court battles to make children's reports less admissible or less credible (Cheit 2014). Like its opponents, the FMSF defined its focus narrowly around child sexual abuse and sought participants from across the political spectrum. Nevertheless, some members' connections to Republican legislators produced a rare moment of challenge to the consensus around child sexual abuse, as we will see.

Participants in the single-issue survivors' movement responded to the countermovement by becoming more overtly political. My interviews with activists in that movement suggest that the self-help and healing-oriented activities for individuals that participants previously saw as apolitical came to seem political in the context of a countermovement that invalidated their accounts of their own experiences (Whittier 2009). They did not link child sexual abuse or survivor identity to other issues—that is, they remained narrow in focus—but they sought to heighten support and mobilization regarding the single issue. As we will see, however, their efforts had no more effect on legislation than those of the countermovement.

More influential organizing developed in the early 1990s around missing children. Parents mobilized around terrible cases of child abductions and murders and worked with law enforcement to establish databases of known sex offenders. They helped form the National Center for Missing and Exploited Children (NCMEC), which was federally funded and mandated to collect and report data on missing children. NCMEC became very influential in passing and expanding sex offender registration and notification requirements. As we will see, it too defined its focus as the single issue and as beyond politics.

By the 2010s, all of these strands coexisted but in diminished form. The FMSF had virtually disbanded and the self-help survivors' groups had shrunk dramatically. Many individuals still identified as survivors, professional therapy thrived, and colleges, mental health centers, and rape crisis centers continued to offer services to adults who had been sexually assaulted as children. Public, organized activism, while still present, was less visible. Small groups used public health techniques to try to decrease child sexual abuse through community-based prevention services.[3] A few groups supported restorative or transformative justice, that is, alternatives to the criminal justice system. With little success, they opposed community registration and notification requirements for sex offenders, the major policy direction of the past 20 years. The focus has remained primarily on familial and acquaintance abuse, with little engagement with stranger abuse. Framing child sexual abuse in the context of race, gender, and class, some more recent organizations are not strictly single issue. But, like earlier initiatives, they frame opposition to child sexual abuse as a given, something that should exist outside politics.

The development of single-issue organizations and the unifying collective identity of survivor led inexorably toward narrow neutrality. Correspondingly, feminist and conservative movement organizations were relatively disengaged and less important than the other two cases.

Women's Movement Engagement with Child Sexual Abuse Activism

Overall, women's movement organizations have focused less on child sexual abuse than on other forms of sexual and intimate partner violence. Mainstream women's movement organizations have had some involvement with child sexual abuse over the years: The National Organization for Women had a Task Force on Child Sexual Abuse in the 1970s and 1980s; NOW's Legal Defense and Education Fund worked for civil settlements for adult survivors in the 1990s; and the Ms. Foundation has funded some organizations in the 2000s. At state and local levels, some child sexual abuse groups worked with women's movement groups and others didn't; some service organizations for adult or child victims collaborated with anti-rape groups or family violence organizations and others didn't. These connections were not central to either the women's or the survivors' movement.

Similarly, feminist press coverage of incest and child sexual abuse has been sparse. Ms., the only feminist publication with a wide readership, published 20 articles on the subject between 1984 and 2013.[4] Not only were there relatively few pieces, but Ms. coverage was also almost indistinguishable from mainstream media coverage. Most articles reflected issues raised by the survivors' movement (such as the prevalence of incest and the importance of breaking silence about abuse and seeking treatment) and suggested resources, including NCMEC, a hotline sponsored by Childhelp, Parents' United, and VOICES. These were single-issue organizations, not feminist ones, perhaps because the feminist survivors' groups that existed were small and informal. But Ms. also published an article on debates over medical evidence of sexual abuse written by noted opponent of the survivors' movement Debbie Nathan, and an article on children's removal from families because of false reports to child protective services. The latter article profiled a parent who founded the southern Colorado chapter of VOCAL (Victims of Child Abuse Laws), an explicitly antifeminist organization, and quoted conservative intellectual Douglas Besharov as an expert on child sexual abuse (Zegart 1989).[5] It is hard to imagine another topic that would lead *Ms.* to quote such conservative sources favorably. Overall, *Ms.* coverage was sporadic and only rarely framed in explicitly feminist terms.

The skepticism about abuse claims in *Ms.* coverage was starkly different from the smaller and more radical feminist *off our backs*, whose coverage of incest and child sexual abuse was much more overtly political and somewhat more in-depth. Between 1982 and 2008, *off our backs* contained 19 articles on incest or child sexual abuse.[6] Overall, the nuanced coverage aimed at readers who were incest survivors or involved in feminist communities where issues of incest were being discussed. Articles dealt in-depth with activist issues related to incest, such as discussion of connections and conflicts between incest survivors' and battered women's organizations (Friday 1983). Many articles focused on lesbian communities or identity, beginning in 1982 with an article on "Lesbian Survivors of Incest" that covered support groups, the relationship between incest and separatism, and effects of incest on sexuality ("Lesbian Survivors" 1982).

Unlike *Ms.* or the mainstream press, *off our backs* did not frame child sexual abuse as a politically neutral issue but emphasized men's power over women and children. Articles presented politicized issues and contexts such as courts' and judges' complicity in mothers' loss of custody to incestuous fathers (Armstrong 1988) and activist organizing against child sexual abuse (Skorczewski 1996). Articles critiqued the "backlash" against survivors, framing the FMSF as a defense organization for offenders ("Backlash" 1994; Jurisfemme 1993). *Off our backs* reached a small audience, one that was still influenced by the feminist self-help and activist strand of organizing. For most survivors and advocates, even those who might read *Ms.*, the definition of child sexual abuse as politically uncontroversial and detached from the feminist ideology dominated. This was largely true for conservatives as well.

Conservative Engagement with Child Sexual Abuse Activism

Except for child pornography, child sexual abuse was not on conservatives' radar prior to the 1980s. Most conservative movement organizations, like women's movement organizations, never made it a central issue. Conservative individuals joined single-issue self-help groups, along with people of all political perspectives. Religious conservative clergy (especially pastoral counselors) and survivors also participated in small religious survivors' organizations and published specialized self-help guides (Whittier 2009). Christian pastoral counselors developed specializations in working with abuse survivors, and religious publications and individuals talked about the spiritual damage that abuse could cause and how survivors could rebuild a relationship with God. As clergy abuse, especially in the Catholic Church, became publicly known, many denominations developed curricula on how to prevent clergy abuse and how congregations could recover from the effects of an abusive pastor (Whittier 2009:106–7).

The influential religious conservative organization Focus on the Family—which had been central in the antipornography campaign—engaged with child abuse in the 1980s, mainly by answering letters from incest victims. In the mid-1990s, Focus on the Family attempted to connect with the survivors' group VOICES and became involved in policy on incest in order to advocate the preservation of "traditional families," under the rationale that stepfathers or boyfriends were more likely than biological fathers to abuse children in their family. This provoked a rare dispute, with feminists I interviewed appalled at Focus on the Family's involvement, which was based on a political agenda rather than participants' identification as survivors and thus departed from the neutrality that enabled cross-ideological cooperation (Whittier 2009). While Focus on the Family linked child sexual abuse to other conservative positions, most grassroots work by religious conservatives was focused on support and resources for individuals and was compatible with the same work done by nonconservatives. Religious conservative rhetoric about the negative effects of pornography on sexual abuse of women and children—and the evangelical women who spoke out about their experiences of sexual assault as children or adults—doubtless fed into evangelical conservative work with child sexual abuse.

Religious conservative publications, like their feminist counterparts, barely covered the issue. *Christianity Today* contained a total of seven articles on incest or child sexual abuse between 1980 and 2013. They were all favorable to the perspective of survivors, with two addressing the effects of child sexual abuse, and most of the others covering accusations of child sexual abuse by clergy or in religious schools.[7] Other Christian publications, especially the mainline Protestant *Christian Century*, covered the clergy sex abuse cases extensively, but there was virtually no religious conservative coverage of other aspects of child sexual abuse.

Secular conservatives, in contrast, argued that child sexual abuse was much rarer than advocates claimed and that many accusations were false, echoing the effective countermovement and also their approach to rape in general, as we will see in Chapter 5. Secular conservative publications contained many articles mentioning child sexual abuse, but they were almost all derogatory of prosecutions, focused on false allegations, or used the issue to critique liberals. The exceptions are stories about clergy abuse and, rarely, stories advocating tougher criminal penalties for sex offenders. The *National Review,* for instance, published 33 articles on child sexual abuse between the mid-1980s and 2013. Of these, only the extensive coverage of the Catholic Church's clergy abuse cases, scathing toward both the Church and the ostensibly gay priests behind the abuse, framed child sexual abuse as a social problem in need of solution. Articles about the ineptitude of child protective services and false allegations were used to critique big government. *Human Events* and *Commentary* had a lower volume of coverage, but all dealt with either false accusations or clergy cases, and most framed child sexual abuse as a problem stemming from gay men in the clergy and elsewhere (e.g., "Conservative Forum" 2000; Coulter 2002). The differences between secular and religious conservatives were stark. It is not surprising, therefore, that religious conservatives had a visible presence in the grassroots survivors' movement, while secular conservatives presumably participated as individual survivors but had no affinity groups.[8]

Child sexual abuse differs from pornography and the Violence Against Women Act because it remained a prominent issue over a longer time period. In the 1970s, when it first emerged as an issue, the women's movement was strong and thus influenced the definition of the issue, the strategies that emerged, and the earliest policy and institutional responses. As social work and other child advocacy professions grew and engaged further with child sexual abuse, they too shaped the issue (Davis 2005). By the 1980s, with the rise of the conservative movement and the weakening of mass feminist mobilization, we would expect that conservatives would exert more influence, but the mainstreaming of the issue prevented a conservative shift. In the 1990s and 2000s, strong religious conservatism did serve as a brake on weaker feminist activism, but both movements were generally disengaged, and it was politically unpalatable for secular conservatives to appear unsupportive of child sexual abuse victims or criminal law, which meant neither movement had much influence.

Because the child sexual abuse case study stretches over a longer period of time than the other two cases, this chapter is organized somewhat differently. In the next section, I analyze congressional hearings, activists' involvement in them, and the politically neutral frames they constructed, focusing on three moments of challenge to narrow neutrality. At each moment of challenge, I show how the narrowly neutral alliance persisted, changed, and facilitated particular kinds of policy. An analysis of authority and emotion follows the discussion of congressional engagement.

CONGRESSIONAL ENGAGEMENT WITH CHILD SEXUAL ABUSE: ROUTINE AGREEMENTS AND MOMENTS OF CHALLENGE

The major federal legislation on child abuse, the Child Abuse Prevention and Treatment Act (CAPTA), was passed in 1974 after extensive 1973 hearings. CAPTA addresses all forms of child abuse and originally focused on physical abuse and neglect. It established a federal center for dealing with child abuse and funded grant programs for research, treatment, and demonstration projects to develop approaches that could be spread to other locations. CAPTA also required states to adopt mandatory reporting laws, requiring that certain professionals working with children (like teachers and physicians) report suspected child abuse to authorities. A large proportion of these reports dealt with sexual abuse, much more than professionals or lawmakers had expected. As a result, hearings, law, and social services for child sexual abuse grew significantly in the later 1970s, at the same time that the grassroots movement of child sexual abuse survivors was beginning to coalesce, setting the wheels in motion for a dramatic rise in attention to the issue in the 1980s.

By and large, members of Congress universally agreed that child sexual abuse was a serious problem and that the federal government should act. At the same time, there were moments when existing programs or directions faced challenge and consensus destabilized. These were actual or potential turning points, when narrow neutrality was challenged and then reasserted, sometimes around different policies. The key moments of challenge occurred (1) in 1981 around a Republican attempt to kill CAPTA; (2) between 1992 and 1999 around feminist organizing regarding child custody cases with abuse allegations and the FMSF attempts to weaken CAPTA; and (3) in 2000 and subsequent years around expansions of sex offender registration and notification requirements. These challenges corresponded to shifts in the framing of child sexual abuse by activist groups and mainstream culture and coincided with change in party control of the presidency or Congress.

One hundred and fifty hearings addressing child sexual abuse were held between 1981 and 2013, an average of 4.5 hearings per year.[9] Some years saw many hearings and others almost none, as Figure 3.1 shows. Republicans and Democrats each controlled Congress half the time between 1981 and 2013, and slightly over half (58 percent) of hearings were held in Republican-controlled congressional chambers.[10] However, Republicans averaged fewer witnesses per hearing, 7.5, compared with Democrats, 10.3. Hearings were also slightly more common under Republican than

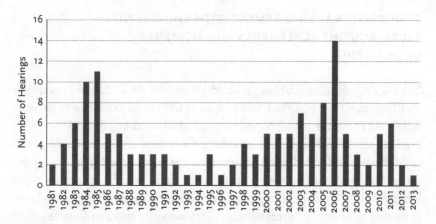

Figure 3.1 Number of Congressional Hearings on Child Sexual Abuse, 1981–2013

Democratic presidents.[11] Hearings did occur around the moments of challenge but not in exceptionally large numbers. Instead, lawmakers demonstrated their commitment to the issue through numerous hearings during periods of routine agreement.

Congressional witnesses included experts and practitioners in the field, such as law enforcement officials, human service and child protective workers from state or local government, researchers, treatment professionals, and experts on the Internet. A steady stream of victims and parents of victims recounted their experiences, along with witnesses from organizations that combined personal and professional expertise, such as Parents Anonymous and Parents United. Few organizations were routine participants.[12] Aside from the National Center on Missing and Exploited Children (NCMEC), no organization appeared more than three times during the studied period. Almost all the organizations that testified before Congress framed child sexual abuse as a single, nonpolitical issue.

Feminist, survivor, and countermovement organizations testified rarely and almost exclusively during moments of challenge. Women's movement organization witnesses appeared at only one (U.S. House 1995b).[13] Three witnesses from small, ephemeral survivors' groups appeared in the late 1980s through mid-1990s,[14] and a handful of witnesses from countermovement organizations appeared at two 1995 hearings challenging CAPTA's reauthorization. Conservative organizations were absent from most child sexual abuse hearings except for those on child pornography, but one witness from a religious conservative organization appeared in 1995 (U.S. House 1995a).

Across all periods and points of view, lawmakers and witnesses relied on experiential knowledge, claims of expert and scientific knowledge, and invocation of emotion as the "glue" to connect them across ideological differences. At each moment of challenge, narratives by individuals with experiential authority made the primary case for continuing, modifying, or expanding federal child sexual abuse law. The content of the narratives varied, however, following the rise and fall of social movements. In the first moment, narratives of incest survivors emphasized psychological aftereffects and treatment, usually not in relation to criminal penalties, just as the grassroots survivors' movement did. In the second moment, narratives by mothers wrongly losing custody of their children and by the falsely accused emphasized the incompetence and overreach of family courts or child protection agencies, albeit in opposite directions. This reflected the rise of the countermovement. In the third moment, narratives from family members of young rape and murder victims emphasized the need to contain sex offenders, who were defined as beyond rehabilitation.

Expert authority and scientific research were nearly universal at the hearings, but were not always influential at potential turning points. Instead, the routine periods of agreement between these challenges relied on expertise alongside experience. Kevin Esterling (2010) finds that witnesses make different kinds of arguments depending on how contentious the hearing issue is. In moderately contentious settings, Esterling finds that witnesses make falsifiable statements, using research and empirical or analytical arguments. In low and highly contentious settings, witnesses are more likely to reference values or experience (which cannot be falsified). To some degree, these patterns hold true for child sexual abuse. Generally it is a low-contention issue. Experiential arguments are indeed common, and they also became the basis for highly contentious discussions. Expert evidence was used in drafting legislation, discussing the scope and patterns of the issue early in the issue cycle, and crafting the intensive punishment for sex offenders in the 2000s.[15]

Congress rarely considered class, race, or gender directly in relation to child sexual abuse. The most frequent mention of race or class was the assertion by witnesses or members of Congress that child sexual abuse "cuts across all income, social, religious, economic, and racial backgrounds."[16] The exception was discussion of Native Americans, the focus of several dedicated hearings because federal law governs the prosecution of Native Americans living on tribal lands. However, legislators and witnesses in these hearings regularly mentioned that abuse is prevalent in non-Indian contexts too. These hearings focused on lack of services and high rates of abuse, with little discussion of specific cultural or structural forces.[17]

Framing child sexual abuse without regard to race or class, or even gender, constructed the issue's apparent political neutrality.[18] This was important because it avoided linking resources for child sexual abuse to social welfare spending in a time of widespread cuts in funding for services for the poor or people of color (Nelson 1984). These constructions tend to create a generic white victim that leads to policy that does not well serve people of color (Richie 2012). Indeed, child protective services and sex offender registration and notification procedures had disproportionately negative effects on people of color (Corrigan 2006; Richie 2012). In addition, white and middle-class offenders are more likely to be viewed as "sick" rather than evil, and thus as amenable to treatment (Leon 2011; Sacco 2009). At the same time, the predominance of white advocates against familial abuse produced punitive measures against white offenders, leading to the uncharacteristic racial balance among sex offenders.

Next, I dissect the three moments of challenge, focusing on how witnesses and lawmakers used experiential narratives to shape narrow, neutral frames in Congress and how grassroots constructions of narrow neutrality affected them. The experiential authority and emotional resonance of personal narratives were powerful enough to foreclose most discursive dissent. But they only influenced law when they were also consistent with other powerful discourses of the time and with federal authority, as we will see. In short, the first moment of challenge reflected discourses of child welfare and crime, as well as the influence of the growing survivors' movement; the second addressed issues that were beyond the scope of the federal government and could not be readily understood through crime or medical discourse; and the third fed off the decline of the social welfare state and the state's punitive and surveillance turn.

MOMENT OF CHALLENGE ONE: 1981 REAUTHORIZATION OF CAPTA AND THE RETURN TO CONSENSUS, 1981–1991

By 1981, CAPTA had been in effect for six years and had generated research and programs addressing all types of child abuse. But the newly elected Republican Senate and President Reagan sought dramatic cutbacks to social programs and an end to dedicated funding streams and federal restrictions on how states could spend their social service funds. This would have included CAPTA. At issue in the 1981 hearings on CAPTA were overall funding cuts, whether child sexual abuse funding should remain a dedicated federal stream or be subsumed in block grants for social services that states could allocate as they chose, and whether NCCAN (National Center on Child Abuse and Neglect) should be eliminated. Ultimately, Congress reaffirmed federal involvement in child sexual abuse prevention and treatment, reauthorizing CAPTA. The moment of challenge and partisan debate in 1981 was quickly supplanted by agreement.

A brief hearing in the Republican Senate and a major hearing in the Democratic House took up the bill. At the Senate hearing, chaired by CAPTA opponent Jeremiah Denton (Nelson 1984), two witnesses spoke in favor of CAPTA. Both appealed to conservative ideals, saying that acting against abuse upheld conservative family values and prevented crime. For example, Earl Forte of the National Committee for Prevention of Child Abuse argued that the importance of child abuse treatment made CAPTA funding a necessary exception to conservative budget cuts. He explained,

> As a conservative businessman, I endorse the goals and approach of the Reagan administration wholeheartedly. . . . [But] unless we do something for our children, future administrations will be trying to solve adult problems that emanate from their youth long after the current administration is dead and gone. . . . I support Federal budget reductions and the discontinuance of many programs, but the dilemma, however, I find myself in is that I believe the National Center on Child Abuse and Neglect is not one that should be discontinued. (U.S. Senate 1981b:145).

His "dilemma" underscores the power of the cross-ideological agreement about child abuse as a politically neutral issue.

Lengthy personal narratives were the centerpiece of the much longer hearing in the Democratic House, although researchers, detectives, and social workers also testified (U.S. House 1981). In 1981, as in the period of agreement that followed, these narratives focused specifically on incest. This is not surprising, since this is the period when the survivors' movement was beginning to receive extensive media coverage, often in the form of personal narratives (Whittier 2009). Hearings on child sexual abuse in the 1970s had likewise focused on familial abuse.[19] During early 1980s hearings, self-help groups like Parents Anonymous and Parents United kept incest front and center. Parents United had strong ties to experts and legislators: their treatment program in Santa Clara County, California, had received a large grant from NCCAN in 1978 to develop a demonstration program for family treatment. They recruited parents and victims to present vivid and moving testimony.

Compelling testimony from "Beth" revealed how she had been "molested by my stepfather" from age 8 or 9 until age 15 or 16. Beth appeared at the 1981 hearing because of her family's treatment through Parents United.

She was accompanied by her mother, stepfather, and a police sergeant who worked with Parents United. Their testimony was among the longest personal narratives in all the congressional hearings. Beth told her story in detail, emphasizing her confusion and isolation. Her narrative closely followed the form of survivor narratives portrayed in mass media, describing bewilderment and secrecy, the healing effects of disclosure and therapy, and the lasting damage that incest could do (Whittier 2009; Davis 2005). As she explained, her stepfather's molestation

> happened fairly frequently over that period of years and it affected me a great deal. . . . When it first began, I didn't really understand what was going on. . . . Normally children aren't told about anything like that . . . what I was told was to stay away from strangers in black cars with candy. And this was a man in my family, and certainly no one I had any means to protect myself from. . . . He was telling me not to tell anyone and it was a big secret. . . . I didn't have anyone to talk to, I didn't have anywhere to go with my problem. I didn't feel that I could talk to my mom. . . . I was really afraid I would break up the family.[20]

Beth went on to describe drug use, sexual promiscuity, having a child that she placed for adoption, and running away, before finally telling her mother, whom she felt "was real supportive of me at that time, and that was a real blessing." But Beth's mother still lived with her stepfather, and they never discussed the abuse. When Beth became involved with Parents United, she reported, "It was a big relief for me to at least have it . . . to where it was something that I could talk about . . . there was a huge relief in knowing . . . that there were a lot of other women who had been molested when they were children, and I finally felt that I had people I could go to who'd understood what had happened to me." Beth especially praised the way that the program brought her family together again.

Beth's abusive stepfather, "Dick," testified after Beth's statement. Although the treatment paradigm at the time made a distinction between incest and sexual assault on nonrelated children, believing that most incest perpetrators were unlikely to molest children outside their family, Dick recounted a lengthy history of sexual violence, saying he "spent 4 years in prison for assault on a woman . . . was out for a very short period of time, was arrested on a child molesting charge." At that point, he was sent to a sex offender treatment program in a state hospital for three years and felt that after leaving, "I was in pretty good shape. I was feeling more confident in myself." But when he married four years later, having disclosed his past convictions to his wife, "[I] found myself overwhelmed with responsibilities, the wife, three small children. It wasn't long after that I started molesting my daughter."[21] Unsurprisingly, after Beth told her mother that Dick had been raping her, their marriage deteriorated; it was a marriage counselor who referred them to Parents United. At that point, Dick said, "things started going uphill again. I now feel that my wife's and my relationship is very, very beautiful, we are getting along fantastically. I have a daughter who loves me, and I love her. We can sit and talk. I feel she looks up to me as a father figure now." Beth's mother, Jo, said that Beth's disclosure was "the most difficult thing I had ever had to deal with" and explained that she "felt a great deal of anger toward my husband" but did not want to "destroy him" with her "rage," and so "kept that in me." She, too, praised Parents United, especially its "self-help component," in which parents help facilitate groups.[22] Like the larger survivors movement of the time, Beth and Jo emphasized the value of speaking out about abuse and of peer support rather than solely professional therapy (Whittier 2009).

Despite Dick's confessing years of raping his daughter and two previous sexual assault convictions, there was no mention of any criminal penalty for him. This would not have happened even a few years later. For Jo, Parents United was the alternative to the criminal justice system. As she said, "I think that without Parents United that today my husband would be in prison, probably for life . . . . I think he would have molested some other child."[23] While Dick might have been imprisoned, Jo thought she would have remained deeply depressed, while Beth might have suffered "numerous broken marriages, prostitution, loss of self-respect, guilt, more child abuse of their own children, physical and sexual abuse, and other sorts of detrimental situations."

Their vivid stories anchored the hearing, confirming Esterling's (2010) proposition that contention increases the likelihood of experiential claims, since they are unfalsifiable. Testimony about direct personal experience was framed as helping legislators understand the issue and, thus, support congressional action. [24] The compelling personal narratives helped create a moral imperative to fund CAPTA despite Republican efforts to cut social programs and devolve control to the states.

Supporting frames bolstered cross-ideological support. Many witnesses emphasized that self-help and services to abused children or to parents would save money—a Republican priority—by preventing future abuse and crime. Elizabeth Elmer, the director of a Parental Stress Center in Pittsburgh, put this concisely: "millions of abused children . . . when they get to be adolescent or a little older, their pent-up anger is going to break forth, and we are going to see a lot more of the crime and delinquency that we now fear" (U.S. House 1981). Small amounts of funding could support self-help groups that, through volunteerism, provided a lot of bang for the buck. As Vanette Graham, the project director of a regional Child Abuse and Neglect Resource Center, explained, "Parents Anonymous costs 88 cents per week per family served" (U.S. House 1981:223). Volunteerism, like cost savings, was a Reagan priority that could also be politically neutral.

Witnesses also suggested that support services could increase criminal prosecution, another Reagan priority. Jo noted that when she told a caller to the Parents United hotline that he could turn himself in to the police department rather than being taken from his home in handcuffs, he did so and subsequently pleaded guilty. CAPTA prioritized "multidisciplinary teams," in which various agencies would work together to provide services, investigation, and prosecution of child abuse. This has since become widespread but was new in 1981. A police officer who had worked with Parents United explained: "[W]e are learning . . . that the more we can deal with all types of offenders, all types of situations, in a more humanistic way, we are much more successful." In fact, the criminal justice system was increasingly integrated with child protective services and other community agencies, providing further justification for funding social services.

There were limits to the politically neutral umbrella. Both liberal and conservative legislators tried unsuccessfully to broaden it. On the liberal side, some witnesses argued that a social safety net against poverty helped prevent child sexual abuse. For example, Vanette Graham, the director of a regional Child Abuse and Neglect Resource Center, explained that child abuse would increase "because of the unstable economy, because of insufficient housing, because of unemployment, and a myriad of social ills and pressures that exist" (U.S. House 1981:117). Dr. Eli Newberger, a pediatrician at Boston Children's Hospital who was influential in the original passage of CAPTA (Nelson 1984), agreed that "child welfare services" like daycare and counseling were crucial to support at-risk parents. This attempt to use a child sexual abuse frame to oppose broader Reagan budget cuts was unsuccessful. There was little uptake of their comments in the hearing itself, and none in the legislation.

On the conservative side, Republicans hoped for broader "pro-family" legislation, or at least to bolster their own pro-family reputations. For example, Rep. Erdahl told a witness that "the most important" institution for preventing abuse "obviously is not the Government, or the church, or the school; it is the home, the family, and yet we seem to take remarkably lackadaisical approach toward preparing people for parenting" (U.S. House 1981:212). He used this statement to *support* CAPTA funding. Similarly, Sen. Denton (R-AL), by then a supporter of CAPTA, opened a 1983 hearing by stating the "basic cause" of child abuse "is a fundamental crisis in the values traditional to our society, particularly the values of love and of respect for the dignity of other human beings, and of the institution of marriage" (U.S. Senate 1983:198). Overall, members of Congress who otherwise opposed social spending supported it in the case of child sexual abuse, justified because of their view of the nature of and remedies for incest.

In sum, even during the 1981 challenge, discourse in Congress was marked by shows of unity and declarations that the issue was beyond politics. Republican and Democratic committee members took a similar approach, emphasizing the needs of victims and the cost-effectiveness of social service interventions. Personal narratives and other discussion of the experiences and needs of victims served as the basis for common ground, foreclosing disagreement. Cross-ideological support also drew on other discourses that justified conservative support for social spending without contradicting Reaganism or conservative Republican principles.

Resolution and Routine Agreement

The challenge in 1981 was resolved by reinforcing the construction of child sexual abuse as beyond politics, deserving of funding because of the importance to victims, and linking it to other widely supported frames. This resolution persisted for a decade. Funding for child sexual abuse did drop, however. Most earmarked funds to the states for child sexual abuse ended in 1981. NCCAN retained funding for its grant programs that supported nonprofits, researchers, and treatment programs, but its grants records show that no funding was granted specifically for sexual child abuse from 1981 until 1984. Funding levels peaked in the mid-1980s and dropped from 1986 forward (Whittier 2009:75).

Over the next decade, Congress consolidated policy regarding child sexual abuse prevention and treatment and established law on the treatment of child victims in the courts. 1987 marked the turnover of both houses of Congress to Democrats, with the presidency held by Reagan (through 1988) and George H. W. Bush until Bill Clinton's 1993 inauguration, but these changes had little effect on child sexual abuse legislation. Fifty-six hearings were held between 1981 and 1991, a mean of 5.1 hearings per year.[25] As Table 3.1 shows, 24 percent of these hearings focused on the renewal of CAPTA and another 20 percent on general issues of child sexual abuse. Thirty per cent of the hearings focused on commercial sexual exploitation (child pornography or prostitution), and only 12 percent focused on criminal justice, including four hearings on improving court procedures for child witnesses. The remaining 14 percent focused on child sexual abuse

Table 3.1 CHILD SEXUAL ABUSE HEARING TOPICS BY YEAR
(PERCENTAGES IN PARENTHESES)

Topic	1981–1991	1992–1999	2000–2013	Total
CAPTA	13 (24)	3 (14)	5 (7)	21 (14)
Sexual exploitation	17 (30)	5 (24)	24 (33)	46 (31)
SORNA/criminal penalties (including NCMEC)	7 (12)	2 (10)	3 (4)	12 (8)
Native Americans	8 (14)	4 (19)	1 (1)	13 (9)
Sex trafficking	0 (0)	3 (14)	35 (48)	38 (25)
General/other	11 (20)	4 (19)	5 (7)	20 (13)
TOTAL	56	21	73	150

Note: Sexual exploitation includes online exploitation but not sex trafficking. Percentages do not add up to 100 due to rounding.

on Native American tribal lands. Familial sexual abuse was at the center of most of the hearings.

There was relatively little legislative action beyond CAPTA and the issue of child sexual abuse in Indian country. CAPTA was renewed three times, in 1981, 1983, and 1988.[26] The 1984 Child Protection Act and the 1986 Children's Justice Act increased penalties and added protections and procedures for the testimony of child victims.[27] The 1984 Missing Children's Act formalized federal involvement in missing children's cases and inaugurated a lasting partnership with NCMEC.

Personal narratives remained important throughout the 1980s. This was a period when survivors' narratives also were broadly disseminated in mainstream media and self-help groups proliferated (Whittier 2009). Stories of abuse were both a general call to action and reinforced the need for treatment for offenders, as with Beth's father Dick. Unlike just a few years later, many incest offenders were seen as treatable rather than irredeemable criminals or pedophiles. For example, at a 1984 hearing on Violence and Abuse in American Families (U.S. House 1984a), Deborah Aal, the executive producer of the TV movie *Something About Amelia*, testified. In the widely watched special, Ted Danson played a father who rapes his daughter. The white, middle-class family goes through family therapy similar to what Parents United provided. Aal reinforced the scope of the problem by recounting the large number of calls from children and adults to hotlines provided after the showing (some of which were staffed by members of grassroots survivors' groups[Whittier 2009]). In a real-life example, a parent testified about how, after her youngest son learned about sexual abuse through a federally funded program at school, he told her about being molested by her older son. She declared, "When my son told me . . . the first words out of my mouth were, 'I believe you, and we need some help.'" The older son entered an "adolescent perpetrator program," while the rest of the family participated in Parents Anonymous groups (U.S. House 1986a:5, 13). The emphasis on speaking out, believing children's accounts, and seeking therapy was consistent with the framing of child sexual abuse by the survivors' movement and mainstream media. The single-issue survivors' movement influenced both the content of the testimony and the fact that the committees called these types of witnesses.

Something About Amelia and the testimony worked as a personal narrative about the importance of family treatment, although it was fictional, and illustrated activists' focus on making abuse in "respectable" families visible. They also, however, reinforced the idea that "respectable" perpetrators were more suited to treatment. In the 1970s, legislators and witnesses had made this case directly. For example, Eugene Brown of the San Jose Police Department said at a 1977 hearing that "a person who is a bank examiner, for example, who has molested his daughter. He is, for all other practical purposes, a good, solid, upright citizen, but he does have this mental problem . . . . I don't think he should be treated like a burglar, a robber, or a dope peddler" (U.S. House 1977:132). These views about which groups were the truly serious threats to children echoed back to Colonial times. They continued into the 1980s and beyond but became much less overt in congressional testimony, particularly as the focus on treatment declined, as we will see.

Survivors were not the only ones using their personal experience to call for action. Police, too, were frustrated by poor child welfare services. Their experiential authority contributed to the ongoing consensus on the need for funding for community organizations. For example, Jerome Miron, of the National Sheriff's Association's Victim Witness Program decried the fact that when children disclose abuse to investigators

> they may have to be taken from their home, taken from the schools that they are at, taken from their local neighborhood, taken from their friends, and placed in the care of the State . . . . Yet, there are no adequate treatment places in this community . . . to which I can place these children so they can get the type of treatment and support they need. (U.S. House 1984a:51–52)

Members of Congress also used their experiences to call for action. For example, Sen. DeWine said in 1989, "[A]s a county prosecuting attorney, I think one of the things that most amazed me, surprised me, shocked me . . . was the number of sexual child abuse cases that I saw." These cases, he said, "had been going on for years—years and years and years—and had not been reported. . . . I know other members of your committee have had the same experiences and seen it firsthand" (U.S. Senate 1989b:9). Some members of Congress also referred to their wife's or daughter's experience.[28] The focus on services in supporting survivors also allowed some opening for feminist witnesses, although they never focused on gender politics. For example, the founder of a South Carolina Rape Crisis Council testified in 1989 about a Victims Witness Assistance Program she directed in Greenville (U.S. Senate 1989b:269).

The consensus was bolstered by the issue of child prostitution and pornography, long-time concerns of conservative movement organizations and legislators. Witnesses in hearings on child pornography and prostitution drew connections to child sexual abuse in the family, encouraging support for CAPTA alongside legislation on child sexual exploitation. For example, multiple witnesses in a 1982 hearing on Teenage Prostitution and Child Pornography (U.S. Senate 1982b) noted that many girls who become prostitutes are victims of incest. Witnesses also framed child pornography as a potential component of incest, unlike later years when they explained it as the work of pimps or Internet seducers. For example, in a 1983 hearing, Detective William Dworin from the Los Angeles Police Department's Sexually Exploited Child Unit described "the incestuous parent, who is also the pedophile, who photographs their child, who seduces other children . . ."[29] A two-part hearing on Child Pornography and Pedophila in 1984 and 1985 (U.S. Senate 1984a, 1985a) centered on extensive testimony from a young man who was molested by his uncle and later became a prostitute, exploring how psychological effects of the abuse shaped his turn to prostitution. Many of the same legislators and committees dealt with both child sexual exploitation and CAPTA, and the narratives that influenced them similarly carried over.

By the late 1980s, the focus was shifting toward prosecution. Republicans and Democrats—still in consensus—strongly framed child sexual abuse as a crime. Whereas in 1981 witnesses and lawmakers praised programs that placed familial abusers in treatment rather than prison, that position was rare by the late 1980s. As Patricia Toth, a former prosecutor and the director of the National Center for Prosecution of Child Abuse, told a 1989 hearing, "[T]here is still a lack of acknowledgment that child abuse is a serious crime in some camps. And that often takes the form of treating child abuse within families as somehow . . . less serious and less deserving of attention in the criminal system than other forms of child abuse" (U.S. Senate 1989b:95). Yet witnesses and legislators still called for social service funding alongside prosecution. Even conservative Sen. Strom Thurmond said both that "[t]hose who violently prey upon childhood innocence must be caught, prosecuted, and sentenced to tough criminal penalties" and that "[t]he victim must be assisted with appropriate medical care and counseling" (U.S. Senate 1989b:13).

Supporting victims became a matter of promoting prosecution. For example, lawmakers framed the 1990 Victims of Child Abuse Act, which dealt with the treatment of child victims in court, in terms of how victims' psychological well-being promoted effective prosecution.[30] Rep. Michaél DeWine explained, "Many, many cases every year are not taken through to trial ... simply because it is ... too tough on the child to go through the judicial process." Protecting child witnesses "makes it more likely that a case will proceed and that ultimately true justice will be done" (U.S. Senate 1989b:10).

Although the veneer of consensus around the issue as ideologically neutral remained, a shift to a stronger crime frame and legislative approach was underway. Bill Clinton's election in 1992 and congressional control shifting to the Republicans in 1994 set the stage for a period of more overt politicization, conflict, and involvement by social movements. But just as survivors' narratives in the 1980s left whiteness implicit, so did the narratives and frames supporting criminalization. Unlike many crimes, the emphasis on the prevalence of child sexual abuse in white families contributed to the relatively high proportion of whites incarcerated for child sexual abuse, as well as a discourse about criminality that emphasized danger from within white, middle-class communities (Lancaster 2011; Leon 2011).

Moment of Challenge Two: Child Custody Disputes and False Allegations, 1992–1999

The years from 1992 to 1999 saw attempts by feminists, survivors' organizations, and the FMSF to redirect federal child sexual abuse law. The emergence of a countermovement made activists and their organizations take notice that law and policy could affect them (Whittier 2009). Survivor organizations tried, mostly ineffectually, to respond with research and public relations. Confrontations occurred at conferences, public talks, and in print, and briefly spilled over into Congress. The countermovement, spearheaded by Victims of Child Abuse Laws (VOCAL), which worked mainly to defend adults accused by children, and the FMSF, which worked mainly to defend adults accused of incest by their grown children, sought to eliminate CAPTA. The FMSF sent witnesses to two hearings in 1995 as part of the Republican House's "Contract with America," which pledged to shrink government agencies and spending. The early 1990s also saw a series of high-profile custody cases, championed by both feminists and adult survivors of incest, in which courts ordered children placed in the custody of their fathers despite allegations of sexual abuse (Chesler 1991). The custody issue led to three hearings held in 1992–1995 that included testimony from small, short-lived protective mothers' organizations and NOW's Sally Goldfarb. The FMSF witnesses also appeared at the last of the custody hearings in 1995. These were not high-profile hearings and produced only small changes in law, but they illustrate a moment of potential politicization of the issue of incest and how it was foreclosed, reinforcing the appearance of neutrality.

In short, these few years saw frames and debates that were not neutral but divisive and contested, and not narrow, but that linked child sexual abuse to other issues. The ruptures were temporary, however, exceptions to the growing consensus on criminal penalties. Twenty-one hearings occurred over the eight years between 1992 and 1999, an average of 2.6 hearings per year.[31] Only 15 percent dealt with CAPTA and 20 percent with general issues, compared with 25 percent on sexual exploitation, mostly online child pornography, 15 percent on sex trafficking, 10 percent on stiffer sentencing and sex offender registration and notification, and 20 percent on child abuse on Native American lands. Republicans took control of both the Senate and House in 1995. In collaboration with Democratic President Clinton, they pushed ever-harsher sentencing requirements, symbolized by, but not limited to, the Omnibus Crime Act of 1994, which included VAWA and the Jacob Wetterling Act establishing sex offender registries, setting the stage for the third turning point.

Incest and Child Custody

Three hearings focused on various attempts to force accountability on fathers who assaulted their daughters. These hearings contained the only overt gender or feminist framing of child sexual abuse in all the post-1980 hearings I analyzed. A 1994 hearing focused on garnishing federal pensions to settle civil judgments against fathers for incest, and two hearings, in 1992 and 1995, focused on mothers who were unable to prevent visitation by fathers accused of incest, some of whom had lost custody. The most notorious case was that of Elizabeth Morgan. Morgan had been jailed for contempt of court after refusing to reveal the location of her daughter, whom Morgan's parents had taken abroad to avoid a custody order assigning visitation to her father, who had allegedly sexually assaulted her.

Morgan was released from prison in 1989 by a special act of Congress and joined her daughter in New Zealand. Morgan was just the best-known of many so-called protective parents, several of whom testified at the hearings.[32] Witnesses included several mothers who had lost custody after alleging that their ex-husbands had sexually abused their children, and the 1992 hearing—unique among those I studied—included an "open mic" for constituents to tell of their experiences (U.S. House 1992c). Their emotional stories critiqued children's powerlessness and the patriarchal family. For example, a witness testifying as a member of an advocacy group called Alliance for the Rights of Children described several such cases and proclaimed, "children are not private property that parents can do with as they wish . . . . Nor should children be divvied up and parceled out by the courts or social services with total disregard for their feelings or their wishes" (U.S. House 1995b:73).

Witnesses and members of Congress directly discussed gender stereotypes and power differentials as relating to child sexual abuse. For example, in 1992 Democratic Rep. Donald Payne asked witness Dr. Mushalater Jayakar,[33] director of a child abuse clinic in Brooklyn, if judges were predisposed to award custody to fathers who sought it because "the stereotypes [are] . . . that [if] a man is willing to share in this responsibility, therefore, he must be all right and this woman is the one who is the bad person because it is unique that this father wants his child on weekends or something, do you think that that kind of psychological thing goes through these courts?" The inarticulate question suggests a struggle simply to put gender stereotyping into words. Dr. Jayakar affirmed that this was the case, and Rep. Payne responded by articulating the basic point more clearly: "So it is really a systemic problem. If a father raises some children, he is really a hero in the community, whereas women do it, you know, every day" (U.S. House 1992c:71). Louise Owens, court clerk at the Brooklyn Family Court, also used a feminist frame, saying, "Some of the psychologists who have been charged with making evaluations of the family. . . usually say that the mother was the one who is hysterical, and the father comes across as a very nice individual, you know, who is really being charged with something that he has not done" (U.S. House 1992c:81).

Sally Goldfarb of NOW testified at the 1994 hearing on civil judgments against fathers awarding damage to their adult daughters. According to Goldfarb, NOW's Legal Defense and Education Fund had a "campaign to obtain legal redress for survivors of child abuse." She framed the issue as one of crime and punishment, stating, "by allowing defendants to avoid paying for the harm that they have caused, the message to perpetrators is that the laws against child abuse can be broken with impunity." She also used a feminist frame, but only at the very end of her testimony, as she said, "We have come a long way since the days when the rape of a spouse or child was not considered a crime because women and children were viewed as a man's property" (U.S. House 1994b:56).[34]

Feminist critiques of patriarchal power did not fit easily into existing discourse. Although they did receive some uptake in individual hearings, they did not appear to affect how the same legislators framed the issue in other hearings. Critiques of gender stereotypes, maltreatment of protective mothers and their children, and fathers' power to mistreat children did not persist into later hearings or shape broader child sexual abuse legislation. For example, Committee Chairman Major Owens (D-NY), after hearing witnesses' testimony, asked rhetorically, "Are we saying that this process is doomed unless we find some way to deal with the basic prejudices of the court, not only the basic prejudice which is sexist, but also class-oriented prejudices?" (U.S. House 1992c:88). The witnesses answered yes, but congressional actions and discourse never targeted these "basic prejudices." The strength of prevailing understandings of child sexual abuse as a medical and criminal issue, of existing law, and the relationships between Congress and advocates and professionals committed to a single-issue approach ensured that feminist moments like this were not ongoing. Opposition by the FMSF made a difference too. One witness from the FMSF, Hollida Wakefield, testified that children were highly suggestible to false allegations of sexual abuse in custody disputes, bolstering the testimony of Morgan's ex-husband who also appeared at that hearing (U.S. House 1995b:34–5). More direct involvement by the countermovement came in 1995 hearings on CAPTA.

False Accusations and the Politicization of the Single Issue

After the 1994 midterm election turned control of both the House and Senate over to the Republicans, House Speaker Newt Gingrich promoted a "Contract with America," promising lower taxes, reduced government, and increased delegation of power to the states. Immediately, the Republican House held a hearing entitled the Contract with America: Child Welfare (U.S. House 1995a) and the Senate held the Child Protection: Balancing Divergent Interests hearing (U.S. Senate 1995a). Unlike any other hearings, these centered on false allegations of abuse and parents' persecution by overzealous child protective services workers. While later hearings would *expand* government surveillance related to child sexual abuse, these hearings focused on the *risks* associated with surveillance and sought limits on state power. These hearings were unique in the direct involvement by activists on both sides of this issue. It is not surprising that they happened at the peak of movement-countermovement battle.

These two hearings were the result of lobbying by the FMSF. Herman Ohme, a board member of the FMSF, claimed credit for arranging some of the testimony and putting false accusations on the agenda, working with Republican Sen. Dan Coats who also opposed CAPTA (Cheit 2014). He wrote in the FMSF newsletter, "when the Republican Party took control of the U.S. House of Representatives in 1994 . . . I saw the opportunity to change the CAPTA laws . . . which had been the root cause of the child sex abuse hysteria and false accusations. I had been an active member of the RNC [Republican National Committee] for years and had some voice with the new party in control."[35]

Many witnesses and legislators at these hearings criticized the approach CAPTA and child protective services took to child sexual abuse. Republican legislators framed the criticism as linked to their larger antigovernment agenda. Subcommittee Chair Duke Cunningham began by stating, "many of us feel that the child abuse prevention system has failed as it is right now, that it currently allows unwarranted and unregulated investigations. It does not adequately protect the children in which it is really aimed to do" (U.S. House 1995a:2). Arkansas Rep. Tim Hutchinson concurred: "As a State legislator in Arkansas for eight years, I heard numerous complaints about our State Department of Human Services . . . from parents and grand-parents who felt that the Department acted as if it were on some kind of witch hunt, barging into people's homes and immediately taking a position that the parents were guilty of abuse or neglect . . . . This over-intrusive, guilty until proven innocent government intervention is exactly what the people of America, I think, were speaking against, rallying against on [the day of the election] November 8" (U.S. House 1995a:11–12).[36] Most witnesses similarly focused on the problems of false accusations and overzealous child protective enforcement. The stars were Carol Hopkins, who had founded a group called the Justice Committee after serving as the deputy foreman of a San Diego grand jury investigating the child protective system for violations of due process (Cheit 2014); James Wade, whose daughter was removed from her family after he was falsely accused of raping her; and Cari Clark, a mother who was reported to child protective services after leaving her three-year-old daughter napping in a car within view and was found to have provided "inadequate supervision" and put on a registry of child abusers.[37] Their testimony vividly illustrated the threat to innocent families and children.

As before, personal experiences were the definitive authority and call to action. Wade recounted his odyssey in painful detail, ending with the conviction of the stranger who had actually raped his daughter, and received applause in the chamber. (There is no indication of who was in the audience, but it is rare for a substantial audience to attend a subcommittee hearing, suggesting the unusual politicization of this one.) After telling her story, Clark complained, "Citing CAPTA, government agents, under cover of immunity, are collecting whatever they want to call evidence and also acting as judge, jury and executioner of innocent parents" (U.S. House 1995:33).

They were joined by witness David Wagner, the director of legal policy for the conservative Family Research Council, who worked regularly with the Republican members of the committee; and academic Richard Wexler, an author of a book that strongly critiqued "child savers" and CAPTA.[38] Wexler was, by his description, "a lifelong liberal Democrat [and] . . . a card-carrying member of the ACLU," while Wagner was a staunch conservative, but both used language from the other position to reinforce the bipartisan nature of the issue. Wexler appealed to the Republican majority "not to allow this to become a partisan issue" but framed his opposition to CAPTA in conservative terms, stating that because of "the principles of the Contract With America" (which Wexler likely opposed) and "the shift of power from Washington to the States, and from government to individuals and private associations, I believe Congress should cut back on the therapeutic establishment's hotline to the Treasury through the Mondale Act, CAPTA, and restore the authority of the States to deal with child abuse and neglect in light of local needs and wishes" (U.S. House 1995:50).[39] He proclaimed, "Child saving combines the worst aspects of liberalism and conservatism. It will take the best of each philosophy to stop it and provide real help and real hope to children in need" (U.S. Senate 1995a:16). Unlike conservatives on the panel, however, Wexler argued—in vain—for social spending to "keep [children] safely in their homes" rather than foster care. Just as the liberal Wexler used conservative language, the Family Research Council's Wagner, unusual for witnesses from that organization, called for stronger due process rights (a more typically liberal concern) and drew on more liberal critiques of "the therapeutic sector of American government" as "a social-service police state" (U.S. House 1995:50).[40]

Wagner also used more typical Family Resource Council arguments about the family, stating, "problems of child abuse are closely related with the problems of breakdown in the family generally, and so anything that we do in public policy to reverse the breakdown of the family . . . [will] have some good side effects in the area of child abuse" (U.S. House 1995:86).

House Republicans attacking CAPTA agreed. Rep. Dave Weldon (R-FL) similarly challenged CAPTA because "the problems that we face as a Nation in the area of family breakdown, [and] increasing amounts of child abuse, appear to me at least to be social problems that are beyond the scope of government to effectively deal with . . . these are problems traditionally dealt with by communities, by churches." But concern for families cut both ways. Sen. Tim Hutchinson (R-AK, testifying before the House panel) worried, "as we witness the continuing dissolution of the American family in our society, I fear that the incidence of child abuse will only increase." Like Hutchinson, Rep. Greenwood (R-PA) saw child abuse as an exception to the principle of devolving services to the states because of the unique vulnerability of children. In his view, "because we're talking about little kids here, and kids in great danger of abuse and neglect, if there's any place for us to be very, very careful about [assuming] . . . that if we let the States protect their own children that they will, in fact, succeed, this is the place where we have to be very careful" (U.S. House 1995:25).

Despite lip service by opponents of CAPTA to the existence of actual abuse, there was little to no sustained discussion about how it should be investigated or federally funded. A few witnesses presented evidence in favor of child protections, but there was little discussion of their points in the hearings, however. Such consideration was discursively difficult within the framing of the hearing around child protection overreach and false accusations.[41]

Briefly, it appeared that the narrowly neutral consensus had fractured, with the single-issue approach to child sexual abuse politicized and disputed. But the 1995 focus on reining in CAPTA and federal intervention into child sexual abuse did not persist in discourse or law, and most of the concerns raised at the hearing were state level, not federal, issues. Opponents achieved a narrower definition of "child abuse" as a "*recent* act or failure to act" [emphasis added] in the revised CAPTA. In addition, the reauthorization decommissioned NCCAN and subsumed its functions to the Children's Bureau, potentially weakening it, established new procedures for appeals, and required expunging false or unsubstantiated reports from sex offender records.[42]

Separate from these conflicts, NCMEC and legislators were moving forward with sex offender law. The first federal sex offender registration law, the Jacob Wetterling Crimes Against Children and Sexually Violent Offender Act (part of the 1994 Omnibus Crime Act), mandated that states create registries for sex offenders. This augured a period of agreement over getting tough on crime through increasing sentences and postincarceration restrictions, including the passage of Megan's Law, which required notifying the community about sex offenders in the area, in 1996. Going forward, the federal government increasingly focused on surveillance and penalties for sex offenders and the dangers to the children of sexual exploitation through the Internet. Overt attention to incest became peripheral, but the new policies pertained to family and strangers alike and in practice affected mostly cases of incest and sexual abuse by acquaintances.

The witnesses and notorious cases discussed here, and those that motivated sex offender laws discussed below, were predominantly white. As Richie (2012) suggests, assaults against children of color are unlikely to become cause célèbres. As others have argued, this ultimately heightened fears about outside threats to white suburban or rural safety (Lancaster 2011; Leon 2011). But because all the laws applied to the far more common familial or acquaintance assailants, the strategic truism that abuse occurs in all families meant that the carceral consequences fell across race and class lines.

Moment of Challenge Three: Online Threats and Sex Offender Policy, 2000–2013

The hearings on false allegations were the last time for more than a decade that familial sexual abuse—or indeed any noncommercial child sexual abuse—was discussed outside the question of how best to track and punish offenders.[43] The focus turned to sex offender registration and notification, monitoring and regulation of the Internet to reduce child pornography and prostitution, and sex trafficking. The earlier focus on prevention and treatment for offenders and victims was largely absent from these new initiatives. Two issues—commercial child sexual exploitation through online pornography and trafficking, and sex offender registration—dominated congressional attention from 2000 into the present. Denunciation of child sexual abuse and congressional committee jurisdiction (mainly the Judiciary Committees' Crime Subcommittees) connected these issues to earlier concerns about child sexual abuse, but different outside advocates were involved, and potential disputes about policy unfolded differently. Religious conservative antipornography organizations and anti-sex-trafficking organizations with both feminist and conservative roots worked against child pornography and trafficking, while parents organizations and NCMEC advocated for stricter sex offender policy. Legislators strongly supported both. The only disagreement, related to child pornography, came from civil liberties organizations, and even they disagreed over constitutional issues, not the evils of child pornography itself.

Increased penalties characterized this period of growing surveillance, which began with George W. Bush's presidential election in 2000 and ended in 2013, during Obama's presidency with a Republican Congress.[44] Party control made little difference to the steady growth of legislation and discourse focused on sex offender policy and threats posed by the Internet. Legislation included several expansions and consolidation of the sex offender registration and notification act, routine renewals of CAPTA, and restrictions on minors' access to the Internet, online pornography, and sex trafficking. Seventy-three hearings were held over 14 years, for a mean of 5.2 hearings per year.[45] Fully three-quarters of the hearings focused on sexual exploitation (mostly online pornography) or sex trafficking. Besides CAPTA reauthorization, the rest focused on enhanced criminal penalties for sex offenders, usually discussed as strangers although in practice, convicted sex offenders include many more acquaintances and family members.

Although most sex offender legislation affected family and acquaintances alongside stranger assailants, the discursive focus on incest was replaced by one on crime. This, too, was a single-issue approach, also defined as beyond politics, and it summoned the same unlikely allies as the earlier approaches. Disagreement on sex offender policy was rare and mainly came from one legislator's challenges over lack of evidence that it was effective. Grassroots activists who opposed sex offender registration and notification law (commonly referred to as SORNA after the Sex Offender Registration and Notification Act, passed in 2006) had no access to the state. Despite the renewed focus on stranger crime, the emphasis was on white victims of white criminals, with relatively little racially coded language. But the focus on external (rather than internal) threats did position white communities as vulnerable to outsiders (Lancaster 2011; Leon 2011).

Maintaining Consensus on Child Pornography

Congressional attention to child pornography, always a point of agreement across the spectrum, grew steadily. One-third of hearings between 2000 and 2013 dealt with child pornography, mostly online, and another 45 percent dealt with sex trafficking, mostly on the Internet. Only conservatives continued to push for a crackdown on general obscenity, but politicians and advocates from all positions came together to denounce child pornography. Unlike other eras and issues, these hearings included little testimony from those who had direct personal experience. Since the issue was uncontroversial, most testimony focused on research or the constitutional ramifications of proposed legislation. For example, psychologist Victor Cline testified that teenage "sexual predators" used "child, adolescent, or adult pornography to stimulate appetite and provide models of sexual abuse, as well as . . . to seduce new victims." Cline's testimony was very convincing to Sen. Dianne Feinstein (D-Calif.), who remarked that evidence that "pornography actually reinforces the individual's ability to go out and commit the act" meant that Congress should, therefore, "stamp this stuff out as much as we possibly can" (U.S. Senate 1996b:118–19).

Antipornography conservative organizations who testified on child pornography and prostitution made their ideological commitments apparent through talk about morality, normative family structure, degeneracy, and the like. But even they couched their testimony in terms of science and expertise, maintaining a veneer of political neutrality. For example, Republican activist Dee Jepsen, appearing under the rubric of the organization Enough is Enough,[46] summarized a study that ostensibly used "brain research" to show how sexually explicit media "trigger excitatory transmitters and a rush of hormones which short-circuit rational left-brain thinking, permanently changing neural pathways . . . neurochemically triggering . . . some vulnerable viewers to engage in criminal and violent sexual conduct" (U.S. Senate 1996b:37–38). With this pseudo-scientific jargon, Jepsen attempted to present the organization as politically neutral, rather than moralistic, in keeping with the predominant neutral definition of the issue of child sexual abuse. This is a hallmark of a narrowly neutral relationship.

Despite opposition from the ACLU and other anticensorship organizations, Congress passed the Communications Decency Act in 1996 prohibiting sending or posting obscene or indecent material online to those under 18; the Child Online Protection Act in 1998, forbidding commercial websites from displaying material "harmful to minors"; and the Children's Internet Protection Act in 2000, the sole law to survive constitutionally, requiring filtering the Internet on library and school computers.[47]

Sex Offender Registration and Notification

There was near universal agreement about increasing punishment and surveillance of sex offenders. Across the ideological spectrum, inside and outside Congress, people agreed that sex offenders were dangerous and that lengthy incarceration and monitoring after release could protect children (Corrigan 2006; Ewing 2011). This cross-ideological agreement again relied on often emotional narratives about personal experiences. Unlike earlier hearings, however, most witnesses recounted experiences of assault by strangers, not family members. For example, in one of the earlier hearings in the post-1990s trend toward tougher sentencing, the mother of Christy Fornoff, who was raped and murdered at 13, recounted the horrifying crime in detail. Advocating mandatory minimum sentencing, she asked the Subcommittee:

> When you and your colleagues are writing laws, Mr. Chairman, please think about people like me. Please think about the fact that every time there is another appeal, another ruling, another hearing, I am forced to think about my daughter's death . . . . Every time I am forced to think about how scared my little girl must have been when she died. (U.S. House 2005a:18)

Making a similar point, Amie Zyla testified about her childhood experience of being sexually assaulted by a minor in a 2005 hearing on a bill mandating sentencing increases and registration requirements for juvenile offenders. She recounted the effects, saying, "My abuser hurt me in my own home, where he had gained a level of trust and then so brutally violated it. He stole my self-esteem, and made me feel so afraid . . . . While it was a very difficult time, I came forward when it happened, to stop him from hurting anyone else ever again." When she discovered he had been released from prison and had committed another sexual assault, she said, "I was scared, and couldn't believe he was out. All those old feelings returned, and I was so sad for all the new victims . . . . I was so mad that what happened to me seemed like it didn't matter." Although Zyla lobbied for specific crime legislation that was very different from "Beth's" goal of family rehabilitation in 1981, she drew from a similar narrative of healing for survivors by breaking the silence and finding connection:

> I pray that by coming forward again sexual abuse victims who can hear the sound of my voice understand that it is not their fault; that they must come forward and find healing and purpose. Stand up to your abusers, and help law enforcement stop them from hurting anyone else. Abuse does not have to affect your whole life. If I can overcome the hurt and trauma, then so can you. (U.S. House 2005c:19–20)

Zyla's narrative was the direct descendent of the survivors' movement but was now linked directly to law enforcement. This reflected growing activism by NCMEC and parents of victims. Many of the laws passed during this period were named after victims whose parents testified in the relevant hearings: for example, Patty Wetterling, mother of Jacob Wetterling, testified in 1994 for the creation of the first national registry; Gail Willard, mother of Aimee Willard testified in 2000 for Aimee's Law, which established a mandatory minimum sentence of life without parole for rape or sexual assault against a child under 14; Marc Klaas, the father of Polly Klaas, testified for many bills. Members of Congress also invoked the names and stories of other horrific child rapes and murders in these hearings, and testimony from NCMEC representatives and law enforcement reinforced the need to track sex offenders and notify their communities of their presence.

Most legislators lined up to support these bills and devise ever-stricter ones. In a 2005 hearing on a bill that would establish a 30-year mandatory minimum sentence for aggravated sexual assault against children, for example, Rep. Mark Green (R-WI) proclaimed that mandatory minimum sentences were necessary because "[s]ome on the bench will be attempted to [sic] coddle sex offenders, to ignore the rights of the law-abiding public to live free from crime in the neighborhoods and seek to deviate from sentencing guidelines with what they feel is reasonable" (U.S. House 2005a:2–3).

Members of Congress and witnesses regularly demonized sex offenders. For example, Chairman Cunningham supported registration but noted, "if I had my way, I won't say on this committee what we'd do to them" (U.S. House 1995a:83). Rep. Jackson-Lee (D-TX), after conceding the need for treatment, said, "I happen to think, let me just say very clearly, one violent predator, one child sexual predator, is one too many for me. I mean, plain and simple. I can't even tolerate the existence of one. I do hope people can rehabilitate their lives. But I would think that Amie [Zyla] . . . would agree that one is one too many" (U.S. House 2005c:31). Rep. Foley (ironically given his subsequent investigation for sexting with an underage page) concurred that SORNA should "send a clear message to anyone contemplating a crime of this nature, that we will make their life a living hell" (U.S. House 2005b:26).

Narrowly neutral relationships need not rest on issue definitions that are weakly held. In the case of child sexual abuse, narrow neutrality entailed a powerful cultural, emotional, and political hegemony that virtually closed out dissent. There were few discursive opportunities to oppose this legislation, given the power of victims' stories and the overall carceral climate. Within Congress, there were rare challenges to community notification of registered sex offenders based on questions about the range of sex offenses or whether registries prevent sex crimes.

First, incest raised concern about sex offender registration and notification. Progressive African-American Democratic Representative Robert (Bobby) Scott (D-VA), one of the only legislators to question these laws, noted in a 2005 hearing on registration requirements (U.S. House 2005c) that sex offender registration and notification bills could have negative consequences in cases of incest. This was important, he said, since, "the vast majority of abusers are either relatives, friends or individuals known to the child and family—90 to 95 percent."[48] Ernie Allen of NCMEC countered: "Most of those children are not members of their own family" (U.S. House 2005c:14). But Fred Berlin, a doctor at Johns Hopkins who specialized in treating sex offenders reiterated that, with community notification,

> [t]here is the risk of inadvertently identifying victims. There is now concern that some victims of incest may be deterred from coming forward. I can give you a brief anecdote of a child that I was aware of, where the teacher, meaning well, read out a sex offender registry in school. The peers of this child looked over at him and said, "Hey, isn't that your dad?" (U.S. House 2005c:22–23)

In addition, he said, mandatory minimum sentences in incest cases were problematic because "[m]any victims don't want their victimizer to go away for a long period of time. That's simply a fact."

Dr. Berlin also argued that not all offenders deserved registration. For example, he said, "Someone who's exposed himself to a child who's 13 can be labeled a predator in many of these statutes . . . a 17-year-old who was involved with a 14-year-old can be labeled a predator" (U.S. House 2005c:23). Rep. Gohmert, speaking in a different hearing, agreed: "I've known of situations where some young kid 'moons' somebody, and his lawyer said, "Just plead 'No Contest.' You get probation.' And the next thing you know, he's got to register as a sex offender" (U.S. House 2005b:30). Rep. Foley concurred, saying, "[T]here are differences between aggravated sexual offenses and things like you described . . . . We could get into familial situations, where a 19-year-old boy takes off with a 17-year-old girl; the father has a problem with it, despite the fact they're consenting; charges him with a crime. His life could be ruined. And facts should prevail in that case to exonerate him from a sexually deviant behavior" (U.S. House 2005b:30).[49]

Whereas legislators agreed that teenage relationships or mooning were not deserving of harsh punishment, they drew the line there. While Dr. Berlin said, bluntly, "nobody needs to figure out what to do about the guy that killed Jessica Lunsford. We all know what to do about that. The issue is the guy who's involved incestuously with his daughter. Are we going to treat him in exactly the same way?" (U.S. House 2005a:29), no one joined him. Child sexual abuse by family members and acquaintances was not the primary justification for increased sentencing, but supporters certainly intended the law to apply to child sexual abuse by family and acquaintances. In his opening statement, Sen. Mark Green not only described horrific cases of abduction, rape, and murder, but also said, "one in five girls and one in 10 boys are sexually exploited before they reach adulthood, yet less than 35 percent of the incidents are actually reported to the authorities" (U.S. House 2005a:2). In the wake of high-profile cases of rapes and murders by previously convicted sex offenders, the idea of moderating penalties was easily countered by vivid personal narratives presented in testimony.

All along, survivor activists had different opinions about the best response to incest. Some thought that programs that diverted offenders to treatment programs rather than prison showed that incest was not taken seriously. Others celebrated treatment programs as providing effective help to victims and, secondarily, offenders and families. The personal narratives by participants in programs of Parents United and Parents Anonymous who made a case for treatment and family unification had vanished by 2000. Resistance to differential treatment for incest was also growing among a new wave of survivor advocacy organizations that lobbied for stricter state laws. Like their federal counterparts, they formed cross-ideological alliances based on narrative neutrality. One influential group, PROTECT, ran successful campaigns in several states for criminalizing incest. It described itself as "focused like a laser on one *single issue:* protecting children" ("PROTECT's Bipartisan Lobby") and listed supporters from across the political spectrum including feminist activist Robin Tyler, about whom the group said: "during the tough days when some liberal groups were unwilling to fight for a Republican-sponsored bill, [Tyler] broke the logjam, relentlessly hammering her old allies to do the right thing and join our coalition" (Tyler 2005). PROTECT argued that incest is the most common form of child sexual abuse, that family therapy and reunification are unfair to victims, and critiqued the formerly influential Parents United for this approach (Weeks 2004). It was behind "Circle of Trust" laws in several states, which repealed laws that provided lesser penalties for incest and encouraged family treatment. But PROTECT did not limit its work to incest. It also was behind the federal PROTECT law of 2008, which established a federal center for tracking child pornography and locating its victims (PROTECT n.d.). In contrast, NCMEC explicitly excluded incest and familial abuse from their definition of "molestation," the issue in their mission.[50]

Debate over data on the efficacy of community notification of sex offenders was the only other point of dispute during hearings on this legislation. Rep. Scott (D-VA)—alone—pressed witnesses hard on this issue in virtually every hearing. For example, in 2005, he repeatedly asked witnesses and the bill's co-sponsors: "Of all of the children abused in America, how many are abused by those who have already been convicted of a sex offense and would be covered by this notification?" (Each time, the answers dealt instead with recidivism, i.e., rearrest for a sex crime after release from prison, which is a different question, as Rep. Scott repeatedly pointed out.) Scott's point was that "if we're trying to reduce child abuse, and a very small percentage [of victims] are being abused by those [previously] convicted, then we're missing most of the target." (U.S. House 2005b:20)[51]

Scott ultimately wrung the admission from cosponsor Rep. Earl Pomeroy (D-ND): "I do not have that figure." Pomeroy challenged the need for data, saying: "Well, look, I think we don't have to have empirical data to tell you it absolutely makes a difference to people concerned about the safety of their children, to be able to have access to information that there might be an elevated risk of a sexual offender down the street" (U.S. House 2005b:21). In other words, Pomeroy relied on experiential authority ("it absolutely makes a difference to people concerned") and an appeal to emotion. Indirectly, Rep. Mark Green (R-VA) did the same. Acknowledging that "we just don't have very good numbers, period," he turned to unfalsifiable knowledge, asking one cosponsor: "Instead of giving us numbers and statistics on a national scale, perhaps you can tell us how your legislation would in fact have made a difference in the case of Jessica Lunsford," who was murdered by a convicted sex offender who worked at her school. Rep. Green concluded that the possibility it would have prevented her murder was "a pretty good purpose for legislation" (U.S. House 2005b:24).[52]

A 2009 hearing, when the Subcommittee was chaired by Rep. Scott, aimed at understanding why most states had not complied with the 2006 Adam Walsh Act, which required them to set up a specific kind of online sex offender registration and notification system that included juvenile offenders and was retroactive (U.S. House 2009). Although Scott was the House's only consistent skeptic of SORNA, three of the seven witnesses appearing were in favor of SORNA, and a fourth mainly disagreed with the unfunded mandate to the states.[53] The three dissenters did not suggest that sex offenders should not be registered with law enforcement but rather questioned the form of that registration, to whom it applied, issues of community notification, and how effective it was in preventing sex crimes. Some opposition also existed behind-the-scenes from former government officials, who issued a statement opposing mandatory minimum sentences.[54] Despite acknowledgement in a hearing on the topic, they had no discernible effect on the legislation. The few movement organizations that disagreed never even entered the federal conversation.[55] Otherwise, opposition to increasing punitive sex offender policy was absent, or excluded, from Congress.

Stronger and more passionate opposition to SORNA came from written submissions to the record by groups that did not testify, including striking written testimony from a man placed on the sex offender registry for a long past statutory rape offense laid out the devastating and unfair consequences to him and his family.[56] This kind of personal narrative rarely made it into hearings—as, indeed, it did not in this case—and indicates the marginalization of experiences by individuals considered unworthy. In contrast, the grim stories told by Ernie Allen from NCMEC and Robert Lunsford, father of a victim, were morally credible and, by extension, so was the sex offender legislation they supported. These cases, with their experiential authority and emotional resonance, were more than enough reason for legislators across the board to support the bill.

In sum, despite continuing recognition that familial abuse was common, there was increasing consensus by the mid-2000s to treat it the same way as stranger abuse.[57] There was similarly broad agreement on mandatory minimum sentencing and community notification about sex offenders. Narrow neutrality and a growing punitive consensus united Congress as it did much of the advocacy movement, embodied in the cross-ideological group PROTECT. Members of Congress touted their bipartisan cooperation around sex offender policy, which Democratic Rep. Jackson-Lee described as "harmony and the spirit of cooperation" (U.S. House 2005b:35) and Rep. Foley said was the "most productive on issues like this" (U.S. House 2005b:34).

Personal narratives were influential throughout in defining child sexual abuse as a nonpolitical issue that was unconnected to more controversial issues, mirroring how the survivors' movement defined that shared experience as superseding difference. Setting aside other disagreements, lawmakers and activists both sought action on child sexual abuse alone. This powerful mandate worked to stifle the moments of challenge that emerged in 1981 over budget cuts, in 1995 over false accusations and feminist challenges, and in the 2000s over sex offender punishment. Throughout, scientific and experiential authority and ritualized emotion helped cement the commitment of otherwise-opposed actors to child sexual abuse policy.

AUTHORITY AND EMOTION

As we have seen, witnesses included experts (researchers or professionals in the field) and people who had been sexually abused as children and their families. Many of the experts who testified were feminists, liberals, or advocates of increased social welfare spending, but they discussed the issue in politically neutral terms, focusing on research, effectiveness of treatment programs, and prevalence of abuse. They kept their political commitments silent and provided a neutral basis for cross-ideological cooperation. It was not only experts who were nonideological. Witnesses who recounted their personal experience also focused narrowly on their experience and the helpful or counterproductive responses they encountered from hospitals, community organizations, and law enforcement. Lawmakers responded with respect and appreciation to these witnesses, whose personal experiences gave them ultimate credibility.

The boundaries between expert and experiential knowledge were blurry and the same witnesses often used both approaches. Survivor activists used their collective experience to make claims about the nature of child sexual abuse, nonexpert witnesses were asked to make policy recommendations, and legislators and expert witnesses invoked their experiences alongside presentation of data. Hearings often include "contests over facts" and "contests about moral qualities" (Nichols 1991). But because the "facts" associated with child sexual abuse have strong normative and moral dimensions, these dimensions were rarely separate. Emotion was also important to legitimation, connected to experiential authority by lawmakers and witnesses of all types. Together, expertise, experiential narratives, and emotion cemented the divergent participants under the narrowly neutral umbrella.

Expertise

Legislators valued expert authority discursively and structurally, to be sure. Expert witnesses appeared at virtually all hearings on child sexual abuse across all three time periods, and legislators regularly cited research to support their positions. Expert witnesses' authority was based on their credentials, which the introducing committee member and witnesses themselves summarized.[58] Expert witnesses included researchers, treatment professionals, and professionals in other fields such as the American Bar Association, which had a division dealing with child abuse. Beyond the live hearings, congressional hearings usually include supplemental materials, and government agencies such as NCCAN and the Government Accounting Office also issued reports on child sexual abuse. While most legislators did not read all this material themselves, their staff members did, providing a route for research (often government funded) to affect congressional approaches to the issue.

During the 1980s, expert authority was the basis for establishing the scope and nature of the problem of child abuse. As sexual abuse of children (vs. physical abuse or neglect) gained attention, experts regularly presented research about its prevalence and nature. By the mid-1980s, sufficient data had been collected by NCCAN and its grantees that the focus shifted to effective prevention and treatment, which remained a major topic throughout the years, along with ongoing issues of recidivism, prosecution, and sentencing. Despite periodic debate, Congress generally agreed on the importance of federal funding for research.[59] Discussion of research in hearings ranged from brief citation of studies (i.e., to establish the frequency of child sexual abuse) to lengthy discussions of the validity of research findings or the need for research funding in specific areas.

Legislators often asked witnesses who were *not* experts in the field of child sexual abuse for expert knowledge. For example, Rep. Wolf (R-VA) questioned Deborah Aal, the producer of the TV movie *Something About Amelia*, about the frequency and causes of child sexual abuse and whether an increase was "because of the complexity of society?" Aal replied that it was indeed increasing "because of the complexity of society" but added, "I feel we are a society that does not love its children . . . our children become adults at a very, very early age [and] . . . they are made to be sexual objects by the media" (U.S. House 1984a:26). When Rep. Dan Coats (R-IN) asked Aal about treatment programs, Aal clarified, "I can't testify as an expert because I am not a psychologist, I am a producer." She nevertheless advocated the kind of family counseling depicted in the film. Similar lines of questioning included Sen. Barbara Boxer asking a United Way representative about the most effective way of "breaking the cycle" of child abuse" (U.S. House 1984a:47) and "Jo's" recommendations for prevention programming (U.S. House 1981). Legislators also treated witnesses from conservative antipornography organizations as experts on the patterns and effects of child pornography and prostitution. For example, Sen. Roth asked Bruce Taylor of Citizens for Decency through Law about the effectiveness of cooperation between federal and local officials and the exchange of information about sex offenders between states.

Experience

Experiential knowledge—the use of experience as the basis for authoritative knowledge—was almost as common throughout the three periods, occurring in between one-third (in the early years) and three-quarters of hearings (in the latter two periods). This included brief invocations of personal experiences, extended personal narratives, and discussion of prior experience prosecuting or providing social services. Experiential narratives were crucial to the narrowly neutral consensus, as we have seen. Perhaps for this reason, many expert witnesses began with case histories that were similar in narrative form and emotional content to those reported by victims themselves. For example, Francine Vecchiola, from Connecticut's Children's Protective Services, recounted several case histories, including "Jane T," "a typical 8-year old." She told how, "When Jane T. was 12, the disbelieving family physician diagnosed the presence of gonorrhea. Only after this diagnosis was made did anyone correctly interpret and accurately piece together the signals Jane had been sending . . . nervousness, loss of appetite, dropping grades, and social discomfort. . . . The horrified physician and angry mother listened as the terrified child revealed her secret. Would they believe her? How could they believe her?" (U.S. House 1981:222). Similarly, Judge Tom McDonald recounted his *own* experience as an abused child removed from his family of origin:

> Unfortunately, the child welfare system all too often does not work in their best interest. I was one of the lucky ones. The system did work for me when as a very young child I was adopted by wonderful, loving parents. I can assure you, however, that if the system had treated me the way it does some of the children who now appear before me, I would not be here before you today. I would be on the other side of the bench, possibly behind bars. (U.S. Senate 1989b:246)

Members of Congress validated these accounts with ritual praise and emotional language. Whereas Allahyari (1997) finds that homeless people had to be explicitly constructed as "worthy" in congressional hearings, legislators treated witnesses who had been sexually abused as children as automatically worthy. In contrast, witnesses who had committed sexual or physical child abuse could contribute perspective to hearings, but their moral status was not negotiable.[60]

The value placed on experiential knowledge was taken for granted, but sometimes legislators stated it directly. For example, Subcommittee Chair Duke Cunningham told a 1995 hearing on child welfare that a witness "represents a sort of opinion that we should value most as we prepare to flesh out productive legislation. She has been affected first hand by the bills that past Congress's [sic] have written and offers true to life perspectives on some of the programs they have created" (U.S. House 1995a:30). Similarly, when Rep. Ted Poe quoted "[o]ne of the victims' grandmothers" as saying, "People have the right to know where sex offenders are living," he intended her voice to carry authority because of her experience (U.S. House 2005b:9).

Occasionally, experts and members of Congress recounted their personal experiences, such as their own or family members' childhood experiences of abuse, their feelings as parents, or their prior professional work in children's services, or as prosecutors or judges. For example, Rep. Thomas Davis (R-VA) described a bill as "a product of my own deepest feelings and knowledge . . . . I know how it feels to be filled with pain as a child. Though years have passed, my memories have not dimmed" (U.S. House 1995b:1). In relation to professional experience, Rep. Greenwood noted that despite the Contract with America's emphasis on returning power to the states, he supported federal guidelines for state child protective services "because of my background" as "a case worker for the County Children and Youth Agency" (U.S. House 1995:26). Here, he relied on experience to justify crossing ideological boundaries. Many participants also invoked parental concern. Dodie Livingston, the commissioner for the Administration for Children, Youth and Families under Reagan, used this strategy to defend herself in a hostile Democratic House hearing in 1986 by saying, "We are all parents here. We recognize the seriousness and the poignance [*sic*] of child abuse, child sexual abuse and child neglect" (U.S. House 1986a:105). Similarly, in a 2005 hearing on SORNA, Rep. Ginny Brown-Waite said, "[A]s a mother and a grandmother, my heart goes out to the Lunsford family in their terrible time of grieving" (U.S. House 2005b:11). Rep. Earl Pomeroy also invoked his experience as a parent in the 2005 hearing, saying, "While I've been serving in Congress, I've been privileged to become the father to two children that I've adopted, and I feel this legislation so deeply and so personally" (U.S. House 2005b:26).

Emotion

Emotion ran throughout these hearings. It was an important source of legitimacy and calls for action. All participants agreed on the emotions associated with child sexual abuse—survivors' pain and triumph, society's horror. Witnesses' descriptions of their emotions and legislators' ritualized invocation of emotion were an important source of common ground across ideology.[61] Witnesses recounting personal experience of sexual assault usually described their emotions. Beth explained, "I was very confused . . . I was really afraid I would break up the family I was scared that somebody would find out . . . . I felt really guilty . . . . I felt very isolated" (U.S. House 1981:88–89). Beth's mother, Jo, similarly named her emotions after finding out that Beth had been abused: "I felt like screaming and running out on the street . . . all of this pain I felt . . . . I felt so helpless as a mother . . . . I also felt a great deal of anger toward my husband. I felt anger as a wife who has found her husband seeking sexual gratification elsewhere. I felt a great deal of rage because this was my child and I had been hurt" (U.S. House 1981:94). Witnesses also acknowledged the expected emotions associated with hearing about child sexual abuse. For example, Dr. Muriel Sugarman, testifying about cases of child sexual abuse in the courts, said, "Let me first state that the subject of child sexual abuse stirs in all of us painful, uncomfortable, difficult, and sometimes overwhelming feelings. The first response of those without direct experience of this topic is horror and disbelief" (U.S. Senate 1989b:109). In doing so, she both suggested what legislators should feel and defused the possible effects of their "disbelief."

Personal narratives had emotional plotlines. Beth, for example, described how the negative emotions she felt contrasted with her desire for "closeness with my family." When she became involved with Parents United, "that closeness started." She vividly described her "big relief" at discussing the issue openly and, she reported, "I feel really good about myself." Former Miss America Marilyn Van Derbur, in a lengthy narrative, described having felt "terrified" and "ashamed," and described the "peaceful[ness]" that the many women who wrote to her about their own experiences said they felt upon telling someone (her) for the first time (U.S. House 1991:8). This was the emotional narrative that self-help participants presented in private interviews and that appeared in mass media, although media accounts tended to emphasize professional therapy over peer support (Whittier 2001). After her assailant was released from prison, Amie Zyla described feeling "so disappointed . . . scared . . . all those old feelings returned and I was so sad for all the new victims." Those feelings changed to anger and action: "I was so mad . . . . I decided my anger . . . needed to be expressed in a positive way," leading to her advocacy for juvenile offenders to be placed on registry and notification lists (U.S. House 2005c:19). While her focus on sex offender policy was different from her predecessors', the transformation of feelings of fear and grief into anger and action was not. The entrance of this emotional trajectory into Congress reflects an indirect influence of the survivors' movement.

Members of Congress ritually invoked emotion at predictable times, particularly when introducing witnesses and at the conclusion of personal testimony. For example, following the testimony by Beth and her family, Rep. Erdahl said, "I want to commend this family for being here. For each of you, it is a courageous thing to do. It is what we might call a 'gutsy' thing to come before us today and share these things with us" (U.S. House 1981:99). Similarly, Rep. Marriott told a witness, "I want to thank you for coming forward and telling your story. It is a courageous thing that you have done" (U.S. House 1984a:21). Rep. Sheila Jackson Lee thanked a witness "for your courage, for your strength of character, and for your can-do attitude. And I'm going to tell you, you're going to beat this. And as you do this, you're going to help educate and encourage and embrace children and young people around the Nation and the world. We applaud you for what you have done" (U.S. House 2005c:30). In introducing Jim Wade, Sen. Ashcroft (R-MO) said, "Obviously, I express my regret to you about the pain and suffering of this tragedy in your family, but it makes my gratitude for your appearance only deeper" (U.S. Senate 1995a:3). Committee Chair Major Owens similarly told witnesses, "you gave life to the statistics, your horror stirred us and has led to our very much wanting to take action" (U.S. House 1992c:50). Following testimony by mothers who had lost custody after alleging that the fathers had sexually abused their children, Rep. Susan Molinari (R-NY), told the witnesses, "At this point I am a little emotionally moved by the stories that you gave . . . thank you for the strength that you have all shown in protecting your children, but also in coming forth today." (U.S. House 1992c:52). These remarks, while likely reflecting genuine gratitude, took a prescribed and consistent form. As official state expression of emotion, they legitimate witnesses' testimony and indicate the expected emotional response.

Legislators also ritually invoked emotion by describing public emotions associated with violence against children. For example, Sen. Mark Green (R-WI) stated that "our country has been shocked and outraged by a series of brutal attacks against our children" (U.S. House 2005a:1); Deputy Assistant Attorney General Laura Partsky stated, "the sexual abuse and exploitation of children is particularly horrific" (U.S. House 2005a:6). In a 2005 hearing on sex offender registration, Committee Chair Howard Coble said in his opening statement, "our hearts go out to the families of those innocent and beautiful children who've been killed, sexually assaulted, or tortured. Too many times, we've had to read gruesome news accounts about these attacks, watch disturbing news reports, or listen to the anguish of the parents of these children" (U.S. House 2005b:2). These reactions were framed as universally shared and helped to establish that the issue and legislation were beyond politics.

The earlier hearings included discussion of a wide range of emotions, including victims' ongoing relationships to offenders, lasting emotional effects of abuse, and paths to healing. By the 2000s, when the focus was on penalties for and surveillance of sex offenders, these emotions were no longer discussed. Instead, emotional appeals mostly directly justified harsh criminal penalties. Subcommittee chair Mark Green made this clear in 2005, saying, "Some might say that we need to treat sex offenders and to rehabilitate them . . . . My view is quite the opposite. One victim, one child harmed, one child raped, one child molested, is one crime too many" (U.S. House 2005a:1). Tracey Henke, deputy associate attorney general, invoked the names of murdered children at the same 2005 hearing: "Names like Jessica Lunsford and Megan Kanka highlight the importance of this new technology. Their smiles, wiped away forever by sex offenders, are a constant reminder that we must keep parents and communities informed and engaged" (U.S. House 2005c:6).

Such emotional appeals made it difficult to oppose increased sentencing and registration/notification requirements. In a rare attempt, opponent Rep. Robert Scott (D-VA) addressed the emotional dimension directly, acknowledging that "[c]hild deaths as a result of sexual abuse or other violence is so tragic as to shock the conscience, and our reaction will be to strike back with all the punitive weight of government. As policymakers, it's also incumbent upon us not to simply strike back after the events have happened, but to see what we can do to reduce the incidence to begin with" (U.S. House 2005c:3). A Seattle police detective and specialist in sex offender management, Robert Schilling, combined expertise, experience, and emotion in a fruitless attempt to argue that sex offender notification laws were ineffective. He proclaimed:

> My experience protecting the public from sex offenders spans two decades. It is not a job to me, it is a passion. Perhaps my most significant experience related to this work comes from the fact that I'm a survivor of childhood sexual abuse. The abuse spanned a 4-year period and, without question, marks the darkest days of my life. I have dedicated my life to doing whatever I can to stop sexual abuse not only in this country, but also around the world. Prior to becoming a detective in the Special Victims Unit, I, like many citizens, believed the only way to manage sex offenders was to put them on a distant island where they couldn't victimize anyone else. My feelings were naive, yet a heartfelt response to a complex problem. (U.S. House 2009a:89)

He went on to say that the SORNA did not make communities safer and suggested more effective ways of spending money to prevent child sexual abuse. This appeal had no effect on the legislation.

We often conceptualize emotion, experience, and science as distinct. But in the congressional hearings and in the child sexual abuse movement they were intertwined. Authority came from both expertise and experience, and the distinction between the two often blurred. Activists developed knowledge about the nature of child sexual abuse and its remedies based on their collective experience. Legislators relied on their experience and observations to form opinions and defend them to each other. Emotion ran throughout these hearings, implicitly and explicitly present in testimony and lawmakers' response to it. Similarly, expressing, processing, and validating emotion was central to the grassroots self-help groups (Whittier 2001; Whittier 2009). Emotion was the "glue" that cemented Congress, advocates, and individuals into their very diverse alliances. Insofar as activists, professionals, and legislators all constructed child sexual abuse as a problem that could affect all children and that produced a common emotional trajectory, they promoted the racially neutral and often implicitly white victim and offender. This, too, helped cement the participation of politically diverse parties under the narrow and neutral umbrella.

NARROW NEUTRALITY IN SUPREME COURT AMICUS BRIEFS

U.S. Supreme Court cases dealing with child sexual abuse include cases related to child pornography, sentencing of offenders against children, and aspects of sex offender registration and notification laws. My search for such cases yielded ten major cases, nine of which had amici.[62] Consistent with the relationships in other aspects of this case, child sexual abuse pulled together ideologically conservative and nominally ideologically neutral groups more than pornography or VAWA.

Child pornography cases drew together otherwise-opposed groups on the antipornography side. (Amici on the anticensorship side were ideologically similar to each other.) All four cases dealing with child pornography (*Stephen Knox v. U.S.* 1993, *U.S. v. X-Citement Video, Inc. and Rubin Gottesman* 1994; *Ashcroft v. Free Speech Coalition* 2001; *U.S. v. Michael Williams* 2006) included antipornography conservative, child welfare, and child sexual abuse survivors' organizations as amici supporting increased restriction or penalties against child pornography. For example, *Knox* had a joint brief from amici including religious conservative groups the Family Research Council and Focus on the Family; survivors' groups Voices in Action and the American Coalition for Abuse Awareness; NCMEC, the PTA, and various child welfare and child advocacy organizations. *X-citement Video* included these same groups and a number of other, more explicitly religious, conservative organizations. Feminist antipornography organizations notably did not weigh in on any of these cases.

Cases dealing with other aspects of child sexual abuse had somewhat more varied amici. The child rape death penalty case, *Kennedy v. Louisiana*, drew amici opposing the death penalty that included state child assault advocacy organizations, social workers associations, anti-sexual-violence groups, the ACLU, the NAACP, and public defenders. Four state child sexual abuse organizations joined this brief, a small minority of such organizations. None of the major antiviolence or survivors' organizations joined either side of the case. The (missing) amici reinforce the picture that we see elsewhere in the movement: an alliance that supports or tolerates punitive state control of offenders and defines that as apolitical. We would not necessarily expect antiviolence organizations to weigh in against the death penalty for rape, but an antiviolence movement that was skeptical of state power would be more likely to do so. The three remaining cases, on the constitutionality of SORNA and civil commitment laws (*Smith v. Doe, Carr v. U.S., and Stagner v. California*) had no nongovernmental amici supporting the statutes and the usual opposing amici, including the ACLU, defense and public offender lawyers, and mental health associations.

In sum, issues that fell under the narrowly neutral umbrella, framed in terms of child sexual abuse and not in terms of other issues, drew no nongovernmental amici in favor of upholding existing law. The pornography cases, which intersected with conservatives' interests in restricting sexually explicit media and survivors' and child welfare organizations' interests in opposing child abuse, drew diverse collaborators. The most contentious death penalty case, which raised issues of race, class, and ability, drew a limited number of unlikely collaborators.

CONCLUSION

Activists against child sexual abuse sought to garner greater attention for the issue, particularly incest, to help both child and adult victims speak up about their experience and recover psychologically, and to end what they saw as societal complicity. As adults who had been sexually abused as children and professionals who worked on child sexual abuse spoke out and were widely heard, they were joined by others from all perspectives and constructed a shared collective identity of "survivor" that prioritized the shared experience of abuse. Drawing on that collective identity, they defined a single-issue politics. In Congress, legislators combined testimony about that experience, from witnesses who were influenced by the activist and professional work against child sexual abuse, with discourses about crime and victimization to define a similarly single-issue approach. This "narrowness" and the strong condemnation of violence against children allowed diverse participants to view the issue as nonpolitical and ideologically neutral.

The narrow, neutral alliance was very different from the collaborative-adversarial relationship between feminist and conservative opponents of pornography. Participants could openly participate in ideologically diverse groups or join with erstwhile opponents, with no implication that they were betraying their cause, because the issue of child sexual abuse was so solidly defined as nonpolitical. The risks to participants' reputations were minimal. The relative detachment of feminist and conservative movement organizations reinforced this, with activists and legislators receiving very little criticism of their work on child sexual abuse. Even feminist critics of the punitive state, who opposed feminist support for VAWA (as we will see in the next chapter), mostly stayed out of the issue of child sexual abuse. The FMSF and its allies were genuine opponents, and they were also ideologically diverse, containing conservatives, liberals, and progressives. Both sides were narrow (focused solely on child sexual abuse) and neutral (defining themselves as only about the issue of child sexual abuse or false accusations, without any larger political agenda).

In Congress, there was more unanimity and more attention paid to child sexual abuse than pornography. Members defined it as highly important and as an issue that transcended political divisions. Legislation and official discourse changed over time, but the insistence that child sexual abuse ought to be beyond politics was constant. The three moments of challenge, around reauthorizing CAPTA in 1981, attempts by feminists and the FMSF to gain support for their battles over custody or false accusations, and questions about the efficacy of sex offender registration and notification, were quickly overcome by the insistence on the political neutrality of child sexual abuse and the importance of federal action.

As we have seen, personal experience and emotion were central to defining the issues and gaining support for action. This was an emotionally "hot" relationship, with intense feelings at the core and frequent invocation of emotion in official contexts. This is not an inherent feature of narrowly neutral relationships. Other narrowly neutral relationships might be emotionally cool. For example, diverse groups might cooperate on issues of traffic or parking, politically neutral issues that they see as a narrow basis for common ground. Although people may have strong feelings about traffic, the intensity and affect are qualitatively and quantitatively different from child sexual abuse even if the type of strange bedfellow relationship might be the same.

The concrete social and legislative changes that occurred around child sexual abuse were significant. In mainstream culture, ideas about child sexual abuse, its visibility, and the availability of resources for adult and child victims increased dramatically (see Whittier 2009 for extended discussion).

In terms of federal legislation and policy, there were gains in terms of funding for organizations, treatment, and prevention programs. There were also more carceral changes in the form of sex offender law, including sentencing guidelines and offender registration and notification requirements. The legal constraints that were so important in the pornography case, limiting action on obscenity and leading to an ultimate decline in congressional attention, were less significant in this case. Congress repeatedly passed laws that it rightly expected might be unconstitutional, those regarding restricting access to the Internet and regulating its contents. Even some components of SORNA, such as applying registration requirements retroactively to convictions before its passage, had a realistic basis for constitutional challenge even though they were upheld (Ewing 2011). The high salience and commitment characterizing this narrowly neutral relationship enabled action despite these legal constraints.

Neither conservative, nor feminist, nor single-issue survivors' organizations sent many witnesses to congressional hearings and likely had little direct influence behind-the-scenes either. Instead, the single-issue survivors' movement had an influence indirectly. The publicity and media attention that movement gained increased congressional attention to child sexual abuse, and the frames promulgated by that movement shaped congressional testimony. Conservative organizations had little influence over child sexual abuse policy because there was little specifically conservative organizing on the subject. Conservative organizations and legislators sought to limit government spending but had trouble making that case for child sexual abuse because of the issue's broad appeal and because conservative survivors generally wanted the same kinds of services as the single-issue survivors' movement. Only around child pornography did religious conservatives have a role. Feminists also had little influence at the federal level. Their frames and discourses were largely absent from Congress along with their organizations. However, they influenced the burgeoning professional sector that addressed child sexual abuse.

Child sexual abuse professionals were the ones who had direct influence through their testimony and work with federal agencies. Feminist social workers, researchers, medical professionals, lawyers, and therapists all testified before Congress, but their political commitments were submerged. Even they rarely spoke directly about gender, except in reporting statistics about assaults. Across the board, no one addressed race, class, or other intersectional issues. Ironically, the tendency to focus on white victims—who were mostly readily seen as innocent—combined with the focus on and prevalence of familial abuse to shape a carceral shift that was less racialized than for most other crimes.

Familial abuse was the priority for most activist and advocacy groups. It was the main focus of the survivors' movement not primarily because of a feminist critique of power in the family, but because simple numbers meant that movement was mostly made up of people who had been abused by family members and acquaintances. In the earlier years, incest also was the main focus of state discourse, law, and intervention, which occurred through child protective services. The influence of the FMSF and VOCAL on mainstream culture and the increasing legislative focus on bills named for notorious cases of assault by strangers substantially decreased the focus on incest by the end of the 1990s. Focus on the "sex offender" and "pedophile" replaced it. The rhetoric of the dangerous stranger, an outsider to the safe community, did have unsubtle overtones of race and class, threats to suburbia, as Leon (2011) and Lancaster (2011) point out. Despite the discursive change, however, those who assaulted family members and acquaintances are the majority affected by sex offender laws. Debates over the consequences and whether incest should be an exception to such laws were a fruitless moment of challenge in the 2000s.

Child sexual abuse policy was shaped by the incredible growth in the criminal and prison apparatus during the 1990s. The rise of sex offender registration and notification has rightly become a paradigmatic case of the dangers of the punitive state and governing through (fear of) crime (Ewing 2011; Lancaster 2011; Leon 2011; Margulies 2013; Roberts 2001; Simon 2007; Waldram 2012). Sex offender policy represents a much more intensely carceral approach to social change than pornography regulation or VAWA or, indeed, earlier policy on child sexual abuse. Criminal meanings reign even in culture and daily life, again in contrast to the broader range of interpretations about the importance of peer support, survivor openness, and therapy that prevailed previously.

Sex offender registration and notification laws that require registration of all offenders, include juveniles, and provide no treatment for sex offenders during incarceration or after release, are expensive and fruitless at best and increase the risk that offenders will commit new crimes at worst (Ewing 2011; Leon 2011). Ironically, it is the strength and form of the narrow and neutral construction of child sexual abuse that makes it virtually impossible to challenge these laws. The power of experiential knowledge, intertwined with emotion and expert authority and the fact that while victims' experiences carry moral power, offenders' experiences do not, left little discursive space for anything that could appear to weaken commitment to preventing abuse.

Despite the fact that a large proportion of rapes and sexual assaults are committed against minors, and that activism on both issues emerged from the same women's movement locations, the issue areas of child sexual abuse and rape have developed along separate paths. At the same time that much of this legislation and activism on child sexual abuse was proceeding, feminists were working hard to pass federal law on violence against women. There was very little overlap between the advocates working on two issues or how they were framed, even though sex offender policy applies to rapes and sexual assaults against adults, as well as children, and VAWA has components that apply to minors. Like child sexual abuse, VAWA saw a bipartisan coalition within Congress, albeit a more contentious one. But unlike child sexual abuse, VAWA included active involvement by women's movement organizations and, not coincidentally, drew more critique from feminists concerned with race and opposing the prison state. The form that the cross-ideological relationship took was quite different.

CHAPTER 4

The Violence Against Women Act and Ambivalent Alliances

When Senator Joseph Biden proposed the Violence Against Women Act in 1990, mass feminist mobilization had waned, but the national women's movement organizations that remained were highly organized, professionalized, and relatively well-funded. Organizations like the National Organization for Women's Legal Defense and Education Fund (henceforth NOW-LDEF) had built connections with primarily Democratic lawmakers on other issues, like workplace and education discrimination (Banaszak 2010; McBride and Parry 2011). These connections paid off, as NOW assembled a broad coalition of movement organizations to help write VAWA and lobby for its passage, which they achieved in 1994. These activists formed a close working relationship not only with key Democratic members of Congress and their staff but also with Republican cosponsors, including some of the most conservative members. There were two alliances across ideological difference in Congress around VAWA. First, fairly common, was the bipartisan group of conservative and liberal lawmakers who sponsored and supported VAWA. Second, less common, was the relationship between feminist organizations working on the law and the conservative members of Congress who promoted and ultimately supported it. Not simply a lobbying relationship, the latter involved lawyers and advocates from NOW working closely with conservative members of Congress and their staff to organize hearings and build support for diverse parts of the law.

The participants in this relationship were undeniably allies, but they were ambivalent ones, wary of the other side and supporting VAWA for different reasons. Conservatives and many liberals in Congress sought to be tough on crime and to protect women from what they came to see as the shockingly common and serious problems of domestic violence and rape. Feminist members of Congress and outside feminist advocates emphasized the need to take domestic violence and rape seriously; to improve the often sexist and dismissive response by law enforcement, medical professionals, and society at large; and to empower women and their advocates. Conservatives' larger goals were improving public safety, punishing criminals, and reinforcing strong families. Feminists' larger goals were reducing the systematic victimization of women and addressing a key dimension of women's oppression, which related not only to how individual women were treated but also to how institutions responded to assaults against women. Bridging these differences, a hybrid frame developed in Congress, a mash-up of feminist and crime discourses that could be understood and deployed in different ways by different sides. This frame promoted VAWA's success by enabling cross-ideological alliance, but, as we will see, it could not accommodate some important feminist goals.

While we might expect that the alliance in Congress would be paralleled by a similar connection between feminists and conservatives outside the state, it was not. Feminists supported VAWA, while conservatives opposed it, albeit both weakly. Like pornography, VAWA was somewhat controversial among feminists, with some criticizing it for its criminal justice dimensions and the kinds of connections and oversight it prescribed between service organizations, like shelters and rape crisis lines, and government institutions, like police and courts. Others objected to the limited scope of its protections for immigrants and other marginalized groups who experienced domestic or sexual violence. By and large, however, women's movement organizations supported VAWA, although it received little attention in the feminist press or at the grassroots. Departing from their elected counterparts, in contrast, conservative pundits and activists objected to many aspects of the law and were near-unanimous in their opposition to VAWA. But like feminists, they were not highly engaged and did little to oppose passage. Outside Congress, when conservative and feminist activists talked about VAWA, they unequivocally connected it to their larger agendas, precluding the ambiguous, multiple interpretations that allowed broad congressional support.

The different alliances inside and outside the state affected each other. Elected officials and feminists working on VAWA had to account for their actions to their constituencies or parent movements. Feminists working on VAWA were part of a multi-issue coalition. Their coalition partners and their own commitments led them to an intersectional approach to violence against women, in which addressing issues like immigration status, sexual identity, race, ethnicity, and age was central to addressing domestic and sexual violence. While conservatives in Congress could accommodate tailoring programs for rural areas or for older or younger victims, they were willing to support only relatively narrow protections for immigrant women and only limited programming for groups like Native American women or LGBT people who were not well served by existing programs. Secular conservatives outside Congress objected to any emphasis on gender in the law and to the idea that sexual and domestic violence were unique compared with other crimes or widespread enough to warrant federal legislation. But it wasn't until 2011 that ideological differences actually threatened the working relationship between congressional conservatives and feminists. Conservative activists' growing influence on Congress through the Tea Party movement—combined with feminists' ongoing push to strengthen VAWA's intersectional dimensions—destabilized congressional agreement on VAWA.

Despite the opposition of outside activists, the relationship between feminists and conservatives was tighter than it was for pornography and more direct and less veiled by political neutrality than it was for the case of child sexual abuse. It was closer in many ways to a conventional coalition. Inside Congress the sides took a pragmatic approach to their collaboration and, at least in public, praised each other's efforts and acknowledged their unlikely common ground with virtually no denigration of conservatism or feminism. Issues of reputation management were muted because of the low salience of VAWA to both grassroots movements. In fact, there were reputational plusses for both sides. Elected officials touted their bipartisanship, while feminist activists claimed influence on legislation and important allies such as Senators Joe Biden and Barbara Boxer.

The outcome of this ambivalent alliance was a significant and influential piece of legislation. VAWA's provisions included increased criminal penalties for sexual and domestic violence; funded police, social service agencies, and local antiviolence groups; provided some protections and routes to legal residency for immigrants who reported domestic violence or rape; mandated collaboration between community-based organizations and law enforcement; and funded training for law enforcement officers, judges, and hospital examiners.[1] The 2000 and 2006 VAWAs increased provisions for immigrants who experienced domestic violence, broadened the definition of stalking, addressed dating violence, and added provisions for services to people in same-sex relationships. The 2006 reauthorization also expanded remedies for Native Americans and set aside a dedicated funding stream for sexual assault, an issue that had been marginalized both within the consideration of the issue and in the legislation itself (Bevacqua 2000; Corrigan 2013).

The law's centerpiece, in the view of Biden and feminist supporters, was Title III, the civil rights provision, which allowed women to sue attackers in federal court for civil damages if they could show that the attack was motivated by gender animus. Essentially, Title III made rape or domestic violence a potential violation of women's civil rights, permitting victims to appeal to federal courts rather than relying on potentially biased local law enforcement or judges. Title III incorporated the notion of rape and domestic violence as violations of women's civil rights—pioneered by MacKinnon and Dworkin in the pornography battles. It reflects the continuity among these issues and their advocates. Supporters presented extensive evidence of gender bias in courts to show the necessity of providing a federal remedy for victims. Title III was more controversial in Congress than the rest of the bill, which saw little opposition. Ultimately, Title III was overturned in 2000 by the Supreme Court, leaving strengthening of criminal procedures and funding for social services as VAWA's main contributions.[2] Although it was symbolically important, even if it had been upheld, its scope and impact—although significant—would have been secondary to the many other components and extensive funding in the rest of the Act.

Feminists gained a great deal of what they sought, but ultimately the legislation entailed two-way compromise. Its noncriminal provisions—especially regarding immigration status—were less than feminists sought and more than conservatives desired, while its emphasis on reaching underrepresented groups, like women of color, and its ultimately overturned civil rights provision were more squarely in the feminist camp. Critics from the Left argued that feminists compromised too fundamentally by supporting VAWA once it was incorporated into the now notorious 1994 Omnibus Crime Act, which expanded mandatory minimum sentencing and failed to pass a measure barring racially inequitable death penalty sentencing. But feminist advocates and congressional supporters of VAWA saw VAWA's inclusion in the Omnibus Crime Act simply as a means of ensuring a vote (Biden 2007).

While VAWA did increase sentencing guidelines for some forms of violence against women and encouraged prosecutors to take on more such cases, these changes paled next to the other parts of the 1994 Crime Act. The Act increased sentences for many crimes, including drug charges, and funded large increases in police forces. The punitive turn did not begin with the 1994 Crime Act (Margulies 2013), but it has become emblematic of the forces that led to the explosion of imprisonment in the United States. By extension, VAWA has come to be seen as a prime example of white feminists' attempting to use the state's carceral powers on their behalf, without attending to the fundamentally racist nature of those powers or the way that law enforcement is more apt to harm women of color or immigrants than to help them (Richie 2012). Bernstein (2010:57; 2012) defines carceral feminism as a feminism that relies on the state's punitive power to advance women's liberation and conceptualizes "social justice as criminal justice." Carceral feminism may be contrasted with intersectional feminism, which emphasizes how social, economic, and political forces interact to shape different experiences and solutions to violence (Arnold 2013; Naples 2009). Despite its inclusion in the 1994 Crime Act, VAWA incorporated both carceral and intersectional feminist elements. The ambivalent alliance between feminist advocates of VAWA and conservatives shaped those outcomes more than a philosophical affinity with carceral feminism.

Overall, feminists enjoyed greater success regarding VAWA than in pornography or child sexual abuse, while conservatives compromised more. This was the result of feminists' strong access and influence on congressional Democrats, and Democrats' control of the Congress or the presidency during much of the relevant period. It was also due to the favorable opportunities for discourse opposing violence against women, with the hybrid gendered crime frame enjoying strong appeal inside and outside the state. The compromises feminists made were a result of similar factors. Intersectional feminist discourse was less readily accepted, and congressional committee jurisdictions that dealt with immigration and Native American affairs were separate from those dealing with crime, increasing the tendency to view these as separate issues.

AMBIVALENT INSTITUTIONAL ALLIANCES

When social movements become institutionalized, they develop close relationships with—or even become absorbed by—societal institutions, including government, schools, hospitals, or businesses. Institutionalization usually entails formal structures with a chain of command and explicit responsibilities at different levels, organizational stability, paid and professional rather than volunteer staff, and linkage between movements' goals and those of institutions' (Meyer 2007). Movements may be connected to or absorbed by government or other institutions (Armstrong and Bernstein 2008). Scholars focus on what accounts for the institutionalization of certain elements of movements, looking at political, institutional, and cultural openings or alignments that movements can exploit or that incline institutional actors to support movement goals for their own ends. For example, as school budgets shrank in the 1980s, schools developed their own child abuse prevention programs rather than contracting with activist groups for such programming (Whittier 2009). Institutionalization can also be initiated by movement organizations, either out of necessity or to expand. As rape crisis centers struggled to maintain themselves, they found offers by hospitals and universities to house and absorb their services appealing. As advocates for victims of rape and domestic violence struggled with police departments, they welcomed initiatives to train local police departments and legislation requiring such training (Corrigan 2013).

Institutions do not simply adopt movement agendas wholesale, nor do activists necessarily determine what aspects of their goals are picked up. Going beyond political opportunities for movements as a whole, selection processes distinguish among the different goals, discourses, and actors within a movement, favoring some and ignoring others (see Whittier 2009 for a detailed discussion; see also Skrentny 2006). As we have seen with pornography and child sexual abuse, the federal government's carceral priorities—criminal law, investigations, and penalties—meant that feminist goals that could be cast as crime were favored over others. VAWA, in which feminist organizations actually helped write the law, also shows the importance of organizational isomorphism, in which groups whose structure and culture are similar to those it seeks to influence are advantaged. NOW's formal organizational structure, legal expertise, allies within the state, and ability and willingness to play the legislative game gave it influence and access far beyond that of grassroots or protest oriented groups (Banaszak 2010; Barakso 2004).

Institutionalization often produces disputes between activists who see it as an achievement and a way of advancing movement goals and those who see it as co-optation, with any achievements more likely to serve the interests of the powerful and to discourage ongoing movement mobilization. These disputes are heightened when alliances across ideological opposition are involved. VAWA was no exception. Many feminist critiques focused on how its provisions advanced the interests of a carceral, neoliberal state (e.g., Bumiller 2008; Richie 2012). But institutionalization is not an either-or process. Movements often institutionalize in some ways and remain outsiders in others. Institutionalization also need not entail simple co-optation but can produce genuine—if limited—change.

As we have seen, the relationships between feminists and conservatives in the other two case studies were unstable and contingent, varying by location, campaign, and time. The relationships themselves did not institutionalize, although in the case of child sexual abuse, they were facilitated by federal funding streams. The VAWA case is different. The relationship between feminist activists and conservatives in Congress—mediated by feminists' relationship with Democratic congresspeople—persisted over time and became somewhat routinized, publicly acknowledged by both sides, and mutually beneficial. This was the case even though the same players simultaneously opposed each other on other issues (like workplace discrimination and abortion). These routinized relationships are generally more influential on legislation than grassroots movement actions like demonstrations (Soule et al. 1999).The policy area of violence against women, like many policy areas, was shaped by an accepted and ongoing interaction among "bureaucrats, legislative personnel, interest groups leaders, researchers, and specialist reporters" (Andrews and Edwards 2004; Baumgartner, Gray, and Lowery 2009; Holyoke 2009; Sabatier 1991:148).

A logic of crime mobilizes certain federal and state institutions (police, courts, prisons, sentencing commissions, surveillance), while a social service logic mobilizes others. Feminist frames about VAWA simultaneously appealed to both logics. VAWA shows not only how crime and neoliberalism intermixed with feminism but also that they contain varying understandings of gender. Inside Congress, feminist discourse and frames for understanding gendered violence combined with criminal justice meanings across the political spectrum. VAWA supported those feminist anti-rape goals that relate to criminal justice and social services—policy changes mostly consistent with state priorities and power structures. Simultaneously, though, feminists also pulled state discourse in less punitive directions and promoted other movement goals regarding invisibility and stigma.

The relative success of each player in a cross-ideological relationship varies. Those with greater structural power and cultural resonance have more leverage. As we have seen, in diverse coalitions outcomes rarely reflect the goals and discourses of all partners equally, but tend to reflect those most consistent with existing state interests, priorities, structures, and power. This was the case for both feminist and conservative movements around VAWA.

PATHS TO VAWA

VAWA did not emerge from nowhere. It grew from many years of state, local, and national anti-rape activism, including state legal reforms and grassroots efforts to provide support to survivors and to work to prevent sexual assault (Bevacqua 2000; Caringella 2009; Corrigan 2013; Martin

2005). In 1970, as the anti-rape movement was beginning, the sparse research that addressed rape conceptualized it as rare, generally the fault of the victim, committed by deranged strangers, and potentially sexually pleasurable for the victim. Women provoked rape, the view went, if they dressed provocatively or frequented dangerous locations. Experts ignored the risks husbands, boyfriends, and acquaintances posed, and most states permitted husbands to rape their wives. Many argued that women could not be raped unless they capitulated (making it essentially impossible to prove a rape charge) and that a woman who did not fight using every method at her disposal had in fact consented. Very few rape cases were prosecuted and even fewer resulted in conviction (Freedman 2013). While domestic violence was recognized, it was believed to be rare and often condoned (Breines and Gordon 1983). Police departments were unlikely to bring charges, trials entailed smearing victims' reputations, medical examinations were inadequate and insensitive, and psychological treatment was virtually nonexistent (Corrigan 2013; Martin 2005; Whittier 2009). State programs that later became widespread had their origins in the rape crisis movement of the 1970s. For example, volunteers from rape crisis centers accompanied women who reported rape to hospitals, and their efforts to reform hospital procedures led to the formation of Sexual Assault Nurse Examiner programs in the late 1970s. These programs, which aimed to produce usable forensic evidence while treating victims with respect, grew steadily; by 2011 there were more than 500 such programs nationwide (Renzetti, Edleson, and Bergen 2011). Organizing against domestic violence also emerged from consciousness-raising groups and from calls to rape crisis centers from women seeking help. It began with grassroots safe houses, which expanded into shelters and ultimately spread widely, often funded by mainstream sources like hospitals or community mental health centers (Matthews 1994).

Both state and national women's movement organizations worked throughout the 1970s and 1980s on reforming state laws about rape. At the local level, feminists and allied professionals pressed city government and police and prosecutors to enforce and prosecute rape and domestic violence and to fund shelters and crisis centers. Existing laws distinguished between rape by strangers and acquaintances, excluded rape by husbands, required corroboration, and had various other provisions that made prosecution and conviction unlikely. Feminists, often spearheaded by NOW chapters, worked to end the exemption for spousal rape and the admissibility of victims' prior sexual history as evidence in rape trials and to make rape convictions more likely (McBride and Parry 2011). Even radical feminists who generally eschewed state-focused or reformist efforts supported and worked for legal change, seeing it as a necessary part of a larger and longer term agenda (Bevacqua 2000). Michigan feminists, working with liberal and conservative state legislators, were the first to pass comprehensive rape law reform in 1974, which then served as a template for other states (Corrigan 2013). Law enforcement and conservative legislators supported these reforms because of their commitment to crime control, in what Corrigan (2013:38) calls a "prickly political alliance" (Spohn and Horney 1992). Rape shield laws, which forbid the use of rape victims' prior sexual behavior in rape cases, resulted from their efforts, as did the end of marital rape exclusions, changes in arrest procedures for domestic violence, and increases in statutes of limitation for child sexual abuse and, in some states, rape (Bevacqua 2000; Freedman 2013). These local- and state-level campaigns also helped activists hone their lobbying skills and primed them for deeper engagement with state and federal government going forward. These efforts, led by feminists with support from conservative lawmakers, were a preview of the ambivalent alliance at the federal level around VAWA.

Connections to the federal government also began in the 1970s. The National Center for the Prevention and Control of Rape (NCPCR) was established within the National Institutes of Mental Health (NIMH) in 1976 after two years of hearings on the Rape Prevention and Control bill, which was passed in 1975. The NCPCR was small, with only three-and-a-half staff in 1978, but influential (U.S. House 1978:558). It made research grants to many feminist authors who produced groundbreaking work on sexual violence, including Diana Russell, Peggy Sanday, Martha Burt, Pauline Bart, Judith Herman, and David Finkelhor. Feminist prevention programs and support services for women who had been sexually assaulted received some governmental funding. These included Columbus's Women Against Rape's Community Action Strategies to Stop Rape (Whittier 1995) and a Los Angeles rape prevention organization (Matthews 1994; U.S. House 1978:548). Groups like Columbus's Women Against Rape also received federal funding through the Victims of Crime Act and were also able to pay some employees through Comprehensive Employment and Training Act funds during the 1970s (Whittier 1995). Most of these funds dried up by the early 1980s. It was not until the passage of VAWA that federal funds began flowing again.

The discussion in the major early Congressional hearing on rape, in 1978, framed rape as an issue that was both social and criminal (Bevacqua 2000). For example, congressmen and witnesses debated whether the National Center for the Prevention and Control of Rape was properly housed in the National Institutes of Mental Health since, as Rep. Robert Walker (R-PA) said, this "has given it an aura that we're dealing with some kind of sexual perversion . . . rather than dealing with it as a violent crime" (U.S. House 1978:554). In response, the head of the NCPCR, Elizabeth Kutzke, replied that violent crime is "only one portion of the larger problem area," which also included "violent behaviors, sex role expectations . . ." (554). Two witnesses affiliated with grassroots feminist antiviolence organizations appeared at the 1978 hearing. Yolanda Bako, who was affiliated with the Women's Survival Space Center for Elimination of Violence in the Family in Brooklyn and NOW's Rape Prevention Committee showed the WAVAW slideshow on pornography (U.S. House 1978:625). While there was some debate between Bako and Rep. Schauer about whether all the images included in the slideshow were violent, this nevertheless represented an unprecedented entrance of the antipornography variety of anti-rape feminism into Congress. Carolyn Sparks of Columbus's Women Against Rape (which had received a large NCPCR grant) briefly summarized their prevention activities. Rep. Schauer asked her for a list of federal legislation she would recommend. She submitted a resolution from a rape workshop conducted as part of Ohio's 1977 organizing for International Women's Year that called for a wide range of both carceral and noncarceral initiatives, including funding for autonomous anti-rape groups, prevention programming, rehabilitation of rapists as a means of prevention, the elimination of the corruption of a minor as a criminal charge, and enhancing punishment by making convicted rapists ineligible for parole or reduced time due to good behavior (U.S. House 1978:663).[3] In contrast to this hearing, the feminist witnesses in VAWA hearings were from professionalized women's movement organizations that had established relationships with Democratic legislators, as we will see.

The National Center for Prevention and Control of Rape not only provided funding but also established a location within the federal bureaucracy for experts and activists on issues of violence against women that helped produce later institutionalized ties (Banaszak 2010). Although the NCPCR was first reduced and then eliminated over the course of the 1980s (Bevacqua 2000), the research it produced helped inform later federal and state policy on sexual assault. Domestic violence, the other major focus of VAWA, had less prior federal support to build on. Some funds went to domestic violence services through the Law Enforcement Assistance Agency, but legislative support was hard to come by. Despite feminists' efforts, legislation introduced in the 1980s and earlier to fund domestic violence shelters faced opposition from conservatives who feared that "funding battered women's shelters would lead to the family's disintegration" ("Symposium" 2010:517). The Reagan Justice Department even withdrew a federal grant to the National Coalition Against Domestic Violence in 1985, charging that it was a radical lesbian feminist organization ("Symposium" 2010:4).[4]

Despite funding shortages throughout the 1980s, by 1990, there were countless state and local organizations dealing with rape and domestic violence. These included battered women's shelters, rape crisis centers, and state-level advocacy and coordination groups (often called CASAs, for Coalition Against Sexual Assault). State and local government had specialized police units for domestic violence and rape, and many hospitals did as well. Mental health providers rounded out the field. (For excellent analysis of this field, see Corrigan 2013; Caringella 2009; Bevacqua 2000.) The number and size of such organizations certainly grew as a result of VAWA funding, which also encouraged connections between these service organizations and government institutions. But the size and integration of the field did not begin with VAWA and, in fact, helped produce the support for VAWA and eased its implementation.

Over time, the institutionalization of women's movement organizations' connections to Congress laid the ground work for the alliance between frenemies over VAWA. Feminists formed alliances with congressional members and staff and learned what resonated with Congress; lawmakers came to see the potential benefits of supporting anti-rape legislation as a means of attacking violent crime. When the overall federal focus on crime increased in the 1990s, along with women's movement organizations' lobbying and legal capabilities, VAWA resulted. The legal framework of Title III also connected back to the framing of pornography and violence against women as a civil rights matter through connections to Catherine MacKinnon's work and the work of MacKinnon's former law students on VAWA (Strebeigh 2009:365).[5] VAWA also connected to policy and advocacy around child sexual abuse, which was key in developing a criminal framework for federal intervention into sexual assault that applied to other forms of sexual violence as well, as we saw in Chapter 3.

Local anti-rape organizations were not highly involved in working for VAWA's passage. Most were absorbed in their day-to-day service work and were not highly politicized despite their origins in feminist organizing (Corrigan 2013). As a result, the tactics used to support VAWA were almost exclusively institutional—lobbying, behind-the-scenes coordination, and occasionally letter-writing campaigns. Similarly, although key leaders, like the presidents of NOW and of NOW-LDEF, brought their organizing and legal skills and institutional connections, they were not highly visible at the grassroots level. On the Right, there was very little coordinated work around VAWA or service provision around violence against women. No organizations were involved, and conservative opposition was confined to a few articles in secular publications without reaching the large and influential Religious Right. The institutionalized women's movement organizations and the institutionalized actors in Congress were the key players, and this shaped both the dynamics of their ambivalent alliance and the outcomes for VAWA.

FEMINIST COALITIONAL LEGISLATION

Hearings on VAWA began in 1990 in the Democratic-controlled Congress during George H. W. Bush's presidency. Joseph Biden, then chair of the Senate Judiciary Committee, proposed an initial version of what became VAWA. Biden's special counsel Victoria Nourse (herself a distinguished lawyer) and Sally Goldfarb of NOW-LDEF did much of the conceptual and organizing work and organized the hearings (Strebeigh 2009). Hearings occurred regularly in the House and Senate without passage until 1994, when VAWA passed the Democratic Senate and House with near-unanimous support and was signed by President Clinton. VAWA passed as part of the Omnibus Crime Act of 1994, but likely would have passed regardless since it enjoyed widespread support in both chambers; later reauthorizations in 2000 and 2006 also saw near-unanimous support.[6]

The feminists working for VAWA were grounded in an intersectional coalition. Biden's staffer Nourse, NOW's Helen Neuborne, and longtime women's movement organizer Pat Reuss assembled a multi-organization task force headed by Reuss to work for VAWA's passage (Strebeigh 2009). Although they ultimately became involved, few anti-rape or domestic violence organizations were engaged at the beginning (Corrigan 2013; Roe 2004). In fact, Neuborne recounted apathy and opposition from other "women's groups." In her telling, "They did not think that this was a big issue facing women . . . . Indeed, some of them were not sure they weren't going to oppose it because it would include criminal penalties against men who abused women" ("Symposium" 2010:515). Reuss also recounted difficulty mobilizing the major antiviolence groups, saying that the National Network to End Domestic Violence had no clear lobbying direction, the sexual assault movement could not afford its own lobbyist, and "victim's rights groups, God bless them. . . had never thought of victims of violence from the gender or feminist lens" ("Symposium" 2010:524). Likewise, Nourse recounted opposition from "both left and right" over issues like "overshadow[ing] other types of discrimination" and bias against men ("Symposium" 2010:522).

Ultimately, however, the task force included most major antiviolence and victims' rights groups, in addition to major national and local "civil rights, labor, religious, youth, and community organizations," the Girl Scouts, YWCA, and others ("Symposium" 2010:521, 528). The National Coalition Against Sexual Assault (NCASA) became involved early on and pushed for VAWA to address rape as well as domestic violence, according to NCASA president MaryBeth Carter (Bevacqua 2000:170). NCASA had significant leadership from Black women whom Richie (2012:150) describes as "relentlessly asserting a radical agenda within a rapidly mainstreaming movement." Task force members helped draft the legislation, organized and prepared congressional witnesses, and lobbied for passage. By all accounts, it was instrumental. After VAWA passed in 1994, the task force adopted the name the National Task Force to End Sexual and Domestic Violence Against Women and continued working to revise and promote the legislation. It remained coalitional as it formalized its organization and established a public presence.[7]

The Task Force's coalitional basis allowed it to broaden support for VAWA beyond traditional women's movement organizations or those focusing mainly on gender and to ensure that issues of immigration, race, sexuality, and other "not-explicitly-gendered policy issues" remained central to feminist advocates, a not uncommon strategy for women's organizations (Goss and Heaney 2010). The Task Force served as a typical "bridging organization" between the various parent movements of its members (Ferree and Roth 1998). Heaney and Rojas (2014) find that hybrid organizations are viewed as legitimate by activists when their identities and issues are seen as a legitimate combination. By the time the Task Force formed, conversations about intersectionality in feminism—and working relationships between women's and other movement organizations—were well developed, making the coalitional group seem logical.

Feminists working on VAWA were grounded in an intersectional approach that was both ideological and organizational. Reuss said she sought to make the Task Force as diverse as possible, aiming "to make sure that every voice and every need and every group is at the table . . . women of color, disabled women, older women, women in the military . . . women in the entertainment industry, women in media . . . . [I]nstead of us speaking for them, we're bringing them to the table" ("Symposium" 2010:528). Lisalyn Jacobs, formerly a staff member in the Federal Office of Violence Against Women, became the chair of the group working on the 2005 VAWA reauthorization, which sought broader provisions for immigrants, Native Americans, and others. She explained that "we figured out what other communities needed to be brought to the table" including "the elder communities, the rural communities, the communities of color, the immigrant communities" ("Symposium" 2010:577–78). As longtime immigration activist Leslie Orloff put it, the coalition included "people ... who hold us accountable and make sure that what we were crafting would really work for immigrant victims" as well as "incredibly strong mainstream allies" ("Symposium" 2010:582).[8] But translating intersectional feminism into law proved difficult, constrained by powerful existing discourses for understanding violence against women, sexual and intimate partner violence against immigrants, same-sex partners, transgender people, and Native Americans.

MEANING CONSTRUCTION IN CONGRESS: GENDERED CRIME

The hearings leading to initial passage of VAWA, between 1990 and 1994, constituted a major increase in attention to violence against women in Congress and a notable change from earlier periods. Building support among Republicans and many Democrats required extensive hearings, including in the district of key Republican Senator Orrin Hatch (in Salt Lake City), as well as in Nevada, Maine, and Boston. Holding Congressional hearings in legislators' home districts allows members of Congress to promote their work and build support among constituents, and could potentially sway them by presenting testimony from affected constituents. Because of the ideological diversity of the congressional coalition around VAWA, witnesses came from a wide range of perspectives. They were a mixture of advocates from nonprofits, shelters, researchers, police and prosecutors, and people who had personally experienced violence, often associated with one of the expert witnesses, such as a service provider or prosecutor, or a resident of the district of lawmakers whose support is needed.

The broad support that developed rested on a frame of gendered crime that emerged in the early 1990s hearings. It invoked both feminist and criminal justice discourses and let different constituencies oppose violence against women in ways consistent with their own ideologies. This frame shaped legislative possibilities, both enabling VAWA and limiting its scope. A gendered crime frame was compatible with a conservative understanding of rape and domestic violence as crimes made particularly heinous by the fact that they targeted women, and feminist views that violence against women was an especially virulent form of women's oppression. Politicians from both perspectives included congenial elements of the other frame, with feminists and liberals using the language of criminal justice alongside that of gender justice, and conservatives decrying the prevalence of violence against women while calling for tougher law enforcement. Little overt opposition emerged. Most of the disagreement over VAWA's components occurred offstage, as legislators negotiated funding levels, specific provisions, and trade-offs for support (Strebeigh 2009). But while this gendered crime frame for understanding violence against women was widely supported over time, intersectional feminist frames were more contested. Activists' goals and frames were refracted through existing discourses and structures in Congress that favored single-issue over intersectional models of gender, and criminal justice over other remedies, shaping both discourse about VAWA and the law itself.

Congressional Hearings, Witnesses, and Party Control

There were 31 committee hearings on VAWA from the first hearing in 1990 through 2013, with 241 witnesses. Figure 4.1 shows the number of hearings that occurred each year.

My analysis of frames draws from a subsample of 14 hearings.[9] Although cosponsors for all versions of VAWA included conservative Republicans and liberal Democrats, Republicans convened fewer hearings on VAWA than Democrats. Only 8 percent of the 31 hearings were held under Republican control, although Republicans controlled the House or Senate 52 percent of the time. Republicans also called fewer witnesses per hearing on average (6.5) than Democrats (7.9).[10] The difference in hearings and witnesses by party is only partly a result of the larger number of hearings held 1990–1994, when the bill was repeatedly introduced in the Democratic Congress. When VAWA came up for reauthorization in 1999–2000 and

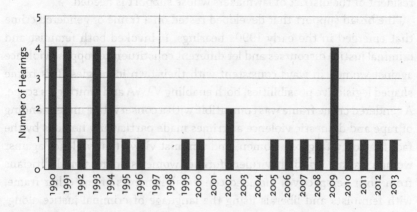

Figure 4.1 Number of Congressional Hearings on VAWA, 1990–2013

2005–2006, under Republican control, fewer hearings were held and fewer witnesses called. When Congress returned to Democratic control in 2007, the number of hearings and witnesses called increased again despite the fact that VAWA was not up for renewal until 2012.[11]

Despite their involvement behind-the-scenes, only six witnesses from NOW or the Task Force testified, at four hearings (all of which are in my qualitative sample), likely a strategic choice to make conservative support more palatable (Chen 2000). Despite conservative lawmakers' support, among all the hearings, no testimony supporting VAWA came from a witness affiliated with a conservative organization.[12] There is no mention of conservative organizations' involvement in any of the existing accounts of VAWA. Further, a list of endorsing organizations presented by House sponsor Barbara Boxer in 1992 included no conservative organizations.[13]

Sarah Soule and her coauthors (Soule and Olzak 2004; Soule and King 2006) show that, in the case of the Equal Rights Amendment, movement organizations were more likely to be called as witnesses early in the consideration of the issue. This was the case with VAWA, where feminist witnesses helped define the issues of domestic violence in the 1970s and 1980s. By the mid-1990s, feminist movement organizations were influential mostly behind the scenes. Service or advocacy organizations working on domestic violence or rape were a regular presence in almost every year, with generally increasing percentages as time went on. Often, these organizations arranged personal testimony by survivors of sexual and domestic violence. This testimony was most common and presumably most influential early in the consideration of VAWA, establishing the scope of the problem and the need for legislation. The majority of such witnesses were survivors of domestic violence; 20 of the survivor witnesses testified about assault by their husbands, compared to only 8 who testified about rape. Even though most domestic violence includes sexual assault, only two witnesses testified about spousal rape.[14] All except one of the survivors of rape testified between 1990 and 1993, early in the issue cycle.

Framing Violence Against Women as Gendered Crime

Gendered crime and crime were the major frames for understanding domestic violence and rape and were used by members of Congress or witnesses in *all* 14 hearings sampled.[15] Feminist frames, in contrast, were used in only six hearings. Overall, 83 percent of speakers, including witnesses and legislators, made statements that were coded as crime, gendered crime, feminist, or a combination of these.[16] Many speakers used more than one frame.

(The figures in the following discussion refer to the percentage of speakers whose statements in a given hearing drew on at least one of these frames.) Feminist frames were not used in the sampled hearings after 2000, that is, during the latter two reauthorizations.[17] Gendered crime and crime frames were used during all reauthorizations at varying rates. Gendered crime was used alone or in combination with other frames by 70 percent of speakers in 1990–1994, 33 percent in 1995–2000, 63 percent in 2001–2006, and 22 percent in 2007–2011. Crime frames were used by 54 percent, 63 percent, 38 percent, and 78 percent of speakers in these periods, respectively. Change over time in the use of gendered crime and crime frames in the hearings is not linear and does not correspond to Republican versus Democratic control of Congress. Further, the much smaller number of witnesses in the latter two reauthorization periods (8 and 9 respectively) in comparison with the first two periods (83 and 30 respectively) makes systematic comparison of frames problematic. I have thus combined hearings across time in the following analysis. Democrats, Republicans, witnesses from women's movement organizations, and witnesses from sexual and domestic violence organizations differed in the frames they used, but their points of overlap helped foster broad support for VAWA.

Crime frames discussed crimes against women as an instance of increasing violent crime in general, including the idea of an epidemic of violent crime, the need to crack down on crime, rising crime rates, and fear of juvenile offenders, all part of the general crime discourse of the 1990s. They emphasized that domestic violence and rape are common, part of a "violent crime epidemic" (U.S. Senate 1990a:19), and equated violence against women to other crimes. Republican Senator Charles Grassley, a cosponsor of the bill, exemplified this approach, decrying widespread "[c]rimes of violence, whether committed against an elderly pensioner or a child abused by a drug-addicted parent, or against women, [which are] the subject of this hearing" (U.S. Senate 1991a:3). Supporters called for greater law enforcement on the grounds that "batterers must be treated like the criminals that they are" (U.S. House 1994a:3). Republicans were the most frequent users of crime frames. The vast majority of Republicans used crime frames alone (55 percent) or in combination with other frames (75 percent), as did half of Democrats (33 percent used crime frames alone). Over half (56 percent) of witnesses from sexual or domestic violence organizations, such as shelters, used crime framing alone or in combination with other frames. For example, Beverly Dusso from the Harriet Tubman Center, a family violence service agency, used a crime frame to tout "the really positive effects of the tough new penalties assuring families necessary Federal protection" (U.S. Senate 1996a:45). No witnesses from women's movement organizations used crime frames. I therefore do not classify crime frames as carceral feminist, because they were not articulated by feminist organizations.

Some supporters used crime frames in later hearings to raise concern about whether the Democratic Clinton administration was sufficiently zealous in enforcing VAWA's criminal provisions. For example, at a 1996 hearing, Senate Subcommittee Chair Orrin Hatch (a key supporter of VAWA) challenged Attorney General Janet Reno, stating, "I am concerned that notwithstanding this administration's commitment to the *social* spending of the VAWA, its enforcement of the act's *criminal* provisions has been limited to only a handful of cases" (U.S. Senate 1996a:1; emphasis added).

Crime frames did not invoke a gender analysis. Whereas some conservative speakers may have eschewed a gender analysis on principle, promoting a broad crackdown on crime, some advocates for VAWA used gender-neutral crime frames to garner support for what could otherwise be dismissed as a matter of gender, not crime. As Maryland legislator Connie DeJuliis stated directly: "[T]his issue . . . is not a woman's issue . . . . It is a crime issue" (U.S. House 1994a:21). As with other crimes, the solution to violence against women in this frame was arrest, conviction, and long sentences. This was consistent with the crackdown on crime during the 1990s and 2000s.

In contrast, *feminist* frames were most common in testimony from women's movement organizations. To be classified as using a feminist frame, statements had to specifically reference gendered power or control or the effects of the gender system on perpetuating violence against women and not emphasize crime. All of the six witnesses from women's movement organizations used feminist frames, alone (33 percent) or combined with gendered crime (67 percent). For example, Kathryn Rodgers, director of NOW-LDEF, stated that the group was "committed to protecting women's rights, and trying to eradicate violence against women has been at the top of our agenda since our inception 26 years ago." She described goals including "creating a sea change in our cultural norms in this country" (U.S. Senate 1996a:75). Some service providers and survivors also used feminist frames, mainly when recounting personal narratives. For example, one witness explained, "my socialization led me to recognize that my worth as a woman would ultimately be measured by looking at the success and quality of my marriage and family. Violence was part of my marriage" (U.S. House 1994a:16). Six percent of witnesses from antiviolence organizations used feminist frames in combination with other frames, although none used only feminist frames.

Liberal lawmakers also sometimes drew from feminism to define violence as a mode of social control of women. None used only feminist frames, but 12 percent of Democrats and 3 percent of Republicans used them along with another frame. Democratic Senator Barbara Boxer's 1992 statement typifies this approach: "every day, women have given up their freedom . . . . I love to walk. But when night comes, I don't walk. I'm so angry about that fact. Look, I'm a Member of Congress and I'm afraid to walk six blocks from here" (U.S. House 1992a:13).

In a 1990 hearing, Biden acknowledged the connection to feminism directly, proclaiming, "I think the Women's movement has done a phenomenal service . . . one of the reasons why we are all here today . . . is because of the women's movement standing up and saying, 'Whoa, wait a minute.' They made women of my wife's generation say . . . stand by one another. It is not 'stand by my man,' it is 'I Am Woman'" (U.S. Senate 1990b:174). Overall, however, lawmakers, like witnesses from antiviolence organizations, rarely used feminist frames. The emphasis on gender much more often emerged in a hybrid understanding of violence against women as a gendered crime.

The *gendered crime* frame was capacious enough to justify broad support for VAWA and could be understood in terms of crime or feminism. Gendered crime frames included the importance of or need for law enforcement responses and/or statements reaffirming that violence against women is a crime *and* at least some claims promulgated by feminists, including the widespread occurrence of violence against women in the family, effects on women such as fear or restriction of activities, gender norms, or male domination (Corrigan 2013; Weldon 2002). Simply mentioning women is not enough to classify a statement as using a gendered crime frame, but stating that "too many women live in fear in their own homes" is. The gendered crime frame was broad, implicitly referencing different underlying ideas or discourses about gender, such as the chivalrous idea that women need better protection, the idea that women are dominated by men in a sexist society, or the need for less gender-biased law enforcement so that violence would not restrict women's freedom. The underlying idea that women's social position shapes crimes against them linked these diverse ideas. The crime frame can be considered "carceral" and the gendered crime frame "carceral feminist." Both emphasize the need for state punishment and enforcement but vary in their additional emphasis on gender.

Statements using a gendered crime frame varied in how much they emphasized crime (i.e., mandatory minimum sentencing, harsh punishment as just and a deterrent, the threat of crime) and gender (i.e., the structural and cultural circumstances shaping violence against women, and its effects on women as a group). Fifty-eight percent of all speakers employed a gendered crime frame in at least part of their testimony. Sixty-three percent of witnesses from antiviolence organizations used a gendered crime frame alone or in combination with other frames. Women who had been assaulted stressed how lack of enforcement and support services had affected them. For example, Yvette Benguerel recounted how law enforcement failed to intervene when her husband attempted to murder her and declared, "Women are not safe in this country, not even from the people they love" (U.S. House 1994a:14). Nicole Snow, who testified in 1990 about being date raped, asked, "Where was the education when I needed . . . the warnings? And where was it after, when I needed the validation of my experience?" (U.S. House 1994a:12). In contrast, she thanked the committee for taking a different approach: "I thank you for listening. I thank you for giving survivors the gift of knowing that you believe in us. That is why I am here today. You have the power to make a big difference. You have the power to make it less frightening for survivors and you have the power to make it a lot more frightening for rapists" (13).

Two-thirds of witnesses from women's movement organizations used the gendered crime frame, often at the same hearing where they also used feminist frames. For example, NOW's Helen Neuborne decried that the "epidemic of violence against women is depriving half of America's citizens of their most basic civil rights" (U.S. Senate 1990a:57). Similarly, 69 percent of Democratic legislators and 41 percent of Republicans used the gendered crime frame. Sen. Biden's statement that "rape is a crime of hate, not of sexual desire . . . battering is a crime of force, not of domestic discord . . . . These are crimes of terror. They instill fear not only in the actual survivors but in every woman in America" is typical (U.S. Senate 1991a:1). Speakers using a gendered crime frame cast arrest as changing the cultural acceptability of men's control over women. As Republican Representative Steven Schiff explained, domestic violence in the past "arose from a feeling that men owned their wives and could take any action they wanted to as virtual slave owners. But that is long past. It is time that enforcement of the law caught up with that" (U.S. House 1994a:5).

Law enforcement witnesses, who often headed sex crimes or domestic violence units, also often used a gendered crime frame to emphasize the role of gender inequality, decrying the "culturally entrenched" attitudes that support domestic violence, as a prosecutor in a Baltimore domestic violence unit put it (U.S. Senate 1990a:85). Like survivors, however, law enforcement personnel also drew on personal experience. For example, Sgt. Mark Wynn, from the Nashville Metropolitan Police, surprised the listeners with personal testimony: "Let there be no doubt I am a supporter of mandatory arrest for incidents of domestic violence! I have a dual perspective of this crime. One as a law enforcement officer; the other as a child survivor of ten (10) years of domestic violence. I might add during that time there were no protective laws, strong police policies. family violence shelters, batterers programs, understanding judges, determined prosecutors or concerned law makers" (U.S. House 1994a:25).

Witnesses' personal testimony apparently made an impact on lawmakers. For example, Orrin Hatch praised the bravery of a panel of women (including one longtime friend of his) who recounted their experience of domestic violence:

> [I want to give] special acknowledgement . . . to the women on the first panel, the witnesses who showed so much courage in coming forward to share their own testimony. Their testimony . . . demonstrates the reality of our problem, and that is that statistics have faces . . . . I was very moved by their testimony. (U.S. Senate 1993a)

Indeed, Nourse told Biden "that Hatch had actually been moved to tears while listening to some of his constituents testify to the pain and humiliation they'd suffered" (Biden 2007:277.). As David Meyer (2005:18) points out, this kind of "conversion" that comes from "exposing recalcitrant legislators to the power of a movement's ideas" can alter legislative calculus, regardless of whether the conversion is genuine. In addition, conservative lawmakers with prior experience in law enforcement or the justice system brought their own observations to the table. For example, Strom Thurmond related his experience as a judge, including hearing two incest cases, and concluded, "I am just sick and tired of seeing these women battered and children abused like they are, and anything we can do we ought to do it" (U.S. Senate 1990b:165). Personal experiences came into play as well, as in Republican Sensenbrenner's opening statement in a 1992 hearing, "I know this is a serious issue because my wife, before we were married, was the victim of an assault against her, and she still bears the scars from that assault 20 years after the fact" (U.S. House 1990a). As with the child sexual abuse hearings, legislators often thanked witnesses for sharing their personal experiences and praised their bravery in sharing them.

Exchanges across ideological lines, particularly between conservative Republicans and supporting witnesses, provide insight into the dialogic process of constructing and debating the meaning of violence against women. For example, Strom Thurmond questioned a witness after arriving late to the hearing; he had apparently read her testimony beforehand.

THURMOND: I understand you were abused, were you?
BUEL: I was, yes.
THURMOND: You are now a prosecutor?

BUEL: I am.

THURMOND: I want to commend you for your spunk and will to keep on keeping on.

BUEL: I could not have done it without the battered women's movement.

THURMOND: What is that?

BUEL: I say I am a product of the battered women's movement in this country. I could not have escaped and I could not have had the empowerment and the support to go to school . . . and the funding for their shelters is crucial to empower other battered women to achieve their dreams.

THURMOND: Well, I am proud of you, the way you have not let it get you down, and that you continued.

BUEL: Thank you, Senator (U.S. Senate 1990b).

While Thurmond emphasized Buel's personal qualities of "spunk" and "will," she focused on collective and political forces. Both perspectives led to support for VAWA, but the underlying analysis of violence against women as an individual problem to be overcome through personal perseverance or a social problem to be overcome through movement organizing reflects very different worldviews and potential solutions.

As the Act was implemented and unfolded, some conservative congresspeople amplified their initial statements of support to connect to their overall political agendas. For example, Orrin Hatch explained in 1999, "I am concerned that the whole issue of violence against women is being misperceived as only a women's issue, even a feminist issue . . . . Domestic and sexual violence is, of course, first about women, since they are most often the victims of it, but it is also about children growing up in an atmosphere of violence and abuse. It is about family and it is about our most basic values as a people; that is, decency and respect" (U.S. Senate 1996a:15).[18] Hatch here was defending his reputation as a conservative by making it clear that he did not support VAWA because of its feminist associations but because of his support for family values. But most maintained the hybrid gendered crime frame. Republican Connie Morella, a chief sponsor of VAWA in the House, emphasized how legislation could improve victims' lives and emotional state in a typical statement:

The Violence Against Women Act of 1994 has created funds for many critical programs for women and children that have raised awareness and given women safe alternatives over the past 5 years . . . . Through these efforts fewer women live their lives ashamed, guilty, and scared . . . . these grants and programs are giving victims a second chance. The crimes of domestic violence and child abuse cannot be tolerated in our society. (U.S. House 1999:46–47)

Morella's emotionally loaded language and praise of VAWA's pragmatic effects, linked with the reminder that domestic violence and child sexual abuse were crimes, were sufficient justification for her support.

The gendered crime frame was compatible with the other frames because, like the crime frame, it drew on crime discourse about the need for increased enforcement against violent crime, and, like both crime and feminist frames, it sought to include violence against women—including in the home—as a violent crime. Even lawmakers and witnesses who did not use the gendered crime frame could and did agree with those who did. The gendered crime frame was widely used outside Congress as well, but the focus on crime remained striking. For example, Hillary Clinton held an event at the White House to promote VAWA's reauthorization in 2000 that reflected the incorporation of crime both structurally and discursively. Structurally, the event was attended by police officers and speakers including a woman sheriff, a state attorney general, and an organizer of a state domestic violence coalition. Discursively, Clinton spoke about violence against women as "not just a women's issue. It's a family issue—and a criminal issue."[19] Republican officials' support for VAWA was generally similar. For example, the secretary for Health and Human Services under Republican President Bush, Tommy Thompson, told the Advisory Committee for the Office on Violence Against Women: "Violence against women harms more than just its direct victim. It also harms the children, the abuser, the entire health of all of our families and communities. And for the health of our country, it's critical that we stop this cycle now."[20] The gendered crime frame signified a cultural change that incorporated the violence women experience into the definition of crime. This entailed, and relied on, speaking out about what had been silent and stigmatized experiences, as with child sexual abuse. In this sense, the frame's ascendance was a success of the women's movement, even as it also narrowed the meaning of violence against women to crime rather than patriarchal and racial power (Freedman 2013; Richie 2012).

Quiet Opposition to Gendered Crime Framing

The concern with undermining the family through domestic violence and marital rape legislation, as well as concern about promoting divorce, hedonism, departure from religion, and infringing on men's rights in custody and divorce, could not be stated directly by the 1990s. However, occasionally it surfaced more obliquely, sometimes in conservative media coverage (discussed later) and more rarely in Congress. For example, the conservative Heritage Foundation's Patrick Fagan subtly raised these critiques in nominally favorable testimony during the 1999–2000 VAWA reauthorization. Although he described "this work" as "very difficult and very needed," he had "a major criticism of the whole framing . . . where the bill is heading." The problem, in his view, was that weakened families led to child abuse and, in turn, to domestic violence. He blamed "a culture of alienation and rejection that is deep within the family and deep between the sexes in America." Because "the traditional family is the safest place for the child . . . by far," he advocated a bill that supported a "deliberate strategy of rebuilding families and communities of care," that would center on "the house of faith with which the person identifies, because that brings them into close contact with neighbors, who are particularly sometimes the very thing you need, somebody to talk with about the abuse that maybe even is beginning to happen, before it gets really bad." In direct opposition to the approaches at the center of VAWA funding, he opposed most mental health practitioners because "they are more antagonistic toward faith-based" work (U.S. House 1999:116, 123, 124), and he did not emphasize criminal justice solutions either. Given the widespread acceptance of the idea that the federal government should pass legislation about violence against women, even Fagan could not oppose that without seeming to favor sexual or domestic violence, an untenable position. Instead, he professed concern about the issue but suggested that VAWA's approach—increased law enforcement and funding for support services for victims—would not work as well as an approach that emphasized the role of religious institutions and the "traditional" family.

Fagen's approach drew little support. Similarly, when other witnesses' frames drew on marginalized discourses, their remarks received little response from members of Congress. M. L. Carr, a former basketball star, appeared at a 2005 hearing, representing the Family Violence Prevention Fund and his own mentoring and prevention program for boys (WARM2Kids). He directly disputed the criminal justice approach, saying, "We can no longer be satisfied with locking people up and saying they didn't get away with it . . . . We must end violence before it starts" (U.S. Senate 2005:24). Carr praised the proposed VAWA funds for prevention. Other than general praise for WARM2Kids and extensive joking about basketball fandom, Carr's remarks received no follow-up, and the discussion after the witness panel remained imbued with a criminal justice focus.

Concern over government spending and expansion of federal power was a more significant strand of opposition both inside and outside Congress.

Chief Justice Rehnquist, whose Supreme Court ultimately overturned Title III, charged that Title III would illegitimately make what should be a state or local concern a federal one, would overload federal courts, and he lobbied for opposition from state and federal associations of judges (Strebeigh 2009:353, 389). As the initial VAWA was being debated, Orrin Hatch and others in Congress raised similar questions about whether Title III infringed on states' rights by providing a federal course of action for offenses that were the province of state law. They were ultimately persuaded to support Title III as it was defined more narrowly and after testimony and reports documented bias in rape charges in many state courts. Others, including most prominently the ACLU, raised concerns over whether a defendant's reading of sexist material (such as pornography) might be evidence of his "gender animus" under Title III, thus infringing on First Amendment rights. This question resonated with the conflict between MacKinnon—the theoretical architect of Title III—and the ACLU over pornography. It underscores the lasting effects of the pornography conflict on other issues of sexual violence. The ACLU did not formally oppose VAWA (U.S. House 1993b) and supported later reauthorizations. But even after the *Morrison* decision overturning Title III, questions about federal spending and authority continued to dog conservative supporters. In the 2005 reauthorization hearings, Hatch defended the law against this critique in his opening statement:

> As a conservative, I understand the limits on Federal power . . . . But domestic violence remains a serious criminal issue that demands a limited Federal response. When people live in fear, when they are not safe in their own homes, when they have to worry about their children growing up in a violent atmosphere, we do not keep the promise of America. We cannot turn our backs on these vulnerable communities, and we should never turn our backs on the small and the weak.[21]

Hatch's statement was almost exclusively framed in terms of crime. The only gender reference was a coded, paternalistic one to "the small and the weak."

Other frames circulated outside Congress, including what Berns (2001) calls the patriarchal-resistance perspective, which denies the prevalence of violence against women. Sen. Biden often referred to the "hate mail" he received from men and "very fundamentalist churches" (U.S. Senate 1996a:50). But these alternative frames never appeared in witness testimony or lawmakers' statements. Even Title III, which was not universally supported, provoked open debate only over whether it was constitutional or would overload federal courts, not over whether violence against women should be conceptualized as an issue of women's rights (U.S. House 1993b; Strebeigh 2009). Public opinion and deal-making in Congress certainly influenced the contents and passage of VAWA, but the gendered crime frame was crucial. Because it could be interpreted broadly and brought together feminist and crime frames, it enabled lawmakers from diverse ideological positions to support VAWA. Provisions regarding immigration and Native Americans were another story.

Despite widespread rhetorical support and votes for VAWA, appropriating the authorized funds was never a sure thing and never complete. In 1996, Senators Orrin Hatch and Arlen Specter worked in the Republican-controlled Congress to secure votes to fund the newly reauthorized act, and they succeeded in part, but some sections remained underfunded. As Lisalyn Jacobs, who worked on lobbying for the 1995 VAWA, as well as working as an early staff person in the OVW, said in 2010, "Congress looked at a very lengthy list of new programs that we presented to it with the reauthorization and said to us, 'Pick five.' A number of these new programs from 2006 still have not received their initial funding." These included the "Sexual Assault Services Program and the National Resource Center that deals with the impact of domestic and sexual violence on the workplace" ("Symposium" 2010:578).

While quiet opposition remained, especially to VAWA provisions that were more closely aligned with feminism, such as studying judges' gender bias, by the 1990s the old concern about undermining the family, promoting divorce, hedonism, and secularism had moved outside the prevailing discourse.[22] In a short time, the discourse about violence against women had shifted.

MOVEMENT INFLUENCE AND HORSE-TRADING: COALITIONS INSIDE CONGRESS

Congresspeople and VAWA advocates sometimes directly acknowledged the maneuvering that led to the bipartisan coalition in favor of the law. Speaking in 2010, Pat Reuss acknowledged, "The Violence Against Women Act wasn't all we wanted it to be. We had some powerful opponents . . . . You don't want to hear about some of this stuff we traded away, you don't want to hear about what Joe Biden promised a member of the House conference committee—I was sitting there next to him and it was something for his brother and I went oh la, la, la, la" ("Symposium" 2010:9). According to Biden, Republican Senator Phil Gramm challenged the inclusion of

Title III at the last minute, but cosponsor Orrin Hatch told Gramm, "Joe's worked very hard on this. And we've got to remember he cares about this. It's a good bill" (Biden 2007:278). Biden and Gramm agreed that Gramm would support VAWA if Biden would agree to cover the cost of the crime bill by reducing the size of the federal work force. In fact, President Clinton did downsize the federal work force, providing VAWA's funding (Biden 2007:279).

Routine lobbying was also important. Pat Reuss explained that Connie Morella, their "sole Republican" sponsor in the House, worked closely with her: "About once a month, she took a call from me and I gave her marching orders and they mostly involved calling Orrin Hatch," the Republican leader of the Senate effort. When judges lobbied against the bill, led by Chief Justice Rehnquist, the women's judges association lobbied in favor (Strebeigh 2009; "Symposium" 2010:525). This continued with reauthorization and funding efforts. For example, in a 1996 hearing, Sen. Biden acknowledged that Sen. Hatch's successful effort to restore full funding for VAWA meant that he "took on his party, took a lot of grief for doing it, as did Senator Spector," and praised Hatch for being "so effective that the person who voted to delete the funding in the appropriation committee asked to cosponsor the amendment restoring funding" (U.S. Senate 1996a:12). Similarly, in 2005 when Hatch was defending VAWA against conservative critics, he noted, "VAWA has always been bipartisan legislation, but when it first became law, there was not as much conservative engagement with the issue as there is today. I am glad to see that groups of varying political stripes are becoming involved in this issue" (U.S. Senate 2005:22).

Conservative members of Congress sometimes readily admitted—and joked about—their unexpected common ground with feminists. For example, in a 1996 hearing, Orrin Hatch, who chaired the newly Republican Senate Judiciary Committee, introduced NOW-LDEF's Kathryn Rodgers by saying, "Ms. Rodgers, you and I do not necessarily agree on every issue—I only say that to protect you—but on the matter of violence against women, we have found a great deal of common ground." Rodgers, in turn, joked, "I would also like to say that I am unhappy to acknowledge all the issues that we agree on" (U.S. Senate 1996a:59).

Even the sole conservative witness supporting VAWA emphasized the importance of coalition. William Schenck, a prosecutor from Ohio who represented the National Organization for Victim Assistance (NOVA) stated:

> I am aware that I'm unlike most of your other witnesses. I am a white male, over
> 40, an accident of birth I keep trying to live with as best I can. I am a conserv-
> ative, a Republican, I've been a leader in the President's election campaign in

my State. I'm an elected official. I suppose then in some ways my presence here says a lot about the victims' movement. . . . With this bill . . . traditional notions of party and ideology have and must continue to be superseded by broader, traditional ideals of compassion and justice. On behalf of NOVA and for the nationwide coalition—tongue in cheek—of "bleeding heart conservatives and hard-nosed liberals" which this organization represents, I thank you for placing women victims of criminal violence on your reform agenda. (U.S. House 1992a)

Another indication of horse-trading in Congress is the larger bills to which VAWA was attached. In 1994, for example, it was a component of the Omnibus Crime Act. In the Republican Congress of 2000, the reauthorization of VAWA was contained as part of the House Victims of Trafficking and Violence Prevention Act and parts of VAWA had been passed in 1998 by the Senate as an amendment to the Child Protection and Sexual Predators Punishment Act of 1998.[23] These were all larger bills that contained numerous elements to ensure broad support and—equally important—that they would actually come to a vote (Biden 2007). Certainly public opinion and political deal-making in Congress influenced the passage of VAWA in 1994. But the gendered crime frame established during the 1990s was also crucial because it enabled both conservatives and liberals to support VAWA from within their own ideological stances and political priorities. Provisions around immigration and LGBT people were another story.

THE 2012 REAUTHORIZATION FIGHT: THE COALITION IN CONGRESS BREAKS DOWN

When VAWA was due for reauthorization in 2011, Congress was highly polarized along party lines, and the Radical Right Tea Party was mobilized inside and outside Congress. For the first time, the bill failed as Republicans and Democrats passed competing versions in the House and Senate. The key distinctions between the bills were visas for battered immigrants, whether LGBT people would be included as an underserved population, and issues affecting Native Americans.[24] The dispute was not over the acceptance of the gendered crime frame, but over these intersectional feminist issues. Both Republicans and Democrats used crime and gendered crime frames for understanding VAWA, even as they took opposing positions on the legislation. Even Republicans who opposed or weakened the bill continued to state their opposition to crime against women. They relied on the gendered crime frame to justify their support for the competing bill. For example, Iowa's Republican Senator Marc Crapo, speaking at a press conference about the unsuccessful reauthorization of the 2011 bill he cosponsored, said, "These dollars go directly to woman and children who have been victimized by domestic violence . . . . The reauthorization of VAWA provides critical services to these victims of violent crime, as well as agencies and organizations who provide important aid to those individuals."[25] Similarly, Rep. Smith (2012) stated that the Republican "bill authorizes hundreds of millions of dollars for valuable services to victims of domestic violence, dating violence, sexual assault, and stalking. Those who have supported VAWA in the past should be eager to support this legislation today." Democrats, meanwhile, framed their bill's disputed provisions around immigration and Native American tribal procedures as gendered crime or crime. Many Democrats made statements similar to Rep. Nancy Pelosi (2012), who said that the Republican bill "fails . . . Native American women, and immigrant victims. All people deserve to be protected from domestic violence."

Instead of disputing the idea of gendered crime, conservatives used frames of opposition to immigration reform and Native American sovereignty as a way of justifying their opposition to VAWA while proclaiming ongoing concern for violence against women. They opposed the provisions on immigration and tribal courts with claims about immigration fraud and constitutional limitations to Native American jurisdiction. Even longtime conservative supporters voted against the bill in 2012. The Senate version, endorsed by the Task Force, passed with only 15 Republicans voting yes. The Republican-controlled House passed its bill, opposed by the Task Force, along party lines, without the disputed provisions regarding immigration, Native Americans, and LGBT nondiscrimination.

Unfortunately for conservative opponents of VAWA, the reauthorization fight took place in the midst of the 2012 elections, during which Democrats effectively charged Republicans of waging a "war on women," and Republican candidates made a series of public remarks that seemed to minimize the problem of rape. Rep. Hank Johnson (D-GA) (2012) charge in the House hearing that the Republican bill "should be renamed WAWA, or 'War Against Women Act.' [Because it] . . . rolls back existing protections and is simply shocking in its callousness towards women and victims of abuse" illustrates this effective rhetoric. Similarly, Rep. Grijalva (2012) said, "Republicans have decided to use this non-partisan issue to push their war on women further than many of us thought possible. This new bill says that if a Native American or immigrant—documented or not—is the victim of abuse, the government should turn a blind eye." Opposition to VAWA fit neatly within this narrative, and a sizeable gender gap contributed to Democratic victories across the ticket. Conservative congresspeople were in a discursive bind: they argued that VAWA's provisions for marginalized groups were about separate issues, not gendered crime, but liberal lawmakers and feminists amplified the gender discourse and public opinion agreed. After the 2012 elections, VAWA, including the Native American provisions and some expansions regarding immigration ultimately passed, with much less Republican support than in previous years (Gray 2013; Keen 2013).[26] The divide reflected long-standing barriers to intersectional feminist frames and the issues they invoked.

BARRIERS TO INTERSECTIONAL FEMINISM

Over time, feminists sought to expand VAWA's components. While reauthorizations and expansions that could be understood through the hybrid gendered crime frame were uncontroversial, those that could not squeeze into that discourse faced opposition. Feminist advocates' growing intersectional agenda, focused on specific issues affecting immigrants, people of color, LGBT people, and Native Americans, increasingly faced barriers. VAWA expanded in several uncontroversial ways that were readily understood through the gendered crime discourse. For example, stalking, readily understood as a form of violence against women, was included in VAWA from the beginning, but revisions expanded both the definition of stalking and the possible interventions against it. Yet other than including it in the list of crimes that speakers deplored, and personal testimony from one woman who had been stalked, there was no discussion of stalking and certainly no controversy.[27] The same was true for dating violence.

The women's movement organizations working for VAWA sought to expand and improve services like culturally appropriate shelters and advocacy to better address the specific needs of women of color, immigrants, youth, and the elderly, LGBT, low income, rural, and disabled people, and others who are marginalized by government and mainstream services (Crenshaw 1991; Gillum 2009; Weldon 2002). Framing these changes in terms of "underserved populations," the Task Force wrote incentives into the original bill for organizations to develop specialized programming. Leslie Orloff reported that Biden's staffer Nourse "literally handed me the bill and said, 'Tell us what we need to include to help immigrant, native women and women of color victims.' I . . . created the first draft of the underserved victim definition of VAWA. We . . . wrote access for underserved victims into the bill everywhere we could think of" ("Symposium" 2010:581).

Underserved populations were not specifically listed but could include people of color, immigrants, rural residents, non-native-English speakers, the elderly, people with disabilities, LGBT people, and Native Americans.[28] While the term "underserved populations" could imply simply including excluded groups, advocates understood these provisions through an intersectional, not simply additive, lens. For example, a Task Force fact sheet explained that underserved groups faced "unique challenges, reluctance to seek support, and few gateways to services" and that "victims often look for assistance from programs in their neighborhoods such as youth centers, senior centers, immigrant and cultural organizations . . . designed to specifically serve the community with which the victim identifies" (Lovelace 2012).

Congressional hearings, however saw little intersectional feminist framing, even from advocates, and little discussion of underserved populations, who were addressed mainly through the Office of Violence Against Women's administrative and grant procedures (Chen 2000). Despite conservative opposition to the 2012 clause prohibiting discrimination in services against LGBT people, there was no discussion of LGBT issues in subcommittee hearings. The only issues addressed at length were immigration and Native American issues, which often were framed as separate from violence against women, rather than intersectionally or as gendered crime, and were administratively separated from the rest of VAWA through congressional committee structure.

Immigration

Activists focusing on immigration emphasized how immigration status, ethnicity, language, class, and gender affected victims and sought measures protecting immigrant women from deportation if they reported domestic violence or sexual abuse (Ammar et al. 2005; Bierria 2007). From the beginning, VAWA included some protections against deportation for immigrants in these situations. The inclusion of such measures came directly from the intersectional feminist coalition pushing for VAWA, which included the National Network to End Violence Against Immigrant Women and several other immigrant women's groups. Leslye Orloff, who was a founder of Ayuda, a DC-based immigrant legal services group, formed the National Network to End Violence Against Immigrant Women in 1991 with NOW-LDEF and several other lawyers and groups working with immigrant women. Orloff explained that

> we worked through the National Network to End Violence Against Immigrant
> Women and the National VAWA Task Force to refine the language and to gain

consensus among all of the women's groups that this was the right thing to do. Once we garnered consensus we took that language back to Victoria Nourse and Senator Biden who took the lead in making sure that . . . the bill would be inclusive and would serve all victims including immigrant and women of color victims. ("Symposium" 2010:581)

Although the Task Force included strong advocates for immigrant women, including immigration provisions in the law was difficult because of the political opposition to any loosening on immigration among Republicans. Orloff recounted how Biden had told advocates early on that they must get Republican support for the immigration components if they were to be included in the bill. Although the "immigration protections have been some of the hardest ones to secure," they did secure bipartisan support, but for lesser protections than they sought ("Symposium" 2010:520).

As VAWA was revised during each reauthorization, provisions for immigrant women increased somewhat. While fairly narrow in scope (Bhuyan 2008), they nevertheless led to sizable numbers of visas granted, as well as the International Marriage Broker Regulation Act (IMBRA), included in the 2006 VAWA.[29] Tahirih, an activist legal center for immigrant women, described itself as "the lead drafter and advocate" for IMBRA in a "coalition of over 200 organizations—representing diverse political, religious, and cultural communities."[30] Legislation like the Women Immigrant Safe Harbor Act permitted access by "immigrant victims of violence against women" to public assistance benefits ("Symposium" 2010:591).

According to Shana Chen's (2000) interviews with participants, activists strategically decided to have antiviolence activists take a more public role than immigration activists in congressional testimony and lobbying in an attempt to bypass conservative opposition to immigration reform. That is, advocates sought to frame the provisions in terms of gendered crime, not immigration. Very little direct discussion about immigration occurred in the hearings leading up to VAWA's initial passage.

In contrast to the minimal differences in frames used by Republican and Democratic lawmakers and feminist witnesses in most VAWA hearings, differences were stark in the case of immigration. *Intersectional frames* were infrequent and were used only by witnesses from advocacy or service organizations and occasional Democratic legislators. For example, Beverly Dusso of the Harriet Tubman Center argued, "The horrors these families face are well beyond typical language and economic barriers. They have the added threats and retaliation and retribution that can be brought to bear through their deportation or losing their children" (U.S. Senate 1996a:46). Leslye Orloff explained succinctly, "control over immigration status, intimidation, isolation with language, cultural barriers, all accentuate the ability to abuse" (U.S. House 2000a:74). Supportive language was sometimes additive, as when a witness from a Florida shelter explained that "immigrant women have special issues. They suffer even more fears, more threats, intimidation and isolation than their American sisters" (U.S. House 2000a:65). The underlying analysis, however, was consistently intersectional, as witnesses emphasized how immigration status, gender, economic marginalization, and national origin together shaped distinct experiences of abuse (Chen 2000; National Network on Behalf of Battered Immigrant Women n.d.; National Task Force to End Sexual and Domestic Violence 2013).

In contrast, Republican lawmakers used only narrow *immigration frames* that did not focus on violence against women, raising objections to any path to legal status for undocumented immigrants and concern over whether VAWA would lead to loopholes and fraud and "open the floodgates" (U.S. House 2000a). For example, House Immigration Subcommittee Chair Lamar Smith worried that expanding protections could "open up our immigration system to widespread fraud as criminal and illegal aliens learn that the way to defeat our immigration laws is simply to claim to be battered" (U.S. House 2000a:24). Opposing witness Dwayne Austin, a former INS official, made the discursive stakes clear as he tried to shift the frame from battered women to immigration, stating: "Any professional public affairs practitioner would tell you that it is unwise, if not foolhardy, to come in here and testify against a bill entitled Protection of Battered Women," but he nevertheless declared that the bill would be "an instrument of fraud" (U.S. House 2000a:46). Similarly in 2012, opponents charged that the U visa and other VAWA provisions were vulnerable to fraud by illegal immigrants. Supporters worked in vain to refocus on a discourse of crime, emphasizing the terrible plight of women who depended on their batterer for legal residency and the importance of the U visa for law enforcement to "help get a rapist off the streets" (Shurtleff and Gansler 2012). In the same vein, Democratic Rep. Conyers (a supporter of the bill) asked an INS witness to reassure the "nervous nellies in Congress" whether the bill would "open the door for everybody to make excuses that my spouse battered me and beat me up and so now I want to become a citizen?" (U.S. House 2000a:45). But Republican Senator Charles Grassley (2012), who had championed earlier VAWAs, said plainly, "We cannot allow people to misuse the VAWA self-petitioning process to obtain a green card."

Opposition to expansion of public assistance to battered immigrants (TANF, food stamps, and other such benefits) also animated debate. The discourse around this opposition mirrored the discourse around public assistance in general. For example, Democratic Rep. Sheila Jackson Lee, who strongly supported the bill in the hearing, questioned witness Maria Ortiz about becoming self-sufficient, asking, "you suffered in isolation as a battered spouse and an immigrant . . . . You are now . . . gainfully employed. You have regained your dignity. Explain how this legislation ties into that and to refute the fear that all we are doing is bringing in more people to be on public assistance." Embarrassingly, Ortiz (who ran a shelter in Immokalee, Florida, and was herself a survivor of domestic violence) informed Lee that she herself was not an immigrant, before explaining the experiences of immigrant women.

Strikingly, only Democrats and supporting witnesses used gendered crime and crime frames in discussions of violence against immigrant women, not Republicans. Advocates attempted to gain Republican votes by framing protections for immigrant women in terms of gendered crime, emphasizing the importance of the visas for law enforcement and protecting women. For example, Orloff argued that "battered immigrant women, when they cannot get out of abusive relationships, cannot call the police, cannot get help . . . their abusers essentially are immune from prosecution" (U.S .House 2000a:58). Democratic lawmakers or advocates used immigration frames only to debate or reassure their Republican colleagues, never to challenge the immigration provisions of VAWA.

Unlike other aspects of VAWA, neither gender nor crime frames defined congressional debate over immigration provisions. Despite Democrats' and advocates' attempts to frame the immigration provisions in terms of gender and/or crime, Republicans opposed them using rather a separate and narrower immigration discourse, in which the provisions were framed as being about immigration, not violence against women. Further reinforcing the separation of the issue, the only hearing with extended discussion of immigration occurred in the Subcommittee on Immigration (U.S. House 2000a). The discursive and institutional separation of immigration and gendered crime in Congress left advocates with little leverage. Supporters, unable to frame immigrants' particular circumstances as a matter of violence against women rather than immigration, could not gain enough Republican votes without compromising their demands. Most activists saw the resulting requirements for successful petitions as too narrow and inadequately addressing the needs of women of color and immigrant women Ammar et al. 2005; Berger 2009; Bhuyan 2008; National Network on Behalf of Battered Immigrant Women n.d.; National Task Force to End Sexual and Domestic Violence 2013; Richie 2012; ("Symposium" 2010; Villalon 2010). But by 2012, the political climate around immigration was polarized, with intense partisan debate over immigration reform. Because immigration was framed as a separate issue, not as a force shaping violence against women, opposition to immigration reform easily carried over into opposition to VAWA.

Protections for Native Americans

Similarly, issues affecting Native American women were an intersectional matter for advocates, but a separate issue for Congress, particularly opponents. Native American women experience high rates of domestic violence and sexual assault and minimal law enforcement or social service response. Tribal lands have an autonomous but underfunded police and court system, and are subject to federal rather than state criminal law (Deer 2006). At issue, especially in the 2012 reauthorization, were assaults committed on reservations by non-Indians. Tribal police and courts did not have the authority to arrest or prosecute non-Indian offenders, such as spouses of Native women, and federal and state authorities rarely prosecuted crimes committed on reservations.

Discussion of violence against Native American women occurred mainly in a 2007 hearing in the Senate Committee on Indian Affairs. It focused on the high rate of violence and the jurisdictional issues that stymie prosecution of non-Native offenders. There was universal denunciation of violence against Native American women, framed in terms of crime by both Republican and Democratic legislators and all the witnesses at the hearing. For example, a witness from Amnesty International explained how jurisdictional and funding inadequacies "delay and prolong the process of investigating and prosecuting crimes of sexual violence" (U.S. Senate 2007:7). Two witnesses from Native American women's organizations also put forward an intersectional analysis, emphasizing indigenous cultural values and practices. For example, Tammy Young, the director of the Alaska Native Women's Coalition, described her group's approach as based on "our customary and traditional ways," explaining that the priority was not just for services to survivors of violence but for "all of our family members . . . to be provided services . . . is what in some ways sets us apart from non-Native agencies" (U.S. Senate 2007:25). The Task Force put forth a similar intersectional analysis in its fact sheets, which called for "preventative cultural practices," "holistic rehabilitation . . . for victims and violent offenders," and "[e]lders' panels and tribal drug courts to restore an Indian sense of justice and fairness" (National Task Force to End Sexual and Domestic Violence 2012).

There was little overt disagreement in the 2007 hearing, which did not lead to a vote. Dispute emerged behind-the-scenes leading up to the 2012 reauthorization however. As with immigration, controversy developed not over violence against women, but because of long-standing single-issue disagreements over tribal jurisdiction. Supporting legislators, speaking in Congress in 2012, framed the issue in terms of gendered crime. For example, Rep. Pelosi (2012) touted the "provisions designed to protect Native American women from sexual and domestic violence," and Rep. Johnson (2012) stated outright, "Native American women, they are women, too." In contrast, opponents framed the issue narrowly in terms of tribal sovereignty and the infringement of accused non-Indians' constitutional rights. For example, Republican Sen. Kyl (2012) said, "Adding this language to the existing law violates basic principles of equal protection and due process." Sen. Coburn (2012) decried the fact that the bill "explicitly provides that the self-governance of a tribe includes the right 'to exercise special domestic violence criminal jurisdiction over all persons'" The problem for him was that "[t]o my knowledge, this is the first time the Federal Government has given Indian courts jurisdiction over 'all persons.'" Congressional committee structure further contributed to the separation of the issue from gendered crime. The only two hearings on the topic leading up to the 2012 reauthorization, including the 2007 hearing discussed earlier, were held in the Senate Committee on Indian Affairs. No extended discussion of Native American women occurred in the general VAWA hearings.

Services for LGBT people

Task Force advocates had long sought to extend services to people in same-sex relationships, both as a matter of equity and in the belief that marginalization based on sexual or gender identity compounded the risks of domestic violence and sexual assault. Task Force members included several municipal LGBT groups and the National Gay and Lesbian Task Force, and had a subcommittee focused on "LGBT Provisions" of VAWA. While grants to organizations serving LGBT people and the inclusion of LGBT people as an underserved group in funded grants had not been controversial previously, opposition arose over a clause in the 2012 VAWA barring discrimination by programs receiving VAWA funds on the basis of sexual orientation or gender identity.[31] Republicans also sought to drop LGBT people from the list of underserved populations (Keen 2013). As with immigration and Native American jurisdiction, debate over the LGBT nondiscrimination clause drew on discourse and tensions around lesbian and gay rights rather than the gendered crime discourse. However, no opponents spoke about the LGBT provisions in either House or Senate floor debates over the bill.

Supporters in Congress drew on discourses about sexual orientation and emphasized the similarity between LGBT people and others, which has been the dominant frame for LGBT rights for at least a decade (Fetner 2008; Stone 2012). For example, supporting Rep. Mike Quigley said about LGBT people, "Do they not feel the same pain?" (quoted in Keen 2013). Senator Blumenthal (2012) also emphasized universality, saying, "In my experience nobody ever asked what the sexual orientation of a victim was when that person was, in fact, battered and brutalized. There is no such question that gay, lesbian, bisexual, and transgender individuals experience domestic violence at the same rate as the general population." So did Senator Feinstein (2012), who said, "I ask those who oppose the bill: If the victim is in a same-sex relationship, is the violence and danger any less real?" Rep. Dicks (2012) proclaimed plainly, "No victim of violence of any kind should be denied assistance simply because his or her sexual orientation. It is wrong that the bill further perpetuates this inequity, and I fear the reasons are purely political." This frame contrasted with the intersectional argument that sexual minorities face specific risks and barriers related to sexual and domestic violence. There was very little direct discussion of the LGBT issues in the hearings or debates, however; most negotiation over the issue occurred offstage. This did not stop Democrats from using the issue against Republicans, as Senator Lautenberg (2012) did in debate, saying, "Apparently, some of our colleagues would vote against protecting women if it means they also have to protect immigrants and people in the gay and lesbian community." Senator Quigley (2012) called out the underlying issue, saying, "I know there are folks who don't want to, in any way, have a pro-gay vote on it, but this is protecting human beings." Until the 2012 vote, the Task Force's efforts to gain support within VAWA for LGBT people's access to services had gone on behind the scenes through the Office on Violence Against Women's grant programs and definition of underserved groups. When it entered the bill through the antidiscrimination clause, it entered public debate and became a matter of the hotly contested issue of LGBT rights rather than the widely supported one of gendered crime.

LACK OF COALITION OUTSIDE THE STATE: HOW CONSERVATIVE AND FEMINIST ACTIVISTS VIEWED VAWA

Unlike their counterparts inside the state, feminists and conservatives outside the state were on opposite sides over VAWA. While most feminists supported it, conservatives opposed it. Neither was highly mobilized, however. Further, religious and secular conservatives took very different approaches to the larger question of sexual and domestic violence, while feminists disagreed over VAWA's carceral approach. These internal divisions and the low salience of the issue to activists meant that the lack of feminist-conservative coalition outside the state did not threaten the feminist-conservative coalition inside Congress.

Conservatives

In contrast to conservative legislators, secular conservatives outside the state opposed the law and sometimes criticized conservatives in Congress for supporting it. However, the critique was mainly confined to pundits and intellectuals, with virtually no mobilizing or campaigning against VAWA. They opposed any special legislation for violence against women, criticizing the focus on crimes against women, arguing that rape was not a serious problem, and claiming that the Act would serve to strengthen feminists. Secular conservatives also framed domestic and sexual violence as an issue that feminists blew out of proportion for their own ends. For example, a typical 1994 article in the *National Review* declared in the subhead: "The New Violence Against Women Act is sexual politics with a vengeance," and the article went on to critique "VAWA's underlying premise . . . that life is pervaded with men's hatred for women, that women are systemically pushed down, that the most intimate relationships are never free of this one-sided power dynamic" (Gutmann 1993). Similarly, after VAWA passed, another *National Review* author reported:

> Boosted by fresh funding from last year's Omnibus Crime Act, feminist advocacy groups are pushing the images of women as victims and men as beasts . . . . A feminist political gender analysis has reframed the problem of violence against women as one of misuse of power by men who have been socialized into believing they have the right to control the women in their lives, even through violent means. (McElroy 1995:74)

Although some conservative pundits opposed VAWA early on, most conservative movement activists and media outlets took little notice. The volume of coverage was low and focused on Title III.[32] After Title III was overturned by the Supreme Court, a typical article celebrated: "The Constitution Prevails Over Congressional Pandering to Feminists" (Rabkin 2000). Secular conservative pundits actively covered false accusations of rape, highlighted what they saw as an overly broad definition of date rape, complained about how liberals refused to publicize rapes by Black men, and criticized the Clintons as apologists for rape because of the accusations of sexual harassment against Bill Clinton (e.g., "The Brawley Gang" 1988; Elder 2003). But, aside from prison rape, there were no articles that addressed rape itself or framed it as a social problem of any kind. These polemics failed to counter the strong and persuasive criminal justice frame that dominated Congress; attacks on the importance of rape also were ineffectual since Republicans in Congress were seeking to prove that they were tough on crime. (In contrast to the climate by 2012, few Republicans were willing to dismiss the seriousness of rape.)

Religious conservative activists and pundits, in contrast, did not engage with VAWA at all: *no* articles in their publications mentioned the law. Unlike secular conservatives, however, they increasingly addressed domestic violence and sexual assault, framed them as widespread problems, suggested resources for victims, and even spoke favorably of feminists' efforts in the area. For example, Tracy (2003:54), in an article on redefining male headship, wrote:

> One way men honor their wives is by protecting them . . . . Unfortunately, secular society and even the Christian church consistently fail to protect women, and often blame women for physical or sexual violence perpetrated upon them . . . . Churches must begin to aggressively confront abusers, pursue all means possible to protect vulnerable women, and teach that male headship means protection, not domination . . . . While feminists *are* correct to highlight the widespread abuses of male power, many of us believe the best solution is not to reject male headship but to clarify it.

A 2015 forum in *Christianity Today* presented three viewpoints about "[a]fter domestic violence, why should a Christian wife call the police, not a pastor, first?" Calling domestic violence "a sin that . . . afflicts 1 in 4 U.S. women," the authors talked about the ability of police to connect women to resources like shelter and legal protection, the importance of legal punishment since "God intends to deal justice" through secular as well as church authorities, and overall, women's right to live without violence (Davis et al. 2015). In 2001, the World Evangelical Fellowship endorsed a sweeping antiviolence campaign in evangelical congregations: "The WEF calls upon the church to denounce abuse from the pulpit, to protect and provide for those in need of safety, to offer healing for victims, and to admonish offenders," especially because "incidents of violence against women are nearly as common in church circles as in wider society" (Stephen 2001).

Unlike feminists, religious conservatives saw traditional heterosexual families and gender positions as protecting women from violence, whether it was redefining "male headship" to mean protecting and respecting women or blaming secular society for rising rates of rape (Wilcox and LeBlanc 2004). But sometimes their language mirrored feminists', as in an article debunking myths about rape in evangelical churches such as, "God protects us if we are living right," "It's no wonder, the way women dress these days," and "That's not a problem in our church." These myths mirrored those presented by secular feminists and, in fact, the author of the article suggested that clergy should work with feminist rape crisis centers, saying, "Pastors may hesitate to refer because most victim-assistance programs and literature have been initiated by feminists, but they still may offer great help." It further suggested that churches should "Recognize that women in the church may be vulnerable because, as a whole, they are uninformed. Traditional Christian teachings that urge women to be meek and submissive can set women up for a rapist who looks for precisely those traits in a victim" (Walters and Spring 1992:31–33). However, religious conservatives' antiviolence work focused on building strong families, religious guidance, and self-help. These were not state-focused strategies and did not bring them into coalition regarding VAWA. This division between religious and secular conservatives probably made conservative congresspeople's support for VAWA easier.

Feminists

If conservative activists thought VAWA was a feminist plot, many feminists outside the state saw it as imperfect at best, and racist and counterproductive at worst, because of the racial and class politics of criminal justice responses to violence against women (Bumiller 2008; Presser and Gaarder 2000; Richie 2012). Feminist activists and scholars criticized VAWA for the way it strengthened a racist criminal justice system, citing VAWA's funding for prosecution and its inclusion in the 1994 Omnibus Crime Act, which failed to pass a measure barring racially inequitable death penalty sentencing and included increased sentencing and numerous measures strengthening the prison system (Burnham 2001; Matsuda 1994). This critique was broadly influential. Karen Rosenberg, for example, who had worked on domestic violence services, initially thought that increased collaboration with law enforcement, greater and more sensitive investigation of domestic violence cases, "federal recognition that violence against women is pandemic, and serious, and worthy of public attention," and VAWA funding were clearly good. But further research led her to critique the symbolism of its inclusion in the crime bill, the proportion of funding that went to "criminal legal system remedies," and particularly the crime bill's failure to include the Racial Justice Act (dealing with death penalty). Conflating VAWA and the larger crime bill, she denounced "feminist acquiescence to the removal of the Racial Justice Act from the final version of VAWA" (Rosenberg 2010).

VAWA's reauthorization as a stand-alone bill rather than as part of a larger crime package made little substantive difference since it remained at least partly grounded in criminal justice. Recall that NOW's Helen Neuborne reported opposition to the initial effort from women's movement groups over the issue of expanded criminal penalties (Symposium 2010). As Matsuda wrote in *Ms.*, "Feminists fight hard for recognition of women as the victims of crime . . . . This necessary focus on crimes against us deflects attention from the crimes of the criminal justice system itself . . . . For women of color, for feminists of all colors . . . . We know that the police are a source of violence in our communities, not just a deterrent to it" (Matsuda 1994:86).

Outside the Task Force, feminist engagement was low. Professionalized activists and authors were more engaged with VAWA than grassroots activists. Even in later reauthorizations, feminist support for VAWA outside the Task Force rarely moved beyond media coverage and small-scale letter-writing campaigns. The Dynamics of Collection Action database, which includes all coverage of protest and public events in the *New York Times*, shows no events on either side of VAWA.[33] In 2005, when the law was up for reauthorization, the National Coalition Against Domestic Violence mobilized its supporters to lobby the congressional representatives for the bill and a large crowd of supporters did show up unexpectedly for the Senate Judiciary Committee hearing.[34] During the later VAWA era, from the 2000s forward, there was relatively high feminist mobilization on the issue, with local Slut Walks against sexual violence and extensive activism on college campuses over sexual assault, but this activism did not explicitly weigh in on VAWA (Reger 2014).

Many others in the women's movement, especially those who worked in domestic violence or anti-rape organizations, viewed VAWA positively because of its funding streams and the way it encouraged police departments to deal with victims more sensitively (Aldrich 2000), although those working on sexual violence were more critical of the lack of emphasis on that issue (Roe 2004). Of course, some also praised the enhanced criminal justice components and saw increased prosecution as a feminist goal, underscoring the ongoing divisions that existed within the women's movement.

Others focused almost exclusively on Title III and praised it as the federal government's codification of feminist goals (e.g., MacKinnon 2005). Even scholars had a tendency to focus on Title III as the "key aspect of the bill" and even to use "VAWA" almost interchangeably with Title III (Sklar and Lustig 2001:1). Media accounts sometimes said that the Supreme Court had overturned VAWA itself. In this case, countermovement opposition increased awareness and support.

Title III was undeniably significant symbolically and for the meaning shift it represented, a victory for the feminist view that sexual and domestic violence were features of patriarchy and represented men's oppression and domination over women rather than simply criminal activity or pathology. If it had survived, it might have been used often enough to effect a broader cultural adoption of this view of violence against women. Legal scholar and key mover for VAWA Sally Goldfarb wrote, "By placing the experience of individual female victims of violence within the category of sex discrimination, VAWA's civil rights provision had the potential to counteract a number of damaging beliefs" such as "that domestic or sexual violence is the victim's fault; that violence against women is a personal, private matter; and that the law and other institutions are justified in ignoring or condoning such behavior." Further, Goldfarb contended that the Title's grounding in the Commerce Clause of the Constitution (empowering federal legislation that dealt with cross-state economic functions) meant that the congressional hearings constructed a detailed account of how sexual and domestic violence affected women's economic and social autonomy and status, another key feature of feminist analyses that remained marginal in prevailing discourse. In addition, she maintained, the discursive shift remained, with the feminist analysis now "a familiar, mainstream concept in law and culture (Goldfarb 2003:255–58). This led, she thought, to some state and local legislation that included including violence against women in hate crimes laws. In the years when Title III was in effect, she said, courts were "surprisingly receptive" in cases brought under the Title and generally found that sexual assaults were motivated by gender.

Despite feminist support and debate over VAWA, there was surprisingly little coverage of VAWA in feminist publications. As with their conservative counterparts, the most common response from women's movement publications during the 1990–1994 period prior to VAWA's passage was silence. Both *Ms.* and *off our backs* covered VAWA's passage in 1994, but only with brief factual articles. After passage, *Ms.* and *off our backs* covered most developments in VAWA briefly, particularly the court challenges to Title III, reauthorizations, and battles for sufficient funding, and few of these short pieces delved into the specific components of the law in depth (e.g., immigration provisions) or raised feminist critiques of it.[35]

All except one article in *Ms.* were positive about VAWA, but superficial. An article by legal scholar Matsuda, in contrast, sharply critiqued VAWA for its criminal justice approach, writing, "[I]t's a paradoxical struggle we feminists find ourselves in. We want to seek safety from the men who harm us, and we want to abolish a patriarchal justice system," and noting that VAWA "came in a package that vastly increased the number of death penalty offenses and failed to require racial equality in death penalty applications." She did not denounce or disown VAWA, however, saying, "For now, feminists must deal with the devil, demanding that the existing criminal justice system protect women from violence, even while working to abolish that system"(Matsuda 1994:86).

Off our backs, in contrast, which aimed at a more activist readership, had in-depth coverage not only of the issues of rape and domestic violence but also of the movements against them, including shelters, crisis services, and feminist prevention activism. Most of these articles were written without reference to VAWA, but a few discussed the law's benefits and drawbacks.[36] For example, a 2001 article told a cautionary "creation story of battered women's shelters" in which the first five days of shelter creation involved feminist social change efforts like "confront[ing] the experts" who blamed women for abuse, helping women and children escape from abusers, challenging lawmakers over protective orders, and so forth. Even "[o]n the sixth day of shelter creating," when "the Feminists secured funding for shelter programs," feminist values prevailed against hierarchy and "shared power among employees was encouraged." The seventh day was when things went wrong. The feminists "were tired and so they decided to rest . . . . But alas, only a short time after the Feminists had fallen asleep, mainstream professionalism infiltrated battered women's programs," leading to organizational hierarchy, professionalization of service providers, and the disempowering and blaming of battered women (Gaddis 2001:15). Although this article did not refer directly to VAWA, which was not the only such funding source, others did. A December 2001 article, "Sisters, We're Doin' It *To* Ourselves," praised the fact that, "with the support of VOCA, VAWA, FEMA, HUD, FBPSA, as well as state and local funding, we have enough funding that we no longer worry about paying the light bills," yet worried, "But are we victims of our success? Are we becoming 'nice girls against domestic violence' instead of radical advocates for battered women?" (Osmundson 2001:14). More directly, Denise Snyder, the executive director of the DC Rape Crisis Center, told an *off our backs* interviewer that VAWA was "good in some ways and bad in some ways." In particular, its "very strong emphasis on prosecution and law enforcement" meant that the many rapes that are not reported to police can't be "included in that focus." Further, she said, because "VAWA is geared to direct service, it is all about putting the band-aids on the survivors and not about genuine prevention." Nevertheless, she concluded, VAWA had "enabled us to expand and do work that needs to be done" (Ruby 2002:16–17). *Off our backs* writers worried about professional and corporate control of the movements against violence against women in general. For example, they published an article critiquing Verizon's "Verizon Clothesline Project" as a depoliticized shadow of the grassroots Clothesline Project (Cumings 2005). *Off our backs* also covered lesbian battering, issues of dealing with men in the antiviolence movement, burnout, and strategy.[37] None of these issues or frames were prevalent in Congress or in *Ms.*

Ms., which aimed for a larger and more general audience, did not cover the movements in much depth, tending more to cover the issues themselves rather than the nitty-gritty difficulties of organizing against them. *Ms.* did publish substantial stories on rape in war and violence against women in the context of the U.S. wars in the Middle East and African civil wars. It also covered various policy and legal issues and had a few long articles on violence against women in the United States on issues like the financial costs of violence against women (in treatment, services, and the criminal justice system), the need for relevant legislation,[38] and the successful campaign to redefine the legal definition of rape used by the FBI. One article called on readers to speak up in support of VAWA's 2005 reauthorization (Emirzian 2005).[39] Despite its extensive coverage of rape and related issues, including legal issues and criminal prosecution, *Ms.* had relatively little coverage of VAWA.

Overall, VAWA was not a frequent topic for either publication. Neither covered it as if it was a central women's movement issue. The sparse feminist media coverage underscores the fact that although VAWA was very important to the professional movement organizations' legal staffers and followed closely by them, the movement was highly segmented. The concern did not translate to the grassroots, which was apparently largely unaware of the issue except when it was challenged in the Title III overturn and the 2012 reauthorization fight.[40] Nevertheless, VAWA produced important effects that reflected the nature and relative power of the unlikely allies in Congress.

Alliances in Amicus Briefs

Amicus briefs filed on major rape cases before the U.S. Supreme Court prior to VAWA, and on the major challenge to VAWA, reflect these overall patterns of feminist—but not conservative—support for VAWA. The test of VAWA's civil rights provision, *U.S. v. Morrison,* was the highest profile case related to rape and domestic violence to come along in a long time. It hinged mainly on obscure questions about what kind of federal action was warranted in what is generally a state matter (criminal law), especially the nature of the clause in the Constitution permitting federal action in areas related to commerce. But while the briefs were often framed in that way, their contents argued over whether domestic and sexual violence were public or private matters, how serious they were, and the significance of their effects on restricting women's actions. Amici supporting VAWA's civil rights clause included two groups that each submitted a brief, one of law professors and one of "international law scholars and human rights experts;" a large group of organizations including sexual and domestic violence organizations, women's professional organizations, Junior Leagues, women's law and policy centers, women's club associations, and unions; and a group of 13 organizations working with immigrant women that submitted a separate brief.[41] The conservative legal organizations that might have filed briefs on other court cases dealing with legislation sponsored by conservative Republican members of Congress were absent.

There were three other major cases related to rape that drew amicus briefs from nonstate actors: *Kennedy v. Louisiana,* in 2007, which ruled the death penalty for child rape was unconstitutional; *U.S. v. Lanier,* in 1996, which dealt with whether rape could be considered interference with bodily integrity;[42] and *Michigan v. Lucas,* in 1990, which dealt with the exclusion of victims' sexual history from trial.[43] *Lucas* drew only one amicus brief, from the Criminal Defense Attorneys Association of Michigan. *Lanier,* which was heard shortly after VAWA's ratification, raised basic assumptions about the nature of rape as an infringement on women's freedom (not just as a crime) and drew many amici from across the coalition that supported VAWA and beyond. Many women's movement, anti-sexual violence and domestic violence organizations, human rights, civil rights, women's religious, and women's legal organizations joined one amicus brief.[44] The ACLU, although it usually did not support cases that would lead to intensified criminal punishment, supported the defense of women's right to bodily integrity in this case and filed its own brief.

Kennedy, dealing with the death penalty, drew a different mixture of amici. As discussed in the chapter on child sexual abuse, while four state organizations against child sexual abuse joined the ACLU in an amicus brief arguing against the death penalty for child rape, they were not joined by other antiviolence organizations. Both *Morrison* and *Kennedy* reveal the limits of unlikely alliances, but not as we might have expected. The submerged conflict between civil liberty and antiviolence feminists, simmering since the porn wars, is reflected in the ACLU's absence from the *Morrison* case despite its relevance for women's rights, an ACLU priority.[45] And the limits of the antiviolence movement in fully critiquing the carceral state's abuses of power are reflected in the very few women's movement or antiviolence organizations joining the brief in *Kennedy*.

CARCERAL AND INTERSECTIONAL FEMINIST OUTCOMES

What was VAWA's impact on the carceral state? To what extent did it strengthen state power, co-opt state power for feminist ends, or both? Overall, VAWA increased criminal justice responses to domestic and sexual violence but also increased shelters' and crisis centers' funding and influence over the state, promoted incorporation of the needs of women of color and other marginalized groups into shelters and services, and shifted discourse about violence against women. The outcomes, overall, are mixed. They include carceral, noncarceral, and intersectional elements. They reflect both unprecedented feminist legislative influence—a result of the ambivalent alliance with Congress—and clear limits to feminist power with countervailing conservative influence in that alliance.

VAWA almost certainly resulted in an *increase in prosecution and conviction* for domestic violence and to a lesser extent for sexual assault. This is impossible to quantify nationwide but numerous local and regional experts reported that VAWA increased federal and state prosecution and conviction for domestic violence and sexual assault ("Symposium" 2010:572). For example, a Michigan prosecutor boasted that, after VAWA-funded training, he "got a conviction in every rape case I tried for almost two years afterward" (quoted in "Symposium" 2010:586). In 1999, Office on Violence Against Women Director Bonnie Campbell reported, "Vigorous prosecution under the VAWA . . . is a top priority" and touted how federal charges could produce "more severe and appropriate punishment for an offender than a prosecution under a similar State law" (U.S. House 1999). Further, the first two iterations of VAWA also contained incentives for law enforcement to adopt mandatory arrest policies, under which assailants must be arrested if police are called to a domestic violence incident. These were widely criticized for reducing victims' agency and accelerating the criminalization of men of color, and were eliminated in the 2006 reauthorization (Presser and Gaarder 2000; Rivera 1995–1996).

Some activists from state and local rape crisis and domestic violence organizations praised VAWA for increasing prosecution. For example, one praised a specialized Washington, D.C. prosecution unit funded by VAWA for increasing domestic violence prosecutions from under 20 per year to over 3,000 ("Symposium" 2010:589). In this view, increasing criminal penalties was an uncontroversial good backed by the logic of gendered crime and serving the dual goals of improving women's social position and reducing crime. This can be considered a carceral feminist outcome, and it was one that Republicans and Democrats in Congress and many feminist advocates agreed on.

Some of the law's most touted accomplishments had to do with changing attitudes and treatment of victims. For example, Lynn Schafran, director of Legal Momentum's (formerly NOW-LDEF) National Judicial Education Program, recounted a training session on reducing gender bias in the courts in which:

> a male judge was listening as our sex offender expert read the transcript of an interview that he had conducted with a male college student who blithely described how he held his arm across his date's windpipe in order to hold her down and have what he perceived as having sex with her. . . . [A] male judge in the group said, "I do not see where there is a rape in that narrative." A female judge jumped up, ran behind her colleague's chair, put him in a chokehold and said, "Do you see it now?" ("Symposium" 2010:587)

VAWA clearly reflected the state's growing punitive approach, but its outcomes also went beyond the carceral. The law itself mandated a balance of funding between criminal justice and social services.[46] VAWA funding added to and supported existing programs for sexual assault survivors. The number of rape crisis centers and statewide domestic and sexual assault coalitions had increased steadily throughout the 1970s, without any major state funding. The first rape crisis center was established in 1972; a year later, they existed in 43 states, and the number increased to 136 in 1975 and 400 in 1976 (Bevacqua 2000). But by the 1990s rape crisis centers were more institutionalized than earlier. Martin (2005) found that in 2004, 10 of the 47 rape crisis centers in Florida were on college campuses; the Justice Department found that one in five colleges had a peer education program on sexual assault in 2005, and by 2009 only one in four of the more than 1,200 organizations nationwide providing rape crisis services were stand-alone centers (cited in Bergen and Maier 2011). The remainder operated within schools, hospitals, and other institutions. VAWA funding for rape crisis services, thus, did not necessarily go to autonomous feminist-run groups. VAWA funding also increased other kinds of professionalized services. A major component of the law was funding for training of specialized sexual assault nurse examiners to conduct examinations of sexual assault victims; such programs grew from 403 in 2001 to more than 500 in 2005 (Bergen and Maier 2011).[47]

Many activists praised the growing collaboration between law enforcement and community rape crisis centers and shelters, which was favored by VAWA funding.[48] Testifying before Congress in 1999, a shelter director proclaimed that VAWA "has created a very, very different environment . . . where people have been forced . . . to begin to work together, people who have been antagonistic; for example, police and domestic violence programs." She continued, "Shelters have not had an easy go of it with the criminal justice system . . . . There are people in this movement that have spent 40 years in the trenches trying to end this crime against women. They have been unacknowledged, unrecognized, and this is the first glimmer of hope. You have given them creativity, you have given them energy, you have given them a belief that we can end violence against women" (U.S. House 1999:101–2). In vivid case examples, she emphasized the importance of police enforcement of protection orders and prosecution of offenders, and women's need for creative and extensive services, counseling, and shelter. A Colorado advocate, Claudia Bayliff, described how "the local district attorney allows the local rape crisis team to sit in . . . when they make . . . charging decisions" ("Symposium" 2010:574). For them, collaboration meant that law enforcement would take their perspective seriously, making prosecutions more likely to go forward, making police, forensic examiners, and others more supportive, and integrating services into the process. But better integrated community organizations did not convert law enforcement to intersectional feminism. Rape crisis centers and shelters are less powerful than police and prosecutors, leaving them with no guarantee of influence, and some—especially those serving immigrants or women of color—preferred to avoid contact with police (Arnold 2013; Corrigan 2013).

A critique of carceral feminism, sees these requirements differently, as *requiring* rape crisis centers and shelters to work with law enforcement. There are two separate issues here. Some critics, with a political and philosophical opposition to colluding with the criminal justice system or the state, opposed all involvement of rape crisis centers and shelters with decision-making, information-sharing, and providing training to police and other law enforcement agencies, and even other institutions like hospitals and schools. In this view, collaboration with law enforcement, state funding, and the discursive incorporation of violence against women as crime into the mainstream can also be understood as strengthening the punitive state and service organizations that work with law enforcement become part of the state's social control and punitive systems, which are more likely to target women of color, immigrants, and queer people than to protect them (Bierria 2007; Richie 2012; Smith 2007; Spade 2011). Even those who do not oppose state intervention on principle raise important doubts about limited access to law enforcement remedies for undocumented immigrants, members of excessively policed groups, and victims who themselves have criminal histories (Bhuyan 2008; Burnham 2001; Villalon 2010).

Most crisis and service workers agreed that crisis centers and shelters should not be required to encourage their "clients" to report to police or to report their own statistics to law enforcement, and most opposed mandatory arrest policies (Corrigan 2013; Matthews 1994). VAWA partially responded to this critique. The 2000 bill noted that VAWA should not simply support "victims through the legal process" but rather assist with "legal, social, and health care services." Further, agencies could be reimbursed for serving victims regardless of whether the assault was reported to police (U.S. House 2000a). Grant guidelines in 2005 went further, excluding certain activities that had been criticized for increasing control over victims by service providers and the state (Crenshaw 1991) because, in the words of the grant guidelines, they "jeopardize victim safety, deter or prevent physical or emotional healing for victims, or allow offenders to escape responsibility for their actions." For example, people could not be excluded from services based on their characteristics, those of their children (including children's age and gender), or "their relationship to the perpetrator." Victims could not be required to participate in counseling; "report . . . crimes to law enforcement," or "participate in criminal proceedings." But other components of the same grant guidelines strengthened criminal justice sanctions, precluding funding for "pre-trial diversion programs . . . court-mandated batterer intervention programs that do not use the coercive power of the criminal justice system to hold batterers accountable for their behavior, [and] . . . anger management programs."[49] These changes, and advocates' support for them, do not reject gendered crime frames or engagement with law enforcement. Instead, they seek to influence law and practice to give survivors and feminist service organizations more power.

Another significant change came from the underserved populations component of VAWA, which provided a strong incentive for rape crisis and domestic violence organizations to expand services for non-English speakers, immigrants, people of color, homeless people, disabled people, men, children in domestic violence households, and other marginalized groups. Many did so, shifting the conditions on the ground, making more widely available services for non-English speakers; shelter for women with teenage sons; reducing coercive counseling programs in shelters; and developing culturally aware programs for multiple ethnic, sexual, and regional groups (Gillum 2009). As Orloff recounted, VAWA funding led to "program after program in communities of color, serving immigrant women, serving deaf women, serving rural communities, serving people that we never dreamed would ever have a part of the pie" ("Symposium" 2010:583). Concretely, an organizer who had worked with a rape crisis organization in Boulder, Colorado, reported that the organization had hired paid staff, started a Spanish-speaking hotline, and trained nurses to serve as specialized examiners for sexual assault ("Symposium" 2010:574). Steering state funding toward more culturally appropriate responses reflects a strategy aimed at reshaping state and nonstate responses along more intersectional feminist lines (Chen 2000; Rivera 1995–1996; Villalon 2010). In the Office on Violence Against Women, a task force focused on underserved populations and worked to address economic needs, such as housing for Native American and immigrant women.[50] In other words, while advocates used gendered crime frames to build connections across difference and gain votes, they were also able to achieve some intersectional feminist goals.

In terms of discursive change, VAWA advanced the idea of violence against women as both crime and a form of gender oppression. Biden's staffer Nourse believed that VAWA "changed the terms of the debate. The idea that women have a right to be free from violence directed at them because of their gender, which was once a novel concept, is now a mainstream, commonplace idea"("Symposium" 2010:522–23). This discursive outcome persisted even after its concrete manifestation—Title III—was overturned. In an editorial column in the *New York Times*, Louise Erdrich (2013) made an eloquent case for the ongoing cultural and discursive change resulting from VAWA: "With each iteration, the act has become more effective, inclusive and powerful. Without it, the idea that some rape is 'legitimate' could easily have been shrugged off by the electorate." These cultural changes were a longtime goal of feminist activists (Arnold 2013). They are both carceral and noncarceral but not explicitly intersectional.

In the end, feminist movement organizations successfully worked with liberals and conservatives in the federal government to produce legislation and discursive focus on the serious nature of sexual and domestic violence. VAWA—especially Title III—was in many ways a stunning feminist achievement. Women's movement organizations helped write the law, introduced testimony that successfully persuaded Congress that rape and domestic violence were pervasive, infringed on women's lives in a way that could be considered gender discrimination, and were subject to discriminatory lack of enforcement in many locales. Funding and incentives under

VAWA expanded and transformed services to women who had been raped or assaulted by intimate partners.

But they achieved only part of their goals, and the aims of factions of the movement that did not work closely with the state were overlooked. The legislation focused more on criminal justice measures than many advocates would have liked; and state frames for understanding violence against women, while they often incorporated elements of feminist frames, also relied heavily on crime discourse. The aspects of movement goals and meanings that entered the state could do so because of the unlikely coordination between feminists and conservative legislators on processes such as the recruitment of witnesses, structure of hearings, position of allies on key congressional committees, and the resonance of some meanings over others.

Conservative lawmakers also got only part of what they wanted. VAWA funded more feminist and feminist-connected organizations than most would have chosen, and contained more protections for immigrants and the antidiscrimination measure for LGBT people, the first to be encoded in federal law. And secular conservative activists, who virulently opposed VAWA, lost altogether. Overall, conservative influence served mainly to scale back provisions regarding immigration and limit overall funding. Even conservative control of the House or the presidency—technically giving them veto power—did not enable them to kill the law or even eliminate provisions they opposed.

The discursive and committee structure of Congress limited feminists' ability to reform immigration for battered women or to comprehensively revise approaches to integrate race or class. In addition, while the women's movement "owned" the issue of violence against women, it did not have authority or early entry on the issue of immigration, where other players for and against already had a strong presence and the political lines were already deeply drawn. But the same forces also limited potential opponents' ability to oppose VAWA. Its assignment, by default, to the Judiciary Committees' Subcommittees on Crime, and its framing as gendered crime, were virtually impossible to counter. Legally, sexual assault and domestic violence already existed as crimes, again both shaping the direction of change and foreclosing opposition.

CONCLUSION

In sum, the feminist coalition that helped write and organize the passage of VAWA was an intersectional one, in which race, citizenship, and other factors were understood as shaping how women experienced sexual and intimate partner violence, what they needed in response, and how state interventions fell short. But the legislation they achieved through working with conservatives and liberals in Congress reflected an official discourse that understood violence against women unidimensionally in terms of crime, not intersectionally. Feminists gained the support of both liberals and conservatives in Congress by collaboratively constructing a frame understanding violence against women as a gendered crime compatible with multiple ideological positions. The gendered crime frame became a dominant way of understanding the issue, linking crime frames to feminist ones, and remained dominant despite Republican votes against VAWA in 2012.

The construction of violence against women as crime is hard to escape, discursively because of the broad appeal of the idea of gendered crime, legally because the law defines sexual and domestic assault as crimes, and institutionally because of the power of the criminal justice system. Nevertheless, the racial, gender, and national politics of VAWA and feminist activism against violence against women do not reflect a simple carceral feminism that overlooks how race and citizenship shape violence. VAWA activists targeted the state for change. They agreed that the criminal justice system failed to serve marginalized groups and sought—with decidedly mixed results—both to improve it and to strengthen community organizations' engagement with women of color and immigrants. Their use of the gendered crime and crime frames in Congress did not reflect a simple embrace of the punitive state but a strategic attempt to gain sufficient votes. Their attempts to expand VAWA and promote intersectional feminist frames in Congress were limited primarily by the material and discursive context of Congress, and the countervailing power of the other members of their ambivalent alliance.

The ambivalent alliance between women's movement organizations and members of Congress was close to a conventional coalition, although, of course, most work on coalitions does not assume an institutionalized political partner (but see Almeida 2010). But both parties were cautious about their relationship. Women's movement organizations acknowledged their success in gaining conservative support, but they did not publicize it. Conservative Republican legislators downplayed the feminist dimensions of the Act and did not tout their work with NOW. They were clearly allies, but the alliance was fraught, and their interactions with each other ambivalent, cooperative but cautious.

Feminists and their erstwhile conservative enemies in Congress were indeed ambivalent about their alliance. The risks to their reputations, however, were minimal. For feminists, the fact that they were working with liberal and feminist Democratic members of Congress, not just conservatives, provided cover. For conservatives, the low salience of secular conservative criticisms of VAWA and religious conservatives' disengagement did the same. Nevertheless, VAWA did nothing to heal the long-standing divisions within the women's movement over working with the state, and may have deepened them. When women's movement organizations worked closely with the state to develop legislation that extended criminal justice enforcement, their relations with more radical feminists, especially those advocating for immigrants and women of color, were strained, and their reputation within the movement was tarnished.

The alliance did not extend to their movement counterparts outside the state. Other ambivalent alliances might carry over from institutionalized politics to outside movements, but the issue of rape was too polarizing, given its firm association with feminism. The potential costs to conservatives' reputation of being seen as allied with feminists were high, with little benefit. Members of Congress, in contrast, could cite their commitment to fighting crime in appealing to a broader range of constituents. In addition, while bipartisan cooperation is positively valued in Congress, there is no positively valued activist equivalent. Feminist and conservative activists had nothing to gain by working together. It is often demands on the state that tend to draw ideological foes into alliance. The women's movement had clear demands on the state regarding violence against women. Conservatives, in contrast, had no demands on the state related to violence against women. Secular conservatives were free, therefore, to remain ideologically pure and oppose VAWA, while religious conservatives developed their own resources for victims in their communities.

The gendered crime frame and the ambivalent alliance behind it remain powerful and continue to shape state actions in several related areas. Sexual assaults in the military and on college campuses have sparked government inquiries, activism, and administrative action. These issues are framed as gendered crimes: both as an affront to women's rights and as crimes that have not been taken seriously. The dominant response to campus sexual assault and sexual assault in the military—that they be taken seriously and prosecuted or administratively investigated and punished through state-mandated campus policies—is a demand that the state use its punitive powers on behalf of women. This carries risks for women of color, undocumented immigrants, and other marginalized groups. For feminists, these campaigns, like VAWA, have both liberatory and regressive potential.

The VAWA case holds useful lessons for understanding the potential and limits of institutional social change. In contrast to the other two cases, the women's movement had considerable access and influence. It faced favorable political and discursive opportunities, could draw on an extensive institutionalized field of service and state-level organizations, and the women's movement organizations at the core of the battle were themselves institutionalized players and well integrated into the liberal legal network that lobbied Congress (Teles 2008). This was probably a best case scenario in the present political system. Yet even though advocates of VAWA were based in a diverse coalition and understood violence against women intersectionally, understandings of violence against women as unidimensionally gendered prevailed over intersectional ones in Congress. Even when advocates emphasized and achieved cultural and organizational change, they also bolstered the criminal justice system. The shape of VAWA was not determined by activists; it emerged from a two-directional process of discursive and material compromise in Congress, in which both feminists and conservatives gained in some areas and lost in others.

CHAPTER 5
Conclusion

The 2016 presidential campaign and election of Donald Trump demonstrated both the effects and the limits of conservative and feminist engagement against pornography and sexual violence. After the devastating critiques of Republicans' comments about rape and opposition to VAWA during the 2012 campaigns, politicians and pundits assumed that seeming to condone sexual violence was political suicide. When recordings surfaced of then-candidate Trump boasting about touching women against their will, followed by numerous women reporting such encounters, it seemed that this would be his downfall. Many called for Trump to exit the race, and Republicans rushed to distance themselves from him. Of course, in the end, it was not a deal breaker. Nevertheless, the fact that even many conservatives framed Trump's actions as sexual assault reflects the impact of the women's movement on attitudes toward sexual violence and conservative politicians' investment in at least appearing to oppose it. Thirty years ago, conservatives—and, indeed, the general public—would have decried Trump's coarseness and sexual immorality but would not have called his actions sexual assault. The long overlap with feminist antiviolence advocates changed the frames and limits on acceptability in conservative circles.

The phrase "politics makes strange bedfellows" has resonated since Shakespeare's time for a reason. The story of social change is a story of frenemies. Their unlikely interactions are more complicated, more fraught, and differently organized than coalitions. Understanding their relationships and consequences for social change has implications for how we think about social movement interactions and social movement outcomes. It also has implications for understanding the trajectory and impact of the women's movement, including the idea of carceral feminism, and for understanding other social change projects involving frenemies.

RELATIONSHIPS AMONG SOCIAL MOVEMENTS

The case studies described here are neither coalitions nor opposing movements. Activism against pornography, child sexual abuse, and violence against women drew ideologically diverse supporters—feminists and conservatives—who were connected to each other and to the state in different ways. Frenemies may be connected through a shared goal, interaction behind the scenes, subscribing to a politically neutral identity or frame, or targeting the same state actors. They operate in varying contexts where their political differences are more or less overt. But they are not connected in the way that coalition partners are. Coalition partners overtly and deliberately interact with one another to plan and execute agreed-upon joint action. When leaders coordinate a coalition, they do not need to conceal it from rank-and-file members and, in fact, coalitions usually entail rank-and-file participation. In contrast, as Table 5.1 shows, all three case studies have at least some movement dimensions for which feminists and conservatives either opposed each other or were uninvolved. They have many dimensions along which their interaction was partial or covert, and one or two on which they had substantial interaction. Coalitions entail interaction along most of these movement dimensions.

While *antipornography* feminists and conservatives covertly cooperated regarding the Indianapolis ordinance, they did not do so otherwise, and each vehemently defended their basis for opposition to pornography. Conservatives briefly employed the feminist frame of pornography's harms to women and children, but mostly framed the issue in terms of the family and sexual morality, while feminists consistently denounced conservative frames. When antipornography feminists tried to influence conservative federal bodies (Congress and the Meese Commission), they did so as outsiders, not coalition partners. Activists against *child sexual abuse*, in contrast, represented a broad range of political inclinations (and many who had no particular political affiliation or ideology), but aside from a short-lived feminist survivors' movement, activism against child sexual abuse took a single-issue approach that eschewed politics and provided a neutral space for participation. This frame traveled easily into Congress. Just as the collective identity "survivor" and the experiential knowledge that grew from it connected participants in the social movement, so too experiential authority and expression of emotion connected diverse supporters in

Table 5.1 DIMENSIONS OF MOVEMENT INTERACTION, COMPARATIVE CASES

Movement Dimension	Type of Interaction or Compatibility		
	Overt, substantial	Covert, partial	None or opposition
Social movement organizations	VAWA	CSA*	Porn CSA VAWA
Leaders or movement elites	VAWA	Porn	CSA VAWA
Participants	CSA	Porn	VAWA
Collective identity	—	CSA	Porn VAWA
Frames	—	Porn VAWA	Porn CSA
Collective action	—	CSA	Porn VAWA
Specific issue and goals	Porn VAWA	CSA	Porn VAWA
Larger goals	—	CSA	Porn VAWA
Elite allies	—	Porn CSA VAWA	—

*CSA is child sexual abuse.

Congress through witness testimony. Feminist organizations working on *VAWA* came the closest to a conventional coalition, forming an ambivalent alliance with conservatives in Congress. They crafted a shared, hybrid frame that combined feminists' concern with gender oppression with conservatives' concern with criminal enforcement. While feminists and conservatives outside Congress took opposing sides on the legislation, lack of conservative activism outside the state mitigated reputational risks for VAWA supporters on either side. Conflict over the passage of the ultimately overturned civil rights Title III indicates the difficulty of maintaining a strong focus on how violence against women connects to the larger gender order. Beyond maintaining a focus on gender, feminists had broader, more intersectional goals than conservative legislators, which they were unable to realize. Table 5.2 summarizes these three types of frenemies.

There are several characteristic features of the relationships between frenemies. First, because they entail contradictory mixtures of cooperation and

Table 5.2 TYPES OF RELATIONSHIPS BETWEEN FRENEMIES

Type of Relationship	Issue	Characteristics of Relationship	Overlapping Frame
Collaborative adversarial relationship	Pornography	Ideological opponents; covert and partial interaction and overt opposition	Harm to women
Narrow neutrality	Child sexual abuse	Ideologically diverse participants under neutral umbrella	Abuse as beyond politics
Ambivalent alliance	VAWA	Coalition within Congress; disengaged movements outside the state	Gendered crime

conflict, participants face risks to their reputations as other members of their parent movements criticize them for "sleeping with the enemy." Both feminist and conservative participants worked to defend their reputations, most strikingly around pornography, but also around the other issues. These reputational risks are unique to frenemy relationships. Second, frenemy relationships rely on hybrid or compromise elements that can appeal to different factions in different ways to hold them together. This might be a hybrid frame, a deliberately apolitical frame, or a specific, narrow goal. For these cases, this entailed harms to women from pornography, child sexual abuse as beyond politics, and violence against women as gendered crime. Third, they come together around a single issue or specific legislative goals. The pornography relationship centered on civil ordinances against pornography as an alternative to obscenity law; when it became clear that those ordinances would not withstand legal challenges, the relationship evaporated. The child sexual abuse relationship centered on the single issue of child sexual abuse, defined narrowly as unconnected to other issues; groups that sought to draw connections to gender, race, or family oppression found no quarter. The VAWA relationship centered on the definition of sexual violence as a matter of gender alone; feminists struggled to bring in issues of race, immigration, or sexuality. Fourth, emotional and personal narratives were important in cementing all three relationships, providing an authority that transcended politics and lent weight to expert knowledge. Fifth, differences in collective identity, ideology, networks, and outside movement allies precluded more extensive collaboration or institutionalization of the relationships. Frenemies' relationships are by nature partial or short-lived or both. Finally, their outcomes must be assessed differently from outcomes for coalitions.

SOCIAL MOVEMENT OUTCOMES

Feminists worried that feminist opponents of pornography facilitated conservative gains by making it appear that opposition to pornography had broad popular support. Evangelical conservatives worried that by referring women to rape crisis centers, they were reinforcing the feminist critique of traditional families. Feminists and conservatives both worried that they might give up too much in VAWA. Relationships between frenemies are indeed risky and often require that both sides make compromises. But it is too simplistic to assume that getting in bed with the enemy always means losing. At the most basic level, *both* sides risk loss and, conversely, both can potentially gain. The outcomes of these relationships depend on the relative power of participants. Like most social movement outcomes, they rarely involve complete success for either side and they often involve partial and unintended outcomes.

Explaining the forces that create social change is always difficult. In the case of frenemies, it is confounded by the fact that partially opposed actors, with overlapping but distinct allies, are trying to shape similar but nonidentical outcomes. Each participant in the relationship faces somewhat different political and discursive opportunities as a result of their connections to different allies, frames that resonate in different ways, and links to different outside movements with different levels of mobilization. Nevertheless, there are some overall patterns for outcomes of campaigns by frenemies. The more powerful participant has more influence on the outcome. A participant is more powerful if it has stronger ties to legislators or other influential allies, a more highly mobilized mass movement or effective professionalized movement organization, or strong cultural resonance. In general, as frenemies come together, they rarely have equal strength. Movements that are larger and more visible have more leverage over politicians as well as more influence over the larger culture. When they have ties to elected officials their strength is increased further. Moreover, movements are not the only advocates working on these issues. Professionals in social services, child welfare, research, schools, hospitals, and government agencies, including the criminal justice system, were integrally involved. The movements' relationship to these professionals and the professionals' influence and agenda also shaped the end results. Opposition from other movements varied across the cases, as did the amount of engagement from participants' parent movements. Finally, cultural and political opportunities, including legal and constitutional constraints specific to each issue, are crucial.

Comparing the outcomes for these three cases indicates how these factors played out. The overall comparison is summarized in Table 5.3. For *pornography*, conservatives had a well-organized movement with a solid infrastructure of organizations and congregations and much stronger

Table 5.3 COMPARATIVE OUTCOMES, PORNOGRAPHY, CHILD SEXUAL ABUSE, AND VAWA

Issue	Power	Cultural Change	Policy Change
Pornography	Conservatives: movement infrastructure; institutional political power; discursive power	Short-term: hybrid frame of "harm" to women temporarily adopted by conservatives	Short term: some legislation and increased enforcement
	Feminists: Grassroots movement organizations; discursive power (but feminist opposition reduced this)	Long term: discussion of and opposition to marital rape and child abuse in evangelical conservative contexts	Long term: Little to none
	Constitutional limits superseded both		
Child sexual abuse	Conservatives: established legal organizations and networks around child pornography, but not other forms of child sexual abuse	Increased visibility; decreased stigma Condemnation of both familial and stranger abuse	Initial: funding and treatment for familial abuse; social welfare supports
	Feminists: submerged ties to experts Nonideological expertise and experience superseded both		Later: stronger punitive policies for both stranger and familial abuse
VAWA	Conservatives: institutional political power; movement organizations disengaged	Violence against women linked to women's rights/civil rights Near-universal condemnation of domestic and sexual violence	Passage of VAWA, with both criminal justice and social service components
	Feminists: Institutional political power through established relationships with Democrats; discursive power; professionalized movement organizations		Limits on change around immigration, Native American, and LGBT issues

ties to policy-makers. Their discourse about pornography and sexual immorality was persuasive, but mainly within conservative and religious circles. Feminists mobilized grassroots organizations and protests and had the discursive advantage with their idea of opposing violence and subordination of women, but internal dissent and the overall decline of the women's movement left them at a disadvantage. Consequently, feminists made some inroads in how pornography was framed, but these were short-lived. Conservative emphases on obscenity enforcement, morality, and the need to protect children dominated both inside and outside the state. Constitutional constraints and opposition from civil libertarians and other feminists narrowed cultural support for antipornography efforts and diminished policy impact. Longer term, the rise in pornography consumption, legal constraints, and growing cultural acceptance of sexually explicit media meant that neither movement achieved most of its goals.

For *child sexual abuse*, the single-issue survivors' movement had mainly indirect ties to legislators through connections to professionals, as did feminist survivor activists. Conservative legal organizations dealing with child pornography had some influence within Congress, but only regarding the issue of pornography. But the experiential narrative's emotional power and its spread through mass media meant that single-issue movement frames had strong cultural resonance. Combined with the structural and discursive power of the idea of child abuse as criminal, this promoted an ongoing policy response. The initial increase in visibility for the issue accompanied funding and treatment for familial abusers, but over time, as the punitive state grew, punitive responses to child sexual abuse did so as well.

For *VAWA*, the women's movement had strong ties to Democratic lawmakers and developed solid ties to Republican cosponsors as well. Established feminist legal organizations built the women's movement's power, as did the fact that feminists had defined violence against women as an issue. Conservative activists, mostly disengaged from VAWA, had little influence. The cultural resonance of gendered crime increased women's movement influence. Lack of mobilization from either feminist or conservative activists at the grassroots enabled the coalition in Congress to continue without outside criticism. Initial outcomes, including passage of VAWA, the expectation that politicians across the spectrum would condemn domestic and sexual violence, and Title III (the civil rights clause) reflected this feminist influence. Long-term, powerful opposition to immigration reform and expansion of rights for Native Americans and LGBT people limited VAWA's reach.

The factors that shaped these outcomes are consistent with what previous work has found (Earl 2004; Soule and Olzak 2004), but all three cases relied much less on protest and mass mobilization than that work has suggested (see Amenta et al. 2010). This is partly gendered; women's movement policy gains historically have been less connected to protest, and there have been fewer feminist protest events reported (Banaszak 2010). It may also be a function of my focus and methodology. The close qualitative analysis of congressional hearings draws our attention to framing and the way that particular constructions of issues refer to larger discourses, suggest particular solutions, and draw on framing efforts by outside advocates. The emphasis on fields that include professionals and media, along with social movement organizations and state targets, draws our attention to mediated processes through which movements affect other actors that, in turn, affect policies (see Armstrong and Bernstein 2008). The child sexual abuse survivors' movement, for example, had virtually no protests or collective actions (Whittier 2009). But it radically transformed the cultural understanding and treatment of adults who had been sexually abused, brought about a huge upsurge in media attention, helped shape a professional research and treatment sector, and thus influenced federal policy. Similarly, the antipornography movement had only a handful of protests and there were no large-scale collective actions around VAWA, yet through lobbying, legal strategizing, writing, and small organizations, activists helped put the issues on the agenda and shaped their outcomes.

In the course of their interactions, movements and the state influence each other not only in concrete goals or policy outcomes but also at the level of meaning. Because frenemy relationships often emerge around movement goals of state intervention, such as law enforcement or legal rights, understanding their interrelation with meaning within the state is key. These unlikely and uneasy interactions rest on constructions of meaning—beliefs about the effectiveness and ideological implications of policies, about political priorities and larger goals; feelings of trust, empathy, wariness, or dislike; identities and affiliation with larger groups, or collective identities, and the questions of reputation that go along with those identities; discourses and frames for talking about and making sense of the world.

The cultural turn in social movement theory has thus far been largely limited to cultural processes within social movements and in civil society. Much work shows the importance of frames, collective identities, emotions, discourses, and interactive processes in social movements and civil society.[1] Yet, while many scholars have studied how social movements and states influence each other, few have studied how interpretive frameworks, collective identities, and emotion operate within the state as it interacts with social movements, nor how they shift as movements form alliances across political difference, nor how movements influence the interpretative frameworks, identities, and emotions of state actors. In this book,

I have attempted to unpack the circulation and construction of frames, emotions, and interactive processes in the state by analyzing congressional hearings. Viewing the state as cultural, as well as structural, shows how meaning is constructed and negotiated by legislators, professionals, outside advocates, and individuals telling their stories. Because of the power of prevailing discourse, emotion, and the construction of authority to shape what frames and policies prevail, this analysis promises to reshape our understanding of how social movements can produce change and why their own cultural processes matter. There is much to be done in theorizing these processes and examining them empirically in other state contexts, including less public ones.

PATHS FOR FEMINISM

In addition to affecting policy, these movements affected each other over time. First, they affected each other's strategies and frames. For example, religious conservatives' sympathy to activism against child sexual abuse and their abstention from VAWA opposition may have been influenced by their endorsement of feminist antiviolence frames around pornography. On a concrete level, key activists from antipornography feminism went on to become central to the movement against sex trafficking, which also drew substantial support from religious conservatives and both liberals and conservatives in Congress and presumably benefited from their earlier, more adversarial, collaboration against pornography (Bernstein 2012). The joint framing of child sexual abuse as beyond politics reinforced claims that everyone should likewise oppose violence against women. This is a kind of social movement spillover across ideological divides (Meyer and Whittier 1994). Second, movements' achievements include shaping political and cultural opportunities for their future incarnations or related movements (Staggenborg 1995). The strange bedfellow relationship complicates this, however, as gains produced by one party in such a relationship may open or foreclose opportunities for the other party. Third, collaborating with an otherwise-opposed movement can negatively affect participants' reputations and ties to their parent movements. The antipornography movement divided the women's movement and separated antiviolence feminism from the rest of the movement going forward (Bevacqua 2000; Corrigan 2013; Duggan and Hunter 1995). The division emerged over the politics of sexuality and the wisdom of seeking state-focused remedies, but charges that antipornography feminists were in bed with the Right fueled and justified the split. Disagreement over MacKinnon's theoretical underpinning for the civil rights ordinances against pornography—that pornography and sexual violence are key to women's subjugation and thus should be penalized as civil rights violations—also shapes some of the most influential critiques of state-focused feminism around issues other than pornography (e.g., Brown 1995).

Debates among feminists about pornography and sex have died down (Love 2015), although some antipornography feminists remain vocal (Dines 2011; Jensen 2007). A growing field of feminist pornography studies moves beyond the debate over "pleasure vs. danger" (e.g., Taormino et al. 2013). Intersectional feminist theorizing of pornography has been particularly productive. Earlier Black feminists analyzed sexually explicit representations of the bodies of women of color as invariably and only about oppression (e.g., Collins 2000; Walker 1981). More recently, authors like Cruz (2016), Shimizu (2007), Miller-Young (2014), and Nash (2008) have complicated that analysis, exploring how agency and power intertwine for both producers and consumers of pornography.

The debates among feminists over pornography played out mainly over the centrality of sexual violence to gender. But the politics of race and intersectional feminism are also a major source of different approaches to these issues. Race structures sexual violence in several ways: the greater vulnerability of women of color to sexual violence and the history of sexual violence against African American, Latino, and indigenous women; the way that white women and children personify innocence and vulnerability to crime; the intra-familial and thus mostly intra-racial nature of child sexual abuse and intimate partner violence; and the shelter from prosecution that race and class can provide for assailants (Freedman 2013; Richie 2012). Conservatives supporting anticrime measures often rely on racially coded language (Baker 2013) or overt opposition to measures addressing issues of race, as in VAWA immigration provisions. This is consistent with the history of racism and nationalism as important conservative strands (Benowitz 2015). Feminists, meanwhile, varied in the degree to which they took intersectional approaches. While antipornography feminists highlighted the greater degradation of women of color in pornography, their general argument was comprehensible without consideration of the intersections of race and gender. The feminist antipornography movement was predominantly white, although prominent Black feminists like Alice Walker and Patricia Hill Collins also developed important feminist antipornography arguments. The narrow neutrality of activism against child sexual abuse entailed omitting discussion of race, gender, and class almost entirely, even as the focus on familial abuse and—implicitly—white, innocent children directed the intensifying punitive response to white offenders more than in other crimes (Leon 2011). VAWA, the most explicitly intersectional feminist movement, drew on the institutional base of women of color in anti-rape and domestic violence movements (Matthews 1994) along with a cross-organizational coalition.

Although feminist activism on these issues was not always intersectional, it also was not simply white feminism. Sexual violence is a major focus of Black feminist writing and activism, including documenting how race and gender together shape sexual violence as a means of subjugation of women of color (e.g., Collins 2000), but also how the state and law enforcement both directly inflict violence and fail to protect women of color from violence (Richie 2012). This clearly precludes simple calls for increased law enforcement as a remedy. However, there are significant strategic differences over targeting the state for reform and to garner funding for services versus disengaging from state-focused activism altogether.

The degree to which feminists advocated intersectional goals and frames affected the amount of conservative support they garnered and the impact they had. Antipornography feminists and opponents of child sexual abuse made no intersectional demands. This facilitated conservatives' adversarial collaboration but also prevented the promotion of strategies or programs to address how race, class, and other issues shape experiences and sources of violence. VAWA, where feminists overtly and strenuously advocated for intersectional demands, came up against spaces in Congress that could accommodate only unidimensional frames and politicians who were adamantly anti-immigration and anti-LGBT. Nevertheless, the persistent focus on the specific needs of women of color, immigrants, and other marginalized groups produced the special funding streams and requirements for "underserved groups," achieving some intersectional goals unobtrusively. Intersectional outcomes, in other words, like other kinds of movement outcomes, are a product of activists' frames and strategies, their alliances, *and* the constraints of what is possible in a given political context.

Sexual violence is an area where profound social change has occurred and where major parts of the feminist agenda remain unachieved. Both the changes and limits are linked to the contradictory power and danger of organizing around issues defined as crimes. Carceral feminism, the attempt to use the state's punitive powers to advance women's freedom, is undeniably a strand within the women's movement. It clearly carries substantial risks for the many people who are targeted by state violence because of nationality, race, gender, class, and sexuality.

The case studies examined in this book suggest two conclusions about carceral feminism. First, we ought to be careful about extending the concept of carceral feminism to other movements without careful analysis.

Bernstein's (2010; 2012) analysis of the anti-sex-trafficking movement—the basis for her analysis of carceral feminism—is a model of how to incorporate research on social movements, law and policy, overarching discourses, and consequences. Similarly close empirical analysis of other cases and their outcomes, as I have done here, suggests variation. As I have shown, the discursive and structural power of crime played out differently in the three cases. Antipornography feminism did not have the full force of the criminal state behind it because the idea that obscenity was a crime was fading by the 1980s. In fact, the rapidly shrinking ability to use criminal law against obscenity is part of why both conservative and feminist opponents of pornography turned in other directions. Child sexual abuse, bound to a politically neutral single-issue approach, was ultimately defined primarily in terms of ever-harsher criminal penalties—child sexual abuse policy is carceral, but not particularly feminist. VAWA, with the strong countervailing force of intersectional women's movement organizing, occupies a middle ground with both carceral and noncarceral feminist outcomes.

Second, alternative approaches to targeting the state's criminal dimensions struggle to succeed because of the structural and cultural power of crime. As Brown (1995) writes, feminists attempt to "exploit and subvert" state power. While these attempts may fail, failure to redirect state power does not equate to endorsement of the use of state power to oppress. Carceral feminist outcomes around sexual violence are not always due to feminists' embrace of the carceral state but can result from their attempt to reform the state's structural and discursive power. Understanding their attempts and the mixed results through social movement theories about outcomes helps clarify the limiting effects of external constraints.

Overall, increased state intervention into sexual violence can be interpreted in different ways. On the one hand, some say that the women's movement has been a handmaiden of increasing neoliberal state power (Bumiller 2008; Fraser 2013). Many feminist and progressive theorists view any kind of movement engagement with the state as depoliticizing in its inevitable collusion with neoliberalism, which can only absorb and co-opt movements and draw them away from more genuinely revolutionary impulses and activity. Consequently, for example, instead of working to criminalize rape on par with other crimes, activists should work to dismantle the prison system (Spade 2011). On the other hand, state intervention represents taking the issue of sexual violence seriously, recognizing that it occurs, is significant, and should not be tacitly permitted. In a culture where criminalization demonstrates the recognition that something is bad, criminalizing sexual violence is a discursive means of saying that it is, indeed, bad, even if the rapist is a husband, father, or acquaintance, or the victim is poor, a person of color, a child, a sex worker, or transgender, lesbian, bisexual, or gay. Because of the importance of meaning-making to state power, the legitimacy conferred on sexual violence by treating it as a crime is significant. When law enforcement does not intervene in violence against people of color, children in families, and low income people, the discursive consequence is to legitimate that violence. This is the case even though many consequences of this criminalized meaning or of law enforcement intervention are far from liberatory for women, people of color, or other oppressed groups.

Refraining from engaging with the state does not negate its power or assure a more transformative outcome. Whether or not activists engage with it, the state's power continues to structure violence and sexuality and to criminalize some forms of violent and sexual behavior. It continues to mete out punishment or permit violence to occur unchecked depending on the race, gender, class, immigration status, and "respectability" of perpetrator and victim. Agents of the state continue to perpetrate violence against people of color, immigrants, and other marginalized groups. Disengaging from the state carries both positive and negative (and intended and unintended) consequences for progressive social transformation. The American state is not benign, but the assumption that a weaker state would be better for women, people of color, or the overall level of surveillance and control, is false. The lack of a strong state is no guarantee of less violence against women or anybody else.

What lessons might activists draw from these case studies? On the one hand, the power of the state and of countervailing movements often outweighs the deep commitments and strategic actions of feminists. This may seem a discouraging lesson. Indeed, I hope one thing that activists will take from this book is greater patience with one another's failures and a hesitance to blame one another for policy shortcomings. On the other hand, these cases show inroads and points of influence. One is the process of meaning construction inside and outside the state. Frames must make sense within existing meaning systems if they are to be adopted by powerful actors or to shape policy, but they can be crafted to stretch these meaning systems. The gendered crime frame used by VAWA activists is one such example; the idea that pornography is used to promote marital rape and child sexual abuse is another. These frames bridge feminist and conservative ideas. While the gendered crime frame promoted the passage of VAWA, it also probably made other legislation and policy more likely over time. This includes the Education Department's promulgation of rules to use Title IX (which prohibits sex discrimination in education) to reform campus sexual assault procedures, led by Vice President Biden, architect of VAWA. The idea of sexual assault as an infringement on women's rights is undeniably important to the Title IX effort. The frame about pornography's links to sexual violence did not change policy or reduce pornography. It did, however, shift religious conservatives' conversations about violence against women and children, which in turn left a more hospitable ground for the support and self-help groups of adult survivors of child sexual abuse, efforts to get clergy to better counsel women who were raped or assaulted by their husbands, and debates over the idea of male headship of the family. This, in turn, left religious conservatives less inclined to oppose legislation on child sexual abuse or VAWA.

Activists who hope to find support across ideological differences should carefully consider the frames they use. One shortcoming of the gendered crime frame was the difficulty activists faced in using it to achieve change that addressed intersections of gender with immigration status, race, or sexuality. Activists working on prison reform, for example, might consider bridging frames that include gender, class, and race. Activists continuing to work on sexual violence might consider how to frame victims' vulnerability to violence in terms of age, race, class, or sexuality, as well as gender. Are there frames about racial inequality that could connect anticrime politicians with antiracist feminists? Such frames hold the most promise for promoting legislation that would more effectively intervene in sexual violence across the board. When working with frenemies, activists should weigh the risks to their reputations and support within their parent movements with the amount of power and potential influence they and their unlikely allies have. The comparison of these three cases suggests that activists may have more influence than their adversarial collaborators when they have more powerful allies, frames that resonate with established discourses, and movement organization or grassroots activism to back them up. Sometimes these conditions favor conservatives, and sometimes they favor feminists or progressives. Clear assessment of these circumstances can help activists determine when cross-ideological work may be worth the risks. The danger of compromise is not only that submerging some elements of activists' larger agenda is risky in itself. In the context of lesser power, activists may lose regardless, but in the context of greater power, they may surrender parts of their agenda unnecessarily.

FRENEMIES BEYOND THE WOMEN'S MOVEMENT

The gendered crime frame remains powerful and shapes state actions in several related areas. Sexual assault in the military and on college campuses has sparked government inquiries, activism, and administrative action (Rondini 2015; Steinhauer 2014). In these cases, the issues are framed as an affront to women's rights and as crimes that have not been taken seriously. The very light sentence imposed on a white Stanford student convicted of rape in 2016, for example, provoked widespread outrage at what many saw as a trivialization of rape as well as the contrast to the long sentences imposed on less privileged offenders. The dominant response to campus sexual assault and sexual assault in the military—that they be taken seriously and prosecuted (or administratively investigated and punished through state-mandated campus policies)—is a demand that the state use its punitive powers on behalf of women. This carries risks for women of color, undocumented immigrants, and other marginalized groups. For feminists, these issues are complex.

Frenemies also come together around numerous other issues: prison reform (Miller 2015; Gingrich and Nolan 2014), same-sex marriage, environmental engineering to reduce climate change, immigration and refugees, and advocacy of polygyny (Heath et al. 2016). Issues that foster overlapping frames and connect to the basic beliefs and interests of different groups are the most likely to see sustained relationships and policy outcomes. For example, frames bridge freedom from state intervention and the right to marry; fiscal savings and the reduction of the prison population; and the religious obligation to steward the natural world with the need to control climate change.

Since the election of President Obama, and even more so since the election of President Trump, the U.S. Congress and American public have been highly polarized. The prospects for collaboration among adversaries certainly vary depending on the context. The contention surrounding the 2012–2013 reauthorization of VAWA illustrates the decline of cooperation across ideological lines in Congress. The election of Trump, however, also produced numerous unlikely connections, such as shifting mutual support between Wikileaks' Julian Assange and the American Right (Doyle 2017), wary interactions between unions and conservative opponents of globalization (Peterson 2000), praise for the CIA and FBI from many organizations on the Left, and a broad-based, ideologically diverse resistance to conservative policy changes. At the municipal level, neighborhood organizing for city services or on issues like traffic or schools is inherently less ideological and can draw otherwise-opposed participants, while refugee resettlement efforts pull in both conservative and liberal religious groups. In analyzing—or seeking to organize with—frenemies, however, we should remember that such relationships take different forms from coalitions. They may involve only leaders or (conversely) rank-and-file collaboration, and they may provoke internal conflict over the risks of collaborating with the enemy. Participants work hard to strategize about all kinds of relationships across difference and their goals. These efforts affect the path of their relationship and the outcomes of their struggles. At the same time, the shifting balance of power—elite allies, resonant frames, and mass mobilization—strongly affects which participants have more influence.

In a highly polarized political environment, the idea that ideological opponents might collaborate at all, no matter how antagonistically, seems quaint. The three variations on relationships between frenemies described in this book suggest some forms to watch for. When ideological opponents collaborate, they may seek to distance themselves from each other and protect their independent reputations, as in the pornography battles. They may carve out a single-issue focus and define it as nonpolitical, as in the child sexual abuse battles. They may collaborate in only one arena, such as in Congress or in state or municipal government, as in the effort to pass VAWA. Both scholars and activists can benefit from closer attention to the complicated ways that strange bedfellows attempt to produce social change.

NOTES

CHAPTER 1

1. For the key social movements literature on coalitions, see Almeida 2010; Bystydzienski and Schact 2001; Gilmore 2008; Isaac 2010; McCammon and Campbell 2002; Obach 2004; Rochon, and Meyer 1997; Rochon and Meyer 1997; Van Dyke 2003; Van Dyke and McCammon 2010.
2. This discussion follows Whittier 2014.
3. Each dimension is a continuum.
4. This is a broader definition of congruence than used in most coalitions literature, which treats radical and liberal feminists as not ideologically aligned (McCammon and Van Dyke 2010).
5. I am indebted for this insight to the work of Margot Canaday (2009), who makes a similar argument about how regulation of homosexuality was central to the development of state bureaucracy from the 1920s forward, the period when US bureaucracy and the form of the late modern state developed.
6. I included but did not systematically analyze coverage in more progressive religious publications, including the *National Catholic Reporter, Christian Century*, and *Sojourners Magazine*.
7. Using the Policy Agendas Project, which codes movement-related stories from the *New York Times*, and my independent search of the *New York Times*, I found very few articles on the case studies, as many of their activities were not of the type required for news coverage. Data available at http://www.comparativeagendas.net/.
8. Banaszak (2010) confirms that there are relatively fewer women's movement protest events captured in large data sets based on media coverage of movement events (i.e., Baumgartner and Mahoney 2005) in part because the women's movement has relied more on litigation and insider activism.
9. These include interviews with 40 activists against child sexual abuse; attendance at three national conferences and several local events organized by activists against child sexual abuse between 1999 and 2003; interviews with 34 activists in the Columbus, Ohio, feminist and anti-rape movement conducted 1989–1990. These data were the primary basis for my books *The Politics of Child Sexual Abuse* and *Feminist Generations*, respectively, and are secondary in this book.
10. The first hearing on VAWA was held in 1990; I also selectively analyzed earlier hearings on rape to understand the background for VAWA. I ended the sample for pornography in 2011. The indexing of congressional hearings moved from Lexis-Nexis to Proquest Congressional during the process of the research.

11. My search process yielded a larger group of hearings on each topic than the procedure used for the Policy Agendas Project, which also does not code witness information.

12. I used the transcripts of the hearings for my analysis, including the verbal presentation by witnesses, members' statements, and question and answer, instead of the prepared testimony for the hearings, in order to get at the collaborative construction of meaning. Witness testimony typically summarized prepared testimony, although some witnesses read it verbatim and others' statements were more loosely connected to their prepared testimony. Details on the qualitative samples are in each chapter. I coded and analyzed these hearings for frames, witness affiliation, emotion, and other variables using Atlas.ti.

13. I eliminated cases that cited case law when dealing with a different issue, had no or few amici, or dealt with sex work but did not engage with obscenity or zoning. I excluded briefs filed by cities, states, governors' or mayors' associations, and the federal government from my counts of briefs. I include briefs filed at the district and appellate levels for one case dealing with a key municipal antipornography ordinance because of its unique substantive importance. Details on each sample are in the substantive chapters.

14. Freedman (2013:1) argues that the connections between race and rape have been important to maintaining structural inequality; as she puts it, "white men's freedom to be sexually violent or coercive lay at the heart of their political power."

15. My discussion in this section is indebted to Estelle Freedman's excellent book, *Redefining Rape*, and Lynn Sacco's excellent *Unspeakable*.

16. Earlier, the 1931 Scottsboro case, in which nine Black men were wrongly convicted of rape, drew international condemnation. Interracial coalitions that included the NAACP, ACLU, and the US Communist Party came together around Scottsboro and, subsequently, "mobilization against interracial rape accusations became a staple among leftists and liberals" (Freedman 2013:257).

17. The trial of Joann Little, an African American woman who killed a prison guard who attempted to rape her, generated a major cross-racial coalition that included NOW, the NAACP, and many grassroots activists (McGuire 2010).

18. So universal was this assumption that even activists who later were squarely in the opposing camp viewed pornography as a form of violence against women. For example, Felice Newman, who later wrote *The Secrets of Lesbian Sex* and lesbian erotica, explained to an interviewer in 1999 that she had "a skeleton in [her] closet." As a founder of the feminist Cleis Press, when she published the anthology *Fight Back*, about the feminist antiviolence movement, she "included pornography in the section on violence against women." Newman further revealed that one of the founders of the lesbian sex magazine *On Our Backs*, Debbi Sundahl, "was part of the anti-pornography movement. So some of us who went on to become great promoters of lesbian erotica used to be anti-porn feminists." "Getting It Interview: The Secrets of Lesbian Sex Interview with Felice Newman by Athena Douris," *Crave*, November 30, 1999, www.gettingit.com/crave, accessed September 15, 2010.

19. Organizations included the Christian Voice, Committee for the Survival of a Free Congress, the National Conservative Political Action Committee, the Conservative Caucus, and Stop ERA (Diamond 1995; Lo 1982). 1976 was a turning point, with the election of President Jimmy Carter, an outspoken evangelical, but grassroots activists were disappointed with his policy directions

and the fact that he appointed few evangelicals to his administration. The election of Ronald Reagan was more satisfactory, although grassroots and leaders remained unhappy with the pace and scope of the changes he introduced. Evangelical conservatives worked for Rev. Pat Robertson's failed 1988 Republican nomination bid, after which participants were organized into the influential grassroots network Christian Coalition, headed by former Robertson organizer Ralph Reed (Lindsay 2008:57).

20. This includes virtually all obscenity prosecutions, since materials are distributed through mail or online.

CHAPTER 2

1. For an exception, see Potter 2012.
2. For more critiques of antipornography feminism, see Bob 1986; Califia 1986; Duggan and Hunter 1995; Duggan 2006; Ferguson 1986; Kaminer 1992; LaCombe 1994; Lynn and American Civil Liberties Union 1986; McHarry 1986; Nobile and Nadler 1986; Page 1986; Rapping 1987; Strossen 1993; Strossen 2000; Vance 1990; Vance 1986b; West 1987.
3. The 1973 Supreme Court ruling in *Miller v. California* established nationwide standards that still guide enforcement today. *Miller* defined obscenity in terms of "whether the average person, applying contemporary community standards would find that the work, taken as a whole, appeals to the prurient interest" and "whether the work, taken as a whole, lacks serious literary, artistic, political, or scientific value" (*Miller v. California*, 413 U.S. 15, 24 [1972]). Over the long term, *Miller*'s use of contemporary community standards to define obscenity has produced a steady narrowing of the definition, as community standards have liberalized and sexually explicit material has become more acceptable. See also Strub 2011.
4. Major hearings were U.S. House 1982; U.S. Senate 1982a, 1982b, 1982c; others included U.S. House 1981, 1983; U.S. Senate 1981a. On child pornography, see U.S. Senate 1982a, a relatively backstage hearing attended only by Specter, Charles Grassley (R-Iowa, who was on the Judiciary Committee but not the Juvenile Justice subcommittee), and three staff members. Following the Supreme Court's 1982 decision in *New York v. Ferber* that allowed greater restriction of sexually explicit photographs of minors, the hearing considered a bill that would prohibit materials that did not "meet the obscenity standard." The debate played out around *Show Me*, a sexuality education book for young people initially published in Germany that included photographs of nude children and adults. Published by St. Martin's Press in 1975, *Show Me* was prosecuted unsuccessfully in several U.S. and Canadian venues and withdrawn by the publisher after *Ferber*, according to testimony of Roy Gainsburg, counsel for St. Martin's Press (U.S. Senate 1982a:123). Grassley suggested "materials such as National Geographic issues" might raise similar issues (5). Witnesses and members of Congress debated the educational value of the book and ramifications of banning it. Ultimately, the 1984 Child Protection Act did not exempt images of nude children with "literary, artistic, scientific, or educational value" (Senator Charles Grassley, speaking in U.S. Senate 1982c). It substantially increased the range of materials subject to prosecution and led to increased prosecution and conviction.
5. In his first three years of the presidency, Reagan mentioned pornography only four times in public speeches. "Remarks Announcing Federal Initiatives Against

Drug Trafficking and Organized Crime," October 14, 1982; "Remarks at the Annual Convention of the National Association of Evangelicals in Orlando, Florida," March 8, 1983; "Remarks at the Annual Meeting of the American Bar Association in Atlanta, Georgia," August 1, 1983. All at http://www.presidency.ucsb.edu/ws/index.php?pid=43127&st=pornography&st1=, accessed October 8, 2010.

6. In his 1984 State of the Union address, child pornography came immediately after religion and the rights of the unborn. Ronald Reagan, "Address before a Joint Session of the Congress on the State of the Union," January 25, 1984, http://www.presidency.ucsb.edu/ws/index.php?pid=43127&st=pornography&st1=, accessed October 8, 2010.

7. There is no clear term for feminist opponents of antipornography feminism, who sometimes called themselves pro-sex, sex positive, or anticensorship. The terms are problematic, because the movement was concerned with issues beyond censorship and because the other side cannot accurately be termed "anti-sex" when the dispute was about modes of sexual expression (see Walters 1996). Despite the awkwardness, I generally use "opponents of antipornography feminism."

8. Cold War campaigns against obscenity included liberal and conservative politicians and included a 1955 special congressional committee report that portrayed pornography as a large, well-organized industry that threatened American youth, investigations under FBI chief J. Edgar Hoover, and hearings in state legislatures (Strub 2011).

9. See, for example, 1977 WAVPM debates over working with San Francisco Mayor Dianne Feinstein on a zoning ordinance (Bronstein 2011:210). Minutes, February 12, 1977, p. 5 and February 19, 1977, p. 3. Box 1: Administrative Files, Folder "Committee Records—General Meeting, 1977–83," Women Against Violence in Pornography and the Media Records, 96-21, The GLBT Historical Society of Northern California. Henceforth cited as WAVPM Papers.

10. E.g., in 1977, they discussed the fact that board member Diana Russell and Susan Brownmiller were "in favor of censorship," and concluded, "violence and brutality to women and children is an abuse of the 1st Amendment," but decided to "use the words 'bannish' [sic] and/or 'abolish' rather than censorship." Minutes, March 12, 1977, p. 2. Box 1: Administrative Files, Folder "Committee Records—General Meeting, 1977–83," WAVPM Papers.

11. Minutes, March 24, 1979, p. 1. Box 1: Administrative Files, Folder "Committee Records—General Meeting, 1977–83," WAVPM Papers.

12. Minutes February 19, 1980, March 23, 1980 and April 7, 1980. Box 1: Administrative Files, Folder "Committee Records—First Amendment Committee," WAVPM Papers.

13. "A Look at the Data," unnamed presenter, possibly Pauline Bart. February 23, 1980. Minutes April 26, 1980, "Questions We Get Asked." Box 1: Administrative Files, Folder "Committee Records—General Meeting, 1977–83," WAVPM Papers.

14. Minutes April 26, 1980, "Questions We Get Asked." Box 1: Administrative Files, Folder "Committee Records—General Meeting, 1977–83," WAVPM Papers. They maintained this stance over the years. For example, in a 1983 discussion of strategy one member "pointed out that WAVPM stays away from legal approaches (censorship) because we do not wish to affect the economic status of women in pornography. It is the women working in pornography who lose business when women protest outside a pornography business, not the men

running it." Minutes May 15, 1983, p. 1. Box 1: Administrative Files, Folder "Committee Records—General Meeting, 1977–83," WAVPM Papers.

15. Letters to the editor in the feminist newspaper *off our backs* illustrate how conflicts following the 1982 Barnard conference set the stage for the disputes over pornography law that followed. Filling the letters sections for three issues in late 1982, most letter writers criticized antipornography and anti-BDSM feminists and the *off our backs* coverage that they saw as biased against the conference. A "Post-Conference Petition" noted that the conference program and sponsorship were withdrawn after the protests (Abraham, et al., "Post-Conference Petition" [letter to the editor], *off our backs* letters section. July 1982, p. 26). Across these three issues, only two people, Lynn Campbell (a member of San Francisco's WAVPM who later went to New York City to work on the startup of WAP, whose letter was printed without affiliation) and Sheila Roher, wrote in support of the OOB position and the protesters at the conference (Lynn Campbell, "Skirting the Issue" and Sheila Roher, "Petition," *off our backs* letters section. August–September 1982, p. 33). Arguing over butch-fem identities, lesbian BDSM, and heterosexual desire, well-known feminists wrote to decry the hostility shown to them by other feminists (Gayle Rubin, "Misquotes and Misperceptions," Amber Hollibaugh, "Patronizing Slander," *off our backs* letters section. July 1982, p. 26; Joan Nestle, "Years of Labels," *off our backs* letters section. August–September 1982, p. 32; Samois, "Samois Corrects"). WAVPM wrote to clarify that their critique of pornography was about power and consent, not sexual explicitness; Cleveland's WAVAW wrote to explain that they were not associated with other WAVAW chapters or with WAVAW's protests at the conference (Laura Boytz, "WAVPM Explains;" Cleveland WAVAW, "Cleveland WAVAW Clarifies," *off our backs* letters section. November 1982. p. 26).

16. Many of the letters came after an appearance by WAP members on the daytime talk show *Phil Donahue* in July 1979, which also probably increased attendance at their march a few months later (Bronstein 2011:194–95). WAP received some funding and other material assistance from groups aiming to "clean up" New York's Times Square (Potter 2012; Van Gelder 1980).

17. Based on my comprehensive database of coverage of pornography in feminist and conservative publications, as detailed in the Introduction.

18. Massachusetts state legislature, March 16, 1992; Los Angeles hearing before the Commission for Women, April 22, 1985 (both reprinted in MacKinnon and Dworkin 1997); Cambridge, Massachusetts, was a referendum question (Duggan and Hunter 1995:26; testimony of FACT member Nancy Ryan, quoted in MacKinnon and Dworkin 1997,:401). According to Brest and Vandenberg (1987:657), the Women's Alliance Against Pornography gathered sufficient signatures to place the Cambridge referendum on the ballot, but the City Council refused to do so on the grounds that the ordinance was unconstitutional. WAAP sued, and the ordinance was placed on the ballot and defeated 13,031 to 9,419.

19. UM Class Finding Porn Violent and Disturbing," *St. Paul Sunday Pioneer Press*, Nov. 13, 1983, cited in Downs 1989:56. A law school professor told journalist Downs that, in Downs's words, "debate about pornography raged in the student paper and in the halls, and professors felt pressure to avoid their usual jokes about sex in class" (Downs 1989:56). The professor, David Bryden, told Downs that "he had not seen such humorless 'subtle censorship' before in his fifteen years at the law school, except during the conflict over the Vietnam War" (218). One assumes that MacKinnon and Dworkin were pleased to exercise "subtle

censorship" over faculty members' "usual jokes about sex in class." Dworkin wrote to Steinem that one of the students in the class was Rosalie Wahl, the first woman Supreme Court Justice in Minnesota. Wahl, appointed to the Court in 1977, "chaired its task forces on gender fairness and racial bias." Minnesota Historical Society, Finding Aid, Rosalie Wahl papers, http://www.mnhs.org/library/findaids/00430.xml, accessed June 20, 2011. Wahl's papers, at the Minnesota Historical Society, include few materials on pornography: 1979 correspondence related to an appellate obscenity case, and materials relating to a National Association of Woman Judges workshop on pornography and the First Amendment, held at its conference, October 12, 1985. On the demonstration, see "Pornography Class Led to Protest Film Star Visit," *Minneapolis Star and Tribune*, Dec. 10, 1983, p. 1B, cited in Downs 1989:57.

Class readings included feminist writing on pornography and rape, theoretical work on gender and sexuality (some of which was critiqued), news articles on pornography and prostitution, case law, and examples of pornography. For example, the section on "Playboy/Penthouse/Hustler" required students to "read one entire current issue," and included supporting and opposing commentary, relevant cases, and reports of feminist activism. A section on privacy included excerpts from Roland Barthes's *Camera Lucida,* Alice Walker's account of the damaging effects of pornography on a heterosexual relationship ("Coming Apart"), nine legal cases, a leaflet by the Kitty Genovese Women's Project, Erving Goffman's *Gender Advertisements*, an article on "wife rape" from *Penthouse,* and a speech by antipornography activist John Stoltenberg. A section dealing with BDSM paraphernalia was followed by many materials on BDSM, with a focus on lesbian BDSM. These included a transcript from a *Phil Donohue* show, articles from mainstream media, writings by lesbian BDSM advocates and theorists including Gayle Rubin and Pat Califia, and articles from the anthology *Against Sadomasochism.* "Pornography" course syllabus, Catharine A. MacKinnon and Andrea Dworkin, Fall 1983, University of Minnesota Law School. Box 202, Folder 6, Gloria Steinem Papers, Sophia Smith Collection, Smith College, Northampton, Mass. Henceforth cited as Steinem Papers. Quoted course description, p. 1; list of topics, p. ii and topic titles in readings list throughout syllabus.

20. Letter from Dworkin to Steinem, November 4, 1983. Box 202, Folder 3, p. 1, Steinem Papers.

21. This was "discrimination by trafficking in pornography" in the first version in Minneapolis. It also allowed action by "any man or transsexual who alleges injury by pornography in the way women are injured by it." It addressed "coercion into pornography," "forcing pornography on a person," and "assault or physical attack due to pornography" (MacKinnon and Dworkin 1997:429). The definition of "coercion into pornography" was broad, essentially defining appearing in pornography as coercion regardless of circumstances, even if: "the person actually consented . . . demonstrated no resistance or appeared to cooperate actively. . . signed a contract, or made statements affirming a willingness to cooperate in the production of pornography; or . . . was paid or otherwise compensated" (MacKinnon and Dworkin 1997:429, 435–36, 442–43). Wording varied slightly among the versions.

22. For example, if a woman's husband forced her to reenact a scene from *Hustler*, or she could show that the attitudes promoted by a specific issue of *Hustler* had a negative effect on the social position of women more generally, she could sue the publisher and distributors of that issue of *Hustler.*

23. "Briefing notes for Minneapolis." Tuesday, July 10 [1984]. Anonymous [possibly Dworkin] to Steinem. Box 202, Folder 7, p. 4, Steinem Papers. Similarly, an article by MacKinnon and Dworkin in a 1983 WAP newsletter makes clear that they believe material that presents women as sexual objects in these ways will be covered: "dehumanizing women as sexual things . . . is fundamental to the subordination and the precondition for the more explicit violence." See also Catharine A. MacKinnon and Andrea Dworkin, "Commentary: The Minneapolis Ordinance," in *Women Against Pornography Newsreport* 6(1) Spr/Sum, 1984. Box 202, Folder 3, p. 2, Steinem Papers.

24. Dworkin to Steinem, November 4, 1983. Box 202, Folder 3, p. 1, Steinem Papers. Emphasis in original.

25. MacKinnon to Steinem, November 18, 1983. Box 202, Folder 3, Steinem Papers.

26. Based on my own count and coding of the witnesses' testimony, as reprinted in MacKinnon and Dworkin 1997. I judged whether witnesses had been recruited by MacKinnon and Dworkin based on their interactions with MacKinnon or Dworkin during the hearing, including introductions, questioning that suggested prior familiarity with the content of the testimony, and submission of exhibits or written materials by MacKinnon or Dworkin based on the testimony. There is no evidence about who recruited Eugene Conway. Brest and Vandeberg (1987:633) reported Conway's retraction.

27. Two brothers who owned numerous pornographic bookstores and theaters in Minneapolis attended but neither they nor their lawyer spoke. Although they expected the ordinance to pass, their lawyer said that they did not consider it to be "a serious challenge to their business," and he looked forward to extensive legal fees in the ensuing successful suit (Brest and Vandenberg 1987:632). The tenuous coalition between gay men and lesbians in 1984 was apparent: some gay men spoke against the ordinance based on the importance of adult bookstores as meeting places for gay men and community and the editor of *GLC Voice*, "accused the proponents of 'gay bashing,'" Meanwhile, "a lesbian" wrote to *GLC Voice*, "Why should we support AIDS research if you don't support the anti-rape movement?" (quoted in Brest and Vandenberg 1987:641).

28. Quoted in Downs 1989:64. Steve Cramer, Minneapolis councilmember, told Downs that the woman had testified for the ordinance (89). The *Star Tribune* later reported that the woman, Ruth Christenson, age 22 or 23, survived with severe burns, and feminist pornography opponents held vigils outside her hospital room and issued a statement asking women not to harm themselves. Christenson lived another six-and-one-half years until she committed suicide in 1990 by setting herself on fire in her apartment (Haga 1990).

29. "Briefing notes for Minneapolis." Tuesday, July 10 [1984]. Anonymous [possibly Dworkin], to Steinem. Box 202, Folder 7, pp. 8–11, Steinem Papers. For example, it included a page and a half detailing what Steinem should say to the bill's new sponsor, Sharon Sayles-Belton, whom the author of the memo saw as an unreliable ally, stating: "It is important that from the conversation she understand that people are watching who know the difference between a bill that will do a lot and one that won't." The document also asked Steinem to call the bill's other cosponsor, Tony Scallon, and simultaneously butter him up and make him realize that the wrong vote would be a mistake, and to call his wife to "ask her for her help in shoring Tony up. Also, please tell her how important it is for there to be visible male leadership on this, and how proud she must be of Tony for taking the leadership." "Kitty" (MacKinnon) and "Andrea" (Dworkin) had

also left telephone messages for Steinem before the first vote with personalized talking points for council members, and Steinem wrote a fundraising letter for Citizens against Pornography. Box 202, Folder 3, Steinem Papers.

30. "Briefing notes for Minneapolis." Tuesday, July 10 [1984]. Anonymous [probably Dworkin], to Steinem. Box 202, Folder 7, pp. 12–19, Steinem Papers. NOW passed a national resolution supporting the ordinance in 1994 and, according to MacKinnon, (1997:13) "hosted testimony on pornography across the nation." MacKinnon cites in a footnote: "NOW Hearings on Pornography, Materials on the Personal Testimony of NOW Activists on Pornography (Lois Reckitt, Twiss Butler, and Melanie Gilbert, eds.) National Org for Women, Inc., May 23, 1986."

31. Downs (1989), the exception, emphasizes the threat to civil liberties.

32. Draft letter, Dorchen Leidholdt to Gloria Steinem, June 22, 1984 and reply from Steinem to Leidholdt, June 26, 1984. Box 202, Folder 3, Steinem Papers. Dworkin and Dorchen Leidholdt did participate in a debate under the auspices of the Library Association with opponents of the ordinance, including Indianapolis feminist attorney Sheila Kennedy who became one of the local lawyers in the later challenge to the ordinance (Downs 1989:116, 129).

33. Neither is included in MacKinnon and Dworkin's collection of testimony from the ordinances (MacKinnon and Dworkin 1997).

34. In subsequent hearings in Boston, Los Angeles, and Cambridge, none of which led to passage, no antipornography conservatives testified. Based on my count and coding of witnesses listed in testimony reprinted in MacKinnon and Dworkin 1997, which MacKinnon says contains all witnesses for these hearings and full testimony of opponents. Besides the two CDL witnesses described by Downs, itis possible that other witnesses were omitted from MacKinnon's anthology; however, she states in her introduction that the records from which she drew the Indianapolis materials were incomplete, and does not say this about the other locations (MacKinnon 1997:n. 24, p. 9). Witnesses from a campaign in Suffolk, New York, by conservatives to pass a differently framed ordinance, which WAP and MacKinnon opposed, are not included.

35. The plaintiffs were the American Booksellers Association, the Association for American Publishers, the Council for Periodical Distributors Associations, the Freedom to Read Foundation (an offshoot of the American Library Association), the International Periodical Distributors Association, Koch News Company (an Indianapolis-based distributor of a range of books, not including pornography), the National Association of College Stores, Omega Satellite Products Co. (a satellite television company), Video Shack (a video cassette rental company), and one individual, Kelly Bentley, described in the court decision as "an adult female resident and citizen of Indianapolis, and a reader and viewer of First Amendment protected material."

36. Dworkin to Steinem, November 4, 1983. Box 202, Folder 3, p. 3, Steinem Papers.

37. Four of these hearings, with 48 witnesses, including 2 antipornography conservatives and 2 antipornography feminists, occurred from 1989 to 1991 under Bush. No hearings were held in 1990, 1992, or 1993. I have included years through 1991 here, even though they are after the peak, to include the final federal efforts of antipornography feminism.

38. Republicans held the Senate through 1986, after which Democrats took control; Democrats held the House for the full period. (Although the 102nd Congress held office through 1992, no hearings were held in 1992.)

39. Witness counts exclude statements by subcommittee members and materials in Appendices. All witnesses are counted for the total, but government employees (prosecutors, inspectors, etc.) and elected officials are not included in the counts of antipornography feminist or conservative witnesses even if they made antipornography feminist or conservative arguments, because they are not movement members. Also omitted from the counts of feminist and conservative witnesses are witnesses who opposed pornography from neither feminist nor conservative perspectives and feminist witnesses who did not oppose pornography. For example, some witnesses testified about their personal experience of coercion into appearing in pornography but did not discuss the effects of pornography on violence against women more broadly or place their statements in the context of women's rights. Feminist witnesses who did not take an antipornography position were mostly from service organizations for rape or domestic violence who were questioned about the relationship of pornography to domestic violence, but specifically rejected analyses of pornography as causal.
40. Based on whether they reported an affiliation in their testimony.
41. There was some crossover in individual testimony between Congress and the Meese Commission. In addition to antipornography feminist leaders, "David," who testified at a 1981 congressional hearing on child exploitation (U.S. Senate 1981a), testified before the Meese Commission (Merrill Hartson, "Pornography," AP, June 18, 1985. Box 14, File "Press Conference 20 May 1986 DOG to Announce the Members of the Attorney General's Commission on Pornography," Edwin Meese Papers, Hoover Institution Archives, Stanford, CA (henceforth Meese Papers).
42. Even noted legal scholar MacKinnon was called at only one other congressional hearing after the antipornography movement, a 1992 hearing on sexual harassment on campus (U.S. Senate 1992). Andrea Dworkin never testified again. Dorchen Leidholdt, who went on to become a prominent antitrafficking activist, testified twice on that topic in 2005 and 2007 (U.S. House 2005d; U.S. Senate 2007b). (U.S. Congress 2005; U.S. Senate October 31, 2007). Other than that, antipornography feminist activists dropped off the federal stage.
43. "Child Protection and Obscenity Enforcement," a 1988 hearing in the Democratic-controlled Senate Judiciary Committee under Acting Chair Dennis DeConcini (U.S. Senate 1988b). The two witnesses coded as influenced by antipornography feminism were Frederick Schauer, who had been on the Attorney General's Commission on Pornography, wrote its recommendations section and argued that the focus of legislation ought to be on violence against women rather than obscenity; and a caseworker (Carol Lavery) who discussed the use of pornography by men who had raped the rape victims with whom she worked. Schauer is a marginal case. A third pseudonymous witness (Susan) reported being coerced into appearing in pornography and had been the star witness for a case brought by a prosecutor who also testified at the hearing. Antipornography conservative witnesses were Jerry Kirk, Larry Braidfoot, Bruce Taylor, and Alan Sears.
44. He called one religious antipornography activist, Gregory Loken, of Covenant House, a Catholic shelter for youth that bridged conservative and liberal religious antipornography activism. The director of Covenant House, Father Bruce Ritter, had been a Meese commissioner and testified before several previous congressional subcommittees dealing with child sexual exploitation;

Covenant House itself served as the location for one such hearing. He also called a number of anticensorship witnesses, but this was not atypical under even much more conservative committee chairs. These included representatives of the ACLU, Al Goldstein (publisher of *Screw*), and two women who appeared in pornography and testified that they were not coerced. At the request of Republican Senator Jeremiah Denton, Specter invited Bruce Taylor, head of CDL, to testify, but Taylor was unable to attend and submitted written testimony.

45. U.S. Senate 1984a. Leidholdt/Specter exchange, p. 55.
46. U.S. Senate 1984a:153–54.
47. The other two women testifying about personal experiences were Valerie Heller, from the incest survivors' group VOICE, and Sue Brown from Minnesota. Heller also testified before the Meese Commission (June 19, 1985). (VOICE, later renamed VOICES, stood at the time for Victims of Incest Can Emerge and later was loosely used to stand for Voices of Incest Survivors.) Brown, who identified herself as "Rev. Susan Wilhem" at the beginning of her statement, was involved in the Minneapolis Pornography Resource Center and said she had initially identified herself as "a victim of marital abuse, and of marital rape" but later realized that pornography was part of this when she was assembling pornographic images as part of her activism and saw an image of a painful sexual position her husband had made her try. Smith, Brown, and Heller focused on child abuse law as a key solution, including statutes of limitation and mandatory reporting. This was a sharp contrast to the witnesses with deeper involvement in the antipornography movement, whose preferred solutions had to do with tackling pornography rather than sexual assaults. U.S. Senate 1984a:174–75, 183–85.
48. ACLU's Lynn, interestingly, relied on sources from feminist opponents of antipornography including two articles, Ellen Willis's "Feminism, Morality, and Pornography" and Alice Echol's "The New Feminism of Yin and Yang," from the feminist anthology that helped define and publicize the sex wars, *Powers of Desire* (U.S. Senate 1984a:268).
49. The previous attorney general, William French Smith, appointed the Commission, which reported to Meese, who was appointed just as the Commission began its work (Attorney General's Commission on Pornography 1986:3).
50. One member, Schauer, who entered the Commission as an advocate for outlawing obscenity, modified his position to favor banning only violent pornography, not sexually explicit (and legally obscene) material.
51. Witness counts are my own. Total Commission witnesses 322. All witnesses are counted in the total, but government employees (prosecutors, inspectors, etc.) and elected officials are not included in the counts of antipornography feminist or conservative witnesses even if they made antipornography feminist or conservative arguments, nor are witnesses who opposed pornography from neither feminist nor conservative perspectives and feminist witnesses who did not oppose pornography. Three witnesses from religious denominations' family life divisions are included in the conservative total. Others included anticensorship feminists; other opponents of the regulation of pornography; religious leaders; prosecutors; officials from customs, the U.S. Postal Service, and the Justice Department; and experts on the effects of pornography.

WAP files contain a list of 28 potential witnesses ("Potential Witness List, Prepared for Alan Sears," n.d. Folder 246, Carton 5, "Attorney General's

Commission," Women Against Pornography Papers, Schlesinger Library, Harvard University). I crosschecked these with the Commission's list of witnesses, using corroborating information about residence and substance of testimony to identify overlapping anonymous witnesses. The overlapping witnesses were Linda Marchiano (who had appeared under the name Linda Lovelace in the film *Deep Throat*), Catherine MacKinnon, Theresa Stanton of Minneapolis, and possibly "Sue W," an anonymous witness. At least seven other antipornography feminist witnesses not on WAP's list appeared, in addition to some of the anonymous witnesses describing their histories, although most such witnesses emphasized religious conservative frames. Bronstein (2011:327) shows that WAP "received a certificate of appreciation" from the Justice Department for this help.

52. Her testimony, printed at the beginning of the "Victim Testimony" section, was introduced as, ". . . the eloquent testimony of Andrea Dworkin on behalf of other victims whose voices were not heard."

53. Of 148 witness statements included in the report, 36 come from the Minneapolis hearings, 4 from statements sent by WAP, and 3 from other women's movement organizations, compared with 3 from conservative organizations and 4 letters from individuals to the Commission. The remaining 98 statements were from testimony before the Commission (Attorney General's Commission on Pornography 1986:ch. 16). Counts are my own.

54. It also recommends including "an affirmative defense of . . . consent" so that people who consent to appearing in pornography cannot then sue for being coerced, contrary to MacKinnon and Dworkin's view.

55. CWA's antipornography activism, which since the 1990s has included an annual Victims of Pornography Month, strengthens its distinct position as a women's organization within the conservative movement. Unsurprisingly, CWA also makes more conventional conservative arguments against pornography (Schreiber 2008).

56. It increased penalties for child pornography, child prostitution, and interstate trafficking of obscene material; extended RICO provisions for obscenity and child pornography offenses; extended obscenity and child pornography provisions to federal jurisdictions (including Indian country); banned obscene "Dial-A-Porn" and obscene material on cable television; added wiretapping provisions for obscenity investigations; and instituted a requirement that producers of pornography keep records of the age of their performers. The initial draft of the bill banned indecent, not just obscene, material on cable television, but this was removed at Meese's direction. The Justice Department debated internally whether the record-keeping provision should extend to simulated sexual activity, which would have applied to R-rated movies and whether it should apply to material that depicted nudity but not sexual activity. Simple nudity was ultimately retained for the sake of restricting child pornography, with the application to publications such as *Playboy* an ostensibly unavoidable by-product. The Justice Department also considered and rejected the Commission's recommendation to extend child pornography restrictions up to age 21 rather than 18. The drafters rejected this recommendation on the grounds that child pornography was subject to special restrictions mainly because its production constituted child abuse and that the change might "call into doubt the constitutionality of the entire child pornography chapter." Weld believed the change would be constitutional but "so controversial as to threaten

the congressional perception of the entire package, and to give an excuse to opponents of the package to disregard it as the product of extremist or over-zealous draftsmen." Memorandum to The Attorney General from William F. Weld, Assistant Attorney General, Pornography Legislation, April 8, 1987, pp. 11–13. Box 109, Folder "Obscenity Enforcement; Nat. Obs. Enf. Unit," Meese Papers.

57. WAP had earlier explored pressuring the FCC to regulate pornography on cable but never mounted a real campaign and had no influence on policy on the issue (Bronstein 2011).

58. It was Title N of the Anti-Drug Abuse Act of 1988. It was considered by the Senate in 1987, as the Child Protection and Obscenity Enforcement Act of 1987, S.2033, in the hearing that also considered the Pornography Victims Protection Act, which was dropped from the House version of the bill. Witnesses who testified before the Senate in support of the CPOE Act did not speak about the PVPA and vice versa. See also ProQuest Legislative History of PL100-690, "Title VII, Subtitle N, the Child Protection and Obscenity Enforcement Act of 1988," accessed February 28, 2014.

59. *American Library Association v. Thornburgh* 1989 overturned the initial provision; *American Library Association vs. Reno* 1994 upheld a revised provision, which has been subject to extensive litigation regarding who is required to keep records (only the initial producers of the material or anyone who distributes it). The provisions relating to cable television and telephone obscenity did not prohibit sexually explicit material, only that which could be found legally obscene, thus permitting what became a wide range of sexually explicit productions.

60. These bills were H.R.5509 in 1986, H.R. 1213 in 1988, and H.R. 1766 in 1991.

61. McConnell's PVCA was voted out of the Judiciary Committee in 1992 but defeated in the full Senate. All Democrats opposed it except Heflin and DeConcini; all Republicans supported it; Specter was not present for the vote. http://library.cqpress.com/cqalmanac/document.php?id=cqal92-1108030, accessed February 28, 2014.

62. When he first introduced the Act, sponsor Specter referenced testimony from children and women who were coerced into appearing in pornography as evidence of the need for action (Specter 1984). Reintroducing the Act in 1987, Specter cited support from a range of "women's and children's" organizations, including several NOW chapters (but not National NOW), Covenant House, and Feminists Fighting Pornography, which included signatures of support from "NOW NY chapter, Women's Institute for Freedom of the Press, DC; National Coalition Against Television Violence, Champaign, IL; V.O.I.C.E.S. Inc (Nat'l Incest Survivors Network), Chicago, IL; TOPP, Task Force on Prostitution and Pornography, Madison WI; Alaska Network on Domestic Violence and Sexual Assault, Juneau Alaska; Covenant House; PRIDE (Family Services), Minn.; N.A.P.C.R.O., National Anti-Pornography Civil Rights Organization, Minn; Genesis House, Chicago; Women in Crisis, Fairbanks, Alaska; IUFA, Independent Union of Flight Attendants, NY; Women's Alliance Against Pornography, Cambridge; Pornography Awareness, Inc., Chapel Hill; S.A.V.E., Sisters Against Violence and Exploitation, LaJolla; Pornography Resource Center, Minn.; NOW San Jose." These include feminist, religious liberal, and service organizations. The major antipornography conservative organizations such as CDL, Morality in Media, and the Religious Alliance Against Pornography are conspicuously absent, as are the major antipornography feminist organizations such as WAP.

63. Press Conference, "Final Report of the Attorney General's Commission on Pornography, Hon. Edwin Meese, III and Henry Hudson," July 9, 1986, p. 44. Box 20, Folder "Press Conf/AG's Porno Comsn Final Report," Meese Papers. The Commission report made the same argument.

64. *Obscenity Enforcement Reporter*, 1987, vol. 1, no. 1, p. 13. Box 109, Folder "Obscenity Enforcement; Nat. Obs. Enf. Unit," Meese Papers.

65. See witnesses in U.S. House 1988.

66. NOW NY did so on the grounds that it relied "heavily upon the . . . useless concept of obscenity." Letter from Marilyn Fitterman, president of NOW's NY chapter, to Senate Judiciary Committee, quoted in Kelly 1992. California NOW said it risked impinging on free speech. Linda Joplin, California NOW, to the Senate Judiciary Committee, referenced in Kelly 1992. The only two feminist witnesses opposing pornography to appear before Congress after 1988 both spoke at the 1991 hearing on the Pornography Victims Compensation and Pornography Victims Protection Acts (U.S. Senate 1991d). The witnesses were Paige Mellish of Feminists Fighting Pornography and Donna Ferguson who testified about her experiences of abuse. Other witnesses may have identified privately as feminists but did not invoke feminist affiliations or language. Dworkin 1992 interview at http://www.andreadworkin.com/audio/moderntimes.html, accessed March 20, 2011.

67. "Tax Dollars Did Fund Annie Sprinkle." Hon. Dana Rohrabacher of CA, remarks in the House of Representatives, Thursday, Feb. 22, 1990. *Congressional Record*, Extensions of Remarks, Feb. 22, 1990, vol. 136, part 2:2841–84. Online at Proquest, accessed March 11, 2014. Search for Mellish and pornography in all congressional records on Proquest shows only her testimony at the 1991 hearing, McConnell's thanks to her, and Rohrabacher's citation of the article in which she is quoted. Feminists Fighting Pornography (FFP) existed in some form from 1984 to 1989, based on the publication dates of its journal, *The Backlash Times*, although it appears that it was nearly a one-woman operation for much of this time. Mellish's relationship with WAP (and WAVPM, for which she was briefly canvass director in September and October 1981) was tense. On WAVPM, see Progress Report, September and November 2, 1981, minutes of Steering Committee. Box 1: Administrative Files, Folder 2, Committee Records—Bd of Directors 1979–82, WAVPM Papers. On WAP, Dworkin disclaimed WAP's connection with FFP in a 1992 NPR interview, available at http://www.andreadworkin.com/audio/moderntimes.html. Mellish was seemingly opportunistic, as evidenced by the list of endorsements she provided the Senate in 1991 under the FFP letterhead. She was charged with obscenity for displaying enlarged posters with images from pornography at her street-side table in New York City, from which she shouted to passersby (ACLU leader Nadine Strossen [1993:1136] reports that Mellish was, ironically, defended by the NY Civil Liberties Union and also reports that Mellish had past arrests.) By 1998, she had evidently left feminism behind, according to an interview reported in the *New York Observer*:

> Page Mellish, who for years worked as a feminist antipornography crusader on the streets of Manhattan, can't believe what she sees around her every day. She has given up her old crusade and spends her days as an animal rights advocate. I found her on St. Mark's Place. "Don't breed!" she yelled. "Too many humans! Sign the petition!" I asked her about the summer fashion habits of women in the city: "I'm through with women," she said. "I'm

through with those ding-dongs! They dress like whores because they are whores!"

In 2004, she was arrested and charged with "scheming to defraud" when she asked for signatures on a petition for animal rights and contributions to "Homeless Cats." See http://law.justia.com/cases/new-york/other-courts/2004/2004-50869.html.

68. When McConnell introduced the PVCA in 1989, he thanked Mellish "for her work and dedication to the cause," as well as thanking MacKinnon "for her efforts to stop the sexual abuse of women by pornography." *Congressional Record,* Senate. June 22, 1989. P. 13091. Online at Proquest, accessed March 11, 2014. Mellish sent materials to senators, urging them to cosponsor the PVCA and included summaries of studies about the impact of pornography on violence against women and excerpts from testimony from the Meese and Minneapolis hearings. The files of Republican Senator H. John Heintz III contain these materials in what appear to be a form sent to numerous senators. Materials sent from FFP, John Heintz III Papers, Carnegie Mellon University Digital Collections, http://doi.library.cmu.edu/10.1184/pmc/heinz/box00024/fld00024/bdl0002/doc0001 and http://doi.library.cmu.edu/10.1184/pmc/heinz/box00024/fld00024/bdl0002/doc0004, accessed March 11, 2014. Endorsements are listed in "Legislative Proposals for Compensation of Victims of Sexual Crimes," (U.S. Senate 1991d:221, 236). Mellish and Subcommittee Chair Biden sparred over the feminist endorsements she claimed, which were chapters of NOW, local rape crisis centers, and shelters, whereas Biden repeatedly asked her if the national NOW, NOW Legal Defense Fund, the National Coalition Against Sexual assaults endorsed the bill. (He likely knew that they did not.) Mellish claimed that she had not "sought their endorsement" (244–45).

69. Press Conference, "Final Report of the Attorney General's Commission on Pornography, Hon. Edwin Meese, III and Henry Hudson," October 22 1986, pp. 8–10. Box 20, Folder "Press Conf/AG's Porno Comsn Final Report," Meese Papers. The NOEU was allotted 15 attorneys, in addition to its executive director, and connected with the FBI, Customs, the IRS, and the Postal Service. Memorandum from H. Robert Showers, Executive Director of National Obscenity Enforcement Unity to Edwin Meese, Bimonthly Report for March and April for the NOEU, p. 2 (Task Force), p. 5 (number of attorneys), N.d. [1988]. Box 109, Folder "Obscenity Enforcement; NOEU," Meese Papers. The training programs got underway quickly, with 6 national and 10 regional programs in 1987, and many others in 1988. *Obscenity Enforcement Reporter,* 1987, vol. 1, no. 1, p. 15. Box 109, Folder "Obscenity Enforcement; Nat. Obs. Enf. Unit," Meese Papers. Memorandum from H. Robert Showers, Executive Director of National Obscenity Enforcement Unity to Edwin Meese, Bimonthly Report for March and April for the NOEU. July 1, 1988, p. 1. Box 109, Folder "Obscenity Enforcement; NOEU," Meese Papers. The NOEU publication, *Obscenity Enforcement Recorder,* went to 10,000 "prosecutors and law enforcement officers and over 2,500 citizen leaders." The NOEU and the NCMEC together published a booklet, "Child Pornography and Prostitution," aimed at summarizing laws and guiding prosecution. *Obscenity Enforcement Reporter,* 1987, vol. 1, no. 1, p. 12. Box 109, Folder "Obscenity Enforcement; Nat. Obs. Enf. Unit," Meese Papers. Memorandum from H. Robert Showers, Executive Director of National

Obscenity Enforcement Unity to Edwin Meese, Bimonthly Report for January and February 1988 for the NOEU. N.d. Box 109, Folder "Obscenity Enforcement; NOEU," Meese Papers.

70. Statement for William A. Webster, Director, Federal Bureau of Investigation, before the Attorney General's Commission on Pornography, U.S. Department of Justice, June 20, 1985. Box 14, Folder "Press Conference 20 May 1986 DOG to Announce the Members of the Attorney General's Commission on Pornography," Meese Papers.

71. "The Facts: FY '87 Prosecutions." *Obscenity Enforcement Reporter*, 1988, vol. 1, no. 2, March/April, p. 14. Box 109, Folder "Obscenity Enforcement; Nat. Obs. Enf. Unit," Meese Papers. Child pornography numbers were 1983 (3), 1984 (61), 1985 (126), 1986 (147), 1987 (249). Not all prosecutions resulted in convictions.

72. 1985 and 1986 figures in Press Conference, "Final Report of the Attorney General's Commission on Pornography, Hon. Edwin Meese, III and Henry Hudson," October 22 1986, p. 4. Box 20, Folder "Press Conf/AG's Porno Comsn Final Report," Meese Papers. 1987 sting operation described in "Meese Announces Multiple Child Pornography Indictments," *Obscenity Enforcement Reporter*, 1987, vol. 1, no. 1, p. 8. Box 109, Folder "Obscenity Enforcement; Nat. Obs. Enf. Unit," Meese Papers. These operations are described in Memoranda from H. Robert Showers, Executive Director of National Obscenity Enforcement Unity to Edwin Meese, "Bimonthly Report for September and October, 1987 Dated Dec. 29, 1987, and May and June 1987 dated August 25, 1987 for the NOEU." Box 109, Folder "Obscenity Enforcement; NOEU," Meese Papers.

73. *Obscenity Enforcement Reporter*, 1988, vol. 1, no. 2, March/April, p. 4. Box 109, Folder "Obscenity Enforcement; Nat. Obs. Enf. Unit," Meese Papers.

74. *Obscenity Enforcement Reporter*, 1988, vol. 1, no. 2, March/April, p. 5. Box 109, Folder "Obscenity Enforcement; Nat. Obs. Enf. Unit," Meese Papers.

75. Press Conference, "Final Report of the Attorney General's Commission on Pornography, Hon. Edwin Meese, III and Henry Hudson," October 22, 1986, p. 37. Box 20, Folder "Press Conf/AG's Porno Comsn Final Report," Meese Papers.

76. Address of the Honorable Edwin Meese, III, before the Pornography Seminar, May 25, 1988. Box 35, Folder "Advanced Obscenity and Child Pornography Conference 25 May 1986 [sic] Arlington VA," Meese Papers.

77. Press Conference, "Final Report of the Attorney General's Commission on Pornography, Hon. Edwin Meese, III and Henry Hudson," October 22 1986, p. 4. Box 20, Folder "Press Conf/AG's Porno Comsn Final Report," Meese Papers. In practice, Meese used a relatively narrow definition of obscenity, for example, excluding "slasher films" for not being legally obscene (October press conference, p. 30). Justice Department attempts to connect pornography to organized crime were largely unsuccessful, but investigators defined the production and distribution of obscenity as organized crime simply because obscenity was a criminal offense. Other officials attempted to connect obscenity to what one termed "traditional organized crime (La Cosa Nostra (LCN))," arguing in a memo that FBI investigations in 1977 had "greatly reduced the control by the LCN of the pornography industry," but that they continued to "have 'agreements'" entailing "extortion or 'street taxation' of pornography dealers." "Talking Points, Commission on Pornography," n.d. , Box 14, Folder "Press Conference 20 May 1986 DOG to Announce the Members of the Attorney General's Commission on Pornography," Meese Papers. See also the press conference on July 9, 1986,

comments by Henry Hudson and Edwin Meese. Press Conference, "Final Report of the Attorney General's Commission on Pornography, Hon. Edwin Meese, III and Henry Hudson," July 9, 1986. Box 20, Folder "Press Conf/AG's Porno Comsn Final Report," Meese Papers.

78. "Talking Points, Commission on Pornography" #3, n.d. , Box 14, Folder "Press Conference 20 May 1986 DOG to Announce the Members of the Attorney General's Commission on Pornography," Meese Papers. Meese noted that the Obscenity Commission's recommendations about child pornography paralleled those of the "attorney general's Task Force on Missing and Exploited Children." Address of the Honorable Edwin Meese, III, before the Pornography Seminar, May 25, 1988, Meese Papers. The U.S. Attorney General's Advisory Board on Missing Children issued reports in 1986, 1987, 1988, and 1989.

79. *Obscenity Enforcement Reporter*, 1987, vol. 1, no. 1, p. 1. Box 109, Folder "Obscenity Enforcement; Nat. Obs. Enf. Unit," Meese Papers.

80. Address of the Honorable Edwin Meese, III, before the Pornography Seminar, May 25, 1988. Box 35, Folder "Advanced Obscenity and Child Pornography Conference 25 May 1986 [sic] Arlington VA," Meese Papers.

81. "Commentary," *Obscenity Enforcement Reporter*, 1988, vol. 1, no. 2, March/April, p. 6. Box 109, Folder "Obscenity Enforcement; Nat. Obs. Enf. Unit," Meese Papers.

82. Address of the Honorable Edwin Meese, III, before the Pornography Seminar, May 25, 1988. Box 35, Folder "Advanced Obscenity and Child Pornography Conference 25 May 1986 [sic] Arlington VA," Meese Papers. Meese did note that the zero-tolerance approach to drugs could not be extended to pornography because of First Amendment limitations.

83. Press Conference, "Final Report of the Attorney General's Commission on Pornography, Hon. Edwin Meese, III and Henry Hudson," July 9, 1986, pp. 6–7. Box 20, Folder "Press Conf/AG's Porno Comsn Final Report," Meese Papers.

84. Press Conference, "Final Report of the Attorney General's Commission on Pornography, Hon. Edwin Meese, III and Henry Hudson," July 9, 1986, pp. 34–35. Box 20, Folder "Press Conf/AG's Porno Comsn Final Report," Meese Papers. According to the report, categories 3 and 4 are nonviolent/nondegrading and nudity, respectively. A reporter followed up, asking about the movie *Debbie Does Dallas*. Noting that the commissioners "must have seen it when you were preparing this report, a great deal of pornographic material," he asked whether viewing it had harmed commissioners. Hudson replied that the effects of such material are stronger on those that are "predisposed to engage in those types of activities."

85. E.g. Press Conference, "Final Report of the Attorney General's Commission on Pornography, Hon. Edwin Meese, III and Henry Hudson," October 22 1986, p. 24. Box 20, Folder "Press Conf/AG's Porno Comsn Final Report," Meese Papers.

86. Press Conference, "Final Report of the Attorney General's Commission on Pornography, Hon. Edwin Meese, III and Henry Hudson," July 9, 1986, p. 13. Box 20, Folder "Press Conf/AG's Porno Comsn Final Report," Meese Papers. The statue and the hypocrisy it implied were mentioned in many published pieces critical of the Commission.

87. Press Conference, "Final Report of the Attorney General's Commission on Pornography, Hon. Edwin Meese, III and Henry Hudson," October 22, 1986,

p. 44. Box 20, Folder "Press Conf/AG's Porno Comsn Final Report," Meese Papers.

88. Address of the Honorable Edwin Meese, III, before the Pornography Seminar, May 25, 1988. Box 35, Folder "Advanced Obscenity and Child Pornography Conference 25 May 1986 [*sic*] Arlington VA," Meese Papers. Press Conference, "Final Report of the Attorney General's Commission on Pornography, Hon. Edwin Meese, III and Henry Hudson," October 22, 1986, pp. 35–36. Box 20, Folder "Press Conf/AG's Porno Comsn Final Report," Meese Papers.

89. Speech to Religious Alliance Against Pornography, November 13, 1985. Box 23, Folder "Religious Alliance Against Pornography 13 Nov 1986 The White House," Meese Papers. The briefing also included the Postal Service, FBI, and Customs.

90. These groups were addressed in September and October 1987. Of the citizen groups listed, only the Kentucky Alliance on Exploited [Children] Association was not a conservative group. Organizations and addresses listed in Memorandum from H. Robert Showers, Executive Director of National Obscenity Enforcement Unity to Edwin Meese, Bimonthly Report for September and October 1987 for the NOEU. Dated Dec. 29, 1987. Box 109, Folder "Obscenity Enforcement; NOEU," Meese Papers. CWA listed in Memorandum from H. Robert Showers, Executive Director of National Obscenity Enforcement Unity to Edwin Meese, Bimonthly Report for July and August, 1987 for the NOEU. Dated Dec. Nov. 23, 1987. Box 109, Folder "Obscenity Enforcement; NOEU," Meese Papers. It also produced a pamphlet aimed at citizens entitled "Pornography: What You Don't Know Will Hurt You." Memorandum from H. Robert Showers, Executive Director of National Obscenity Enforcement Unity to Edwin Meese, Bimonthly Report for January and February 1988 for the NOEU. Box 109, Folder "Obscenity Enforcement; NOEU," Meese Papers.

91. Press Conference, "Final Report of the Attorney General's Commission on Pornography, Hon. Edwin Meese, III and Henry Hudson," October 22, 1986, p. 12. Box 20, Folder "Press Conf/AG's Porno Comsn Final Report," Meese Papers. Only three of the letters preserved in Meese's papers were opposed.

92. Letter from Rev. Clarence G. Weber to Meese, Aug. 7, 1985. Box 117, Folder "Pornography," Meese Papers.

93. Letter from Robert Bowman to Meese, June 21, 1985. Box 117, Folder "Commission on Pornography 1985," Meese Papers. In addition to Protestant and Catholic clergy, letters came from representatives of organizations including CDL chapters, the Florida Coalition for Clean Cable, and the Michigan Conservative Caucus, among others.

94. Letter from Wendy K. Decker to Meese, July 1, 1986. Box 120, Folder "Pornography," Meese Papers.

95. Four other briefs supporting the expansion of enforcement were filed by ideologically neutral organizations dealing with child pornography, and one by Marchiano with a nonfeminist lawyer. Most remaining briefs opposed expansion of antipornography law.

96. MacKinnon's was the only supporting brief at the district level (*American Booksellers Association v. Hudnut* 598 F. Supp. 1316 [S. Dist. Ind. 1984]).

97. Dworkin's suit was filed first at the district level, with the first judgment in a complicated series of judgments about jurisdiction and other issues entered in 1985. Leidholdt's initial district decision was entered in 1986, and Ault's on March 9, 1987. At the appellate level, *Leidholt* and *Ault* were heard and decided on the same day, and before *Dworkin*. *Ault v. Hustler Magazine* 860 F.2d 877 (9th Cir. 1988), online

at Open Jurist, http://openjurist.org/860/f2d/877/ault-v-hustler-magazine-inc, accessed January, 29, 2014; *Leidholdt v. Lfp, Inc.* 860 F. 2d 890 (9th Cir. 1988), online at Open Jurist, http://openjurist.org/860/f2d/890/leidholdt-v-lfp-inc accessed January, 29, 2014; *Dworkin v. Hustler Magazine* 867 F. 2d 1188 (9th Cir. 1988), online at Open Jurist, http://openjurist.org/867/f2d/1188/dworkin-v-hustler-magazine-inc accessed January, 29, 2014. It is possible that additional district- or appellate-level decisions had overlapping briefs of this sort. However, a search on Open Jurist (which covers appellate decisions) shows no cases where briefs by CDL were filed along with briefs by feminists or by prominent feminist lawyer MacKinnon (according to subject search for CDL and "feminist" or CDL and MacKinnon), and no other notorious court cases included APF plaintiffs or defendants.

98. Finan, Christopher, "He Who Laughs Last . . ." *Playboy*, n.d. Box 109, Folder "Obscenity Enforcement/Porn Commission," Meese Papers.

99. From 1992 to 2011, there were 55 hearings (vs. 33 between 1981 and 1991). Only 18 were held during the Clinton administration, with 32 under Bush II and the remaining 5 in Obama's first two years. Counts for 2009–2011 may be low as congressional records are not immediately indexed and digitized. Republicans controlled 55 percent of congressional chambers during those years.

100. A search of all hearings on pornography or obscenity (as well as a search for hearings with any mention of women or feminism in full text) showed only four from 1992 forward where witnesses were associated with any women's or feminist organization. Black feminist witnesses Delores Tucker and Faye Williams of the National Congress of Black Women, Black feminist academic Tracy Sharpley-Whiting, and Lisa Bediako of the media watchdog organization Industry Ears emphasized the pervasiveness of racialized misogyny in both rap music and mainstream white media and society and the negative effects on children and on Black women. Their argument focused on the use of the public airwaves, and sometimes called on the FCC to regulate content, but also on Black women to stop supporting offensive media. All three witnesses emphasized powerful, white-owned conglomerates' control of the media and a broad range of problems associated with racism and sexism, not just media representations. They testified at three of these hearings: Music Lyrics and Commerce (U.S. House 1994c) and Shaping Our Responses to Violent and Demeaning Imagery in Popular Music (U.S. Senate 1994b), both in 1994, and From Imus to Industry: The Business of Stereotypes and Degrading Images in 2007 (U.S. House 2007a). Concerned Women for America, a conservative women's group, testified before one hearing in 2004, "Online Pornography: Closing the Door on Pervasive Smut" (U.S. House 2004).

101. This included the Communications Decency Act in 1996 prohibiting sending or posting obscene or indecent material online to those under 18, the Child Online Protection Act in 1998, forbidding commercial websites from displaying material "harmful to minors" (overturned); and the Children's Internet Protection Act in 2000, the sole law to survive constitutionally, requiring filtering of the Internet on library and school computers.

102. Brief of Amicus Curiae Feminists For Free Expression in Support of Respondent, *City of Erie, Pennsylvania, et al. vs. PAP'S A.M.* 20 S. Ct. 1382 (Mar. 29, 2000) 1998 U.S. Briefs 1161 and 1999 U.S. S. Ct. Briefs Lexis 136. September 30, 1999.

103. The cases were *United States v. X-Citement Video, Inc., and Rubin Gottesman* 115 S. Ct. 464, 472, 130 L.Ed.2d 372 (1994) and *Stephen Knox v. United States of America* 114 S. Ct. 375 (1993).

104. DC Feminists Against Pornography did so on the *Webster* abortion case
(*Webster v. Reproductive Health Services* 109 S. Ct. 3040 [1989]) as part of Brief
Of Seventy-Seven Organizations Committed To Women's Equality As Amici
Curiae In Support Of Appellees. WAVPAM and WAP joined an amicus brief
against the Hyde Amendment, which banned Medicaid funding of abortion,
Williams and Diamond v. Zbaraz, et al. 100 S. Ct. 2694 (1980). Prominent
antipornography feminists Dorchen Leidholdt and Norma Ramos of WAP,
among others, filed an amicus brief in support of the government requirement
that groups receiving international aid to prevent HIV/AIDS must explicitly
oppose sex work (*Agency for International Development v. Alliance for Open
Society International, Inc.* 133 S.Ct. 2321 [2013]). Signatories included a range
of antitrafficking organizations, including Coalition Against Trafficking in
Women, the National Women's Coalition Against Violence and Exploitation
(with a broad antiviolence mission but most programs focused on trafficking),
and Equality Now (also with a broad antiviolence and exploitation mission and
a large focus on trafficking)
105. The National Strategy for Child Exploitation Prevention and Interdiction.
A Report to Congress. U.S. Department of Justice, 2010, http://www.justice.gov/
criminal/ceos/downloads/natstrategyreport.pdf, accessed February, 6, 2014.
106. The Supreme Court's 1982 *Ferber* ruling found that child pornography was not
protected by the First Amendment even if it was not obscene by the *Miller*
definition regarding overall merit and community standards (*New York v. Ferber*,
458 U.S. 747 [1982]).
107. It did crop up occasionally, as in Specter's 1984 "Effects" hearing (U.S. Senate
1984a:313–22, when a woman who performed in pornography described in
detail how she had explored her fantasies about bondage and submission
through a photoshoot as Specter referred to her photograph and she and
another witness with experience in pornography discussed the prevalence
of rape fantasies, their underpinning of consent, and the difference from
actual rape.
108. The exception was witnesses specifically recruited to provide a different
perspective, such as the ACLU and producers of pornography.
109. Witness testimony is available only in the National Archives files from the Meese
Commission. Some witnesses opposed to the commission provided information
that was incorporated into the final report. For example, John Weston, counsel
for the Adult Film Association of America, is cited in numerous footnotes in the
chapter on "Production and Distribution of Sexually Explicit Material," as the
source for facts about the preparation and marketing of films, and their contents
(e.g., "The most important part of the movies is considered by the trade to be the
male ejaculation scene"), but not about his reasoning for opposing regulation of
obscenity. The report's section on "First Amendment Considerations" contains
no testimony or summary of testimony from witnesses from the ACLU, FACT,
or other opponents of censorship, and makes a strong case that obscenity is
not subject to First Amendment protections. Anticensorship views are reflected
only obliquely in some individual commissioners' statements, notably the
two women whose joint statement dissented from many of the Commission's
recommendations (Attorney General's Commission on Pornography 1986:348).
Antipornography feminist critiques of obscenity or zoning restrictions are not
reflected in the report, although MacKinnon later reported that she had testified
about this (MacKinnon 1997).

In contrast, congressional testimony is published in full and hence not subject to the same kind of selectivity and framing through publication. However, although available to the public, transcripts of congressional hearings are rarely viewed.

110. Brest and Vandenberg (1987:65–66) describe the letter as "widely distributed" and list signatories including "Robin Morgan, Kathleen Barry, Mary Daly, and Pauline Bart, among others."

111. The story began with the assumption that feminists disagreed about the issue of pornography and explored all points of view, raising questions about free speech, coalition with the right, the use of the law, and whether pornography is central to violence against women and gave space to both proponents and opponents. (Hunter: "Theoretically, the pornography ordinance suggests that women somehow *can't* consent . . . . I think that infantilizes women." MacKinnon: "We're talking about a situation where if a woman can be forced to fuck a dog, she can be forced to sign a contract" (Blakely 1985:120).

112. Letter to Gloria Steinem from Dorchen Leidholdt. Box 151, Folder 7. April 24 [1985], Steinem Papers.

113. In a footnote, MacKinnon states that Coughenour was "chosen by Mayor William Hudnut to shepherd the bill through the process largely because of her political skills, which were exceptional" (MacKinnon and Dworkin 1997:11–12). Hudnut, a hardline conservative, was a darling of the Christian conservative press for his anti-obscenity work, and his role in selecting Coughenour is hardly a sign that her ideology was irrelevant. She also claimed that Indianapolis Mayor "Hudnut has always supported a woman's right to choose an abortion" (MacKinnon and Dworkin 1997:401). Hudnut may have been pro-choice, but he was no liberal.

114. For example, contrast the accounts of the municipal antipornography ordinances given by Duggan and Hunter 1995 and MacKinnon 1997. On journalists, see, e.g., MacKinnon's criticism of Downs and the *New York Times*.

115. Instead, Leidholdt debated, in her words, "the editor of Penthouse's Forum, a pimp named Philip Nobile" (Leidholdt 1985:26). Leidholdt cited relatively concrete instances of overlap between FACT and sexually explicit media, such as, "The article by FACT brief signatory Karen Decrow [not actually a signatory] in the April issue of Penthouse, which Penthouse issued as a press release (headlined "Former President of N.O.W. Denounces Radical Feminists in Penthouse") and FACT hands out as literature, Penthouse logo and all. Naiad Press's deal with Penthouse to serialize Lesbian Nuns in Forum." But she also cited other instances of sexual practices that she saw as nonfeminist, particularly, "[r]ecent event connected with NYC's Gay Pride March, advertised as 'Lady Smut Night' (don't they sound just like the Right?!), which turned out to be a big gathering in a loft plastered with pornography. The entertainment was real women performing naked in leather bondage gear," and went on to say that FACT was no longer simply "fronting" for pornographers, but had become pornographers. (Notice the slippage between FACT, the larger pro-sex or sex radical movement, and the gay pride march.)

Funding from the Playboy Foundation was a broader issue in the women's movement during the 1980s. The Playboy Foundation offered some grants for anti-rape work and other feminist efforts, many of which were turned down (see Whittier 1995 for an account of this in Columbus, Ohio). WAVPM unsuccessfully applied for a grant from the Playboy Foundation in 1978 and discussed how they would consider it "retribution money—money for all the damages done to us by 20 years of pornography magazines." Two years later, WAVPM received a $10 check for membership from Margaret Standish, then director of the Playboy Foundation, which they accepted after discussion. Minutes January 7, 1978, p. 2. Box 1, Administrative, Folder "Committee Records, General Meeting." Minutes, WAVPM Board Meeting, January 10, 1980. Box 1 Administrative, Folder "Committee Records," WAVPM Papers. Playboy awarded the 1980 Hugh Hefner Award to feminist and Mormon dissenter Sonia Johnson, who ultimately refused after initially saying she planned to accept. Meanwhile, Gloria Steinem and Christie Hefner, the president at the time of Playboy Enterprises, exchanged cordial letters in 1980 about their mutual opposition to Reagan and their support for Democratic candidates. Box 87, Folder 18, Steinem Papers.

116. Nan Hunter, "Modern McCarthyism," *off our backs* letters section, vol. 15, no. 11, December 1985, p. 26. Lisa Duggan, "The Binds that Divide," *off our backs* letters section, vol. 15, no. 11, December 1985, p. 26. Both Hunter and Duggan called for greater tolerance of difference within the women's movement. Hunter writes: "WAP would like to pretend that all true feminists agree with them. We don't. That's settled. Let's move on and discuss the issues."

117. Antipornography feminist writing and blogging continued but wasn't accompanied by substantial mobilization.

118. A newer and vibrant literature on pornography includes several works complicating the analysis of the intersections of race and gender in pornography. See Nash 2008, Miller-Young 2014, and Shimizu 2007.

119. Only new empirical work by Bronstein 2011 and Potter 2012 has examined antipornography feminism on its own terms.

CHAPTER 3

1. See Whittier 2009 for a detailed discussion.
2. See Whittier 2009 for full analysis.
3. Some such efforts were funded by state or local government, including the federal Centers for Disease Control, or by foundations, and some fell under the aegis of domestic violence or anti-rape organizations.
4. These included first-person accounts by survivors, coverage of custody disputes where mothers accused fathers of incest, civil suits by daughters against their fathers, clergy abuse, and one article on SORNA. Twenty other articles from *Ms.* come up with a keyword search for incest, but all dealt with incest in the context of abortion rights. *Ms.* also published two articles, including a cover story, on child pornography in 1977. Indexing of *Ms.* is incomplete prior to 1984, and it is possible that my count of earlier articles may be inaccurate.
5. Besharov was the first director of NCCAN, but by the time *Ms.* published this article, he was a fellow at the conservative American Enterprise Institute. See Whittier 2009 for further discussion.
6. There were five articles on civil suits or other incest court cases, three book reviews, two short reports, and nine broad articles Two very brief international news reports appeared prior to 1982; none appeared after 2001. *Off our backs* folded in 2008.
7. One 2009 article discussed dilemmas when sex offenders sought to participate in a congregation, talking about how to "balance grace and accountability" (Ross 2009).
8. To my knowledge, based on fieldwork, interviews, and publication reviews (Whittier 2009).

9. Eight additional hearings on child sexual abuse were held between 1973 and 1980; not included in counts above. The qualitative analysis is based on 36 hearings held between 1973 and 2006. I purposively sampled for key hearings leading to legislation, especially extensive hearings, hearings that included witnesses from advocacy or movement organizations, and early or definitional hearings. They are U.S. House 1973, 1977, 1978, 1981, 1982, 1983a, 1983b, 1984a, 1984b, 1984c, 1986a, 1988, 1991, 1992c, 1994b, 1995a, 1995b, 2000b, 2001 2005a, 2005b, 2005c; U.S. Senate 1981a, 1982a, 1984a, 1984b, 1986a, 1988a, 1988b, 1989b, 1990e, 1994a, 1995a, 1995b, 1996b, 2006. CAPTA's name has varied over the years. It was reauthorized as the Child Abuse Prevention and Treatment and Adoption Reform Act (CAPTARA) in 1978.
10. One hearing, with four witnesses, was a joint commission.
11. Seventy-four percent of hearings were held under Republican Presidents and 26 percent under Democrats; Democrats held the presidency 39 percent of the years between 1980 and 2013.
12. Prior to the 1990s, longstanding child welfare organizations and the National Committee for the Prevention of Child Abuse retained a role; by 2000, only NCMEC remained influential. Child welfare organizations included the American Humane Association, American Medical Association, Child Welfare League, the National Association for the Education of the Young Child. Organizations focused on sex trafficking also sent witnesses, including Linda Smith (Shared Hope International); Carol Smolenski (ECPAT-USA), and Mohamed Mattar (Protection Project).
13. They also appeared twice in the 1970s. First, at a 1977 hearing on Sexual Exploitation of Children, Melba Watson of NOW's Task Force on Child Sexual Abuse presented one of the only discussions of power imbalance in all the years of testimony, framing child pornography in terms of feminist opposition to pornography in general, stating, "It is using children in the same way women have been used, just as objects and tools" (U.S. House 1977:175). Second, feminist witnesses at a 1978 hearing on research into violent behavior were there to speak about rape and included children tangentially, consistent with the feminist approach during that period, which conceptualized child sexual abuse and rape of adults in the same category (Whittier 2009).
14. They were Linda Hull (Formerly Abused Children Emerging in Society, 1987); Denise Gooch (Mothers Against Raping Children, 1988); and former Miss America Marilyn Van Derber (1991), who was associated with the American Coalition Against Abuse and One Voice, although she did not identify this in her testimony.
15. Burstein (2014) finds, in contrast, that research-based evidence was rarely used in the hearings he sampled.
16. Quote is from William Dworin, LAPD Sexually Exploited Child Unit, U.S. House 1983b:23. Similarly, Rep. Michael DeWine (R-OH) said in 1989, "in any area of the country, in any part of our economic strata it exists" (U.S. Senate 1989b:9); Jeffrey Dupilka of the Postal Service similarly said, "This most despicable of crimes . . . cuts across all social and economic classes" (U.S. Senate 1996b:21). Some argued that class disadvantage could increase child abuse, as Rep. Donald Payne (D-NJ) said, "As you know, during these difficult economic times, family problems often worsen as a result of increased stress and anxiety. For this reason, it is more important than ever that we emphasize child abuse prevention and early intervention programs" (U.S. House 1992c:5).

Only two or three witnesses, over all the hearings in my qualitative sample, presented data on how race and class affected reporting or response to child sexual abuse.

17. Hearings include U.S. Senate 1985b, 1986b, 1986c, 1989a, 1990e, 1990c, 1990d, 1993b, 1994a, 1995b, 1996c, 2006. The specialized legislation is the Indian Child Protective Services and Family Violence Prevention Act, passed in 1990 and renewed since. The major issues discussed were child sexual abuse in reservation schools, lack of law enforcement, lack of foster homes or child protective services, and lack of mental health treatment. Some early hearings were very lengthy, but later ones were brief. Witnesses occasionally raised issues of tribal sovereignty (e.g., a tribal official at a 2008 hearing called the mandate to enforce the Adam Walsh Act an infringement on sovereignty) and lack of funding to comply with mandates.

18. The occasional direct discussion of race used frames terms seldom heard in Congress. For example, in 1983 Dr. Neuberger reported that hospitals underreported cases of physical abuse in "white and more affluent families," contributing "to a widespread myth in this country that the families who abuse their children are poor people, members of ethnic minorities, and members of socially margin populations" (U.S. Senate 1983:234). After his testimony, there was no follow-up on this point in the lengthy hearing, indicating the difficulty even expert witnesses faced in introducing alternative frames. A 1992 witness talked about racism in the foster care system arguing that "95 percent of the children in foster care are black and Hispanic. . . . This is a deliberate move to destroy families, to destroy the family structure." (U.S. House 1992c:89). There was no further discussion of the idea of deliberate destruction of Black and Hispanic families, again showing the difficulty of introducing frames about racism into congressional discourse.

19. Even at a 1977 hearing dealt with commercial sexual exploitation, i.e., pornography and prostitution, the emphasis on familial abuse remained. One expert witness noted, "What we are hearing is the pornography part. We are not hearing [about] those hundreds and maybe thousands of families where there may be incest . . . that can be treated, that can be helped," and another said that incest was "what is under the tip of this iceberg that . . . in terms of pornography" (U.S. House 1977:111).

20. U.S. House 1981. The family's testimony is pp. 87–96.

21. Under questioning, Dick revealed that he had been molested as a child by a sister, but attributed his "problems" to a range of forces, including an "overprotective mother" and stress from work.

22. Despite what Beth and her parents described as a positive family relationship, when Rep. Erdahl asked about forgiveness, Beth demurred: "I can never say it is OK that he abused me. I can say we have grown closer now and have a much better relationship, but to me the word 'forgiveness' implies some things I don't feel fit."

23. Rep. Austin Murphy asked why Dick had not sought help sooner. Dick blamed the threat of criminal prosecution: "I felt if I went to the authorities or a psychiatrist, I would be turned in, I would lose my family, lose my job, and probably end up back in jail."

24. Witnesses who testified based on their expertise as psychotherapists, social workers, and medical professionals told stories from cases. For example, Francine Vecchiola, who worked with Connecticut Child Protective Services,

recounted vivid case studies, including one of a girl raped by her grandfather (U.S. House 1981).

25. Seventeen of these are in my fully coded qualitative sample. I read all the hearings, even those I did not code, and included all hearings with substantial involvement by activists in my qualitative sample.

26. Child Welfare Information Gateway 2011.

27. The Child Protection Act was included in the 1984 Victims of Crime Act.

28. E.g., Judiciary Chair Biden said his wife had told him about compositions her students had written about their sexual or physical abuse (U.S. Senate 1989b:140); Rep. Payne (D-NJ) referenced his daughter, a kindergarten teacher who had "taken several cases to the Division of Youth and Family Services (DYFS), in New Jersey, and reported abuse" (U.S. House 1992c:71).

29. He distinguished such "pedophiles" from those who only assaulted children within their own household, who might be treatable (U.S. House 1983b:23).

30. The Act expanded related laws from 1984 and 1986.

31. Seven were in my qualitative sample. Three hearings during this period were on sex trafficking. I included sex trafficking hearings in the quantitative totals if they addressed children but omitted them from the qualitative samples and analyses.

32. In an interesting twist, Morgan was engaged to Sen. Arlen Specter's chief of staff. The Act releasing her from jail is a movement outcome—protective parents and the mothers' "underground railroad" had become a cause both for the survivors' movement and the larger women's movement. It was presumably facilitated by Morgan's engagement to Specter's staffer. Amy Neustein's battle with her ex-husband, who was awarded custody in an allegedly biased and irregular family court proceeding after she reported corroborated sexual abuse of their daughter, also framed the 1992 hearing. More on Neustein's case at http://www.mothers-of-lost-children.com/neustein.htm; http://amyneustein.com/amy.htm.

33. The name is spelled as both Jayakar and Jayaker in the transcript.

34. Goldfarb was working closely with Congress on VAWA at the same time. See Chapter 5.

35. Ohme arranged Clark's and Gardner's testimonies, the latter submitted in writing. Ohme aimed to "delet[e] the 'mandatory reporting' feature" of CAPTA and perhaps kill the law altogether. His efforts were likely aided by the fact that two Republicans, Subcommittee Chair Cunningham and Representative Duncan Hunter, represented San Diego. Hunter had referred several cases to Hopkin's grand jury. Herman Ohme, "It felt something like the WTC Towers 9-11 attack," *Ohio Association of Responsible Mental Health Practices* March 2002. Memory Debate Archives, "Viewpoints," www.tmdarchives.org, accessed June 28, 2007.

36. Hutchinson acknowledged there was also a serious "problem of too little intervention in certain situations," citing serious physical abuse and murder and "stories" that he heard from foster parents about "children being returned to abusive situations."

37. Such registries were not public at that time but would have become visible if Clark had undergone a background check.

38. Wade, Wexler, Hopkins, Spivak, Weber, and Morton testified at the "Divergent Interests" hearing, and Clark, Hopkins, Wagner, and Donnelly at the "Contract with America" hearing. According to Cunningham, "Mr. Wagner's organization has provided us with some very valuable information in the past and I'm sure will do so again" (U.S. House 1995a:30).

39. Opponents sometimes referred to CAPTA as "the Mondale Act" after its 1974 sponsor Walter Mondale. I have never encountered a supporter referring to it thus; Nelson (1994) argues that opponents sought to associate it with the then-unpopular politician. Richard Gardner's submitted testimony referred to the Mondale Act throughout.

40. Wagner was influenced by Andrew Polsky's work on the therapeutic state, which he included in his bibliography with the descriptor: "The author is not a conservative, and his critique goes far beyond familiar conservative condemnations of 'big government'" (U.S. House 1995:63).

41. Dr. Betty Spivak reported on child deaths due to abuse; Anne Donnelly of the National Committee to Prevent Child Abuse and two child welfare specialists supported enhancing training and funding for child protective workers. More marginalized, the survivors' movement organization American Coalition for Abuse Awareness submitted a lengthy position paper for the record but was not asked to testify. They used a crime frame to advocate mandated reporting and prosecution of familial abuse, writing, "Child abuse in any form perpetrated by any one is a crime and should be named, identified, and prosecuted as one." They also challenged the idea of false allegations and sought to discredit the FMSF board members who appeared before Congress, citing investigations of Ralph Underwater's deceptive and unscientific research practices and his apparent defense of pedophilia in the Dutch journal *Paedika*, and Richard Gardner's court testimony "on behalf of accused pedophiles" (U.S. Senate 1995a:126–28).

42. NCCAN, March 12, 1997. U.S. Department of Health and Human Services Administration for Children and Families, "Availability of Fiscal Year (FY) 1997 State Grant Funds Under the Child Abuse Prevention and Treatment Act," http://www.acf.hhs.gov/programs/cb/laws_policies/policy/pi/capi9701.htm, accessed May 29, 2008.

43. One CAPTA hearing examined child sexual abuse, including incest, in depth (U.S. Senate 2011).

44. Party control of Congress shifted several times during this period. Congress was divided in 2001–2002 during the beginning of George W. Bush's presidency, controlled by Republicans until 2006, then by Democrats from 2006 through the beginning of President Obama's term in 2008, until 2011 when Republicans again took control of the House. I ended the period in 2013 because of the timing of this book. Increasing penalties and surveillance continued to be important after 2013.

45. Eight of these hearings are in my qualitative data set. Numerous other hearings, dealing with children's exposure to sexually explicit media and music, shared similar discourses but are not included here.

46. "Enough is Enough!" was a women's antipornography organization, linked to conservative activists, that the hearing misleadingly described as "nonpartisan." Jepson had served as President Reagan's liaison for women's issues and worked actively with her husband, Republican Senator Roger Jepsen. "Dee Jepsen," "Enough is Enough," http://www.enough.org/inside.php?tag=N40EUMNE, accessed July 8, 2015.

47. Subsequent hearings were similar (U.S. House 2005a, 2005b, 2005c, 2011b).

48. Rep. Scott (D-VA) complained that "as usual, every 2 years we are pontificating about child crimes and dramatically increasing Federal sentences, . . . despite the fact that crimes against children prosecuted in Federal Court constitute a miniscule percentage of such crimes and represent none of the horrendous

crimes against children that have been in the media in recent months." He presented evidence on low recidivism and the disproportionate impact of federal sentencing on Native Americans (U.S. House 2005a:4). Witness John Rhodes, a federal defense attorney in Montana who worked with many Native American clients, agreed that this would make penalties for Native American defendants disproportionate to crimes prosecuted at the state level.

49. In practice, these fine distinctions did not make it into law (Ewing 2011; Leon 2011).

50. On NCMEC's exclusion of familial child sexual abuse, see testimony by Michelle Collins (U.S. Senate 2011).

51. Scott also regularly pointed out that the bills did not address rehabilitation, had no cost estimates, and that states with similar bills showed no reduction in child sexual abuse (U.S. House 2000b; U.S. House 2005b).

52. Witnesses John Rhodes (a federal defender) and Dr. Fred Berlin agreed with Scott that data did not suggest that community notification reduced recidivism (U.S. House 2005c).

53. Supporters included the former director of the Department of Justice's office dealing with sex offender management, Ernie Allen of NCMEC, and Mark Lunsford, father of victim Jessica Lunsford. Opponents were a Louisiana assistant attorney general, a Seattle detective, a representative from the Ohio Public Defender's office, and a representative from a nonprofit dealing with sex offender management policy.

54. Rep. Foley cited " recommendations released today by a group of bipartisan . . . scholars and high level current and former public policy makers, including former Attorney General Ed Meese, and former Deputy General Phil Hayman."

55. The 2011 Senate hearing focused on child sexual abuse by family and acquaintances. It responded in part to the widely-publicized case of sexual assaults by Penn State Assistant football coach Gary Sandusky against multiple children. Because University administrators and Sandusky's in the football and athletic departments had been aware of Sandusky's actions but not reported them, the case raised issues of mandatory reporting, the focus of the 2011 hearing. The 2008 and 2009 CAPTA reauthorization hearings (for the 2010 reauthorization) contain very little discussion of sexual abuse, as opposed to child abuse in general.

56. These included the American Bar Association; the National Congress of American Indians; the Coalition for a Useful Registry (which argued for a more limited and scaled registry); and the Association for the Treatment of Sex Offenders, a juvenile public defenders' group.

57. Differences remain in how the law is implemented. For example, familial abusers are assessed as lower risk when assigning sex offender to tiers (Corrigan 2006). Some incest exceptions and differences in pleading and sentencing remain at the state level.

58. For example, Sen. Biden introduced Judge Charles B. Schudson as "a Circuit Court Judge in Milwaukee, WI, who is widely recognized as a leading expert on laws protecting children in the courts. He is a coauthor of 'On Trial: America's Courts and Their Treatment of Sexually Abused Children,' and he is a frequent lecturer" (U.S. Senate 1989b:73–74). A typical witness opening is "My name is Elizabeth Elmer and I am director of research and training at the Parental Stress Center in Pittsburgh, Pa. In addition I have an academic title, associate

professor of child psychiatry, social work [*sic*], School of Medicine, University of Pittsburgh; and I am on the executive board of the National Committee for Prevention of Child Abuse, a private voluntary organization" (U.S. House 1981:28). Some witnesses established the authority of their organization, such as Hubert Williams, who began, "This morning, I am representing the 100-member Police Chiefs and Sheriffs' Association from the larger jurisdictions who are members of the Police Executive Research Forum. A national professional organization dedicated to improving the quality of police services, the Forum has been working since 1978 to improve police officers' capabilities to handle domestic violence calls" (U.S. House 1984a:32).

59. In a typical exchange, in 1995, Rep. Greenwood asked Ann Donnelly of the National Committee to Prevent Child Abuse whether "the Federal Government [is] not doing enough in the way of research and dissemination of information?" Donnelly replied with specific information, but also stated, "I think all of us should feel a tremendous burden to try and improve that knowledge base [so that federal spending] really is effective and has the kind of outcomes we want" (U.S. House 1995:89).

60. They could, however, be constructed as acting in response to their own childhood abuse. This "cycle of abuse" narrative was common and was used to justify expenditures for prevention and treatment as cost-effective because they would prevent victims from becoming offenders.

61. There is little indication of nonverbal display of emotion in the hearing transcripts, except occasional notations about applause or chairs' requests that an audience remain silent.

62. They were *Stephen Knox v. United States of America* 114 S. Ct. 375 (1993), *United States v. X-Citement Video, Inc., and Rubin Gottesman* 115 S. Ct. 464, 472, 130 L.Ed.2d 372 (1994), and *The United States of America, Petitioner, V. Michael Williams*, 2006 U.S. Briefs 694 (2007), on child pornography; *Ashcroft v. Free Speech Coalition* 535 U.S. 234 (2001) on the Child Online Protection Act (COPA); *Kansas v. Hendricks*, 521 U.S. 346 (1997) on civil commitment; *Stogner v. California*, 539 U.S. 607 (2003), on statutes of limitations; *Smith v. Doe*, 538 U.S. 1009 (2003), *Carr v. U.S.*, 560 U.S. 438 (2010), and *Connecticut Department of Public Safety v. Doe*, 538 US 1 (2003), with no amici) on sex offender registration and notification laws; and *Kennedy v. Louisiana* 2007 U.S. Briefs 343; 2008 U.S. S. Ct. Briefs 246 on the constitutionality of the death penalty for child rape. I identified cases through subject and keyword searches on LexisNexis and Questia and through secondary sources.

CHAPTER 4

1. Increased criminal penalties included "new offenses and penalties for the violation of a protection order" and stalking that crosses state lines, requirements for states "to enforce protection orders issued by other states," increased sentences for "repeat federal sex offenders," pretrial detention requirements for federal child pornography cases, funding for training programs for prosecutors and probation and parole officers dealing with sex offenders, and "mandated restitution to victims" of sexual abuse and child sexual abuse. Grant programs covered prevention, law enforcement training and increased prosecution, the National Domestic Violence Hotline, shelters, court-appointed special advocates, and many other specific programs (Seghetti and Bjelopera 2012).

2. In *Morrison*, the court voted 5-4 to overturn Title III on the grounds that violence against women was not within the authority of the federal government; criminal law is the purview of the states unless it crosses state lines or is relevant to one of the areas of federal authority. Lawyers for the government argued that violence against women affects interstate commerce—an area of legitimate federal intervention—but the majority disagreed.

3. Many of the legal demands on this list have since been met, such as elimination of spousal immunity, barring use of the victim's past sexual history in trial, uniform evidence-collection kits in hospitals, and making female physicians and nurses available for victims.

4. A bill introduced in 1980 failed under such opposition.

5. For example, Sen. Charles Schumer (D-NY)'s staff member David Yassky had been a student of MacKinnon's (Strebeigh 2009:365).

6. The 1994 Act was titled the Violent Crime Control and Law Enforcement Act and commonly referred to as the Omnibus Crime Act. VAWA came up for reauthorization in late 1999 and was voted as a part of the Victims of Trafficking and Violence Protection Act (P.L. 106-386), passing the Republican Senate unanimously and the Republican House 371-1, and again in the Republican-controlled Congress in 2005 as freestanding legislation (The Violence Against Women and Department of Justice Reauthorization Act PL 109-162), where it was again unanimously passed in the Senate and nearly so (415-4) in the House. The 2000 Act increased funding dramatically, although not all funds were appropriated (Roe 2004). It also added programs for "elderly and disabled women," required a portion of funds "to be used exclusively for rape prevention and education programs," and increased programs around dating violence and stalking (Seghetti and Bjelopera 2012:9). The 2006 VAWA (P.L. 109-162) created a Deputy Director of Tribal Affairs in the Office of Violence Against Women (U.S. Senate 2005:11) and increased other provisions for immigrants and Native Americans (Seghetti and Bjelopera 2012). VAWA expired in September 2011 and faced a lengthy reauthorization battle before ultimately passing in March 2013, as discussed later in this chapter.

7. By 2013, membership included "national, tribal, state, territorial and local organizations . . . civil rights organizations, labor unions, advocates for children and youth, anti-poverty groups, immigrant and refugee rights organizations, women's rights leaders, education groups, and others focusing on a wide range of social, economic and racial justice issues." A smaller steering committee was more focused but still coalitional, made up of "national organizations whose primary purpose is to end domestic violence, dating violence, sexual assault, and stalking as well as a limited number of allied organizations who have historically focused significant time, resources and energy to ending violence against women." It included "title chiefs" responsible for assessing implementation, revising, and promoting reauthorization of each component of the Act. These included representatives from the National Alliance to End Sexual Violence, National Alliance to End Domestic Violence, National Council of Juvenile and Family Court Judges, Legal Momentum (NOW's legal arm), youth-focused organizations Break the Cycle and Futures Without Violence, Pennsylvania Coalition Against Rape, Washington State Coalition Against Domestic Violence, the National Law Center on Homelessness and Poverty, two groups focusing specifically on immigrant women (Casa de Esperanza and the Tahirih Justice Center), two representatives from National Congress of American Indians

Taskforce on Violence Against Women, Sisters of Color Ending Sexual Assault, the New York City Gay and Lesbian Anti-Violence Project, and the LA Gay & Lesbian Center (National Task Force to End Sexual and Domestic Violence Against Women, "About NTF"). NOW-LDEF submitted to Congress a long list of additional endorsing organizations in support of the 2000 reauthorization, including liberal religious organizations, the National Gay and Lesbian Task Force, ethnic organizations, the Black Women's Health Project, the NAACP, and numerous local and national organizations related to domestic violence and immigration. Significantly, they did not include any conservative, crime-focused, or even victims' rights organizations (which had participated in the initial early 1990s effort) (U.S. House 2000a).

8. Orloff specifically cited their need to convince Senators Simpson, Hatch, Abraham, and Brownback and Representatives Smith and Sensenbrenner. In lobbying Wyoming Senator Simpson, Orloff reported allying with the Wyoming Coalition Against Domestic Violence (Anonymous 2010:520).

9. I coded all 31 hearings for date, chamber (House or Senate), subcommittee, party control, and witnesses' affiliation and position on VAWA and read them all for background understanding. To construct the sample, I selected 9 of the 19 hearings that are part of VAWA's legislative history, meaning that VAWA was assigned to that committee for official consideration. Specifically, I selected hearings from all four reauthorization cycles and from both House and Senate in cycles when both chambers held hearings. I selected the longest hearings from each cycle and purposely sampled all hearings at which witnesses affiliated with women's movement organizations appeared. I added four other hearings that addressed VAWA outside the official legislative history, three because they were especially extensive, and one in the Senate Committee on Indian Affairs because of the topic. Hearings in the qualitative sample, for which full information is in the references, are U.S. House 1992a, 1993, 1994a, 1999, 2000 and U.S. Senate 1990a, 1990b, 1991a, 1993a, 1996a, 2005, 2007, 2009.The added hearings were U.S. House 1993b, 1994, and U.S. Senate 1996, 2007. Because of delay in availability of hearing transcripts, I include hearings from 2012 in the overall sample but not the qualitative subsample.

10. Between 1990 and 2013, Republicans held control for 10 years, Democrats for 9 years, and Congress was divided in 2001–2002 and 2010–2013; three of the five hearings during divided control were in the Democratic chamber. Both Democratic and Republican lawmakers touted their support for VAWA in websites and speeches. Even Mitch McConnell, who voted against VAWA in 2013, touted his support (Bendery 2014).

11. During the 2011–2013 reauthorization, the Democratic-controlled Senate held three hearings and the Republican-controlled House held two hearings (one of which had only one witness, the director of the OVW).

12. One supporting witness, representing a victims' rights organization, invoked conservatism. The sole other conservative witness during this period was an opponent, Patrick Fagen from the Heritage Foundation (U.S. House 1999).

13. Rep. Barbara Boxer (D-CA) (U.S. House 1992a).

14. Spousal rape witnesses are counted as sexual assault here. An additional five witnesses testified about stalking and physical attack by nonpartners; three were relatives of adult victims of murder by intimate partners or strangers.

15. I also coded for intersectional feminist frames, operationalized as explanations of how statuses besides gender affect experiences of or desired responses to

violence against women. These were rare. I also coded for any mention of race, LGBT issues, immigration, Native Americans, or other specific groups, like youth or the elderly. There were almost no mentions of race or other specific groups and none of LGBT issues. I coded discussions of immigration and Native American women for intersectional or issue-specific frames of general immigration issues or tribal sovereignty. I also coded for any other frames, including public health and fiscal savings, which were rare. I also coded for any opposition to VAWA, which occurred almost solely around Title III.

16. Other speakers used a variety of infrequent frames, e.g., fiscal savings associated with providing services to victims of violence.

17. Feminist frames, alone or in combination, were used by 14 percent of speakers in the first reauthorization cycle and 17 percent in the second.

18. See also Hatch's statement U.S. Senate 2005:22.

19. "Remarks at the Violence Against Women Act (VAWA) Reauthorization Event," June 12, 2000. White House, Office of the Press Secretary, http://clinton4.nara. gov/WH/EOP/First_Lady/html/generalspeeches/, accessed December 16, 2010. Similarly, in a column Clinton wrote for the White House website, she underscored the point that "[v]iolence against women is not only wrong, it is a crime," and she stressed the widespread nature of violence against women. Hillary Rodham Clinton. "Talking It Over," June 14, 2000. White House, http://clinton5.nara.gov/ WH/EOP/First_Lady/html/columns/2000/hrc, accessed February 16, 2010.

20. Remarks of Health and Human Services Secretary Tommy Thompson at the Spring Meeting of the National Advisory Committee on Violence Against Women, April 24, 2003, https://www.justice.gov/archive/ovw/docs/hhs_ secremarks_sprngmeeting.htm, accessed April 21, 2017.

21. U.S. Senate 2005, p. 22.

22. On the study of judges' gender bias, see Biden's remarks in U.S. Senate 1996a.

23. On the 1998 bill: Hon. John Conyers, Jr. of Michigan in the House of Representatives Tuesday, January 19, 1999, *Congressional Record*, 106th Congress, accessed through Thomas.loc.gov, June 3, 2014. On the 2000 bill, H.R. 3244, Victims of Trafficking and Violence Protection Act of 2000: Bill Summary & Status 106th Congress (1999—2000) H.R.3244 All Congressional Actions, accessed through Thomas.loc.gov, 6/3/2014.

24. Sponsors introduced a reauthorization bill unsuccessfully in the fall of 2011 and again in early 2012. Whereas previous versions had broad bipartisan support, the 2011–2012 version initially had only two Republican cosponsors in the Senate, Mike Crapo (R-ID) and Mark Kirk (R-IL) ("VAWA Reauthorization First Legislative Order of Business in 2012 For SJC" January 23, 2012, http://www.leahy.senate. gov/press/vawa-reauthorization-first-legislative-order-of-business-in-2012-for- sjc, accessed June 10, 2014. When it came to a vote in the Senate in April 2012, there were 8 Republicans among its 61 cosponsors (Helderman 2012a). The final vote was 68-31 with 15 Republicans (Kellman 2012). An alternative bill, sponsored by Republican Senator Kay Bailey Hutchison, failed in the Senate, as did an amendment requiring mandatory minimum sentences in domestic violence (Helderman 2012b). Ultimately, funding for VAWA also was cut by 17 percent, with bipartisan agreement and little controversy, although advocates were critical (Helderman 2013a). The House passed a Republican-sponsored bill that would have reauthorized VAWA without the disputed provisions dealing with immigration, discrimination against LGBT people, and Native American authority over offenders on reservations; it also did not include the Campus Sexual Violence

Elimination Act, but this was not a high-profile dispute at the time (Grasgreen 2012). It drew a veto threat from President Obama and died with the end of the congressional session (Helderman 2013b; Kellman 2012). The Senate passed its version of the Act again with a larger margin (78-22) in February 2013, after the November 2012, elections in which Republicans' objections to VAWA had become a campaign issue. Ultimately, the House permitted a vote on the 2013 Senate bill, which passed at the end of April despite extensive ongoing Republican opposition, 286 to 138, with all Democratic Representatives and 87 Republicans voting in favor and only Republicans voting against (Helderman 2013a; 2013b). Pundits attributed the Republican House leadership's willingness to permit the vote to a desire to improve support among women, who voted strongly in favor of Democrats in the 2012 elections (e.g., Abrams 2013; Helderman 2013b).

25. "Leahy, Crapo Introduce Bipartisan Bill to Reauthorize Landmark Violence Against Women Act," November 30, 2011, htty://www.leahy.senate.gov/press/ leahy-crapo-introduce-bipartisan-bill-to-reauthorize-landmark-violence-against-women-act, accessed June 10, 2014.

26. The contested ban on discrimination against LGBT people also passed. After the Act finally passed in 2013, many Republicans who voted for one or both of the Republican versions of VAWA but opposed the Senate version that became law claimed to support VAWA. These included Michele Bachman (who called it "the stronger House version" of VAWA) and several others who issued statements about their support for VAWA and the issues it addressed (Gray 2013).

27. For example, at 1996 and 1999 hearings held in part to consider antistalking legislation saw virtually no discussion of the stalking provisions (U.S. Senate 1996a; U.S. House 1999). Even a provision to prosecute people for possessing a handgun if they were subject to an order of protection against them did not provoke controversy, although it most likely would have in later years (U.S. House 1999).

28. VAWA 2005 defined "populations underserved because of geographic location, underserved racial and ethnic populations . . . special needs (such as language barriers, disabilities, alienage status, or age), and any other population determined to be underserved by the Attorney General," 42 U.S.C. § 13925(a) (33). The Department of Justice guidelines also state, "To date, OVW has declined to issue a definitive list of 'underserved populations,' because we believe that these populations vary by State and community." The Department of Justice reported that a VAWA grant program for "culturally and linguistically specific services" had "funded organizations serving, among others, the African American, Latino/Hispanic, Native American/Alaska Native, Asian/Pacific Islander, African immigrant, Arab, Deaf and Hard of Hearing, Lesbian Gay Bisexual and Transgender (LGBT), Orthodox Jewish, and Portuguese-speaking communities." Quoted in "Frequently Asked Questions on Stop Formula Grants," updated January 2013, http://www.justice.gov/sites/default/files/ovw/legacy/ 2013/01/14/stop-formula-faq.pdf, accessed August 5, 2014. Special grants, amounting to 30 percent of overall VAWA funding were available for service and law enforcement initiatives with underserved communities; at least 10 percent of STOP grants for victim services were required to go to community-based organizations working with underserved communities, and programs that aimed to serve underserved populations were required to "ensure that they offer full linguistic access and culturally specific services." Ohio Office of Criminal Justice Services, "Violence Against Women Act Funding," 2012 request for proposals, http://www.ocjs.ohio.gov/FY2012_VAWA_RFP.pdf, accessed June 20, 2014.

29. There were more than 30,000 self-petitions, 1,500 trafficking victims visas, and an additional 12,000 pending petitions as of 2010 (Anonymous 2010:583). Early years saw modest increases each year, from 1,210 in 1997 to 1,921 in 1999, with an increase to approximately 3,500 in 2000 (U.S. House 2000a:43); figures provided by Barbara Strack, acting executive associate commissioner for Policy and Planning, INS. Prior to the 2012 reauthorization, battered women could apply for legal residency either under VAWA or through the U visa, which required them to cooperate with law enforcement in (and which also extended to victims of other types of crimes) (Constable 2012). The 2012 VAWA bill increased the number of U visas by up to 5,000 from the 10,000 visas that could be issued annually previously (Helderman 2012a).

30. According to Tahirih, enforcement and implementation of IMBRA remained highly insufficient in 2014, Tahirih Justice Center, IMB Campaign http://www.tahirih.org/advocacy/policy-areas/imb-campaign/, accessed June 9, 2014.

31. This was reportedly the first time federal law would contain such an antidiscrimination clause.

32. Based on comprehensive search in conservative media outlets, as detailed in the Introduction. There were 17 articles discussing VAWA in the secular conservative media sample between 1990 and 2015. Some focused on VAWA itself, others used VAWA as an example to criticize Republicans or to make other points (e.g., about federalism). For example, Lowry 1997; O'Beirne 1995; Ponnuru 1997. The *Weekly Standard* and *American Spectator* favorably covered the *Morrison* case that overturned Title III (Rabkin 2000; Turk 1999). The *National Review*'s only coverage of *Morrison* was a short paragraph in a news of the week summary, June 5, 2000. Between 1975 and 1990, *National Review* published 33 other articles on rape; *Commentary* and *Human Events* covered sexual violence in the 1990s. There is little difference in the content of pre- and post-VAWA articles.

33. Data are publicly available at http://web.stanford.edu/group/collectiveaction/cgi-bin/drupal/.

34. National Coalition Against Domestic Violence, Public Policy Update, August 9, 2005, http://www.ncadv.org/files/AugustUpdate.pdf, accessed June 9, 2014.

35. Based on comprehensive subject searches, as discussed in the Introduction. *Ms.* published 15 mostly short pieces 1990–2015; *off our backs* published 9 short pieces and 2 slightly longer ones on VAWA from 1990 through its folding in 2008, almost all announcing reauthorizations or the court challenges to Title III. Major liberal and progressive publications such as the *Nation* and the *Progressive* generally had no more than one or two articles on VAWA, if any, mostly focused on Title III.

36. When these articles were mainly about the movement, not VAWA, I did not code them as VAWA articles.

37. The focus on lesbian battering seems to have emerged first from anti-SM activists who framed SM as lesbian-lesbian violence, but became more general.

38. It called for support for the SAFE Act, H.R. 3271, which was introduced in 2012 and failed in the Republican House; it would have provided job protections and unemployment benefits for those who have to miss work due to domestic violence (Burk 2013).

39. The article dealt with a brief campaign to get viewers to speak up in support of VAWA 2005, in connection with the film *North Country*, which was sponsored by the production company, NOW, the Family Violence Prevention Fund, and the Feminist Majority Foundation.

40. Jo Reger (2012 and personal communication) found no mention of VAWA in her interviews with young feminists in the early 2000s.

41. Thirty-six states submitted a brief, and Sen. Biden submitted his own brief. The brief by immigrant women's organizations also included the National Association of Women Lawyers.

42. *Lanier* deals with a case in which a judge was convicted of rape in his chambers under a statute barring the state from interfering with bodily integrity and raised the question of whether freedom from sexual assault is constitutional right; appeals court had ruled that rape was not interference with bodily integrity.

43. In addition, *Felkner v. Jackson* dealt with the exclusion of African American jurors from a rape trial, but the case drew no amici. 2010 U.S. Briefs 797.

44. In addition, Catherine MacKinnon served as counsel for an amicus brief from the victim in the original case. Amici included: NOW-LDEF, Anti-Defamation League, Ayuda, Inc., Center For Women Policy Studies, Connecticut Women's Education And Legal Fund, Inc., The DC Rape Crisis Center, Jewish Women International, National Alliance Of Sexual Assault Coalitions, National Council Of Jewish Women, National Organization For Women Foundation, Inc., National Women's Law Center, Northwest Women's Law Center, People for the American Way, Virginians Aligned Against Sexual Assault, Women's Law Project, Women's Legal Defense Fund.

45. This is partly due to differences of opinion in how best to ensure women's rights legislatively, which were at play in the pornography wars as well.

46. For example, in 2000, the text of the bill specified a division in funding under which at least 35 percent would go to victims' services and a maximum of 50 percent to law enforcement, prosecution grants, and state court systems combined (U.S. House 1999).

47. Caringella (2009) argues that, despite these changes, conviction rates remain low and rape survivors are often mistreated by hospitals, prosecutors, and in court.

48. VAWA funding required law enforcement agencies to include community-based organizations in their work, and grants favored groups that worked with community-based organizations. It specified in 2000 that reimbursement to agencies serving victims would not be "contingent upon the victim's report of the sexual assault to law enforcement or upon the victim's cooperation in the prosecution of the sexual assault." Further, instead of simply supporting "victims through the legal process," the proposed amended law mandated "providing advocacy and assistance for victims seeking legal, social, and health care services" (U.S. House 1999).

49. Ohio Office of Criminal Justice Services, "Violence Against Women Act Funding," 2012 request for proposals, http://www.ocjs.ohio.gov/FY2012_VAWA_RFP.pdf, accessed June 20, 2014.

50. National Advisory Committee on Violence Against Women, OVW, Justice Department. "Expanding the Reach of Victim Services," https://www.justice.gov/archive/ovw/docs/execsum-evs.pdf, accessed April, 21, 2017.

CHAPTER 5

1. See Blee 2012; Goodwin, Jasper, and Polletta 2001; Lichterman 1995; Snow and Benford 1998; Steinberg 1999; Taylor and Whittier 1992; Taylor et al. 1995.

REFERENCES

Abrams, Jim. 2013. "Senate again Focuses on Domestic Violence." *The Washington Post*:A15.

Abrams, Philip. 1988. "Notes on the Difficulty of Studying the State." *Journal of Historical Sociology* 1:58–89.

Aldrich, Liberty. 2000. "Sneak Attack on VAWA (Violence Against Women Act of 1994 Services Threatened)." *The Nation* 271:6.

Alexander, Michelle. 2010. *The New Jim Crow.* New York: New Press.

Allahyari, Rebecca A. 1997. "The Micro-Politics of Worthy Homelessness: Interactive Moments in Congressional Hearings." *Sociological Inquiry* 67:59–71.

Almeida, Paul. 2010. "Social Movement Partyism: Collective Action and Oppositional Political Parties." Pp. 57–73 in *Strategic Alliances: Coalition Building and Social Movements*, edited by Nella Van Dyke and Holly McCammon. Minneapolis: University of Minnesota Press.

Amenta, Edwin, Neal Caren, Elizabeth Chiarello and Yang Su. 2010. "The Political Consequences of Social Movements." *Annual Review of Sociology* 36:287–307.

Ammar, Nawal H., Leslye E. Orloff, Mary A. Dutton and Giselle Aguilar-Hass. 2005. "Calls to Police and Police Response: A Case Study of Latina Immigrant Women in the USA." *International Journal of Police Science & Management* 7:230–44.

Andrews, Kenneth T. and Bob Edwards. 2004. "Advocacy Organizations in the U.S. Political Process." *Annual Review of Sociology* 30:479–506.

Aretxaga, Begoña. 2001. "The Sexual Games of the Body Politic: Fantasy and State Violence in Northern Ireland." *Culture, Medicine & Psychiatry* 25:1–27.

Aretxaga, Begoña. 2003. "Maddening States." *Annual Review of Anthropology* 32:393–410.

Armstrong, Elizabeth and Mary Bernstein. 2008. "Culture, Power, and Institutions." *Sociological Theory* 26(1):74–99.

Armstrong, L. 1988. "Child Sexual Abuse: Fighting to End Rape." *Off our backs* 18:22.

Arnold, Gretchen. 2013. "Reframing the Narrative of the Battered Women's Movement." *Violence Against Women* 19(5):557–78.

Attorney General's Commission on Pornography [AGCP]. 1986. *Final Report of the Attorney General's Commission on Pornography.* Nashville, TN: Rutledge Hill Press.

"Backlash Against Survivors/False Memory Syndrome Foundation." 1994. *Off our backs* 24:10–13.

Bailey, Beth. 1999. *Sex in the Heartland.* Boston: Harvard University Press.

Baker, Carrie. 2013. "Moving Beyond 'Slaves, Sinners, and Saviors'." *Journal of Feminist Scholarship* 4 (Spring):1–23.

Banaszak, Lee A. 2010. *The Women's Movement Inside and Outside the State*. New York: Cambridge University Press.

Barakso, Maryann. 2004. *Governing NOW*. Ithaca, NY: Cornell.

Baumgartner, Frank, Virginia Gray and David Lowery. 2009. "Federal Policy Activity and the Mobilization of State Lobbying Organizations." *Political Research Quarterly* 62:552–67.

Baumgartner, Frank and Christine Mahoney. 2005. "Social Movements, the Rise of New Issues, and the Public Agenda." Pp. 65–86 in *Routing the Opposition*, edited by David S. Meyer, Valerie Jenness and Helen Ingram. Minneapolis: University of Minnesota Press.

Beckett, Katherine. 1997. *Making Crime Pay*. New York: Oxford University Press.

Bell, Joyce. 2014. *The Black Power Movement and American Social Work*. New York: Columbia University Press.

Bendery, Jennifer. 2014. "Mitch McConnell Touts Support for Violence Against Women Act, Which He Repeatedly Opposed." *Huffington Post*. Retrieved June 19, 2016 (http://www.huffingtonpost.com/2014/08/05/mitch-mcconnell-violence-against-women-act_n_5651334.html).

Benowitz, June Melby. 2015. *Challenge and Change*. Gainesville: University Press of Florida.

Bergen, Raquel K. and Shana Maier. 2011. "Sexual Assault Services." Pp. 227–42 in *Sourcebook on Violence Against Women*, edited by Claire Renzetti, Jeffrey Edleson and Raquel K. Bergen. Thousand Oaks, CA: Sage.

Berger, Susan. 2009. "(Un)Worthy: Latina Battered Immigrants Under VAWA and the Construction of Neoliberal Subjects." *Citizenship Studies* 13:201–17.

Bernstein, Elizabeth. 2010. "Militarized Humanitarianism Meets Carceral Feminism: The Politics of Sex, Rights, and Freedom in Contemporary Antitrafficking Campaigns." *Signs* 36:45–71.

Bernstein, Elizabeth. 2012. "Carceral Politics as Gender Justice? The 'Traffic in Women' and Neoliberal Circuits of Crime, Sex, and Rights." *Theory and Society* 41:233–59.

Bevacqua, Maria. 2000. *Rape on the Public Agenda*. Boston: Northeastern University Press.

Bevacqua, Maria. 2008. "Reconsidering Violence Against Women: Coalition Politics in the Antirape Movement." Pp. 163–77 in *Feminist Coalitions: Historical Perspectives on Second-Wave Feminism in the United States*, edited by Stephanie Gilmore. Champaign: University of Illinois Press.

Bhuyan, Rupaleem. 2008. "The Production of the 'Battered Immigrant' in Public Policy and Domestic Violence Advocacy." *Journal of Interpersonal Violence* 23:153–70.

Biden, Joseph. 2007. *Promises to Keep*. New York: Random House.

Bierria, Alisa. 2007. "Pursuing a Radical Anti-Violence Agenda Inside/Outside a Non-Profit Structure." Pp. 151–164 in *The Revolution Will Not Be Funded*, edited by INCITE! Women of Color Against Violence. Cambridge MA: South End Press.

Blakely, Mary K. 1985. "Is One Woman's Sexuality Another Woman's Pornography?" *Ms.* 13:37.

Blee, Kathleen. 1991. *Women of the Klan*. Berkeley: University of California Press.

Blee, Kathleen. 2012. *Democracy in the Making: How Activist Groups Form*. New York: Oxford University Press.

Blee, Kathleen and Kimberly A. Creasap. 2010. "Conservative and Right-Wing Movements." *Annual Review of Sociology* 36:269–86.

Blumenthal, Richard. 2012. 158 Cong Rec S 2761. April 26.

Bob, Murray L. 1986. "The Right Questions about Obscenity: An Alternative to the Meese Commission Report." *Library Journal* 111:39.

Brasher, Holly. 2006. "Listening to Hearings: Legislative Hearings and Legislative Outcomes." *American Politics Research* 34:583–604.

"The Brawley Gang v. Us." *National Review* 40:18.

Breines, Wini. 2002. "What's Love Got to Do With It? White Women, Black Women, and Feminism in the Movement Years." *Signs* 27:1095–133.

Breines, Wini and Linda Gordon. 1983. "The New Scholarship on Family Violence." *Signs* 8:490–531.

Brest, Paul and Ann Vandenberg. 1987. "Politics, Feminism, and the Constitution: The Anti-Pornography Movement in Minneapolis." *Stanford Law Review* 39:607–61.

Bronstein, Carolyn. 2011. *Battling Pornography: The American Feminist Anti-Pornography Movement, 1976–1986*. New York: Cambridge University Press.

Brown, Wendy. 1995. *States of Injury*. Princeton, NJ: Princeton University Press.

Brownmiller, Susan. 1999. *In Our Time: Memoir of a Revolution*. New York: Delta/Dell.

Bumiller, Kristin. 2008. *In an Abusive State*. Durham, NC: Duke University Press.

Burk, Martha. 2013. "The Cost of Violence." *Ms.* 23:50.

Burnham, Margaret. 2001. "The Role of the State, Globalization, Race, Class, Gender and the Violence Against Women Act: Lessons from an 'Ordinary Case.'" *Guild Practitioner* 58:7–10.

Burns, Gene. 2005. *The Moral Veto*. New York: Cambridge University Press.

Burstein, Paul. 2014. *American Public Opinion, Advocacy, and Policy in Congress*. New York: Cambridge University Press.

Burstein, Paul and C. E. Hirsh. 2007. "Interest Organizations, Information, and Policy Innovation in the U.S. Congress." *Sociological Forum* 22:174–99.

Bystydzienski, Jill and Steven Schact. 2001. *Forging Radical Alliances Across Difference: Coalition Politics for the New Millennium*. Lanham, MD: Rowman and Littlefield.

Califia, Pat. 1986. "The Obscene, Disgusting, and Vile Meese Report." *The Advocate* 457:42.

Campbell, John L. 2002. "Ideas, Politics, and Public Policy." *Annual Review of Sociology* 28:21–38.

Canaday, Margot. 2009. *The Straight State: Sexuality and Citizenship in Twentieth-Century America*. Princeton, NJ: Princeton University Press.

Caringella, Susan. 2009. *Addressing Rape Reform in Law and Practice*. New York: Columbia University Press.

Chancer, Lynn. 1998. "Playing Gender Against Race through High-Profile Crime Cases." *Violence Against Women* 4:100.

Cheit, Ross. 2014. *The Witch-Hunt Narrative: Politics, Psychology, and the Sexual Abuse of Children*. New York: Oxford University Press.

Chen, Shana W. 2000. "The Immigrant Women of the Violence Against Women Act: The Role of the Asian American Consciousness in the Legislative Process." *Georgetown Journal of Gender & the Law* 1:823.

Chesler, P. 1991. "Mothers on Trial. [Cover Story]." *Ms.* 1:47.

Christenson, Reo M. 1981. "It's Time to Excise the Pornographic Cancer." *Christianity Today* 25:20–23.

Coburn, Tom. 2012. 158 Cong Rec S 2761. April 26.

Cole, Elizabeth R. and Zakiya T. Luna. 2010. "Making Coalitions Work: Solidarity across Difference within US Feminism." *Feminist Studies* 36(1):71–98.

Collier, Cheryl N. 2008. "Neoliberalism and Violence Against Women: Can Retrenchment Convergence Explain the Path of Provincial Anti-Violence Policy, 1985—2005?" *Canadian Journal of Political Science* 41:19–42.

Collins, Patricia Hill. 2000. *Black Feminist Thought*. New York: Routledge.

Comack, Elizabeth. 2006. "The Feminist Engagement with Criminology." Pp. 22–56 in *Criminalizing Women*, edited by Gillian Balfour and Elizabeth Comack. Nova Scotia: Fernwood.

Combahee River Collective. 1983. "A Black Feminist Statement." Pp. 264–74 in *Home Girls, A Black Feminist Anthology*, edited by Barbara Smith. New York: Kitchen Table Press.

"Conservative Forum." 2000a. *Human Events* 56:20.

Constable, Pamela. 2012. "U.S. Laws a Lifeline from Abuse." *The Washington Post*:B01.

Corrigan, Rose. 2006. "Making Meaning of Megan's Law." *Law & Social Inquiry* 31:267–312.

Corrigan, Rose. 2013. *Up Against a Wall: Rape Reform and the Failure of Success*. New York: New York University Press.

Coulter, Ann. 2002. "Liberals, Priests and Boy Scouts." *Human Events* 58:6.

Crenshaw, Kimberle. 1991. "Mapping the Margins: Intersectionality, Identity Politics, and Violence Against Women." *Stanford Law Review* 43(6):1241–90.

Critchlow, Donald. 2005. *Phyllis Schlafly and Grassroots Conservatism*. Princeton, NJ: Princeton University Press.

Cruz, Ariane. 2016. "Playing with the Politics of Perversion: Policing BDSM, Pornography, and Black Female Sexuality." *Souls* 18(2-4):379–407.

Cumings, Susan. 2005. "Taking Back the Clothesline: Fighting Corporate Claims on a Grassroots Movement." *Off our backs* 35:13–17.

Currie, Elliott. 2013. *Crime and Punishment in America*, 2nd Edition. New York: Picador.

Das, Veena. 1996. "Sexual Violence, Discursive Formations and the State." *Economic and Political Weekly* 31:2411–23.

Davis, Joseph. 2005. *Accounts of Innocence*. Chicago: University of Chicago Press.

Davis, Tawana, Owen Strachan, Lindsey Holcomb and Justin Holcomb. 2015. "After Domestic Violence, Why Should a Christian Wife Call the Police, Not a Pastor, First?" *Christianity Today* 59:26–27.

Deer, Sarah. 2006. "Federal Indian Law and Violent Crime." Pp. 32–41 in *Color of Violence: The INCITE Anthology*, edited by INCITE! Women of Color Against Violence. Cambridge, MA: South End Press.

DeGregorio, Christine. 1994. "Professional Committee Staff as Policy Making Partners in the U.S. Congress." *Congress & the Presidency* 21:49.

Diamond, Sara. 1995. *Roads to Dominion: Right Wing Movements and Political Power in the United States*. New York: Guilford Press.

Dicks, Norm. 158 Cong Rec H 2745. May 16.

Diermeier, Daniel. 2000. "Information and Congressional Hearings." *American Journal of Political Science* 44:51–65.

Dines, Gail. 2011. *Pornland*. Boston: Beacon Press.

Douglas, Carol A. 1986. "Pornography: The Meese Report." *Off our backs* 26:5.

Downs, Donald A. 1989. *The New Politics of Pornography*. Chicago: University of Chicago Press.

Doyle, Sadie. 2017. "It's Time to Take Sexism Seriously as a Political Force." *Elle*, January 11, Retrieved January 13, 2017 (www.elle.com/culture/career-politics/a4204/putn-trump-and-julian-assange-sexism).

Duggan, Lisa. 1985. "The Danger of Coalitions. [Cover Story]." *Ms.* 13:47.

Duggan, Lisa. 2006. "Censorship in the Name of Feminism." Pp. 29–39 in *Sex Wars*, edited by Lisa Duggan and Nan Hunter. New York: Routledge.

Duggan, Lisa and Nan D. Hunter. 1995. *Sex Wars: Sexual Dissent and Political Culture*. New York: Routledge.

Dworkin, Andrea. 1976. *Woman Hating*. New York: Plume.

Dworkin, Andrea. 1983 [1978]. *Right-Wing Women*. New York: Wideview/Perigee.

Dworkin, Andrea. 1991 [1979]. *Pornography: Men Possessing Women*. New York: Plume.

Earl, Jennifer. 2004. "The Cultural Consequences of Social Movements." Pp. 508–30 in *The Blackwell Companion to Social Movements*, edited by David Snow, Sarah Soule and Hanspieter Kriesi. Malden, MA: Blackwell.

Edwards, Bob and Sam Marullo. 1995. "Organizational Mortality in a Declining Social Movement: The Demise of Peace Movement Organizations in the End of the Cold War Era." *American Sociological Review* 60:908–27.

Elder, Larry. 2003. "Playing the Race Card." *Human Events* 59:18.

Emirzian, Aislinn. 2005. "A "Participant" Against Violence." *Ms.* 15:41.

Enke, Anne. 2007. *Finding the Movement*. Durham, NC: Duke University Press.

Erdrich, Louse. 2013. "Rape on the Reservation." *New York Times:*A:25.

Esterling, Kevin. 2010. "Identifying Conditions for Falsifiable Discourse." *Legislative Studies Quarterly* 35 (May):169–98.

Evans, Sara M. 1980. *Personal Politics*. New York: Vintage.

Ewing, Charles. 2011. *Perverted Justice*. New York: Oxford University Press.

Feinstein, Dianne. 2012. 158 Cong Rec S 2761. April 26.

Ferguson, Ann. 1986. "Pleasure, Power and the Porn Wars." *The Women's Review of Books* 3:11–13.

Ferguson, Ann. 2000. *Bad Boys*. Ann Arbor: University of Michigan Press.

Ferree, Myra M. 2003. "Resonance and Radicalism: Feminist Framing in the Abortion Debates of the United States and Germany." *American Journal of Sociology* 109:304–44.

Ferree, Myra M. and Carol M. Mueller. 2004. "Feminism and the Women's Movement: A Global Perspective." *Blackwell Companion to Social Movements*, edited by David Snow, Sarah Soule and Hanspieter Kriesi. New York: Wiley-Blackwell.

Ferree, Myra M. and Silke Roth. 1998. "Gender, Class and the Intersection between Social Movements." *Gender & Society* 12(6):626–48.

Fetner, Tina. 2008. *How the Religious Right Shaped Lesbian and Gay Activism*. Minneapolis: University of Minnesota Press.

Fligstein, Neil and Doug McAdam. 2012. *A Theory of Fields*. New York: Oxford University Press.

Frame, Randall L. 1984. "Citizens Battle a Booming Pornography Business: Opponents Call Boycott of 7-Eleven, Retailer of Explicit Magazines." *Christianity Today* 28:72–73.

Frame, Randall L.1986. "Unlikely Allies in a Common War." *Christianity Today* 30:54–55.

Fraser, Nancy. 2013. "How Feminism Became Capitalism's Handmaiden—and How to Reclaim it." *The Guardian*, 13 October 13, Retrieved January

15, 2014 (http://www.theguardian.com/commentisfree/2013/oct/14/
   feminism-capitalist-handmaiden-neoliberal).

Frazier, Claude A. 1977. "Child Abuse: Society's Symptom of Stress." *Christianity Today* 21:6–8.

Freedman, Estelle. 2013. *Redefining Rape*. Cambridge, MA: Harvard University Press.

Freeman, Jo. 1975. *The Politics of Women's Liberation*. New York: Longman.

Friday, Marty. 1983. "Surviving and Stopping Incest: Bringing the Issue of Incest into
   the Anti-Violence Movement." *Off our backs* 13:16.

Friedman, Andrea. 2000. *Prurient Interests*. New York: Columbia University Press.

Fuselier, Daniel, Robert Durham and Sandy Wurtele. 2002. "The Child Sexual
   Abuser: Perceptions of College Students and Professionals." *Sexual Abuse*
   14(3):271–80.

Gaddis, Patricia. 2001. "In the Beginning . . . A Creation Story of Battered Women's
   Shelters." *Off our backs* 31:14–15.

Gardner, Christine J. 2001. "Tangled in the Worst of the Web." *Christianity Today*
   45:42–49.

Gavey, Nicola. 2009. "Fighting Rape." Pp. 96–124 in *Theorizing Sexual Violence*, edited
   by Renee Heberle and Victoria Grace. New York: Routledge.

Gerhard, Jane. 2001. *Desiring Revolution*. New York: Columbia University Press.

Gerstein, Josh. 2011. "Eric Holder Accused of Neglecting Porn Fight." *Politico*.
   Retrieved February 6, 2014 (http://www.politico.com/news/stories/0411/
   53314.html).

Gerstein, Josh.2013. "X-Rated Video Maker Ira Isaacs Gets 4-Year Prison Term."
   Politico. Retrieved February 6, 2014 (http://www.politico.com//blogs/under-
   the-radar/2013/01/xrated-video-maker-gets-year-prison-term-154463.html).

Giddings, Paula. 2008. *Ida, A Sword among Lions*. New York: Amistad/Harper Collins.

Gillum, Tameka. 2009. "Improving Services to African American Survivors of IPV."
   Violence Against Women 15(1):57–80.

Gilmore, Stephanie. 2008. *Feminist Coalitions: Historical Perspectives on Second-Wave
   Feminism in the United States*. Champaign: University of Illinois Press.

Gingrich, Newt and Pat Nolan. 2014. "An Opening for Bipartisanship on Prison
   Reform." *Wall Street Journal* (July 15):A15.

Giugni, Marco. 2007. "Useless Protest?" *Mobilization* 12:53–77.

Goldfarb, Sally. 2003. "Applying the Discrimination Model to Violence Against
   Women." *American University Journal of Gender, Social Policy & the Law*
   11:251–71.

Goodwin, Jeff, James Jasper and Francesca Polletta, editors. 2001. *Passionate Politics*.
   Chicago: University of Chicago Press.

Goss, Kristin. 2013. *The Paradox of Gender Equality*. Ann Arbor: University of
   Michigan Press.

Goss, Kristin and Michael Heaney. 2010. "Organizing Women as Women: Hybridity
   and Grassroots Collective Action in the 21st Century." *Perspectives on Politics*
   8(1):27–52.

Gottschalk, Marie. 2006. *The Prison and the Gallows: The Politics of Mass Incarceration
   in America*. Cambridge, UK: Cambridge University Press.

Gould, Kenneth A., J. Timmons Roberts and Tammy Lewis. 2004. "Blue
   Green Coalitions: Constraints and Possibilities in the Post 9-11 Political
   Environment." *Journal of World Systems Research* 10:91–116.

Grasgreen, Allie. 2012. "Sexual Assault Survivors Tell Congress to
   Increase Protections in VAWA." Inside Higher Education. Retrieved

July 26, 2013 (http://www.insidehigihered.com/news/2012/
sexual-assault-survivors-tell-congress-increase-protections-vawa).

Grassley, Charles. 2012. 158 Cong Rec S 2761. April 26.

Gray, Kaili J. 2013. "Republicans Who Didn't Vote for Violence Against Women Act
Say They Did Anyway Because Why Not?" *Daily Kos*. Retrieved March 6, 2013
(http://www.dailykos.com/story/2013/03/04/1191486/-Republicans-who-
didn-t-vote-for-Violence-Against-Women-Act-say-they-did-anyway-because-
why-not).

Gring-Pemble, Lisa. 2003. "Legislating a 'Normal, Classic Family': The Rhetorical
Construction of Families in American Welfare Policy." *Political Communication*
20:473–98.

Grijalva, Raoul. 2012. 158 Cong Rec H 2745. May 16.

Gross, Neil, Thomas Medvetz and Rupert Russell. 2011. "The Contemporary American
Conservative Movement." *Annual Review of Sociology* 37:325–54.

Gutmann, Stephanie. 1993. "Are All Men Rapists?" *National Review* 45:44–47.

Haga, Chuck. 1990. "Peace Came at a Terrible Price to a Soul Pained by Injustice." *Star
Tribune* (Minneapolis, MN).

Haney, Lynne. 2000. "Feminist State Theory: Applications to Jurisprudence,
Criminology, and the Welfare State." *Annual Review of Sociology* 26:641–66.

Harris, Angela. 1989. "Race and Essentialism in Feminist Legal Theory." *Stanford Law
Review* 42:581–93.

Heaney, Michael and Fabio Rojas. 2014. "Hybrid Activism: Social Movement
Mobilization in a Multimovement Environment." *American Journal of Sociology*
119 (4):1047–103.

Heath, Melanie, Jessica Braimoh and Julie Gouweloos. 2016. "Judging Women's
Sexual Agency: Contemporary Sex Wars in the Legal Terrain of Prostitution
and Polygamy." *Signs* 42(11):199–225.

Heins, Marjorie. 2001. *Not in Front of the Children*. New York: Hill and Wang.

Helderman, Rosalind S. 2012a. "GOP Shifts Strategy regarding Violence Against
Women Act." *The Washington Post*:A04.

Helderman, Rosalind. 2012b. "Senate Votes to Reauthorize Violence Against Women
Act." *The Washington Post*:A03.

Helderman, Rosalind. 2013a. "Anti-Violence Act Is Approved." *The Washington
Post*:A12.

Helderman, Rosalind. 2013b. "House to Consider Bills on Violence Law." *The
Washington Post*:A03.

Hill, Rebecca. 2009. *Men, Mobs, and Law: Anti-Lynching and Labor Defense in U.S.
Radical History*. Durham, NC: Duke University Press.

Holland, Sharon P. 2011. "The "Beached Whale"." *GLQ: A Journal of Lesbian & Gay
Studies* 17:1–95.

Hollander, Jocelyn. 2001. "Vulnerability and Dangerousness." *Gender & Society*
15:83–109.

Holyoke, Thomas T. 2009. "Interest Group Competition and Cooperation at
Legislative Hearings." *Congress and the Presidency* 35:17–38.

Irvine, Janice. 1995. "Reinventing Perversion Sex Addiction and Cultural Anxieties."
Journal of the History of Sexuality 5(3):429–50.

Isaac, Larry. 2010. "Policing Capital: Armed Countermovement Coalitions Against
Labor in Late Nineteenth-Century Industrial Cities." Pp. 22–49 in *Strategic
Alliances: Coalition Building and Social Movements*, edited by Nella Van Dyke and
Holly McCammon. Minneapolis: University of Minnesota Press.

Jabour, Anya. 2013. "Prostitution Politics and Feminist Activism in Modern America." *Journal of Women's History* 25:141–64.

Jacobs, Ronald and Sarah Sobieraj. 2007. "Narrative and Legitimacy: U.S. Congressional Debates about the Non-Profit Sector." *Sociological Theory* 25:1–25.

Jensen, Robert. 2007. *Getting Off: Pornography and the End of Masculinity.* Boston: South End Press.

Jones, Bryan D. and Frank Baumgartner. 2004. "Representation and Agenda Setting." *Policy Studies Journal* 32:1–24.

Johnson, Hank. 2012. 158 Cong Rec H 2745. May 16.

Jurisfemme. 1993. "FMS: The Latest in Sexual Abuse Defense Ploys." *Off our backs* 23:6.

Kaminer, Wendy. 1992. "Feminists Against the First Amendment." *The Atlantic* November.

Kantzer, Kenneth S. 1986. "The Power of Porn." *Christianity Today* 30:18–20.

Katzenstein, Mary. 1999. *Faithful and Fearless.* Princeton, NJ: Princeton University Press.

Keen, Lisa. 2013. "Inclusive Violence Against Women Act Passes House." *Between the Lines*:12.

Kellman, Laurie. 2012. "GOP Revises Anti-Violence Bill, Draws White House Veto Threat." *The Washington Post*:A19.

Kelly, David. 1992. "Feminist Group Calls Premise of Measure 'False.'" *The Hollywood Reporter.* Accessed through LexisNexis, August 22, 2017.

Kennedy, John W. 2008. "Help for the Sexually Desperate: More and More, Christian Men are Admitting They've Been Caught in a Vicious Cycle." *Christianity Today* 52:28–35.

King, Brayden G., Keith G. Bentele and Sarah Soule. 2007. "Protest and Policymaking: Explaining Fluctuation in Congressional Attention to Rights Issues, 1960–1986." *Social Forces* 86:137–63.

Kolb, Felix. 2007. *Protest and Opportunities.* Chicago: University of Chicago Press.

Kyl, Jon. 2012. 158 Cong Rec S 2761. April 26.

LaCombe, Dany. 1994. *Blue Politics: Pornography and the Law in the Age of Feminism.* Toronto: University of Toronto Press.

Lancaster, Roger. 2011. *Sex Panic and the Punitive State.* Berkeley: University of California Press.

Lautenberg, Frank. 2012. 158 Cong Rec S 2761. April 26.

Leidholdt, Dorchen. 1985. "A Small Group." *Off our backs* 15:26.

Leon, Chrysanthi. 2011. "Sex Fiends, Perverts, and Pedophiles." New York: New York University Press.

"Lesbian Survivors of Incest." 1982. *Off our backs* 12:16–.

Levi, Margaret and Gillian H. Murphy. 2006. "Coalitions of Contention: The Case of the WTO Protests in Seattle." *Political Studies* 54:651–70.

Levine, Judith. 2002. *Harmful to Minors: The Perils of Protecting Children from Sex.* Minneapolis: University of Minnesota Press.

Levy, Ariel. 2005. *Female Chauvinist Pigs: Women and the Rise of Raunch Culture.* New York: Free Press.

Lichterman, Paul. 1995. "Piecing Together a Multicultural Community: Cultural Differences in Community Building Across Grass-Roots Environmentalists." *Social Problems* 42:513–34.

Lindsay, Michael. 2008. *Faith in the Halls of Power.* New York: Oxford.

Lo, Clarence. 1982. "Countermovements and Conservative Movements in the Contemporary U.S." *Annual Review of Sociology* 8:107–34.

Lohmann, Susanne. 1998. "An Information Rationale for the Power of Special Interests." *American Political Science Review* 92(4):809–28.

Love, Heather. 2015. "Pornography Porn." *Public Books*. Retrieved March 24, 2017 (www.publicbooks.org/pornography-porn).

Lovelace, Tanya. 2012. "Reaching Underserved Populations through VAWA." Washington, D.C.: National Task Force to End Sexual and Domestic Violence Against Women. Retrieved October 7, 2015 (http://www.scribd.com/doc/138768134/Final-RevUnderserved-VAWA-Fact-Sheet-Feb1-12#).

Lowry, Rich. 1997. "Dysfunctional Republicans." *National Review* 49(3):20.

Lynn, Barry W. and American Civil Liberties Union. 1986. *Rushing to Censorship*. Washington, D.C: American Civil Liberties Union, Washington Office.

MacKinnon, Catharine. 1997. "The Roar on the Other Side of Silence." Pp. 3–24 in *In Harm's Way*, edited by Catharine MacKinnon and Andrea Dworkin. Cambridge, MA and London: Harvard University Press.

MacKinnon, Catharine A. 2005. *Women's Lives Men's Law*. Cambridge, MA: Belknap Press of Harvard University Press.

MacKinnon, Catharine A. and Andrea Dworkin. 1997. *In Harm's Way: The Pornography Civil Rights Hearings*. Cambridge, MA: Harvard University Press.

Maney, Gregory. 2000. "Transnational Mobilization and Civil Rights in Northern Ireland." *Social Problems* 47:153–179.

Margulies, Joseph. 2013. *What Changed When Everything Changed*. New Haven, CT: Yale University Press.

Martin, Patricia Y. 2005. *Rape Work*. New York: Routledge.

Matsuda, Mari. 1994. "Crime and Punishment." *Ms.* 5:86.

Matthews, Nancy. 1994. *Confronting Rape*. New York: Routledge.

McBride, Dorothy and Janine Parry. 2011. *Women's Rights in the USA*. New York: Routledge.

McCammon, Holly J. and Karen E. Campbell. 2002. "Allies on the Road to Victory: Coalition Forming between the Suffragists and the Woman's Christian Temperance Union." *Mobilization: An International Journal* 7:231–51.

McCammon, Holly and Nella Van Dyke. 2010. "Applying Qualitative Comparative Analysis to Empirical Studies of Social Movement Coalition Formation." Pp. 292–315 in *Strategic Alliances*, edited by Holly J. McCammon and Nella Van Dyke. Minneapolis: University of Minnesota Press.

McCammon, Holly J., Courtney S. Muse and Harmony D. Newman. 2007. "Movement Framing and Discursive Opportunity Structures." *American Sociological Review* 72:725–49.

McCarthy, John. 2005. "Velcro Triangles: Elite Mobilization of Local Antidrug Issue Coalitions." Pp. 87–116 in *Routing the Opposition*, edited by David S. Meyer, Valerie Jenness and Helen Ingram. Minneapolis: University of Minnesota Press.

McCaughey, Martha. 1997. *Real Knockouts: The Physical Feminism of Women's Self-Defense*. New York: New York University Press.

McElroy, Wendy. 1995. "The Unfair Sex?" *National Review* 47:74–88.

McGirr, Lisa. 2001. *Suburban Warriors*. Princeton: Princeton University Press.

McGuire, Danielle. 2010. *At the Dark End of the Street: Black Women, Rape, and Resistance*. New York: Knopf.

McHarry, Mark. 1986. "The Meese Commission: Ominous Implications for Gay Men and Lesbians." *Gay Community News* 14:5.

Meiners, Erica. 2009. "Never Innocent." *Meridians* 9:31–62.

Meyer, David S. 2003. "Political Opportunity and Nested Institutions." *Social Movement Studies* 2(1):17–35.

Meyer, David S. 2004. "Protest and Political Opportunities." *Annual Review of Sociology* 30:125–45.

Meyer, David S. 2005. "Social Movements and Public Policy." Pp. 1–26 in *Routing the Opposition*, edited by David S. Meyer, Valerie Jenness and Helen Ingram. Minneapolis: University of Minnesota Press.

Meyer, David S. 2007. *The Politics of Protest*. New York: Oxford University Press.

Meyer, David S. and Suzanne Staggenborg. 1996. "Movements, Countermovements, and the Structure of Political Opportunity." *American Journal of Sociology* 101:1628–60.

Meyer, David S. and Nancy Whittier. 1994. "Social Movement Spillover." *Social Problems* 41:277–98.

Meyer, David S., Nancy Whittier and Belinda Robnett. 2002. *Social Movements: Identity, Culture, and the State*. Oxford; New York: Oxford University Press.

Miller, Jake. 2015. "An Unlikely Alliance Forms Between Koch Brothers and Liberal Groups." *CBS News*, February 19, Retrieved April 5, 2017 (www.cbsnews.com/news/Koch-brothers-conservative-liberal-groups-unite-on-criminal-justice-reform/).

Miller, Lisa L. 2004. "Rethinking Bureaucrats in the Policy Process: Criminal Justice Agents and the National Crime Agenda." *Policy Studies Journal* 32:569–88.

Miller-Young, Mireille. 2014. *Brown Sugar*. Durham, NC: Duke University Press.

Minkoff, Debra. 1993. "The Organization of Survival: Women's and Racial-Ethnic Voluntarist and Activist Organizations, 1955–1985." *Social Forces* 71:887–908.

Minnery, Tom. 1985. "Antipornography Conference Signals Growing Commitment to Combat Obscenity." *Christianity Today* 29:37–41.

Minnery, Tom. 1986. "Pornography: The Human Tragedy." *Christianity Today* 30:17–22.

Minnery, Tom. 1987. "Porn Again: Final Report of the Attorney General's Commission on Pornography." *Christianity Today* 31:62, 318.

Moen, Matthew. 1992. *The Transformation of the Christian Right*. Tuscaloosa: University of Alabama Press.

Molotch, Harvey L. and Deirdre Boden. 1985. "Talking Social Structure: Discourse, Domination and the Watergate Hearings." *American Sociological Review* 50:273–88.

Naples, Nancy. 1997. "The 'New Consensus' on the Gendered 'Social Contract': The 1987–1988 US Congressional Hearings on Welfare Reform." *Signs* 22:907–45.

Naples, Nancy. 2003. "Deconstructing and Locating Survivor Discourse." *Signs* 28:1151–85.

Naples, Nancy. 2009. "Teaching Intersectionality Intersectionally." *International Feminist Journal of Politics* 11:566–77.

Nash, Jennifer C. 2008. "Strange Bedfellows: Black Feminism and Antipornography Feminism." *Social Text* 26:51–76.

National Network on Behalf of Battered Immigrant Women. N.d. "What Women Immigrants Need from a Comprehensive Immigration Reform Bill." Retrieved

June 5, 2014 (http://www.immigrantwomennetwork.org/Resources/What%20
Women%20Need%20From%20CIR-Network.pdf).

National Task Force to End Sexual and Domestic Violence. 2012. "Sexual Assault in
Rural Indian Country." Washington, D.C.: National Task Force to End Sexual
and Domestic Violence. Retrieved October 7, 2015 (https://www.scribd.com/
doc/138754377/Sexual-Assault-in-Rural-Indian-Country-2-2012).

National Task Force to End Sexual and Domestic Violence. 2013. "How
Comprehensive Immigration Reform Affects Immigrant Survivors." Retrieved
June 5, 2014 (http://4vawa.org/comprehensive-immigration-reform/).

National Task Force to End Sexual and Domestic Violence Against Women. "About
NTF." Retrieved June 5, 2014 (http://4vawa.org/about/).

Nelson, Barbara. 1984. *Making an Issue Out of Child Abuse*. Chicago: University of
Chicago Press.

Nichols, Lawrence T. 1991. "'Whistleblower' Or 'Renegade': Definitional Contests in
an Official Inquiry." *Symbolic Interaction* 14:395–414.

Nickerson, Michelle. 2012. *Mothers of Conservatism*. Princeton: Princeton
University Press.

Nobile, Philip and Eric D. Nadler. 1986. *United States of America Vs. Sex: How the Meese
Commission Lied about Pornography*. New York: Minotaur Press.

Nordlinger, Jay. 2001. "Getting Aroused." *National Review* 53:44–45.

Obach, Brian. 2004. *Labor and the Environmental Movement: The Quest for Common
Ground*. Cambridge, MA: MIT Press.

Obach, Brian. 2010. "Political Opportunity and Social Movement Coalitions: The Role
of Policy Segmentation and Nonprofit Tax Law." Pp. 197,197–218 in *Strategic
Alliances: Coalition Building and Social Movements*, edited by Nella Van Dyke and
Holly McCammon. Minneapolis: University of Minnesota Press.

O'Beirne, Kate. 1995. "Who's What in Congress." *National Review* 47(23):91.

Ogas, Ogi and Sai Gaddam. 2012. *A Billion Wicked Thoughts: What the Internet Tells Us
about Sexual Relationships*. New York: Plume.

Olzak, Susan and Sarah Soule. 2009. "Cross-Cutting Influences of Environmental
Protest and Legislation." *Social Forces* 88:201–25.

Osmundson, Linda A. 2001. "Sisters, Are Doin' It to Ourselves: Florida and the Future
of Our Sheltering Movement." *Off our backs* 31:14–18.

Page, Sharon. 1986. "Feminists Stand Divided on Meese Commission Report." *Gay
Community News* 14:1–11.

Pelosi, Nancy. 2012. 158 Cong Rec H 2745. May 16.

Peterson, Jonathan. 2000. "Unlikely Anti-Trade Warrior." *Los Angeles Times*,
October 2:A1.

Ponnuru, Ramesh. 1997. "Fortune Favors the Brave." *National Review* 49(Mar. 10).

Potter, Clare. 2012. "Taking Back Times Square." *Radical History Review* 113:67–80.

Presser, Lois and Emily Gaarder. 2000. "Can Restorative Justice Reduce Battering?
Some Preliminary Considerations." *Social Justice* 27:175.

"PROTECT's Bipartisan Lobby." N.d. Retrieved June 8, 2016 (http://protect.org/
lobby).

Putnam, Robert D. 2000. *Bowling Alone*. New York: Simon and Schuster.

Quigley, Mike. 2012. 158 Cong Rec S 2761. April 26.

Rabey, Steve. 1984. "Christian Leaders Take Steps to Combat the Porn Epidemic."
Christianity Today 28:47, 318.

Rabkin, Jeremy. 2000. "Sex, Violence, and the Supreme Court: The Constitution
Prevails Over Congressional Pandering to Feminists." *Weekly Standard* 5:18–19.

Rapping, Elayne. 1987. "Meese Commission Report Left a Chill in the Air." *The Guardian* 39:7.

Ray, Raka. 1999. *Fields of Protest*. Minneapolis: University of Minnesota Press.

Reese, Ellen. 2005. "Policy Threats and Social Movement Coalitions." Pp. 259–87 in *Routing the Opposition*, edited by David S. Meyer, Valerie Jenness and Helen Ingram. Minneapolis: University of Minnesota Press.

Reger, Jo. 2012. *Everywhere and Nowhere: Contemporary Feminism in the United States*. New York: Oxford University Press.

Reger, Jo. 2014. "Micro-Cohorts, Feminist Discourse, and the Emergence of the Toronto SlutWalk." *Feminist Formations* 26:49–69.

Rentschler, Carrie A. 2011. *Second Wounds: Victims' Rights and the Media in the U.S.* Durham, NC: Duke University Press.

Renzetti, Claire M., Jeffrey L. Edleson and Raquel K. Bergen, editors. 2011. *Sourcebook on Violence Against Women*. 2nd Edition. Thousand Oaks, CA: Sage.

Richie, Beth. 2012. *Arrested Justice: Black Women, Violence, and America's Prison Nation*. New York: New York University Press.

Rivera, Jenny. 1995–1996. "The Violence Against Women Act and the Construction of Multiple Consciousness in the Civil Rights and Feminist Movements." *Journal of Law and Policy* 4:463–511.

Roberts, Dorothy. 2001. *Shattered Bonds: The Color of Child Welfare*. New York: Basic Books.

Rochon, Thomas. 1998. *Culture Moves*. Princeton, NJ: Princeton University Press.

Rochon, Thomas and David S. Meyer, editors. 1997. *Coalitions and Political Movements: The Lessons of the Nuclear Freeze*. Boulder, CO: Lynne Rienner.

Rodriguez, Dylan. 2006. *Forced Passages: Imprisoned Radical Intellectuals and the U.S. Prison Regime*. Minneapolis: University of Minnesota Press.

Roe, Kristen. 2004. "The Violence Against Women Act and Its Impact on Sexual Violence Public Policy: Looking Back and Looking Forward." Retrieved February 24, 2012 (http://new.Vawnet.org/assoc_files_vawnet/vawa-Svpubpol.Pdf).

Rondini, Ashley. 2015. "Tracing the Trajectory of Federal Initiatives Addressing Campus Sexual Violence." *ASA Footnotes* May/June:13.

Rosen, Ruth. 2000. *The World Split Open: How the Modern Women's Movement Changed America*. New York: Penguin.

Rosenberg, Karen. 2010. "Compromising Positions: Reflections on the Violence Against Women Act." *The Society Pages*. Retrieved February 4, 2011 (http://thesocietypages.org/sexuality/2010/07/18/compromising-positions-reflections-on-the-violence-against-women-act/).

Ross, Bobby. 2009. "Modern-Day Lepers: Churches Try to Balance Grace and Accountability toward Sex Offenders." *Christianity Today* 53:16, 318.

Roth, Benita. 2003. *Separate Roads to Feminism*. Cambridge: Cambridge University Press.

Rubin, Gayle. 1994. "Thinking Sex." Pp. 267–319 in *Pleasure and Danger*, edited by Carole Vance. Boston: Routledge.

Rubin, Gayle. 2011. "Blood under the Bridge: Reflections on 'Thinking Sex.'" *GLQ: A Journal of Lesbian & Gay Studies* 17:1–48.

Ruby, Jennie. 2002. "Interview: What It Would Really Take to End Rape?" *Off our backs* 32:16–19.

Sabatier, Paul. 1991. "Toward Better Theories of the Policy Process." *PS: Political Science and Politics* 24:144,144–156.

Sacco, Lynn. 2009. *Unspeakable: Father-Daughter Incest in American History*. Baltimore, MD: Johns Hopkins Press.

Schlafly, Phyllis and U.S. Attorney General's Commission on Pornography. 1987. *Pornography's Victims*. Westchester, IL: Crossway Books.

Schreiber, Ronnee. 2008. *Righting Feminism*. New York: Oxford University Press.

Seghetti, Lisa and Jerome Bjelopera. 2012. "The Violence Against Women Act: Overview, Legislation, and Federal Funding." *Congressional Research Service* May 10.

Selle, Robert. 1984. "Pornography Warehouse Target of Irate Protesters." *New York City Tribune*. (In Edwin Meese Papers, Box 120, Folder "Pornography.")

Semonche, John. 2007. *Censoring Sex*. New York: Rowman and Littlefield.

Shimizu, Celine Parreñas. 2007. *The Hypersexuality of Race*. Durham, NC: Duke University Press.

Shurtleff, Mark and Doug Gansler. 2012. "Weakening Violence Against Women Act Betrays Immigrant Victims." *Politico*. Retrieved September 17, 2012 (http://www.politico.com/news/stories/0912/81048.html).

Simon, Jonathan. 2007. *Governing through Crime*. New York: Oxford University Press.

Sklar, Kathryn K. and Suzanne Lustig. 2001. "Introduction, How Have Recent Social Movements Shaped Civil Rights Legislation for Women? The 1994 Violence Against Women Act." Binghamton, NY: Center for the Historical Study of Women and Gender at the State University of New York, Binghamton, and Alexander Street Press of Alexandria, Virginia. Retrieved March 17, 2010 (http://womhist.alexanderstreet.com/vawa/intro.htm).

Skorczewski, D. 1996. "No More Shame: Marie Cartier and the Dandelion Warriors." *Off our backs* 26:6.

Skrentny, John D. 2006. "Policy-Elite Perceptions and Social Movement Success." *American Journal of Sociology* 111:1762–815.

Smith, Andrea. 2007. "Introduction." Pp. 1–18 in *The Revolution Will Not Be Funded*, edited by INCITE! Women of Color Against Violence. Cambridge, MA: South End Press.

Smith, Lamar. 2012. 158 Cong Rec H 2745. May 16.

Snitow, Ann, Christine Stansell and Sharon Thompson, editors. 1983. *Powers of Desire: The Politics of Sexuality*. New York: Monthly Review Press.

Snow, David and Robert Benford. 1998. "Master Frames and Cycles of Protest." Pp. 133–155 in *Frontiers in Social Movement Theory*, edited by Aldon Morris and Carol M. Mueller. New Haven, CT: Yale University Press.

Soule, Sarah and Brayden G. King. 2006. "The Stages of the Policy Process and the Equal Rights Amendment, 1972–1982." *American Journal of Sociology* 111:1871–909.

Soule, Sarah, John McCarthy, Doug McAdam and Yang Su. 1999. "Protest Events: Cause or Consequence of the U.S. Women's Movement and Federal Congressional Activities, 1956–1979." *Mobilization* 4(2):239–56.

Soule, Sarah and Susan Olzak. 2004. "When Do Movements Matter? The Politics of Contingency and the Equal Rights Amendment." *American Sociological Review* 69:473–97.

Spade, Dean. 2011. *Normal Life: Administrative Violence, Critical Trans Politics, and the Limits of Law*. New York: South End Press.

Specter, Arlen. 1984. 130 Cong Rec S 29169. October 3.

Spohn, Cassia and Julie Horney. 1992. *Rape Law Reform*. New York: Plenum.

Springer, Kimberly. 2005. *Living for the Revolution: Black Feminist Organizations, 1968–1980*. Durham, NC: Duke University Press.

Staggenborg, Suzanne. 1995. "Can Feminist Organizations Be Effective?" Pp. 339–55 in *Feminist Organizations*, edited by Myra M. Ferree and Patricia Y. Martin. Philadelphia: Temple.

Steinberg, Marc. 2003. "The Intellectual Challenges of Toiling in the Vineyard." Pp. 121–33 in *Rethinking Social Movements*, edited by Jeff Goodwin and James Jasper. New York: Rowman and Littlefield.

Steinberg, Marc W. 1999. "The Talk and Back Talk of Collective Action: A Dialogic Analysis of Repertoires of Discourse among Nineteenth-Century English Cotton Spinners." *American Journal of Sociology* 105:736–80.

Steinhauer, Jennifer. 2014. "Lawmakers Broadening Their Focus to Fight Against an Array of Sex Crimes." *New York Times*, April 21, Retrieved April 22, 2014 (www.nytimes.com/2014/04/22/us/politics/lawmakers-broaden).

Stephen, Anil. 2001. "Muslim Leader Appeals to Evangelicals." *Christianity Today* 45:24–25.

Stone, Amy L. 2012. *Gay Rights at the Ballot Box*. Minneapolis: University of Minnesota Press.

Strebeigh, Fred. 2009. *Equal: Women Reshape American Law*. New York and London: W. W. Norton.

Strossen, Nadine. 1993. "A Feminist Critique of 'the' Feminist Critique of Pornography." *Virginia Law Review* 79 (5):1099–190.

Strossen, Nadine. 2000. *Defending Pornography: Free Speech, Sex, and the Fight for Women's Rights*. 2nd Edition. New York: New York University Press.

Strub, Whitney. 2011. *Perversion for Profit: The Politics of Pornography and the Rise of the New Right*. New York: Columbia University Press.

"A Symposium Celebrating the Fifteenth Anniversary of the Violence Against Women Act." 2010. *Georgetown Journal of Gender & the Law* 11:511–92.

Taormino, Tristan, Celene Parreñas Shimizu, Constance Penley and Mireille Miller-Young, eds. 2013. *The Feminist Porn Book*. New York: The Feminist Press.

Tarrow, Sidney. 1994. *Power in Movement*. New York: Cambridge University Press.

Taylor, Verta and Nancy Whittier. 1992. "Collective Identity in Social Movement Communities." Pp. 104–29 in *Frontiers in Social Movement Theory*, edited by Aldon D. Morris and Carol M. Mueller. New Haven, CT: Yale.

Taylor, Verta and Nancy Whittier. 1995. "Analytical Approaches to Social Movement Culture." Pp. 163–87 in *Social Movements and Culture*, edited by Hank Johnston and Bert Klandermans. Minneapolis: University of Minnesota Press.

Teles, Steven. 2008. *The Rise of the Conservative Legal Movement*. Princeton, NJ: Princeton University Press.

Tilly, Charles. 2004. *Social Movements*. Boulder, CO: Paradigm.

Tong, Rosemarie. 1986. "Review: Brief Encounter." *The Women's Review of Books* 3:7–9.

Tracy, Steven R. 2003. "Headship with a Heart: How Biblical Patriarchy Actually Prevents Abuse." *Christianity Today* 47:50–54.

Turk, Craig D. 1999. "Violence Against the Constitution." *The Weekly Standard*:17.

Tyler, Robin. 2005. "Silent No More: A Veteran Political Activist's Perspective." Retrieved June 8, 2016 (http://protect.org/articles/silent-no-more-veteran-political-activists-perspective).

Van Dyke, Nella. 2003. "Crossing Movement Boundaries: Factors That Facilitate Coalition Protest by American College Students, 1930–1990." *Social Problems* 50:226–50.

Van Dyke, Nella and Holly McCammon. 2010. *Strategic Alliances: Building Social Movement Coalitions*. Minneapolis: University of Minnesota Press.

Van Gelder, Lindsy. 1980. "Confronting Street Porn for the First Time." *Ms.* 8:62–66.

Vance, Carole, ed. 1984. *Pleasure and Danger*. Boston: Routledge and Kegan Paul.

Vance, Carole. 1986a. "Meese Commission: The Porn Police Attack." *Gay Community News* 4:3, 6, 12.

Vance, Carole. 1986b. "Porn in the U.S.A.: The Meese Commission on the Road." *The Nation* 243:65.

Vance, Carole. 1990. "Negotiating Sex and Gender in the Attorney General's Commission on Pornography." Pp. 118–134 in *Uncertain Terms*, edited by Faye D. Ginsburg and Anna L. Tsing. Boston: Beacon Press.

Villalon, Roberta. 2010. *Violence Against Latina Immigrants*. New York: New York University Press.

Waldram, James. 2012. *Hound Pound Narrative: Sexual Offender Habilitation and the Anthropology of Therapeutic Intervention*. Berkeley: University of California Press.

Walker, Alice. 1981. *You Can't Keep a Good Woman Down*. New York: Harcourt, Brace, Jovanovich.

Walters, Suzanna. 1996. "From Here to Queer: Radical Feminism, Postmodernism, and the Lesbian Menace." *Signs* 21(4):830–70.

Walters, Candace and Beth Spring. 1992. "The Wounds of Rape: How Your Church Can Help Victims of Sexual Assault Find Healing and Hope." *Christianity Today* 36:30–33.

Weeks, Grier. 2004. "Redressing California's Betrayal of Child-Abuse Victims." Retrieved June 8, 2016 (http://www.protect.org/articles/redressing-californias-betrayal-of-child-abuse-victims).

"We've Got Porn." 2000b. *Christianity Today* 44:32–33.

Weldon, S. Laurel. 2002. *Protest, Policy, and the Problem of Violence Against Women*. Pittsburgh: University of Pittsburgh Press.

West, Robin. 1987. "The Feminist-Conservative Anti-Pornography Alliance and the 1986 Attorney General's Commission on Pornography Report." *American Bar Foundation Research Journal* 12:681–711.

Whittier, Nancy. 1995. *Feminist Generations*. Philadelphia: Temple University Press.

Whittier, Nancy. 2001. "Emotional Strategies: Oppositional Emotions in the Movement Against Child Sexual Abuse." Pp. 267–81 in *Passionate Politics*, edited by Jeff Goodwin, James Jasper and Francesca Polletta. Chicago: University of Chicago Press.

Whittier, Nancy. 2002. "Meaning and Structure in Social Movements." Pp. 289–308 in *Social Movements: Identities, Culture, and the State*, edited by David S. Meyer, Nancy Whittier and Belinda Robnett. New York: Oxford University Press.

Whittier, Nancy. 2009. *The Politics of Child Sexual Abuse: Emotion, Social Movements, and the State*. New York: Oxford University Press.

Whittier, Nancy. 2012. "The Politics of Visibility: Coming Out and Individual and Collective Identity." *Making History: Movements, Strategy, and Social Change*, edited by Jeff Goodwin, Rachel Kutz-Flamenbaum, Gregory Maney and Deana Rohlinger. Minneapolis: University of Minnesota Press.

Whittier, Nancy. 2014. "Rethinking Coalitions: Anti-Pornography Feminists, Conservatives, and Relationships between Collaborative Adversarial Movements." *Social Problems* 6(2):175–93.

Whittier, Nancy. 2015. "Where Are the Children? Theorizing the Missing Piece in Gendered Sexual Violence." *Gender & Society* 30(1):95–109.

Whittier, Nancy. 2016. "Carceral and Intersectional Feminism in Congress: The Violence Against Women Act, Discourse, and Policy." *Gender & Society* 30(5):791–818.

Wilcox, W. B. and Douglas LeBlanc. 2004. "Affectionate Patriarchs: In the Popular Imagination, Conservative Evangelical Fathers are Power-Abusing Authoritarians. A New Study Says Otherwise." *Christianity Today* 48:44–46.

Willentz, Sean. 2008. *The Age of Reagan.* New York: Harper Collins.

Wired Safety. N.d. "About Wired Safety." wiredsafety.org. Retrieved July18, 2013.

Wright, Melissa W. 2011. "Necropolitics, Narcopolitics, and Femicide: Gendered Violence on the Mexico-U.S. Border." *Signs* 36:707–31.

Yongjoo, Jeon and Donald Haider-Markel. 2001. "Tracing Issues Definition and Policy Change: An Analysis of Disability Issue Images and Policy Response." *Policy Studies Journal* 29:215–31.

Zegart, Dan. 1989. "Solomon's Choice." *Ms.* (June):78–83.

Congressional Hearings

U.S. House. 1973. To Establish A National Center On Child Abuse And Neglect. Hearings before the Committee on Education and Labor, Select Subcommittee on Education. Oct. 1, Oct. 5, and Nov. 12.

U.S. House. 1977. Sexual Exploitation of Children. Hearings before the Committee on Education and Labor, Select Subcommittee on Education. Los Angeles CA, May 27 and 28, New York, NY May 31, and Washington, D.C. June 10.

U.S. House. 1978. Research into Violent Behavior: Overview and Sexual Assaults. Hearings before the Committee on Science and Technology, Subcommittee on Domestic and International Scientific Planning, Analysis and Cooperation. Jan. 10, 11, and 12.

U.S. House. 1981. Reauthorization of the Child Abuse Prevention and Treatment and Adoption Reform Act. Hearings before the Committee on Education and Labor, Select Subcommittee on Education. Mar. 9.

U.S. House. 1982. Teenage Prostitution and Child Pornography. Hearings before the Committee on Education and Labor, Select Subcommittee on Education. Hearings Held in Pittsburgh, PA, April 23, and Washington, D.C., June 24.

U.S. House. 1983a. Protection of Children Against Sexual Exploitation. Hearing before the Committee on the Judiciary House, Subcommittee on Crime. June 16.

U.S. House. 1983b. Children, Youth, and Families in the Southwest. Hearings before the Select Committee on Children, Youth, and Families. Dec.7.

U.S. House. 1984a. Violence and Abuse in American Families. Hearings before the Select Committee on Children, Youth, and Families. June 14.

U.S. House. 1984b. Title IV, Missing Children's Assistance Act. Hearing before the Committee on Education and Labor, Subcommittee on Human Resources. Hearing held in Chicago, IL, Apr. 9.

U.S. House. 1984c. Child Abuse What We Know About Prevention Strategies. Hearings before the Select Committee on Children, Youth, and Families. Mar. 12.

U.S. House. 1986a. Child Abuse and Neglect and Child Sexual Abuse Programs. Hearings before the Committee on Government Operations, Subcommittee on Intergovernmental Relations and Human Resources. Mar. 12.

U.S. House. 1986b. Sexual Abuse Act of 1986: Hearing on H.R. 596 and H.R. 4745. Hearings before the Committee on the Judiciary, Subcommittee on Criminal Justice. Apr. 29.

U.S. House. 1987. Women, Violence, and the Law. Hearings before the Select Committee on Children, Youth, and Families. Sept. 16.

U.S. House. 1988. Child Protection and Obscenity Enforcement Act of 1988, on H.R. 1213 (Pornography Victims Protection Act of 1987), 1438 (Omnibus Family Decency Protection Act of 1987), H.R. 2605 (Children's Home Video Protection Act of 1987, H.R. 3889 (Child Protection and Obscenity Enforcement Act of 1988), and H.R. 4257 ("Pornographic Mail Prohibition Act"). Hearings before the Committee on the Judiciary, Subcommittee on Crime. Apr. 28, June 16, and Aug. 11.

U.S. House. 1991. Child Abuse Prevention and Treatment in the 1990s, Keeping Old Promises, Meeting New Demands. Hearings before the Select Committee on Children, Youth, and Families. Sept. 15.

U.S. House. 1992a. Violence Against Women. Hearings before the Committee on the Judiciary, Subcommittee on Crime and Criminal Justice. Feb. 6.

U.S. House. 1992b. Hearing on the Child Abuse Prevention, Adoption, and Family Services Act. Hearings before the Committee on Education and Labor, Subcommittee on Select Education. Feb. 27.

U.S. House. 1992c. Field Hearing on Child Abuse. Hearings before the Committee on Education and Labor, Subcommittee on Select Education. New York, NY, Apr. 20.

U.S. House. 1993b. Crimes of Violence Motivated by Gender. Hearings before the Committee on the Judiciary, Subcommittee on Civil and Constitutional Rights. Nov. 16.

U.S. House. 1994a. Domestic Violence: Not Just A Family Matter. Hearings before the Committee on the Judiciary, Subcommittee on Crime and Criminal Justice. June 20.

U.S. House. 1994b. H.R. 3694, the Child Abuse Accountability Act, and H.R. 4570, the Child Support Responsibility Act. Hearings before the Committee on the Post Office and Civil Service, Subcommittee on Compensation and Employment Benefits. July 12.

U.S. House. 1994c. Music Lyrics and Commerce. Hearings before the House Committee on Energy and Commerce, Subcommittee on Commerce, Consumer Protection, and Competitiveness. Feb. 11 and May 5.

U.S. House. 1995a. Hearing on the Contract with America: Child Welfare and Childcare. Hearings before the Committee on Economic and Educational Opportunities, Subcommittee on Early Childhood, Youth, and Families. Jan. 31.

U.S. House. 1995b. Hearing on H.R. 1855, To Amend Title 11, D.C. Code, To Restrict the Authority of the Superior Court over Certain Pending Cases Involving Child Custody and Visitation Rights. Hearings before the Committee on Government Reform and Oversight, Subcommittee on the District of Columbia. Aug. 4.

U.S. House. 1998. Child Protection and Sexual Predator Punishment Act of 1998 and Related Proposals. Hearings before the Committee on the Judiciary, Subcommittee on Crime. Apr. 30.

U.S. House. 1999. Violence Against Women Act of 1999, Stalking Prevention and Victim Protection Act of 1999. Hearings before the Committee on the Judiciary, Subcommittee on Crime. Sept. 29.

U.S. House. 2000a. Battered Immigrant Women Protection Act of 1999. Hearings before the Committee on the Judiciary, Subcommittee on Immigration and Claims. July 20.

U.S. House. 2000b. Aimee's Law, Matthew's Law, Two Strikes and You're Out Child Protection Act and Stop Material Unsuitable for Teens Act. Hearings before the Committee on the Judiciary, Subcommittee on Crime. May 11.

U.S. House. 2001. Two Strikes and You're Out Child Protection Act of 2001. Hearings before the Committee on the Judiciary, Subcommittee on Crime. July 31.

U.S. House. 2004. Online Pornography: Closing the Door on Pervasive Smut. Hearings before the Committee on Energy and Commerce, Subcommittee on Commerce, Trade, and Consumer Protection. May 6.

U.S. House. 2005a. Protection Against Sexual Exploitation of Children Act of 2005, and the Prevention and Deterrence of Crimes Against Children Act of 2005. Hearings before the Committee on the Judiciary, Subcommittee on Crime, Terrorism, and Homeland Security. June 9.

U.S. House. 2005b. House Bills on Sexual Crimes Against Children. Hearings before the Committee on the Judiciary, Subcommittee on Crime, Terrorism, and Homeland Security. June 9.

U.S. House. 2005c. Protecting Our Nation's Children from Sexual Predators and Violent Criminals: What Needs To Be Done? Hearings before the Committee on the Judiciary, Subcommittee on Crime, Terrorism, and Homeland Security. June 9.

U.S. House. 2005d. Combating Trafficking in Persons: An International Perspective. Hearings before the House Committee on Financial Services, Subcommittee on Domestic and International Monetary Policy, Trade, and Technology. June 22.

U.S. House 2007a. From Imus to Industry: The Business of Stereotypes and Degrading Images. Hearings before the House Committee on Energy and Commerce, Subcommittee on Commerce, Trade, and Consumer Protection. Sept. 25.

U.S. House. 2007b. Combating Modern Slavery: Reauthorization of Anti-Trafficking Programs. Hearings before the Committee on the Judiciary. Oct. 31.

U.S. House 2009a. Sex Offender Notification and Registration Act (SORNA): Barriers to Timely Compliance by States. Hearings before the Committee on the Judiciary, Subcommittee on Crime, Terrorism, and Homeland Security. Mar. 10.

U.S. House. 2009b. Preventing Child Abuse and Improving Responses to Families in Crisis. Hearings before the Committee on Education and Labor. Nov. 5.

U.S. House. 2011a. Reauthorization of the Adam Walsh Act. Hearings before the Committee on the Judiciary, Subcommittee on Crime, Terrorism, and Homeland Security. Feb. 15.

U.S. House. 2011b. Protecting Children from Internet Pornographers Act of 2011. Hearings before the Committee on the Judiciary, Subcommittee on Crime, Terrorism, and Homeland Security. July 12.

U.S. Senate. 1981a. Exploitation of Children. Hearings before the Committee on the Judiciary, Subcommittee on Juvenile Justice. Nov. 5.

U.S. Senate. 1981b. Oversight on Community Services Administration, Child Abuse Prevention and Treatment, and Adoption Opportunities, and Native American Programs Act. Hearings before the Committee on Labor and Human Resources, Subcommittee on Aging, Family, and Human Services. Apr. 23.

U.S. Senate. 1982a. Child Pornography: Hearing on S. 2856, Bill to Amend the Sexual Exploitation of Children Act of 1977. Hearings before the Committee on the Judiciary, Subcommittee on Juvenile Justice. Dec. 10.

U.S. Senate. 1982b. Problems of Runaway Youth. Hearings before the Senate Committee on the Judiciary, Subcommittee on Juvenile Justice. July 22.

U.S. Senate. 1982c. Exploitation of Children. Hearing before the Committee on the Judiciary, Subcommittee on Juvenile Justice. Nov. 5.

U.S. Senate. 1983. Child Abuse Prevention and Treatment and Adoption Reform Act Amendments of 1983. Hearings before the Committee on Committee on Labor and Human Resources, Subcommittee on Family and Human Services. Apr. 3.

U.S. Senate. 1984a. Effect of Pornography on Women and Children. Hearings before the Committee on the Judiciary, Subcommittee on Juvenile Justice. Washington, D.C., Aug. 8, Sept. 12 and 25, and Oct. 30, 1984; Pittsburgh, PA, Oct. 18.

U.S. Senate. 1984b. Child Pornography and Pedophilia, Part One. Hearings before the Committee on Governmental Affairs, Permanent Subcommittee on Investigations. Nov. 29 and 30.

U.S. Senate. 1985a. Child Pornography and Pedophilia, Part Two. Hearings before the Committee on Governmental Affairs, Permanent Subcommittee on Investigations. Feb. 21.

U.S. Senate. 1985b. Sexual Molestation of Children in Indian Country. Hearings before the Committee on the Judiciary. Nov. 19.

U.S. Senate. 1985c. Child Abuse Victims' Rights Act. Hearing on S. 985: A Bill to Protect the Rights of Victims of Child Abuse. Hearings before the Committee on the Judiciary, Subcommittee on Juvenile Justice. Sept. 24.

U.S. Senate. 1986a. Child Sexual Abuse and Pornography Act of 1986, S. 2398, A bill to amend Title 18 of the United States Code to ban the production and use of advertisements for child pornography or solicitations for child pornography. Hearings before the Committee on the Judiciary, Subcommittee on Juvenile Justice. Aug.11.

U.S. Senate. 1986b. Native American Children, Youth, and Families. Hearings before the Select Committee on Children, Youth, and Families. Jan. 7 and 9.

U.S. Senate. 1986c. Sexual Abuse of Indian Children. Hearings before the Committee on the Judiciary, Subcommittee on Criminal Justice. Dec. 30.

U.S. Senate. 1988a. Child Abuse and Neglect. Hearings before the Select Committee on Indian Affairs. Nov. 22.

U.S. Senate 1988b. Child Protection and Obscenity Enforcement Act and Pornography Victims Protection Act of 1987. Hearings before the Senate Judiciary Committee. June 8.

U.S. Senate. 1989a. Federal Government's Relationship with American Indians: Sexual Abuse of Indian Children. Hearings before the Select Committee on Indian Affairs. Feb. 21, 22, 23, and 27.

U.S. Senate. 1989b. Child Abuse. Hearings before the Committee on the Judiciary. May 16.

U.S. Senate. 1990a. Women and Violence, Part 1. Hearings before the Committee on the Judiciary. June 20.

U.S. Senate. 1990b. Women and Violence, Part 2. Hearings before the Committee on the Judiciary. Aug. 29 and Dec. 11.

U.S. Senate. 1990c. Indian Child Protective Services and Family Violence Prevention Act. Hearings before the Select Committee on Indian Affairs. June 7.

U.S. Senate. 1990d. Child Physical and Sexual Abuse in Indian Country. Hearings before the Committee on Indian Affairs. Apr. 3.

U.S. Senate. 1990e. Child Sexual Abuse in Indian Country. Hearings before the Select Committee on Indian Affairs. Phoenix, AZ, Sept. 5.

U.S. Senate. 1991a. Violence Against Women: Victims of the System. Hearings before the Committee on the Judiciary. Apr. 9.

U.S. Senate 1991b. Domestic Violence: the Struggle for Survival. Hearings before the Committee on Appropriations, Subcommittee on Departments of Labor, Health and Human Services, Education, and Related Agencies. Feb. 12.

U.S. Senate. 1991c. Behind Closed Doors: Family Violence in the Home. Hearings before the Committee on Labor and Human Resources, Subcommittee on Children, Family, Drugs, and Alcoholism. July 9.

U.S. Senate. 1991d. Legislative Proposals for Compensation of Victims of Sexual Crimes. Hearings before the Committee on the Judiciary. July 23.

U.S. Senate. 1992. University Responses to Racial and Sexual Harassment on Campuses. Hearings before the Senate Committee on Labor and Human Resources. Sept. 10.

U.S. Senate. 1993a. Violent Crimes Against Women. Hearings before the Committee on the Judiciary. Apr. 13.

U.S. Senate. 1993b. Indian Child Protection and Family Violence Prevention Act. Hearings before the Committee on Indian Affairs. Oct. 28.

U.S. Senate. 1994a. Indian Child Protection and Family Violence Prevention Act. Hearings before the Committee on Indian Affairs. May 24.

U.S. Senate. 1994b. Shaping our Responses to Violent and Demeaning Imagery in Popular Music. Hearings before the Senate Committee on the Judiciary, Subcommittee on Juvenile Justice. Feb. 23.

U.S. Senate. 1995a. Child Protection: Balancing Divergent Interests. Hearings before the Committee on Labor and Human Resources, Subcommittee on Children and Families. May 25.

U.S. Senate. 1995b. Indian Child Protection and Family Violence Prevention Act. Hearings before the Committee on Indian Affairs. Mar. 22.

U.S. Senate. 1996a. Combating Violence Against Women. Hearings before the Committee on the Judiciary. May 15.

U.S. Senate. 1996b. Child Pornography Prevention Act of 1995. Hearings before the Committee on the Judiciary. June 4.

U.S. Senate. 1996c. Indian Child Protection and Family Violence Prevention Act. Hearings before the Committee on Indian Affairs. Dec. 16.

U.S. Senate. 2005. Reauthorization of the Violence Against Women Act. Hearings before the Committee on the Judiciary. July 19.

U.S. Senate. 2006. Indian Child Protection and Family Violence Prevention Act Amendments. Hearings before the Committee on Indian Affairs. Mar. 15.

U.S. Senate. 2007. Examining the Prevalence of and Solutions to Stopping Violence Against Indian Women. Hearings before the Committee on Indian Affairs. Sept. 27.

U.S. Senate. 2008. Protecting Children, Strengthening Families: Reauthorizing CAPTA. Hearings before the Committee on Health, Education, Labor, and Pensions, Subcommittee on Children and Families. June 26.

U.S. Senate. 2009. The Continued Importance of the Violence Against Women Act. Hearings before the Committee on the Judiciary. June 10.

U.S. Senate. 2011. Breaking the Silence on Child Abuse: Protection, Prevention, Intervention, and Deterrence. Hearings before the Committee on Health, Education, and Labor. Dec.13.

INDEX